T0181524

Lecture Notes of the Institute for Computer Sciences, Social Informatics and Telecommunications Engineering 459

More information about this series at https://link.springer.com/bookseries/8197

Telex Magloire Ngatched Nkouatchah ·
Isaac Woungang · Jules-Raymond Tapamo ·
Serestina Viriri (Eds.)

Pan-African Artificial Intelligence and Smart Systems

Second EAI International Conference, PAAISS 2022
Dakar, Senegal, November 2–4, 2022
Proceedings

 Springer

Editors
Telex Magloire Ngatched Nkouatchah [ID]
Memorial University
Corner Brook, NL, Canada

Isaac Woungang [ID]
Ryerson University
Toronto, ON, Canada

Jules-Raymond Tapamo [ID]
University of KwaZulu-Natal
Durban, South Africa

Serestina Viriri
University of KwaZulu-Natal
Durban, South Africa

ISSN 1867-8211　　　　　　　ISSN 1867-822X (electronic)
Lecture Notes of the Institute for Computer Sciences, Social Informatics
and Telecommunications Engineering
ISBN 978-3-031-25270-9　　　　ISBN 978-3-031-25271-6 (eBook)
https://doi.org/10.1007/978-3-031-25271-6

This Springer imprint is published by the registered company Springer Nature Switzerland AG
The registered company address is: Gewerbestrasse 11, 6330 Cham, Switzerland

Telex Magloire Ngatched Nkouatchah ·
Isaac Woungang · Jules-Raymond Tapamo ·
Serestina Viriri (Eds.)

Pan-African Artificial Intelligence and Smart Systems

Second EAI International Conference, PAAISS 2022
Dakar, Senegal, November 2–4, 2022
Proceedings

 Springer

Editors
Telex Magloire Ngatched Nkouatchah ⓘ
Memorial University
Corner Brook, NL, Canada

Isaac Woungang ⓘ
Ryerson University
Toronto, ON, Canada

Jules-Raymond Tapamo ⓘ
University of KwaZulu-Natal
Durban, South Africa

Serestina Viriri
University of KwaZulu-Natal
Durban, South Africa

ISSN 1867-8211   ISSN 1867-822X (electronic)
Lecture Notes of the Institute for Computer Sciences, Social Informatics
and Telecommunications Engineering
ISBN 978-3-031-25270-9   ISBN 978-3-031-25271-6 (eBook)
https://doi.org/10.1007/978-3-031-25271-6

This Springer imprint is published by the registered company Springer Nature Switzerland AG
The registered company address is: Gewerbestrasse 11, 6330 Cham, Switzerland

Preface

We are delighted to introduce the proceedings of the second edition of the Pan-African Artificial Intelligence and Smart Systems Conference (PAAISS 2022). This conference brought together leading academic research scientists, industry practitioners, independent scholars, and innovators from across the African continent and the world to explore, exchange, and discuss the challenges and opportunities of harnessing the capabilities of Artificial Intelligence (AI) and Smart Systems (SS), which have emerged as the engine of the next wave of future innovations.

The theme of PAAISS 2022 was "Advancing AI Research in Africa". The technical program of PAAISS 2022 consisted of 27 full papers, carefully selected from 70 submissions. Each submitted paper went through a rigorous evaluation by at least 3 members of the Technical Program Committee in a blind review process. In oral presentation sessions at the conference tracks: Track 1: Artificial Intelligence (Theory and Framework), Track 2: Smart Systems Enabling Technologies, Track 3: AI Applications in 5G/6G Networks, and Track 4: Applied AI and Smart Systems. Each submitted paper went through a rigorous evaluation by at least 3 members of the Technical Program Committee in a blind review process. Apart from the presentations of high-quality technical papers, the technical program also featured four keynote speeches, one tutorial presentation, and two panel discussions. The four keynote presenters were Ndapa Nakashole, University of California, San Diego, USA; Christophe Bobda, University of Florida, Gainesville, USA; Muyinatu Bell, Johns Hopkins University, USA, and Gervais Mendy, University Cheikh Anta Diop, Senegal.

An international conference of this size requires the support and hard work of many people to produce a successful technical program and conference proceedings. Our general chair, Thomas Ndousse-Fetter, was essential to the success of the conference. We sincerely appreciate his vision, constant support, and guidance. It was also a great pleasure to work with an excellent organizing committee, including Ousmane Thiare, Hamidou Dathe, Oumar Sock, Mame Binta Gayei, and Massamba Ndiaye, and the Technical Program Committee. We are grateful to our webmaster, Justice Owusu Agyemang, for his diligence and hard work. We are also honored that the Academy of Science and Technology of Senegal accepted to co-organize and sponsor the conference. Finally, we would like to thank all the authors who submitted their papers to the PAAISS 2022 conference.

We strongly believe that the PAAISS conference will continue to be an excellent forum for all researchers, developers, and practitioners to discuss the related up-to-date science, technology, and practical aspects of Artificial Intelligence and Smart Systems. We also expect that the future PAAISS conferences will be as successful and stimulating as this year's, as shown by the contributions presented in this volume. We do hope that you enjoy reading these proceedings.

Isaac Woungang
Telex M. N. Ngatched
Jules-Raymond Tapamo
Serestina Viriri

Organization

Steering Committee

Thomas Ndousse-Fetter	Department of Energy, USA
Isaac Woungang	Ryerson University, Canada
Telex M. N. Ngatched	Memorial University of Newfoundland, Canada
Jules-Raymond Tapamo	University of KwaZulu-Natal, Durban, South Africa
Serestina Viriri	University of KwaZulu-Natal, South Africa

Organizing Committee

General Chair

Thomas Ndousse-Fetter	Department of Energy, USA

General Co-chairs

Isaac Woungang	Ryerson University, Canada
Ousmane Thiare	Gaston Berger University of Saint-Louis, Senegal

Technical Program Committee Co-chairs

Telex M. N. Ngatched	Memorial University of Newfoundland, Canada
Jules-Raymond Tapamo	University of KwaZulu-Natal, Durban, South Africa
Serestina Viriri	University of KwaZulu-Natal, South Africa

Sponsorship and Exhibit Chair

Hamidou Dathe	Cheikh Anta Diop University, Senegal

Local Chair

Mame Binta Gayei	National Academy of Sciences and Techniques of Senegal, Senegal

Workshops Chair

Serestina Viriri   University of KwaZulu-Natal, South Africa

Publicity and Social Media Chair

Oumar Sock   National Academy of Sciences and Techniques of
                                    Senegal, Senegal

Publications Chair

Telex M. N. Ngatched   Memorial University of Newfoundland, Canada

Web Chair

Justice Owusu Agyemang   Kwame Nkrumah University of Science and
                                    Technology, Ghana

Panels Chair

Attahiru S. Alfa   University of Manitoba, Canada

Tutorials Chair

Ernest Parfait Fokoue   Rochester Institute of Technology, USA

Technical Program Committee

Cheikh Ahmadou Bamba Gueye   University Cheikh Anta Diop of Dakar, Senegal
Assane Gueye   Carnegie Mellon University Africa, Rwanda
Jean Marie Dembele   Gaston Berger University of Saint-Louis, Senegal
Youssou Faye   University Assane Seck of Ziguinchor, Senegal
Cheikh Sarr   University Iba Der Thiam of Thies, Senegal
Mamadou Bousso   University Iba Der Thiam of Thies, Senegal
Youssou Dieng   University Assane Seck of Ziguinchor, Senegal
Cheikh Talibouya Diop   Gaston Berger University of Saint-Louis, Senegal
Moussa Lo   Université virtuelle du Sénégal, Sénégal
Dame Diongue   Gaston Berger University of Saint-Louis, Senegal
Ousmane Sall   Université virtuelle du Sénégal, Sénégal
Ibrahima Niang   University Cheikh Anta Diop of Dakar, Senegal
Gervais Mendy   Ecole Supérieure Polytechnique de Dakar,
                                    Senegal
Ado Adamou Abba Ari   University of Maroua, Cameroon
Hippolyte Michel T. Kenfack   University of Yaoundé I, Cameroon
Moussa Diallo   Ecole Supérieure Polytechnique de Dakar,
                                    Senegal

Mourad Gueroui	Université de Versailles Saint-Quentin en Yvelines, France
Jupiter Romuald N. Bakakeu	Alteryx, USA, and University of Erlangen, Germany
Jules Merlin Mouatcho Moualeu	University of the Witwatersrand, South Africa
Olutayo Oyeyemi Oyerinde	University of the Witwatersrand, South Africa
Alain Richard Ndjiongue	Memorial University of Newfoundland, Canada
Telex M. N. Ngatched	Memorial University of Newfoundland, Canada
Sylvester B. Aboagye	Memorial University of Newfoundland, Canada
Majid H. A. Khoshafa	Queens University, Canada
Lilatul Ferdouse	Ryerson University, Canada
Mkhuseli Ngxande	Stellenbosch University, South Africa
Ignace Tchangou Toudjeu	Tshwane University of Technology, South Africa
Raphael Angulu	Masinde Mulino University of Science and Technology, Kenya
Clement Nyirenda	University of Western Cape, South Africa
Narushan Pillay	University of KwaZulu-Natal, South Africa
Ruppa K. Thulasiram	University of Manitoba, Canada
Marcelo Luis Brocardo	University of Santa Catarina, Brazil
Amir Mohammadi Bagha	Ryerson University, Canada
Isaac Woungang	Ryerson University, Canada
Juggapong Natwichai	Chiang Mai University, Thailand
Nitin Gupta	University of Delhi, India
Neeraj Kumar	Thapar Institute of Engineering and Technology, India
Ilsun You	Soonchunhyang University, South Korea
Mehrdad Tirandazian	Ryerson University, Canada
Danda B. Rawat	Howard University, USA
Chen Ding	Ryerson University, Canada
Zelalem Shibeshi	University of Fort Hare, South Africa
Glaucio Haraldo Da Silva de Carvalho	Sheridan College, Canada
Joel Rodrigues	University of Beira Interior, Portugal
Andrea Visconti	University of Milan, Italy
Sanjay Kumar Dhurandher	University of Delhi, India
Alagan Anpalagan	Ryerson University, Canada
Vinesh Kumar	University of Delhi, India
Cui Baojiang	Beijing University of Post and Telecommunications, China
Chamseddine Talhi	École de technologie supérieure, Canada
Rohit Ranchal	IBM Watson Health Cloud, USA
Hamid Mcheick	Université du Québec à Chicoutimi, Canada

Contents

Artificial Intelligence Applications in Medicine

Remote sensing and AI in Agriculture

IoT and Enabling Smart System Technologies

A Certificate-Based Pairwise Key Establishment Protocol for IoT Resource-Constrained Devices

Mounirah Djam-Doudou[1], Ado Adamou Abba Ari[1,2]([envelope]),
Joel Herve Mboussam Emati[1], Arouna Ndam Njoya[3], Ousmane Thiare[4],
Nabila Labraoui[5], and Abdelhak Mourad Gueroui[2]

[1] Department of Computer Science, University of Maroua,
P.O. Box 46, Maroua, Cameroon
[2] DAVID Lab, Université Paris-Saclay, University of Versailles
Saint-Quentin-en-Yvelines, Versailles, France
adoadamou.abbaari@gmail.com
[3] Department of Computer Engineering, University Institute of Technology,
University of Ngaoundéré, P.O. Box 455, Ngaoundéré, Cameroon
[4] LANI Lab, Gaston Berger University of Saint-Louis,
P.O. Box 234, Saint-Louis, Senegal
[5] STIC Lab, Abou Bakr Belkaid University of Tlemcen,
P.O. Box 230, 13000 Chetouane, Tlemcen, Algeria

Abstract. In this paper, we address the problem of security in communication between IoT resource-constrained devices. We propose a peer-to-peer key establishment protocol based on implicit certificates and elliptic curves for low-capacity devices such as sensors. Using an AVL tree, we formulate the relationship between nodes in the same group as a certification chain. We propose a strategy that distributes the load of cryptographic computation over all nodes in the group. The group leader is the root certification authority of its group, and constructs an AVL tree from which a certification chain is established in an ordered fashion with an intermediate certification authority at each level of the tree. The primary nodes of each level are intermediate certification authorities. This trust chain will be used by the nodes to create and exchange implicit certificates on an elliptical curve. For communication between nodes, symmetric keys are derived from the certificates thus created. A realistic implementation of the protocol with TelosB sensors on the TOSSIM simulator shows the robustness of the protocol. In the worst case, the maximum size consumed for RAM is 4101 bytes and 24944 bytes for ROM. When we consider that a TelosB node offers up to 48 kb of ROM for 10 kb of RAM, we can conclude that the protocol is light enough to accommodate resource-constrained devices. Finally, we compare our proposal to three other well-known protocols.

Keywords: IoT · Elliptic curve cryptography · AVL tree · Implicit certificate · Keys management

© ICST Institute for Computer Sciences, Social Informatics and Telecommunications Engineering 2023
Published by Springer Nature Switzerland AG 2023. All Rights Reserved
T. M. Ngatched Nkouatchah et al. (Eds.): PAAISS 2022, LNICST 459, pp. 3–18, 2023.
https://doi.org/10.1007/978-3-031-25271-6_1

1 Introduction

The Internet of Things (IoT) is an infrastructure that interconnects objects called sensors via wireless communication networks for data collection, hosting and processing platforms [3,14]. The data produced in this way is used to provide a service to users via an application, for example. In other words, thanks to the Internet of Things, devices connect to each other and exploit the data they exchange [1,18,24]. However, security of communications in resource-poor devices is a real concern and cryptography is used among other solutions to address the security and privacy issues in such kind of networks [17,19,25]. Unfortunately, the use of cryptographic keys raises the problem of key management [9,30].

Indeed, key management is the process by which keys are generated, assigned, stored, protected, verified, revoked, renewed and destroyed in order to secure routing and improve cooperation between network nodes [23]. There are two main families of cryptographic solutions, symmetric cryptography and asymmetric cryptography. Symmetric cryptography is powerful in terms of calculation and uses small keys. However, in order to communicate, the parties must share the same key for encryption and decryption. Distribution to the different parties is therefore a critical operation whose sensitivity increases with the number of nodes in the network. Asymmetric cryptography requires the use of much longer keys and more complex calculations. Its requirements are not a serious problem for systems without resource constraints. However, sensors are resource-poor devices (memory, computing power, energy), which makes the use of traditional cryptographic key management protocols difficult in this context s [9,23,30]. Among the asymmetrical systems still called public key systems or PKI, we distinguish the asymmetrical cryptosystem RSA, which is very widely used. However, to ensure a fairly robust security it requires a key whose length is between 1024 and 2048 [7,31].

Furthermore, we also have Elliptic Curve Cryptography (ECC) which is particularly interesting for low-resource devices, as it can offer the same robustness as RSA with a much shorter [9,11,23]. Moreover, its performance can be improved by mathematical methods. Finally, an important factor for cryptographic key management between nodes is the approach. There are several approaches, such as the probabilistic approach in which nodes just have a certain probability of establishing shared keys with other nodes [2]. The knowledge-based approach to deployment. In this scheme, nodes are pre-arranged to improve the probability of establishing keys with neighbours. Another approach is the one that focuses on the dynamic mechanism in key management [33]. We have for instance the one based on AVL trees which are balanced binary trees [12,28,32]. For this approach, the nodes are grouped in clusters organised around a leader [4,10,13]. With such a topology, fixed around a special node, this node can act as a Certification Authority (CA) for the nodes in its cluster. However, such an approach is not suitable for homogeneous networks and is not without consequences on the dynamism of the network. In this paper, we address the problem of secure communication between resource-constrained devices. We propose a protocol to establish pairwise keys between nodes of the same group. To do so, we use an AVL tree that is constructed by the leader of a group of devices based on the signal strength received from the group members. The leader of the group is the root CA of its group and the leaders of each level of the tree are intermediate CAs for the subtrees they control.

The rest of the paper is organized as follows. Section 2 presents the related works. Section 3 presents the system model that includes design goal and the proposed key establishment scheme. Section 4 presents the proof of security of the early proposed scheme. Section 5 presents the performance evaluation in order to demonstrate the effectiveness of our proposal. We then proceed to comparison with other schemes in Sect. 6. Finally, the conclusion and future research is given in Sect. 7.

2   Related Works

In this section we present the concepts and previous work that inspired our protocol.

In [20], the authors proposed a theoretical protocol that uses implicit ECDH certificates to ensure key establishment. However, the protocol is communication-intensive. In addition, after deployment, nodes cannot renew the established certificates. In the scheme proposed by [6], ECC is used in a hybrid management of heterogeneous nodes and pre-distribution of keys. The topology is developed around a leader node that is deemed to be unassailable and has superior capabilities to ordinary nodes. To establish keys, ordinary nodes must request the leader. This solution forces the use of a static network around the leaders. In addition, the protocol uses a high number of communications to establish the keys.

In [34], the authors proposed a method of randomly pre-distributing keys using two AVL trees, one at the cluster level and another at the whole network level. AVL trees offer the possibility to change the position of nodes in the tree dynamically. In this approach, the network is hierarchical and the nodes are organized into clusters by the cluster-head. To establish session keys, the nodes by exchanging their individual keys and identifiers each can then calculate the key. The protocol requires a lot of communication to establish the keys and the workload is largely supported by the cluster-head which must change regularly depending on the energy, thus causing extra communication to reconfigure the system to zero [29] offer within the clusters formed using the LEACH protocol [15], a preload of identifiers and public keys in each node, which are then stored in an AVL tree. To communicate, nodes look up their public keys in the tree and generate a session key. The workload relies largely on the cluster-head, which must build the tree with the public keys of the nodes sent to it beforehand by the nodes, which has a non-negligible cost in terms of radio communication and therefore energy consumption. In addition, the protocol does not present a method for adding a new node to the network.

In [7] the authors proposed a protocol that uses an AVL tree to store the keys and positions of nodes in clusters. Each node is associated with a leaf of the tree, and it stores only the keys along the path from the node to the root of the AVL tree. To create a shared key between two nodes they exchange the numbers of their positions in the tree and use the first common key in the tree hierarchy to construct the key. However, in addition to the shared keys, the nodes must store the keys along the path from the node to the root of the tree, which has a cost in terms of storage. In addition, the process of creating symmetric keys requires a considerable amount of exchange which is costly in terms of communication. The protocol proposed by [27] uses implicit certificates and elliptic curves. Like done in [3,4,10,13], the topology is organized with clusters. The cluster-heads are provided with special capabilities which make the topology static around them. Nodes establish their shared keys by exchanging their implicit certificates from which the keys are derived. To be valid, the certificates must be signed by the cluster-head which is the CA. The way the protocol works places the burden of cryptographic operations solely on the CA. The obligation to have the certificates signed by the CA alone makes the solution dependent on a fixed topology around a leader with particularly high capacities compared to the other members of the cluster.

3   Vocabulary and System Model

3.1   Design Parameters and Vocabulary

In the rest of this work, we will use the notations and expressions summarized in Table 1.

3.2   Design Goal

The chosen method is based on elliptic curve cryptography. The principle of certificate generation is inspired by those explained in [8,26] which defines the standard for implicit certificates. Key management is based on the principle of the AVL tree for which the creation, insertion and deletion operations are of the order of $O(logn)$, which represents a significant time saving. Before deployment, the elliptic curve parameters are preloaded in each node with a unique identifier U and a global key K used to identify the nodes of the network. After the formation of the groups (cluster) and the designation of the leader, each cluster member sends a membership message to its leader as done by Ari et al. in [4,5]. In the end, the cluster leader uses the strength of the signals received from his cluster members to build an AVL tree, the structure of which only he knows. In each cluster, the cluster leader is the root CA. At each level of the tree, the main node of the level is an intermediate certification authority (ICA) for the nodes that depend on it and so on. When a cluster member wants to obtain a certificate or renew it, it first creates it. Then it sends its certificate in a request to its local certification authority (ICA), which is its first direct node in the tree hierarchy. The ICA signs the certificate with its private key and sends the signed certificate back to the applicant. This certificate is sent back

Table 1. Vocabuary

Notation	Description
U	node identifier
K	Global network key used for node authentication
rU	Random secret number generated by node U
R_U	Value of the point on the EC curve for the certificate requested by the node U
$Cert_U$	Implicit Certificate of the node U
$TrustChain_U$	Trusted list of node U
$HTrustChain_U$	Contains the hash value of the trusted list of node U
$CertChain_U$	certificate chain of node U
e	Contains the hash value of the certificate
s	Value used to calculate the private key of the requesting node
d_U	Private key of node U
Q_U	Public key of node U
N_U	Random cryptographic nonce generated by node U
K_{UV}	Key shared between nodes U and V
$rootCA$	Certification Authority
ICA	Intermediate Certification Authority

with the certificate chain ($CertChainU$) from the CA to the relevant node. The cryptographic workload is thus spread over the entire network and not on a particular node (root CA). The implementation of the chain of trust starts with the root CA CA which initiates it. It first self-generates a certificate from which it derives its key pair, then sends it to an external entity (e.g. a sink) by encrypting it with the global key K of the network. Then, the nodes in position 1 (those just below the root CA) according to the tree make a certificate request to the root CA. Once done, they initiate the same process for the next lower level nodes which in turn request certificates and so on up to the last level of the tree. The principle of the resulting certificate chain is the same as that of the RFC5280 standard [16]. At each step, the signing authority returns the signed certificate contained in $CertChain$ (the certificate chain from the root CA to the requesting node). Finally, the CH sends to each node of the cluster a message (encrypted with the global key) containing $TrustChain_U$ (the trust list of the node, i.e. the set of identifiers of the intermediate CAs along the path from the concerned node to the root CA of the tree), as well as $HTrustChain_U$ (the digest obtained by signing $TrustChain_U$ with the private key of the root CA).

3.3 Proposed Key Establishment Scheme

To set up its certificate, the CH follows these steps:

1. It generates two random number:

$$rCA1 \in [1, n-1] \cap \mathbb{N} \text{ and}$$
$$rCA2 \in [1, n-1] \cap \mathbb{N}$$

(1)

2. Calculates its certificate

$$Cert_{CA} = rCA1 + rCA2 \times G \tag{2}$$

3. Then it computes

$$
\begin{aligned}
e &= H(Cert_{CA}) \text{ and} \\
s &= erCA1 + erCA2 \ (mod \ n)
\end{aligned}
\tag{3}
$$

where H is a hash function

4. The node finally calculates its private key

$$
\begin{aligned}
e &= d_{CA} = erCA1 + s \ (mod \ n) \text{ and its public key} \\
s &= Q_{CA} = d_{CA} \times G
\end{aligned}
\tag{4}
$$

5. The node then sends its key pair to an external entity (for example a base station) using the global key K

3.4 Setting Up the Certificates and the Symmetric Key

To create a certificate, the node takes the following steps:

1. It generates a random number as done in Eq. 5

$$
\begin{aligned}
rU &\in [1, n-1] \cap \mathbb{N} \text{ and calculates} \\
R_U &= rU \times G
\end{aligned}
\tag{5}
$$

2. Then it produces a random nonce NU and computes

$$MAC_K[RU, N_U, U, TrustChain_U] \tag{6}$$

3. Then the node transmits U, $HTrustChain_U$, $TrustChain_U$, R_U and N_U with the MAC in a request to its local CA which is the first direct node in the tree hierarchy

4. At each level, when a CA i receives the request message, it checks the validity of the trust chain and the MAC of the requester. If the verification is successful, the Authority generates a random number $rCA_i \in [1, n-1] \cap \mathbb{N}$ and calculates the certificate

$$Cert_U = R_U + rCA_i \times G \tag{7}$$

5. Then, computes s using $Cert_U$, rCA_i and its own private key (d_{CA_i}),

$$
\begin{aligned}
e &= H(Cert_U) \text{ and} \\
s &= erCA_i + d_{CA_i} \ (mod \ n)
\end{aligned}
\tag{8}
$$

with H which is a hash function

6. The CA sends back to the requesting node U, $CertChain_U$ (this is its own certificate chain to which it has added the newly created certificate $Cert_U$), a random nonce N_{CA_i}, s, with

$$MAC_K[CertChain_U, N_{CA_i}, s, U] \tag{9}$$

When the message is received, node U checks the MAC and the chain of trust digest $HTrustChain_U$ and $TrustChain_U$ receives from the root CA. If everything is correct then U calculates $e = H(Cert_U)$. It uses the same hash function as her local CA

7. The node then computes its private key $d_U = erU + s(mod\ n)$ and its public key $Q_U = d_U \times G$

4 Proof of Security

Let be the nodes U and V, $TrustChain_U$ the list containing the elements of the chain of trust of U, $TrustChain_V$ the list containing the elements of the chain of trust of V, $HTrustChain_U$ and $HTrustChain_V$ the respective signatures associated with the lists of trusts of the nodes U and V generated with the private key of the root CA.

When node U wants to communicate with node V, it sends it a request containing a random Nonce N_U, with its $CertChain_U$, $TrustChain_U$ and $HTrustChain_U$. When V receives the request message from U, it first uses root CA's public key to verify the signature of the $HTrustChain_U$ hash chain.

Then, if the signature verification succeeds, then node V crosses its list with the received one by performing the Eq. 10.

$$TrustChain_U \cap TrustChain_V \tag{10}$$

If the operation result is $\neq \{\varnothing\}$, then it can verify the authenticity of the certificate by calculating the initiator's public key according to the following Eq. 11. In addition to obtaining the public key, this calculation ensures that the certificate chain is valid. Indeed, the certificates being linked to each other by the hierarchical signature, if an invalid certificate were to be found in the chain, it would make the calculation fail.

$$Q_{U_i} = d_{U_i} G$$
$$= (e_i r U_i + s_i (modn))G$$
$$= (e_i r U_i + e_i r C A_{i-1} + d_{C A_{i-1}} (modn))G$$
$$= e_i (r U_i G + r C A_{i-1} G(modn)) + d_{C A_{i-1}} G(modn)$$
$$= e_i (r U_i G + r C A_{i-1} G(modn)) + (e_{i-1} r U_{i-1} + e_{i-1} r C A_{i-2} + d_{C A_{i-2}})G(modn)$$
$$= e_i (r U_i G + r C A_{i-1} G(modn)) + e_{i-1} (r U_{i-1} G + r C A_{i-2} G(modn)) +$$
$$d_{C A_{i-2}} G(modn)$$
$$= e_i (r U_i G + r C A_{i-1} G(modn)) + e_{i-1} (r U_{i-1} G + r C A_{i-2} G(modn)) + \cdots$$
$$+ (e_{i-m} r U_{i-m} + e_{i-m} r C A_{i-m-1} + d_{C A_{i-m-1}})G(modn)$$
$$= e_i (r U_i G + r C A_{i-1} G(modn)) + e_{i-1} (r U_{i-1} G + r C A_{i-2} G(modn)) + \cdots$$
$$+ e_{i-m} (r U_{i-m} G + r C A_{i-m-1} G(modn)) + d_{C A_{i-m-1}} G(modn) \tag{11}$$
$$= e_i (R U_i + r C A_{i-1} G(modn)) + e_{i-1} (R U_{i-1} + r C A_{i-2} G(modn)) + \cdots$$
$$+ e_{i-m} (R U_{i-m} + r C A_{i-m-1} G(modn)) + d_{CA} G(modn)$$
$$= e_i Cert_{U_i} + e_{i-1} Cert_{U_{i-1}} + \cdots + e_{i-m} Cert_{U_{i-m}} + d_{CA} G$$
$$= \sum_{j=0}^{m} e_{i-j} Cert_{U_{i-j}} + d_{CA} G$$
$$= \sum_{j=0}^{m} e_{i-j} Cert_{U_{i-j}} + Q_{CA}$$
$$= \sum_{j=0}^{m} H(Cert_{U_{i-j}}) Cert_{U_{i-j}} + Q_{CA}$$
$$m \in \mathbb{N}$$

More generally we have:

$$Q_U = d_U G$$
$$= \sum_{i}^{CertChain_U} H(Cert_{U_i}) Cert_{U_i} + Q_{CA} \tag{12}$$

If the verification is successful for node V, then it sends the similar information to node U, which proceeds with the same verification in the same way. Each node can now calculate the pairewise key which is the product of their private key and the public key of the other. So node V computes $K_{VU} = d_V Q_U = d_V d_U G$ while node U computes $K_{UV} = d_U Q_V = d_U d_V G$.

5   Performance Evaluation

5.1   Simulation Parameters

For the simulation we use TOSSIM simulator with TelosB (16-bit architecture, 8 MHz maximum CPU speed, 48 kB flash, 10 kB RAM) with CC2420 radio chip, and the SHA1 algorithm for hashing. The message has the size 84 bytes and a structure such as in the Table 2.

Table 2. Message component

Component	Size (bytes)
EC	44
nodeID	2
random nonce	4
MAC	10
$timestamp$	6
$TrustChain$	4
$HTrustChain$	4
$CertChain$	6

5.2   Results

The measurements are made in terms of execution time and memory consumption. The simulation is done by alternating between the activation and deactivation of all the optimization options and the Shamir's trick. The simulation is conducted with seven TelosB nodes that form a cluster. We obtain the results as shown in Fig. 1, Fig. 2 and Fig. 3.

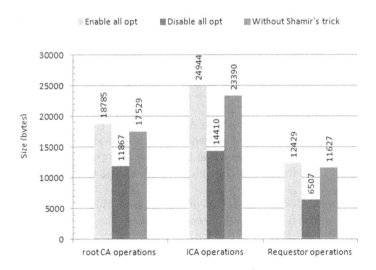

Fig. 1. ROM consumption

It can be seen that, in general, the highest consumption of resources (RAM, ROM, key calculation) is recorded at the level of the intermediate certification authorities, which in this case process two nodes each. While the lowest consumption is recorded at the requester level. Intermediate consumption is observed at

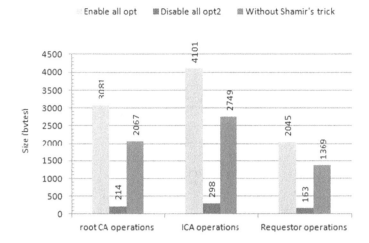

Fig. 2. RAM consumption

the root CA. This trend illustrates the distribution of the workload over all nodes as opposed to a root CA centric solution where the CA would have been in charge of all the calculations to personally issue certificates for all nodes in the network. One might legitimately ask what would happen if one node received far too much work while another received far less. This cannot be a problem because the distribution of nodes is based on a balanced tree, which implicitly guarantees a certain fairness in the distribution of workloads. Furthermore, as each node addresses its local CA directly, the protocol ensures that for certificate generation and key establishment, the communication cost is reduced to two direct message exchanges without intermediaries, which would not have been the case with an organisation around a fixed CA for which, in a large network, several relays between nodes would have been needed to route requests and processing.

The simulation results show that we obtain the lowest ROM and RAM consumption by disabling the optimisation techniques. On the other hand, enabling these techniques results in over-consumption. Disabling the Shamir trick alone produces a resource gain compared to enabling all techniques. Similar trends have already been observed in [27]. We also observe that the work time measured directly on the nodes for all operations follows the same trend Table 3. In the end, whatever the type of operation, for the worst case complexity, the maximum size consumed for RAM is 4101 bytes and 24944 bytes for ROM. When we know that a TelosB node offers up to 48 kb of ROM for 10 kb of RAM, we can conclude that the protocol is light enough to adapt to devices with limited resources.

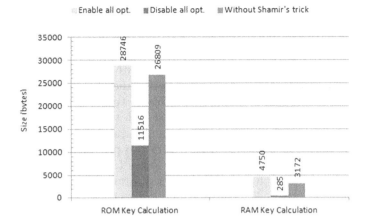

Fig. 3. Key calculation

Table 3. Execution time

Operation	Disable all opt (ms)	Enable all opt (ms)	Without Shamir's trick (ms)
Initialization	2,33	12596	6524
Certificate request generation	99531	6729	6949
Certificate generation	201766	13558	13565
Certificate verification	9864	6728	6935
Key computation	212745	13745	13758

5.3   Scalability Analysis

When a new node wishes to join the cluster, it sends a request to the CA which, after a successful verification, partially or totally rebuilds the tree according to the value of the newcomer's signal. The reconfiguration operations are accelerated by the tree construction time which is of the order of $O(logn)$. The impacted nodes receive new trust chains and can then obtain certificates from their local certification authorities. The same thing happens when a node is removed from the cluster. This has the advantage of causing a key refresh, which is a good thing for security. The new node can therefore establish a peer key with its neighbours using its certificate, which ensures that all are authenticated in the same cluster. The protocol therefore does not require nodes to be pre-loaded with all the keys in the network or neighbourhood. Moreover, the workload for node allocation does not require a cluster head with special capabilities, so the network can expand without problems. It is even possible to consider a periodic change of leader as in the LEACH protocol.

5.4   Security Analysis

Before deployment, all nodes are preloaded with the network key K. After the deployment time T, all communications are encrypted. Each node stores only the keys shared with the nodes it communicates with. If a node is compromised, the tree is reconfigured and all keys shared with other nodes are changed. With this approach, the adversary will not be able to trade with the other nodes. Each message contains a MAC authenticated with the global network key plus a timestamp value to preserve the integrity and freshness of the information. In addition, the shared keys are calculated from two pre-calculated values which ensures implicit trust and legitimacy, a legitimacy further enhanced by the use of chains of trust. Regarding availability, it is guaranteed by the possibility for nodes to establish a secure key pair to communicate in addition to the workload (key calculation, memory usage, etc.) that is distributed over the whole cluster, which can improve its lifetime and does not require defining a network with special nodes. The non-repudiation property is satisfied by the use of certificates; thus, no node can deny its responsibility. Confidentiality is guaranteed by the use of pairwise keys. With respect to attacks, if a node U is captured, the adversary can reveal Q_{CA}, $Cert_U$, Q_U, d_U, $TrustChain_U$, $HTrustChain_U$, $CertChain_U$. However, with the public key of its ICO, an adversary cannot create a new valid certificate because it does not have the private key of the ICO. More importantly, the creation of a certificate as well as the establishment of a pairwise key requires the verification of the valid TrustChainU which is accompanied by its signature $HTrustChain_U$ both issued only by the CA from its private key. This ensures that no node can generate a certificate otherwise. However, a compromised node can continue to establish pairwise keys with its neighbours, so we assume as [27] that a malicious node can be identified as such using the techniques proposed in [17,22]. When a node is identified as malicious, its identifier is broadcast to all the nodes in the network which revoke its certificate and block its identifier.

6   Comparison with Related Work

In this section, we compare our solution to the ECDH, EDSA [21] and [27] protocols that have most influenced our work. This comparison will be done in terms of time and memory consumption. We are particularly interested in the best results of our simulations, i.e. those obtained by deactivating only the Shamir's trick optimization. From Fig. 4, we can notice that in front of ECDSA we register a respective gain 1013 bytes of ROM and 217 bytes of RAM for the requestors (leaf node in the tree). On the other hand, we observe an increase with the root CA and the ICA. However, this increase is not a counter performance if we compare the number of operations performed by the concerned nodes i.e., for the root (certificate auto-generation, signing of two certificates for the ICA), for the ICA (certificate solicitation, signing of two certificates). In fine, the type of node whose operations are of the order of ECDSA is the Requestor which shows a clear improvement compared to ECDSA. Let us also recall that in our solution, these loads are quasi fixed loads because of the distribution on the

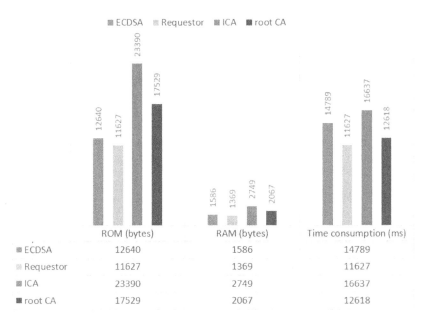

	ROM (bytes)	RAM (bytes)	Time consumption (ms)
ECDSA	12640	1586	14789
Requestor	11627	1369	11627
ICA	23390	2749	16637
root CA	17529	2067	12618

(a) Comparaison with ECDSA

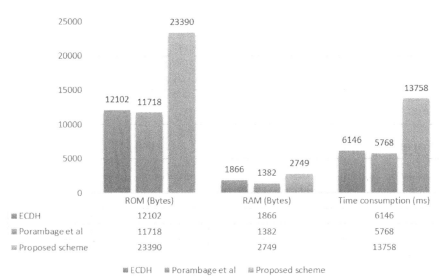

	ROM (Bytes)	RAM (Bytes)	Time consumption (ms)
ECDH	12102	1866	6146
Porambage et al	11718	1382	5768
Proposed scheme	23390	2749	13758

(b) Comparaison with ECDH and [27]

Fig. 4. Comparaison with other schemes

whole network compared to that of [27] which normally sees the load of the CA increasing as the cluster grows since it is the only one in charge of the signature of all the certificates of the cluster. We observe a similar variation with the EDCH protocol. The trend is also similar for the processing time as can be seen in Fig. 4. We notice that the ECDSA and ECDH schemes do not address the possibility of network scalability [21]. If the scheme proposed by [27] supports network scalability, it concentrates the workload of the cluster on the leader, which is consequently obliged to have special capabilities. Our solution guarantees scalability for all types of networks (homogeneous or not). The workload (cryptographic operations) is distributed over all the nodes in the network, which removes the constraint on the obligation to have a leader with special resources.

7   Conclusion

In this paper, we have proposed a certificate-based peer-to-peer key establishment protocol for low-capacity devices that provides good protection, given the limited characteristics of the devices. The approach used is a certificate chain structure to allow devices to generate elliptic curve symmetric keys from implicit certificates. This structure is built on an AVL tree to define the hierarchy of certificates stored in the network keys. Each node in the tree stores, in addition to its certificate, its chain of trust and its signature. It only generates keys with those neighbours with whom it wishes to communicate securely. This considerably reduces storage and greatly reduces communication and calculation. The communication and computation operations are decentralised to all the nodes in the tree, which makes the structure independent of a node with particular properties. The security analysis of the performances carried out has shown the robustness of the protocol for possible attack situations. In a perspective, we consider the use of the protocol in a key management solution by integrating routing, clustering and energy saving operations.

References

1. Aitsaadi, N., Boutaba, R., Takahashi, Y.: Cloudification of the internet of things. Ann. Telecommun. **72**(1), 1–2 (2017)
2. Albakri, A., Harn, L., Song, S.: Hierarchical key management scheme with probabilistic security in a wireless sensor network (WSN). Secur. Commun. Netw. **2019** (2019)
3. Ari, A.A.A., Djedouboum, A.C., Gueroui, M., Thiare, O., Mohamadou, A., Aliouat, Z.: A three-tier architecture of large-scale wireless sensor networks for big data collection. Appl. Sci. **10**(15), 5382 (2020)
4. Ari, A.A.A., Labraoui, N., Yenké, B.O., Gueroui, A.: Clustering algorithm for wireless sensor networks: the honeybee swarms nest-sites selection process based approach. Int. J. Sens. Netw. **27**(1), 1–13 (2018)
5. Ari, A.A.A., Yenke, B.O., Labraoui, N., Damakoa, I., Gueroui, A.: A power efficient cluster-based routing algorithm for wireless sensor networks: honeybees swarm intelligence based approach. J. Netw. Comput. Appl. **69**, 77–97 (2016)

6. Azarderskhsh, R., Reyhani-Masoleh, A.: Secure clustering and symmetric key establishment in heterogeneous wireless sensor networks. EURASIP J. Wirel. Commun. Netw. **2011**, 1–12 (2011)
7. Boumerzoug, H., Amar Bensaber, B., Biskri, I.: A key management method based on an AVL tree and ECC cryptography for wireless sensor networks. In: Proceedings of the 7th ACM Symposium on QoS and Security for Wireless and Mobile Networks, pp. 57–62 (2011)
8. Campagna, M.: SEC 4: elliptic curve Qu-Vanstone implicit certificate scheme (ECQV). Standards for Efficient Cryptography, Version 1 (2013)
9. Chatterjee, U., Ray, S., Khan, M.K., Dasgupta, M., Chen, C.M.: An ECC-based lightweight remote user authentication and key management scheme for IoT communication in context of fog computing. Computing 1–37 (2022)
10. Djedouboum, A.C., Ari, A.A.A., Gueroui, A.M., Mohamadou, A., Thiare, O., Aliouat, Z.: A framework of modeling large-scale wireless sensor networks for big data collection. Symmetry **12**(7), 1113 (2020)
11. Djerassem, L., Tieudjo, D.: On congruent numbers elliptic curves. IOSR J. Math. **16**(3), 1–5 (2020)
12. Gautam, A.K., Kumar, R.: A comprehensive study on key management, authentication and trust management techniques in wireless sensor networks. SN Appl. Sci. **3**(1), 1–27 (2021). https://doi.org/10.1007/s42452-020-04089-9
13. Gbadouissa, J.E.Z., Ari, A.A.A., Titouna, C., Gueroui, A.M., Thiare, O.: HGC: hypergraph based clustering scheme for power aware wireless sensor networks. Future Gener. Comput. Syst. **105**, 175–183 (2020)
14. Hamidouche, R., Aliouat, Z., Ari, A.A.A., Gueroui, A.: Mobile sink path planning in heterogeneous IoT sensors: a SALP swarm algorithm scheme. KSII Trans. Internet Inf. Syst. **15**(6), 2225–2239 (2021)
15. Heinzelman, W.R., Chandrakasan, A., Balakrishnan, H.: Energy-efficient communication protocol for wireless microsensor networks. In: Proceedings of the 33rd Annual Hawaii International Conference on System Sciences, p. 10. IEEE (2000)
16. Housley, R.: Internationalization updates to RFC 5280. Technical report (2018)
17. Jokhio, S.H., Jokhio, I.A., Kemp, A.H.: Node capture attack detection and defence in wireless sensor networks. IET Wirel. Sens. Syst. **2**(3), 161–169 (2012)
18. Keivani, A., Ghayoor, F., Tapamo, J.R.: Collaborative mobile edge computing in Ev2x: a solution for low-cost driver assistance systems. Wirel. Pers. Commun. **118**(3), 1869–1882 (2021)
19. Khedim, F., Labraoui, N., Ari, A.A.A.: A cognitive chronometry strategy associated with a revised cloud model to deal with the dishonest recommendations attacks in wireless sensor networks. J. Netw. Comput. Appl. **123**, 42–56 (2018)
20. Kotzanikolaou, P., Magkos, E.: Hybrid key establishment for multiphase self-organized sensor networks. In: Sixth IEEE International Symposium on a World of Wireless Mobile and Multimedia Networks, pp. 581–587. IEEE (2005)
21. Liu, A., Ning, P.: TinyECC: a configurable library for elliptic curve cryptography in wireless sensor networks. In: 2008 International Conference on Information Processing in Sensor Networks (ipsn 2008), pp. 245–256 (2008). https://doi.org/10.1109/IPSN.2008.47
22. Lu, R., Li, X., Liang, X., Shen, X., Lin, X.: GRS: the green, reliability, and security of emerging machine to machine communications. IEEE Commun. Mag. **49**(4), 28–35 (2011)
23. Majumder, S., Ray, S., Sadhukhan, D., Khan, M.K., Dasgupta, M.: ECC-CoAP: elliptic curve cryptography based constraint application protocol for internet of things. Wirel. Pers. Commun. **116**(3), 1867–1896 (2021)

24. Myoupo, J.F., Nana, B.P., Tchendji, V.K.: Fault-tolerant and energy-efficient routing protocols for a virtual three-dimensional wireless sensor network. Comput. Electr. Eng. **72**, 949–964 (2018)
25. Ngangmo, O.K., Ari, A.A.A., Alidou, M., Thiare, O., Kolyang, D.T.: Guarantees of differential privacy in cloud of things: a multilevel data publication scheme. Int. J. Eng. Res. Afr. **56**, 199–212 (2021)
26. Poornima, A., Amberker, B.: Tree-based key management scheme for heterogeneous sensor networks. In: 2008 16th IEEE International Conference on Networks, pp. 1–6. IEEE (2008)
27. Porambage, P., Kumar, P., Schmitt, C., Gurtov, A., Ylianttila, M.: Certificate-based pairwise key establishment protocol for wireless sensor networks. In: 2013 IEEE 16th International Conference on Computational Science and Engineering, pp. 667–674. IEEE (2013)
28. Prakasha, K., Muniyal, B., Acharya, V., Krishna, S., Prakash, S.: Efficient digital certificate verification in wireless public key infrastructure using enhanced certificate revocation list. Inf. Secur. J. Glob. Perspect. **27**(4), 214–229 (2018)
29. Qin, Z., Zhang, X., Feng, K., Zhang, Q., Huang, J.: An efficient key management scheme based on ECC and AVL tree for large scale wireless sensor networks. Int. J. Distrib. Sens. Netw. **11**(9), 691498 (2015)
30. Rana, M., Mamun, Q., Islam, R.: Lightweight cryptography in IoT networks: a survey. Future Gener. Comput. Syst. **129**, 77–89 (2022)
31. Suárez-Albela, M., Fernández-Caramés, T.M., Fraga-Lamas, P., Castedo, L.: A practical performance comparison of ECC and RSA for resource-constrained IoT devices. In: 2018 Global Internet of Things Summit (GIoTS), pp. 1–6. IEEE (2018)
32. Sun, Y., Yin, S., Liu, J., Teng, L.: A certificateless group authenticated key agreement protocol based on dynamic binary tree. Int. J. Netw. Secur. **21**(5), 843–849 (2019)
33. Yousefpoor, M.S., Barati, H.: Dynamic key management algorithms in wireless sensor networks: a survey. Comput. Commun. **134**, 52–69 (2019)
34. Zhang, Y.Y., Yang, W.C., Kim, K.B., Park, M.S.: An AVL tree-based dynamic key management in hierarchical wireless sensor network. In: 2008 International Conference on Intelligent Information Hiding and Multimedia Signal Processing, pp. 298–303. IEEE (2008)

Reinforcement Learning-Based Dynamic Path Allocation in IoT Systems

Arouna Ndam Njoya[1]([✉])(iD), Uriel Nguefack Yefou[2](iD),
Ado Adamou Abba Ari[3,6](iD), Rockefeller[4], Assidé Christian Djedouboum[5,6](iD),
Wahabou Abdou[7], and Ousmane Thiare[8](iD)

[1] Department of Computer Engineering, University Institute of Technology,
University of Ngaoundéré, P.O. Box 455, Ngaoundéré, Cameroon
ndanjoa@gmail.com
[2] African Institute for Mathematical Sciences, South West Region, Crystal Gardens,
P.O. Box 608, Limbe, Cameroon
[3] DAVID Lab, Université Paris-Saclay, University of Versailles
Saint-Quentin-en-Yvelines, 45 Avenue des États-Unis, 78000 Versailles, France
[4] Department of Mathematical Sciences, Stellenbosch University,
Private Bag X1, Matieland, 7602 Stellenbosch, South Africa
[5] Department of Computer Science, University of Moundou,
P.O. Box 206, Moundou, Chad
[6] Department of Computer Science, University of Maroua,
P.O. Box 814, Maroua, Cameroon
[7] LIB EA7534, University Bourgogne Franche-Comté, 9 Avenue Alain Savary,
21078 Dijon, France
[8] LANI Lab, Gaston Berger University of Saint-Louis,
P.O. Box 234, Saint-Louis, Senegal

Abstract. With an increasingly interconnected world, Internet of
Things (IoT) technologies are progressively turning into an integral part
of our day-to-day lives. IoT systems, which can be seen as a set of sensor nodes connected to each other to exchange information, are subject
to energy limitations. As a result of that, efficient delivery schemes for
data transmission between sensor nodes are required in order to extend
the network lifetime, and therefore reduce nodes' energy drain. Various studies have been conducted to address this issue. However, only a
few of them propose strategies that take into account the energy context in the network during data transmission. A lot of attention has
drifted towards reinforcement learning lately, especially given its success in addressing problems that involve clustering and data collection
challenges. This paper focuses on its application in Dynamic Path
Prediction: an approach through which an agent, operating in a network, achieves a behavior that allows the selection of an optimal path
for data transmission while minimizing network energy consumption. We
performed a comparative analysis between the proposed approach and
the traditional heuristics, including Dijkstra and A star. The results
obtained show that our model increases the network lifetime by a factor
of 2.26 compared to 1.58 obtained with A star and Dijkstra algorithms.

© ICST Institute for Computer Sciences, Social Informatics and Telecommunications Engineering 2023
Published by Springer Nature Switzerland AG 2023. All Rights Reserved
T. M. Ngatched Nkouatchah et al. (Eds.): PAAISS 2022, LNICST 459, pp. 19–38, 2023.
https://doi.org/10.1007/978-3-031-25271-6_2

Keywords: Internet of things · Wireless sensor network · Network lifetime · Reinforcement learning

1   Introduction

At its core, communication involves sending information from one location to another. It takes three pieces for communication to happen: A sender, a message, and a recipient. Communication has evolved into a vital human activity that plays a significant role in our daily lives. Though this may sound like a straightforward process, recent developments in making communication between two entities neater and neater, have brought along some layers of complexity. Relating it to this context, pieces of equipment for instance, that are connected to the Internet can also communicate with one another in a shared environment, hence the attribute IoT. IoT Communication refers to the infrastructure, technologies, and protocols that connect IoT devices, gateways, and cloud platforms [1,2]. We are increasingly witnessing the emergence of new Information and Communication Technology (ICT), gadgets with sensors that capture a large amount of data. Therefore, companies, governments, and administrations share information with one another and with specific individuals. As a result of that, a great deal of information is disseminated every day, every minute, and every second. One of the key challenges in communications, is to come up with strategies to transfer or convey information with short latency and minimal energy [3,4]. Fortunately, dynamic path prediction has proven to be a viable solution for conserving energy and ensuring that the majority of the network's paths are used.

The limited capacity of IoTs [5] in terms of computation and energy makes their spatial distribution constantly dynamic. This dynamic attribute is also enhanced by the mobility of IoT nodes. Therefore, conventional routing algorithms which consist in selecting a static path for data transmission based solely on the shortest path can no longer be systematically applied in such an environment. Constraints related to the characteristics of IoT nodes and to the dynamism of the topology must be taken into account during data routing operations. However, there is an emergence of routing protocol which consists of the dynamic assignment of network segments to data flows in transit through the network.

The idea behind dynamic routing is to generate a routing path from a source node to a destination node, incorporating the requirements of the application, resources, and spatial configuration of the network. This concept refers to dynamic path planning. Specifically, it is about performing automatic routing operations based on the network context [6]. In the current context, in addition to the availability of network resources, the positions of nodes in the network also refer to the data carried in the network. Taking into account these pieces of information, it is possible to design a machine learning algorithm that is able to minimize the usage of network resources like the network energy consumption [7,8]. A couple of existing methods have proposed mechanisms that take into account the energy context in the network. However, our methodology consists of designing dynamic data path prediction and establishment, in which the path is created as and when the flow moves from one subnetwork to another using IoT context information.

1.1 Limitations and Challenges

When referring to path planning in the network, the main optimization parameter that comes to mind is the length of the path that the traffic will take. However, the fact remains that, in the context of IoTs and therefore sensor networks, energy is one of the most important metrics to consider. When it comes to extending the lifetime of such a network, it is common practice to limit the transmission activities of nodes as much as possible because they promote their energy depletion. Routing algorithms that take into account the network lifetime extension and nodes' energy consumption have been the subject of deep comparative study in [9]. Apart from the fact that the routing problem is NP-hard, it is inappropriate to consider solving it using deterministic algorithms [9,10]. Many algorithms, including meta-heuristic ones like Particle Swarm Optimization(PSO), and genetic ones like Ant Colony Optimization (ACO) have been used to tackle that. More recently machine learning approaches such as Encoder-Decoder Neural Network and Long Short Term Memory (LSTM) are being increasingly used as alternative methods to address this problem.

In this work, we use Reinforcement Learning algorithms in order to detect and forecast in an IoT sensor network where the information will flow next time in order to minimize the energy consumption in the network.

1.2 Authors' Contributions

Our main objective in this work is to design a machine learning model that exploits the Spatio-temporal distribution of sensor nodes and uses context energy from IoT to detect and predict the next network segment of the incoming flow. Performing this task would come with the advantage that the energy consumption in the network will be minimized during the data transfer and therefore the network's lifetime is set to be extended, as it remains one of the major problems in IoT. One of the unique features of Reinforcement Learning is that it does not require prior knowledge of the system's underlying dynamics, and there is no constraints on the reward metrics to be used when setting a goal to achieve. Moreover, the agent is the component that interacts in an environment and makes decisions based on a certain reward or punishment it receives.

The contribution of this paper includes:

– Proposing an algorithm that is used to derive the best path for a request based on energy consumption;
– Proposing a new feature engineering representation that gives to the RL agent useful information;
– Designing a model using RL for path planning prediction.

The rest of the paper is organized as follows. Section 2 presents the methods used in path planning prediction. Section 3 states the dynamic path prediction problem as well as the mathematical formulation of it, followed by a general description of the entire proposed Machine Learning (ML) model. Section 4 is devoted to simulations and results where we present the different results that we obtained using the model that we have built. Section 5 presents the conclusion as well as future work.

2   Related Work

Some research has already been conducted on the dynamic path prediction problem. As mentioned previously, the main constraint here is the energy consumption in the network. The related work exposed below is divided into two parts based on the approach used to solve the problem.

Studies have been conducted for dynamic path prediction in IoT wireless networks using heuristic and metaheuristic approaches.

To extend the network lifetime, it is proposed in [11] a routing algorithm through multi-hop cluster-based architecture structured around a base station. The approach adopted was firstly to develop a PSO routing algorithm by carrying out a multi-objective formulation of the problem terms of linear programming, as described in Eq. 1. That also includes minimizing the maximum transmission distance between two nodes and the maximum number of hops to the base station.

$$
\begin{aligned}
\text{minimize} \quad & W = \alpha \times MaxDist + \beta \times MaxHop \\
\text{subject to} \quad & dis(g_i, g_j) \times a_{ij} \le d_{max}, \\
& \sum_{j=1}^{M+1} a_{ij} = 1, 1 \le i \le M \\
& \forall\ g_j\ \in\ \xi \cup \{g_{M+1}\} \text{ and } i \ne j
\end{aligned}
\tag{1}
$$

where $\alpha = \beta - 1$, α is the parameter that controls the total path distance and β is the parameter that controls the total hop count.

The maximum distance between two nodes is given by Eq. 2:

$$
MaxDist = Max\left\{ dis(g_i, NextHop(g_i))|\ \forall\ i, 1 \le i \le M, g_i \in \xi \right\}, \tag{2}
$$

The maximum HopCount of the gateway is given by Eq. 3:

$$
MaxHop = Max\left\{ HopCount(g_i)|\ \forall\ i, 1 \le i \le M, g_i \in \xi \right\}, \tag{3}
$$

ξ is the set of gateways, $NextHop(g_i)$ is the gateway g_j, $HopCount(g_i)$ denotes the number of next hops required to reach the base station from g_i and d_{max} denotes the maximum communication range of the gateways. a_{ij} be a Boolean variable such that $a_{ij} = 1$ if the sensor node s_i is assigned to the cluster head g_j and $a_{ij} = 0$ if it is not.

The second approach tackles the design of a PSO clustering algorithm to extend the lifetime of the network by expressing it in a nonlinear programming fashion, as a minimization of the communication distance between a node and its cluster head and a reduction of energy consumption of cluster head. The considered lifetime model is one that assumes that the network is alive if no gateway (cluster head) is dead. For evaluation, two scenarios were generated and a comparative study was conducted with the genetic algorithm [10], where the formalization of the optimization problem is given by Eq. 4. The heuristic computes the shortest path from a sensor to its cluster head [12] and the greedy load-balancing clustering algorithm [13]. Simulation results have shown that in addition to extending the lifetime of the network, the proposed algorithms maximize the number of packets transmitted and reduce the number of inactive sensors, i.e. sensors that can no longer communicate with a gateway. Although these results are suitable, it is important to note that most of the studies are based on the number of hops, which in this case takes into account either the direction of data transmission or application requirements as outlined in [14].

$$
\begin{aligned}
&\text{minimize} && L = \max\left\{ L_i \mid \forall\, g_i \in \xi \right\} \\
&\text{subject to} && \sum_{g_j \in \xi} a_{ij} = 1 \mid \forall\, S_i \in S \\
& && \sum_{S_i \in S} d_i \times a_{ij} \le L \mid \forall\, g_j \in \xi,
\end{aligned}
\tag{4}
$$

with L_i the load of the cluster, S, the set of sensors and d_i the traffic load contributed by a sensor node S_i.

These shortcomings can result in excessive use of the same path and rapid degradation of network lifetime. In order to improve the end-to-end delay, routing overhead and data packet delivery, the polymorphism-aware routing algorithm (APAR) was proposed in [15]. The method is a combination of the ACO and dynamic source routing algorithm (DSR) previously proposed in [16]. Considering a tree topology around a sink with nodes composed of Radio Frequency IDentification (RFID) tags, RFID readers, and sensors, it is proposed in [17] a fuzzy logic dynamic route selection technique including four metrics (Expected Transmission Count, Number of Hops, Delivery Ratio and Energy Consumed). Each metric is used to determine a route likely to satisfy an application requirement. In [18], the network lifetime is studied by performing an analysis of the impact of the direct transmission from the cluster head to the base station and the policy of choosing the cluster head during routing operations. In [19], a model for data aggregation in a dense Wireless Sensor Network (WSN) with a single sink is developed, and the lifetime of the system is maximized by minimizing the maximum proportionate energy consumption across all nodes using a linear programming problem.

For a while, machine learning methods have been employed in IoT networks to improve the network's energy consumption during path selection.

For Sequence to Sequence path prediction, an Encoder Decoder Neural Network has been developed in [20]. A proposed deep learning approach exploits data for an IoT monitoring system deployed inside the museum to predict the movements of visitors. One of the important results of this study is the generation of a visit graph that indicates the most visited positions and the most used paths in the museum. In the same vein, in order to control traffic in IoT networks and thereby path usage, an LSTM-based strategy has been proposed in [21]. The proposed method uses data properties through time to implement a data fusion mechanism to monitor the traffic load on each road segment. In [22], the authors proposed a deep Q-learning-based method for saving energy in smart buildings. The choice of whether to buy or sell energy from the storage system is made by the Deep Q Learning agent.

3   System Model

This section presents the proposed machine learning algorithm method and metrics computation for solving the problem of path planning prediction in a dynamic graph. The organization is as follows: Subsect. 3.1 presents our network assumptions and different topology of node arrangement in a WSN. The IoT Network is well represented in Subsect. 3.2 using the concepts of graphs on which our model is based. Subsection 3.3 focuses on design goal and problem formulation, Subsect. 3.4 gives a description of various terminologies used in the computation of our model and the last subsection gives in detail our reinforcement learning framework.

3.1   Network Assumptions

In this project, the network is assumed to be dynamic, consisting of non-mobile homogeneous fully functional sensor nodes capable of performing tasks of sensing, computing, and communication. The number of sensor nodes in the network exerts a significant impact on energy consumption as well as on sensing performance. Nodes arrangements in a deployment area can either be flat or have a hierarchical pattern. In our case, we work with the flat Architecture more precisely the Multi Hops architecture where we have one sink and the nodes are connected together and some of them to the sink which suits well with the problem to solve.

3.2   Graph Theory Representation of IoT Network

An IoT Network can be described using a graph theory representation with links also called edges or vertices and nodes. Our graph is denoted by $G = (V; E)$, where:

- V is a set of vertices (also called nodes or points)
- $E \subseteq \{\{k,l\} \mid k,l \in V \text{ and } k \neq l\}$, a set of edges or links between each node in the IoT network, which are unordered pairs of vertices (that is, an edge is associated with two distinct vertices).

The number of nodes is denoted by $N = |V|$ and the number of links $L = |E|$. The diameter of a network is the greatest number of connected links that make a path, whereas the degree of a node is the number of links that are connected to it.

Let $G = (V; E)$ be a graph, we define the weight matrix of G as a matrix $W(G)$, with rows and columns representing the nodes of G given by Eq. 5.

$$W(v_a, v_b) = w(l_{ab}), \tag{5}$$

where l_{ab} denotes the link between nodes v_a and v_b. Also, we can define the average degree of a node denoted by $< K >$ as:

$$< K >= \frac{2 V|}{|E|} \tag{6}$$

3.3   Design Goal and Problem Formulation

This model was created in order to accurately anticipate the dynamic path in the IoT Network as specified in Sect. 3.2 via graph representations. Furthermore, given that each of these sensor nodes runs on limited battery power, which is not always rechargeable, there is a need to develop a model that reduces energy consumption for data transmission in order to reduce delay, power loss, packet loss, and re-transmission, thereby extending the network's lifespan.

Transmission Energy. A radio model which defines the energy required for data transmission has been given by [23]. If we consider that all the sensor nodes have the same initial energy E_i over a given distance d to transfer k bit of information, we can then define transmission energy by Eq. 7:

$$E_{Tx}(k, d) = \begin{cases} kE_{elec} + k\varepsilon_{fs}d^2, & \text{if } d < d_0 \\ kE_{elec} + k\varepsilon_{amp}d^4, & \text{if } d \geq d_0, \end{cases} \tag{7}$$

where E_{elec} reperesents the electronic energy consumption, ε_{fs} and ε_{amp} represent the amplifier energy when the distance is less or greater than a certain threshold value d_0 respectively.

To receive the data sent from another sensor, there is an amount of energy required called Reception Energy, the Reception energy is given by the Eq. 8:

$$E_{Rx} = kE_{elec}. \tag{8}$$

Total Energy Consumption. The total energy consumption E_{Tc} in a path where n is the number of nodes situated in the transfer path can be calculated using Eq. 9:

$$E_{Tc} = E^1(k,d) + \sum_{i=1}^{n} E^{2i}(k,d), \tag{9}$$

where

$$E^1(k,d) = E_{Tx}(k,d) \tag{10}$$

is the transmission energy from the source node to the node directly linked to the source node and

$$E^{2i}(k,d) = E_{Tx}(k,d) + E_{Rx} \tag{11}$$

is the energy consumption of a node situated on the transfer path.

Remaining Energy. After transmitting the data, the remaining energy of the node can be calculated in two ways:

If the node is the source node, the remaining energy is given by:

$$E^{iupdate} = E_i - E_{Tx}. \tag{12}$$

where E_i is the initial energy level of node i

In the other case, if the node is situated on the transfer path, this remaining energy is computed as follows:

$$E^{iupdate} = E_i - E_{Tx} - E_{Rx}. \tag{13}$$

3.4   Terminologies

Table 1 shows us the set of parameters necessary for our problem formulation.

Table 1. Terminologies of the mathematical formulation

Notations	Description
S	Set of sensor nodes in the IoT Network
W_{ij}	Weight between source node i and destination node j
E_i	Initial Energy level of node i
N	Total Number of nodes
k	Data packet size
A	Network Size
BS	Base station
E_{Tx}	Transmission Energy
E_{Rx}	Reception Energy
ε_{amp}	Transmit amplifier
ε_{fs}	Transmit amplifier
E_{elec}	Electronic Energy Consumption

3.5   Reinforcement Learning Framework

To address the Dynamic Path prediction problem, we used the Deep Q Learning algorithm in conjunction with an agent that behaves in the environment similar to that of a real network provisioning environment. When the agent obtains the state S_t from the environment at time t, it performs an action A_t and receives a reward R_{t+1}. This operation $(\cdots, S_t, A_t, R_{t+1}, S_{t+1}, A_{t+1}, \cdots)$ is repeated by the agent until the provisioning is completed. The design of the environment, state space, and action space representations, as well as the design of the reward function, are all critical for the overall success of Reinforcement Learning algorithms. The four main aspects are listed as follows:

Design of the Path Planning Environment. The proposed Dynamic Path Environment architecture is presented in Fig. 1. The Deep Reinforcement Learning (DRL)-agent interacts with the environment by making use of the defined functions. To design the environment, a certain number of steps is required as it is illustrated in Fig. 1.

- **Initialize Network Topology**: The topology of the network is represented by a graph that we have generated randomly. The link between each node represents the euclidian distance between them, and an initial energy of $2J$ is allocated to each of these nodes.
- **State your sources nodes and Sink**: Since the network topology is already set up, the attributes of the nodes in the network are partitioned into two categories: One node is chosen as the Sink and all the remaining ones are our potential sources nodes also called active nodes.
- **Make a Random Request**: We randomly generate some requests in the Network by choosing randomly one node among all the active nodes.
- **Find all Possible paths to accomplish the request**: After making the request, we find all possible paths that can be used to forward data from the selected source node to the sink.
- **Compute the Energy consumption for all possible paths**: For all the possible paths that we got previously, we compute the energy consumption for all these paths using the Eqs. 9, 10, 11.
- **Choose k paths out of all possible paths based on energy consumed**: Having the energy consumed for all the possible paths, we will sort the energy in increasing order and select the k paths having the minimum energy consumed.
- **Design the state representation**: The state representation contains meaningful information about the state of the agent, more explanation is given in Subsect. 3.5.
- **Select one path out of the k precomputed paths:** Take one path out of the k precomputed paths that we have selected before and Check the feasibility of this path.
- **Check if a path is feasible**: A path is feasible if:

- For the source node: The remaining energy of the source node is greater than the transmission energy used by the source node to transmit the data to the next one.
- For the intermediate node: The remaining energy of the intermediate node is greater than the transmission energy used by the node to transmit the data to the next one plus the reception energy used to receive the data from the previous node.

In the event of the path's **Feasibility**, we grant the request and give a positive reward to the agent otherwise the request is rejected and we punish the agent.

- **Update sensors energy:** When a path is feasible, after granted the agent, update sensors energy of the nodes situated in the transfer path using Eqs. 12, 13.

State Space. Figure 2 shows us how to design the RL agent, at the Input, we have the state representation. The state representation contains meaningful information that will help the agent to choose a good policy in order to maximize his reward.

Our state representation is an array which contains the encoding of the active nodes and the corresponding energy of these encoded active nodes.

$$S_r = [A_e, R_e], \tag{14}$$

where $A_e = [0, 0, \cdots, 1, 0, 0]$ is the encoding of the active nodes of the network, 1 is situated at the index of the source node of the request.

$R_e = [E_0, E_1, \cdots, E_{N-1}, E_N]$ is the remaining energy of each of the active nodes and N is the total number of active nodes.

In the middle, we have the Deep Neural Network (DNN) which is composed of the Hidden Layer, we will present it in more detail in the next section.

Action Space. Once the state space is defined, the action space $\mathcal{A}_f$ of the dynamic path prediction problem is straightforward.

$$\mathcal{A}_f = \left\{ A_{s_t} / A_{s_t} = \left\{ p_k \mid p_1, \cdots, p_{|K|} \right\}, t \leq T \right\}, \tag{15}$$

where A_{s_t} is the action at time t, and T is the maximum number of steps per episode. p_k denotes that the agent selects the path with the highest Q-value at time step t given the set of K pre-computed paths of request d. So given a request, the possible action at each time step is either to choose a path or to reject the request.

Reward Function. The design of the reward may have an influence on provisioning policies, which is important for policy training. The incentive at each time step should aid in guiding real provisioning efforts, and the cumulative long-term reward should also represent the overall provisioning goal. Knowing

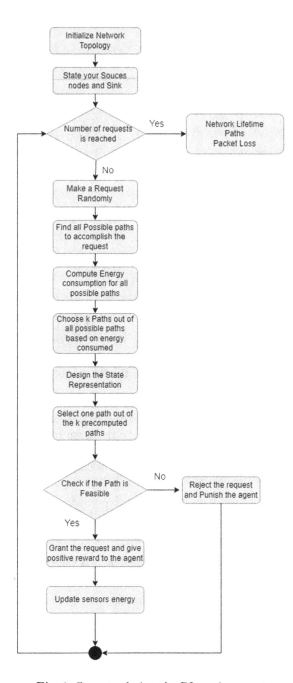

Fig. 1. Steps to design the RL environment

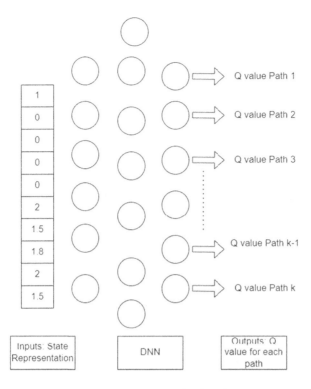

Fig. 2. Steps to design the RL Agent

that when we receive a request, the agent chooses one of the K-pre-computed pathways that may be utilized to transfer the data, we have two potential outcomes at a given time t: i) the request is granted, or ii) the request is refused since the path is not viable. Based on our knowledge, we defined the reward function as follows:

$$R_{t+1} = \begin{cases} 1/E_{Tc}^{(k)}, & \text{if path } k \text{ is feasible} \\ 0, & \text{otherwise} \end{cases} \tag{16}$$

where R_{t+1} is the immediate reward at time t, E_{Tc}^{k} is the total energy consumption in the path k at time t.

Neural Network Architecture. After testing many parameters (activation function, number of layers, number of neurons) in our model, the best architecture was finally obtained. Table 2 shows the architecture of our DNN, where we have 3 layers with 128 neurons each and the Rectified Linear Unit (ReLU) activation function.

Our system model has been presented in the above section.

Table 2. Neural network architecture

Layer	Activation	Number of Neurons
1	ReLU	128
2	ReLU	128
3	ReLU	128

4 Simulation

In this section, we analyse and report the numeric results obtained from the proposed algorithm for the dynamic path prediction problem and then compare it with both the A star algorithm and the Dijkstra algorithm.

4.1 Network Topology and Parameters of Simulation

Seven differents topologies have been used, i.e., Graph20, Graph25, Graph30, Graph35, Graph40, Graph45 and Graph50 (random graphs with respectively 20, 25, 30, 35, 40, 45 and 50 nodes). Figures 3 and 4 give us an illustration of the network with 20 and 25 nodes respectively. Each topology's key characteristics (the number of links and nodes; diameter (Δ); mean, minimum and maximum node degrees; average link length are detailed in Table 3. The columns labeled 'Avg.deg', 'Max.deg' and 'Min.deg' represent the mean node degree, the maximum node degree and the minimum node degree respectively.

Fig. 3. Network with 20 nodes

Fig. 4. Network with 25 nodes

Table 3. Key topology characteristics

Datasets	$|N|$	$|L|$	Δ	Avg.deg	Max.deg	Min.deg	Avg.Link
Graph20	20	55	3	5.5	11	3	1.86
Graph25	25	83	3	6.64	12	3	1.82
Graph30	30	125	3	8.33	15	3	1.78

The Table 4 below shows us the values of the differents parameters used for the simulation.

Table 4. Parameters of simulation

Parameter	Value
Sensor nodes	20, 25, 30, 35, 40, 45, 50
Initial Energy of sensor nodes	2.0 J
Number of simulations iterations	1000
E_{elec}	50 nJ/bit
ε_{fs}	10 pJ/bit/m^2
ε_{amp}	0.0013 pJ/bit/m^4
d_0	87 m
Packet size	4000 bits

4.2   Quantitative Evaluation

In our topology which uses the Deep Q Network (DQN), we conduct a Grid-Search on several parameters, and the best values are selected. The discount factor γ was fixed at 0.95, the learning rate α at 10^{-4}, and both Adam's optimizer and Mean Square error (MSE) was used. We used the ε-greedy approach for action selection (choose a random action with the probability ε and action that corresponds to the maximum value of Q with the probability $1 - \varepsilon$). According to Fig. 5, we can say that the right value of ε to be taken is 0.05 because the curve for this value of epsilon looks more stable. The agent has been trained for 150 episodes on a 2.7 GHz CPU with 12 GB of RAM.

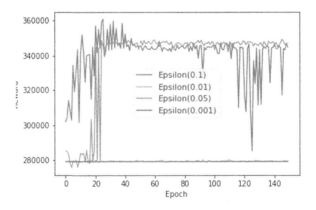

Fig. 5. Selection of the value of ε

4.3   Statistical Data Analysis

The Pearson Coefficient of Variation (PCV) has been used as a 95% confidence level measure of dispersion to capture the spread or the variability of the data relative to their average value. The PCV has been chosen since it is a relative measure of variability that is independent of the unit of measurement used, where the observed unit of data may change but the value stays constant. The PCV is measured by the relationship between the standard deviation and the mean of data from the same sample [17].

$$PCV = \frac{\sigma}{\bar{X}} \times 100, \tag{17}$$

where

- PCV is the Pearson Coefficient of Variation
- σ is the standard deviation of the series data
- $\bar{X}$ is the average of the series data

The mean network lifetime, the standard deviation, and the PCV for 1000 runs of the algorithms are computed by changing the number of sensor nodes. The result is presented in Table 5 for 20, 25, 30 sensors nodes. For the energy consumption measurement, the Table 5 reveals that RLDPP presents a lower value in the PCV with 32.62% when compared to A Star and Dijkstra (41.47%) for 20 nodes, the very same observation can be made when we used 25 sensors nodes and 30 sensors nodes just because our method during the path planning takes the path with small consumption of energy.

For the energy consumed metric, Table 5 shows that RLDPP presents a lower value in the coefficient of variation with 32.62% when compared to A Star and Dijkstra (41.47%) for 20 nodes, the same observation can be made when we used 25 sensors nodes and 30 sensors nodes because our method during path planning takes the path with small energy consumption.

Table 5. Statistical analysis of energy consumption

Algorithms	20 sensors nodes			25 sensors nodes			30 sensors nodes		
	Mean (μJ)	SD (μJ)	PCV	Mean (μJ)	SD (μJ)	PCV	Mean (μJ)	SD (μJ)	PCV
RLDPP	1078	352	32.62%	607	263	43.24%	726	257	35.45%
A Star	754	313	41.47%	862	427	49.5%	816	385	47.13%
Dijkstra	754	313	41.47%	862	427	49.5%	816	385	47.13%

Figures 6 and 7 show us that RLDPP achieved lower consumption energy approximately 0.8 J with 20 nodes and 0.6 J with 25 nodes at the end of the simulation when compared to the A star and Dijkstra algorithms which achieved consumption rates of 1.2 J with 20 nodes and 0.9 J with 25 nodes.

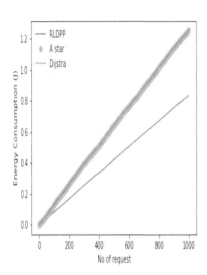

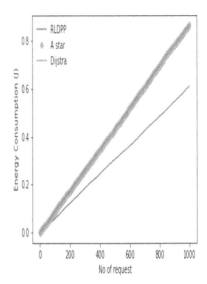

Fig. 6. Energy consumption for 20 nodes

Fig. 7. Energy consumption for 25 nodes

It can be observed from Fig. 8 where we used 10 sensors nodes for the simulation that the number of active sensors nodes for 25000 requests is 7 sensors nodes for the RLDPP Algorithm but for the A star and Dijkstra Algorithms is 4 sensors nodes; this difference continues to be significant, up to 48000 requests where all the sensors nodes for the three algorithms die.

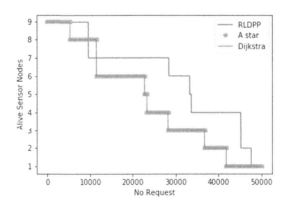

Fig. 8. Comparison in terms of Alive Sensors nodes

The same observation can be made in Fig. 9 where we did the simulation for 20 sensor nodes half of the sensor nodes die after approximately 47000 requests, this number of nodes remains constant for the RLDPP algorithm up to 68000 requests but it is not the case for A Star and Dijkstra Algorithms where this number falls to 9 sensors nodes up to 62000 requests. Between 22000 requests and 45000 requests, the number of active sensor nodes is the same for all the algorithms. First, we ran the algorithms for comparing the lifetime of the net-

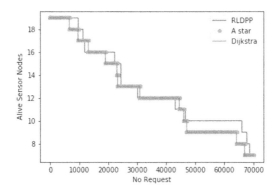

Fig. 9. Comparison in terms of Alive Sensors nodes

work by varying the sensor nodes for 20, 25, 30, 35, 40, 45, 50. Figure 10 and Fig. 11 show the comparison of the proposed RLDPP-based algorithm with A star and Dijkstra in terms of network life. It can be observed from Fig. 10 that the proposed algorithm has a better network lifetime than the A star and Dijkstra algorithms.

Figure 11 shows us that our algorithm RLDPP still performs well across the 4 network topologies used.

The Table 6 gives a clear overview about what we observed in Fig. 10 and Fig. 11 where for all the number of sensors used for the simulation, the RLDPP algorithm outperformed the other algorithms with the number of requests.

Table 6. Network lifetime with differents sensors nodes and algorithms

Algorithms	Number of sensor nodes						
	n = 20	n = 25	n = 30	n = 35	n = 40	n = 45	n = 50
RLDPP	9469	21467	14444	19749	26571	21723	25514
A Star	6550	10388	13407	8163	5412	10372	9361
Dijkstra	6550	10388	13407	8163	5412	10372	9361

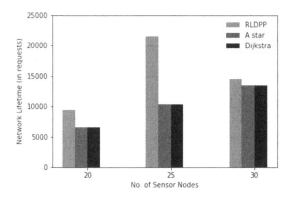

Fig. 10. Comparison in terms of network lifetime in requests

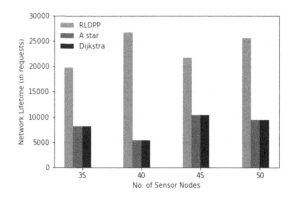

Fig. 11. Comparison in terms of Network Lifetime in requests

5   Conclusion

In this work, we proposed a Reinforcement Learning algorithm to solve a crucial problem faced by the IoT industry nowadays, which is related to Path prediction in IoT systems. The idea was to design an intelligent agent with a global vision of the network activity. Any new request characterized by its throughput, source, and destination must be feasible in order to be granted. The agent, trained in three different environments, has succeeded in finding the best policy that employs the path related to the small energy consumption when transporting information across the network. This results in extending the lifetime of the network topology.

We parameterized the path planning policy with a Neural Network and train it under three network topologies. Using the DQN Algorithm and the ε-greedy method with ε equal to 0.05, experimental results show that the proposed algorithm provided good solutions when compared to the others algorithms named A Star and Dijkstra.

With the three different topologies that comprise various amounts of nodes (20 nodes, 25 nodes, 30 nodes, 35 nodes, 40 nodes, 45 nodes, 50 nodes), we have observed that the energy consumption in the network is being minimized and, this, therefore, ensures an extension of the network lifetime. A graphical evidence of the obtained results is shown in form of the amount of alive nodes as a number of requests increases.

Furthering this investigation, we will essentially rely on four main axes:

- Making use other Reinforcement Learning algorithms like REINFORCE and Advantage Actor Critic (A2C) and training the related agents under the same circumstances.
- Comparing the findings with our approach and using the learning outcomes to develop some robustness around our method.
- Running a comparative analysis on a different ground, using evolutionary algorithms.
- Scale our technique and adapt it to other complex IoT network environments with a relatively high number of nodes.

References

1. Saidi, H., Labraoui, N., Ari, A.A.A.: A secure health monitoring system based on fog to cloud computing. Int. J. Med. Eng. Inform. (2022)
2. Tchagna Kouanou, A., et al.: Securing data in an internet of things network using blockchain technology: smart home case. SN Comput. Sci. 3(2), 1–10 (2022)
3. Njoya, A.N., Thron, C., Awa, M.N., Ari, A.A.A., Gueroui, A.M.: Lifetime optimization of dense wireless sensor networks using continuous ring-sector model. Future Gener. Comput. Syst. 129, 212–224 (2022)
4. Njoya, A.N., Thron, C., Awa, M.N., Ari, A.A.A., Gueroui, A.M.: Power-saving system designs for hexagonal cell based wireless sensor networks with directional transmission. J. King Saud Univ. Comput. Inf. Sci. 1–12 (2022)
5. Njoya, A.N., et al.: An efficient scalable sensor node placement algorithm for fixed target coverage applications of wireless sensor networks. IET Wirel. Sens. Syst. 7 (2017)
6. Sun, N., Shi, H., Han, G., Wang, B., Shu, L.: Dynamic path planning algorithms with load balancing based on data prediction for smart transportation systems. IEEE Access 8, 15907–15922 (2020)
7. Ari, A.A.A., Labraoui, N., Yenke, B.O., Gueroui, A.: Clustering algorithm for wireless sensor networks: the honeybee swarms nest-sites selection process based approach. Int. J. Sens. Netw. 27(1), 1–13 (2018)
8. Njoya, A.N., et al.: Hybrid wireless sensors deployment scheme with connectivity and coverage maintaining in wireless sensor networks. Wirel. Pers. Commun. 112(3), 1893–1917 (2020)
9. Al Aghbari, Z., Khedr, A.M., Osamy, W., Arif, I., Agrawal, D.P.: Routing in wireless sensor networks using optimization techniques: a survey. Wirel. Pers. Commun. 111, 2407–2434 (2020)
10. Kuila, P., Gupta, S.K., Jana, P.K.: A novel evolutionary approach for load balanced clustering problem for wireless sensor networks. Swarm Evolut. Comput. 12, 48–56 (2013)

11. Kuila, P., Jana, P.K.: Energy efficient clustering and routing algorithms for wireless sensor networks: particle swarm optimization approach. Eng. Appl. Artif. Intell. **33**, 127–140 (2014)
12. Bari, A., Jaekel, A., Bandyopadhyay, S.: Clustering strategies for improving the lifetime of two-tiered sensor networks. Comput. Commun. **31**(14), 3451–3459 (2008)
13. Low, C.P., Fang, C., Ng, J.M., Ang, Y.H.: Efficient load-balanced clustering algorithms for wireless sensor networks. Comput. Commun. **31**(4), 750–759 (2008). Algorithmic and Theoretical Aspects of Wireless ad hoc and Sensor Networks
14. Liu, X.: A deployment strategy for multiple types of requirements in wireless sensor networks. IEEE Trans. Cybern. **45**(10), 2364–2376 (2015)
15. Yu, Y., Ru, L., Chi, W., Liu, Y., Yu, Q., Fang, K.: Ant colony optimization based polymorphism-aware routing algorithm for ad hoc UAV network. Multimedia Tools Appl. **75**, 1–26 (2016)
16. Johnson, D., Maltz, D., Broch, J.: DSR: the dynamic source routing protocol for multi-hop wireless ad hoc networks. Ad Hoc Netw. **5**, 01 (2002)
17. Araujo, H.D.S., et al.: A proposal for IoT dynamic routes selection based on contextual information. Sensors **18**, 353 (2018)
18. Al-Shalabi, M., Anbar, M., Wan, T.-C., Alqattan, Z.: Energy efficient multi-hop path in wireless sensor networks using an enhanced genetic algorithm. Inf. Sci. **500**, 259–273 (2019)
19. Njoya, A.N., Thron, C., Awa, M.N., Ari, A.A.A., Gueroui, A.M.: Lifetime optimization of dense wireless sensor networks using continuous ring-sector model. Future Gener. Comput. Syst. **129**, 212–224 (2022)
20. Piccialli, F., Giampaolo, F., Casolla, G., Cola, V.S.D., Li, K.: A deep learning approach for path prediction in a location-based IoT system. Pervasive Mob. Comput. **66**, 101210 (2020)
21. Fathalla, A., Li, K., Salah, A., Mohamed, M.F.: An LSTM-based distributed scheme for data transmission reduction of IoT systems. Neurocomputing **485**, 166–180 (2022)
22. Kim, S., Lim, H.: Reinforcement learning based energy management algorithm for smart energy buildings. Energies **11**(8) (2018)
23. Abdollahzadeh, S., Navimipour, N.: Deployment strategies in the wireless sensor network: a comprehensive review. Comput. Commun. **91–92**, 06 (2016)

Reduction of Data Transmission in an IoT Wireless Sensor Network

Arouna Ndam Njoya[1(✉)] , Amina Salifu[8] ,
Assidé Christian Djedouboum[3,5] , Allassan A. Nken Tchangmena[2],
Ado Adamou Abba Ari[4,5] , Amine Mohamed Adouane[6] , Wahabou Abdou[7],
and Abdelhak Mourad Gueroui[4]

[1] Department of Computer Engineering, University Institute of Technology,
University of Ngaoundéré, P.O. Box 455, Ngaoundéré, Cameroon
ndanjoa@gmail.com

[2] African Institute for Mathematical Sciences, South West Region, Crystal Gardens,
P.O. Box 608, Limbe, Cameroon

[3] Department of Computer Science, University of Moundou,
P.O. Box 206, Moundou, Chad

[4] DAVID Lab, Université Paris-Saclay, University of Versailles
Saint-Quentin-en-Yvelines, 45 Avenue des États-Unis, 78000 Versailles, France

[5] Department of Computer Science, University of Maroua,
P.O. Box 814, Maroua, Cameroon

[6] Department of Computer Science, University of Algiers 1,
2 Rue Didouche Mourad, 16000 Alger Ctre, Algeria

[7] LIB EA7534, University Bourgogne Franche-Comté,
9 Avenue Alain Savary, 21078 Dijon, France

[8] African Institute for Mathematical Sciences, Senegal,
P.O. Box 1418, Mbour-Sénégal, Cameroon

Abstract. A Wireless Sensor Network (WSN) is a collection of spatially separated and specialized sensors that work together to monitor, record, and transmit information about the physical state of the environment to an internet-based location. To improve WSN power consumption, this work proposes a classification technique where K nearest neighborhood was applied in those clusters to select the best nodes. The purpose of the classification technique is to divide the network into various node-groupings. We calculated the correlation matrix for one node in each group and cluster, and we also applied the RNN model to get a better prediction within each node in each cluster, so only one node of data will be sent from each cluster to the base station. Furthermore, the experimental results reveal that, based on a suitable choice of nodes, our proposed model performs accurate predictions, with a minimum error of 0.01 measured using the Root Mean Squared Error (RMSE). The radio-energy transmission model used in this work also shows that a suitable choice of cluster head reduces the amount of energy consumed by the entire network, and by so doing improves it's life-time. This has been proven in our network's lifetime algorithm.

Keywords: Data reduction · IoT · Network lifetime · Machine learning

T. M. Ngatched Nkouatchah et al. (Eds.): PAAISS 2022, LNICST 459, pp. 39–57, 2023.
https://doi.org/10.1007/978-3-031-25271-6_3

1 Introduction

The world is evolving and expanding tremendously and a lot of things are changing and people are looking for different means of making the earth a better place to live. Technology is now the day-to-day thing, everyone including scientists, researchers, banks, and entrepreneurs looking for information here and there through the internet and now about 99% of devices are connecting to the internet to access information and self-driving technology to make things easier all aspects of life. The upgrades that innovation has brought and is as yet bringing to our general public can't be overemphasized. These staggering devices are the internet of things(IoT) [15,16].

In today's world, a ton of areas have acknowledged and begun valuing devices of IoTs. Furthermore, presently IoT is not too far off and is developing quickly as a comprehensive worldwide processing network in which everybody and all that will connect to the internet [4]. By a long shot, the majority of Internet affiliations generally are gadgets used straight by individuals, similar to PCs and flexible handsets. The major correspondence structure is human. In a relatively close future, everything can be related. Things can exchange information without assistance from any other person and the amount of "things" related to the web will be much greater than the amount of "people" and individuals could transform into the minority of generators and authorities of traffic [21]. IoT is an incorporated piece representing things to come, the internet that could be characterized as a self-supporting worldwide network foundation designing capacity based on guidelines and interoperability [22,23].

Every physical device of IoT is embedded with sensor nodes which are stored with data received and transferred. However, the massive transfer of data to base stations decreases the lifetime of sensor nodes, increases data loss due to failure of nodes, and hence the maximum amount of energy is lost [1,7]. The proposed solution should therefore be able to minimize the maximum energy consumption during data transfer and increase the lifetime of the nodes.

The main objective of this project is to propose a machine learning model. Thus, predicting the sensing data for a set of nodes within clusters have a crucial advantage that the sensor data collected at the node level will only be transferred on the off chance that the distinction between the anticipated and noticed upsides of the information surpasses a predefined edge state thus, information transmission to the base station is restricted to a sensible measure of data move.

1.1 Contributions

Our contribution to this work includes:

– Initiate a data pre-processing technique based on data stationarity and data normalization to remove erroneous values and suggesting a k-nearest neighbors(k-NN), finding the k values from clusters nodes and also predict multiple output data of a sensor node using recurrent neural network (RNN);

– Evaluate the effectiveness of the proposed model by doing a comparative analysis with a number of clusters of the sensor nodes.

The remainder of this paper is organized as follows. Section 2 presents the related work on data transmission reduction in IoT wireless networks. Section 3 focuses on developing a data reduction model based on k-NN and RNN. In Sect. 4, we conducted a case study where simulations were performed to verify the performance of the model, and thereafter results and discussions were presented. Section 5 provides a conclusion of the present work and proposes future directions.

2   Related Work

The method of diminishing the size of unique data may be addressed in a most modest space as Data reduction. While diminishing data, its techniques guarantee data trustworthiness. The time spent on data reduction ought not to be ignored for the time saved by data mining on the more modest data set. It can further develop stockpiling effectiveness while likewise bringing down costs. Capacity limit is regularly depicted as far as crude limit and powerful limit, which alludes to data after it has been diminished. There are a few methods for lessening data. A portion of the data reduction techniques includes processing, data compression, and data prediction. base on the correlation between temperature and humidity in sensor node 2 from other researchers was –0.72 which is a strong negative correlation and We use multivariate correlation to decrease prediction errors by means of multiple linear regression which was 0.03

Data Compression Approaches

Numerous IoT frameworks create an immense and changed measure of information that should be handled and answered in an exceptionally brief time-frame. One of the significant difficulties is the high energy utilization because of the transmission of information to the cloud and subsequently, Data compression is useful for expanding information stockpiling and remote correspondence energy effectiveness. With its effect on energy, there will be a lot of massive savings of energy in large data [24]. Since the nodes are controlled by incredibly hard batteries that are to supplant or re-energize for a huge scope, the conservation of the energy is the issue at hand. Moreover, it is used typically in savings of energy nodes since information transmission consumes the vast majority of the energy node and the energy expected for communicating a lone piece is generally identical to the energy expected for the execution of 4000 directions [18].

The most broadly perceived estimation used to overview the adequacy of data compression algorithms is the compression ratio [13]. Regardless, compacting information will in general expand the computational energy consumed, particularly nodes with restricted assets. What's more, consequently, there is an undeniable tradeoff between the energy computation expected for compression and the energy hold reserves related to sending stuffed information rather than the original information. We can't just pick a high-compression-ratio algorithm to guarantee genuine energy effectiveness; all things considered, we should consider the general energy productivity of data reduction. In other words, we need to make sure that the energy used to convey how much information is saved by compression is more obvious than the energy needed to pack the information to save it. Information reduction achieves energy efficiency in information compression calculations, and as a result, the higher the information compression energy productivity, the more energy is saved by compressing information. [11]. Data compression has its significance and weaknesses and in WSN, energy is exceptionally relied upon hardware nodes regardless of the way that WSNs are information-driven while thinking about human-driven applications [26], the energy efficiency of nodes changes as the hardware or boundaries change. Subsequently, the data compression algorithm's energy efficiency assessment conspire in WSNs should be founded on hardware and software considerations. While assessing the energy efficiency of data compression, there are two forms of energy to consider. The initial segment is the saved energy by diminishing how much data is sent, which is connected with the algorithm's compression ratio. The subsequent part is the energy utilized by compression algorithms being used. The latest examination on compression algorithm execution assessment just thinks about the compression ratio or joins the compression ratio with the complexity of algorithms as well as compression error [9].

Data Prediction Approaches

WSNs are comprised of a few asset-obliged sensor nodes. Some sensor nodes gather data from the rest of the world and send it to the sink, including temperature, humidity, and light. The data is sent in hops (intermediate nodes) until it arrives at the sink. Data traffic is an issue in WSN because of high energy consumption [6]. Classically, the information is forwarded by multi-hops until it arrives at the sink. Data traffic, then again, is an issue in WSN due to high energy consumption [20].

To store energy, effective conventions need to discover the relationship between data assembled by way of a sensor node and its neighbors, as properly as the connection between data gathered by way of the sensor node itself over the lengthy haul and consequently, the cause for data expectation is to reduce data traffic to the sink and assist in bringing down the network's commonplace strength utilization [12]. The coefficients of linear regression are decided using an algorithm mounted inside the sensor node. These coefficients are named β and α and signify a collection of variable samples amassed via the sensor, such as temperature. Accordingly, alternatively, then sending the grouping of variable samples, the sensor node sends the coefficients to the sink. When β and α arrive at the sink, they are used with the aid of linear regression characteristics established inside the sink. The checking framework which is considered underneath, then predicts the studying sequence [2]. Every sensor node assembles a sample of every variable and enumerates coefficients of the Simple linear regression function given the variable and the epoch. Then, it just spends coefficients to the sink at each cycle. Only one variable to be expected and solely one variable to predict the based variable are usually taken into account in this method. For instance, the time variable, contrasted with, is with variables like temperature, humidity, and light and usually is not the correlated variable. Multi-linear regression can also be applied on data transmission prediction [2].

3   Methodology

This section is devoted to the mathematical formulation and implementation of the solution to study the data transmission problem in IoT wireless network. We also introduce the level of energy consumption during data transfer from the sensor nodes to the base stations.

3.1   Data Transmission Problem Formulation

In the following, we formulate the data transmission problem based on the knowledge clustering algorithm. The mathematical proposal presents the set of parameters (see Table 1) necessary for our problem formulation. Consider N-nodes spatially distributed across the coverage area defined in Eq. 1.

$$S = \{n_i\}_{0 \leq i \leq N} \ where \ (n_i = node\, i) \tag{1}$$

S is the set of sensor nodes. Intuitively the clustering function H maps the node n_i to a cluster $\mathcal{C}_k$ (as presented in Eq. 2) where $\mathcal{C}_k$ is a subset of nodes in S.

$$H(n_i) = C_k. \tag{2}$$

Summarily, let n_i be the node i, then, $\exists$ k such that $H(n_i) = C_k$.

Table 1. Variables for the mathematical description

Variable	Description
S	Set of sensor nodes across the WSN
H	Clustering function
n_i	node i
$\mathcal{C}_k$	Cluster k
k	Cluster index
N	Number of sensors

3.2 k-Nearest Neighbours (k-NN)

To perform the clustering, we use a k-nearest neighbors algorithm (k-NN). In short, the k-NN is a non-parametric supervised learning method for classification and regression problems. The output of the K-NN algorithm is calculated using the k closest training examples. K-NN computes the distance between all points in close proximity to the unknown data and eliminates those with the shortest distances. As a result, it's sometimes called a distance-based algorithm. We must first determine the value of k in order to correctly classify the results. In classification, the output is a class membership. An object is classified by a majority vote of its neighbors, with the object being assigned to the class most common among its k nearest neighbors. By applying this algorithm in data transmission, we can group into clusters. This help to investigate the correlation between data belonging to the same cluster before transmission to the base station.

As the k-NN is a distance-based algorithm, Euclidean distance is a commonly used distance function. By using the below formula in Eq. 3, it measures a straight line between the query point and the other point being measured from the datasets.

Consider an inner product space $(V, < \cdot, \cdot >)$. Then

$$d(x, y) := \sqrt{< x - y, x - y >} = \sqrt{\sum_{i=1}^{n} (y_i - x_i)^2} \qquad (3)$$

For $x, y, \in V$ is the distance between x and y. The distance is called Euclidean distance if the dot product is used as the inner product.

After performing the clustering, using the information correlation between the nodes, we want to reduce the amount of data to send to the sink by predicting the data of some nodes from the others. To this end, we use a recurrent neural network (RNN).

3.3 Recurrent Neural Network (RNN)

An RNN is a type of artificial neural network that uses sequential or time series data. When there is a sequence of data and the temporal dynamics that link the data are more significant than the spatial content of each frame, this architecture is used. Sent in the form of sequences that follow a temporal distribution at various time steps t, the data collected by sensor nodes in WSNs is suitable for RNN processing. The input x, hidden h, and output unit o makes up the fundamentally three main components of an RNN. RNN can handle sequential data and does not consider only the current input and can memorize previous input [5] (Fig. 1).

RNN is governed by equations which include:

$$m^{(t)} = b_1 + W h^{(t-1)} + U x^{(t)} \qquad (4)$$

$$h^{(t)} = \sigma(m_{(t)}) \qquad (5)$$

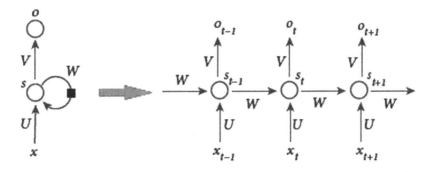

Fig. 1. A recurrent neural network model [19].

$$o^{(t)} = b_2 + Vh^{(t)} \tag{6}$$

where b_1 and b_2 are the vectors added to the weight matrix U, V and W, which are respectively the input-to hidden, hidden-to-output and hidden-to-hidden weights. The activation function is denoted by σ. Similarly, a loss function given by Eq. 7 is defined in terms of the inputs, the hidden and output units.

$$L = \frac{1}{T} \sum_{t=1}^{T} l(o^{(t)}, y^{(t)}). \tag{7}$$

where $l(o^{(t)}, y^{(t)})$, is the loss function at time step t, $y_{(t)}$ is the true output.

The various parts of the weight matrices U, V, and W must also be updated, which calls for the use of an optimizer. Updates are made for time t because of the data temporal distribution, which introduces the idea of "backward propagation through time" (BPTT). The dynamic of BPTT is carried out using various sets of equations which include:

$$\frac{\partial L}{\partial v} = \sum_{t=1}^{T} \frac{\partial L}{\partial o} h^{(t)^T} \tag{8}$$

$$\frac{\partial L}{\partial U} = \sum_{t=1}^{T} \frac{\partial L}{\partial h} x^{(t)^T} \tag{9}$$

$$\frac{\partial L}{\partial W} = \sum_{t=1}^{T} \frac{\partial L}{\partial h} h^{(t)^T} \tag{10}$$

Unfortunately, RNN has two main issues. First, learning a long and complex sequence of information becomes tiresome when the gradient is too small, making weight updates insignificant. The term "vanishing gradient descend" refers to this phenomenon. Additionally, if the gradient is very large, exploding gradient descent will result in significant weight updates. Long-short-term memory

(LSTM) is a model architecture that can forget and remember information over a set amount of time proposed as a solution to this issue to predict accuracy (Fig. 2).

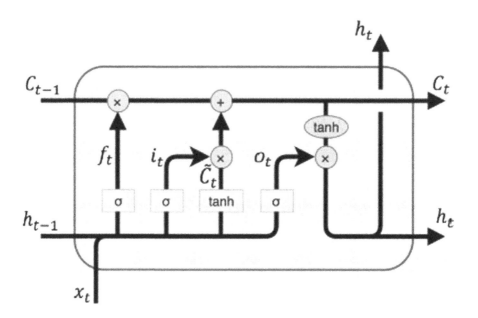

Fig. 2. Long short-term memory scheme [17].

3.4 Energy System

Transmission and Reception Radio Model

To send an $b - bits$ through a distance d, the Eq. 11 described in [3, 10, 14] was adopted.

$$E_{Tx(b,d)} = \begin{cases} b(E_{elec} + \varepsilon_{fs}d^2), & d < d_0 \\ b(E_{elec} + \varepsilon_{amp}d^4), & d \geq d_0 \end{cases} \tag{11}$$

where $E_{elec} = 5 \times 10^{-8}$ J/bit defines the energy consumed in filtering, modulation, and coding to transmit or receive one bit of message. $\varepsilon_{fs} = 10^{-11}$ J/bit/m^2 and $\varepsilon_{amp} = 1.3 \times 10^{-15}$ J/bit/m^4 denote the energy required by the amplifier to transfer a single bit to the receiver node in direct transmission or multi-hop transmission respectively. $d_0 = \sqrt{\frac{\varepsilon_{fs}}{\varepsilon_{amp}}}$ represents the distance threshold.

The amount of energy required to receive $b - bits$ is given by

$$E_{Rx(b)} = bE_{elec} \tag{12}$$

Power Consumption Optimization

Our objective in this work includes ensuring an effective data transmission process that can save a significant amount of energy in order to extend the network lifetime. We used the energy radio model to compute the energy difference between each cluster. We then calculate the minimum energy required by each node on each cluster From Fig. 4 to transfer data to the base station. We saved the other nodes' lives by doing this because they all have similar information, and even if one node fails, we still have other nodes that can replace the failed node.

From Fig. 4, we check the energy consumption or the energy of each node by calculating the minimum energy required to transfer data to the base station in each cluster.

Firstly, to check for the minimum amount of energy in each cluster C_k, we use the Eq. 13.

$$E(C_k) = min\{E_{n_1}, E_{n_2}, ..., E_{n_m}\} \tag{13}$$

where $E_{n_{1 \leq i \leq m}}$ represents the energy required by node i to transfer information to the base station. The variable m denotes the number of sensors in a given cluster.

Secondly, the lifetime of a cluster k is inversely proportional to the energy

$$lifetime(C_k) \propto \frac{1}{E}. \tag{14}$$

where C_k is cluster k. E is the total energy consumption of the network at a particular time.

Thirdly, we compute the lifetime of the entire network as

$$\sum_{k=1}^{K} lifetime(C_k). \tag{15}$$

where K is the number of clusters.

Finally, the pseudo-code of the Algorithm 1 is used in order to compute the network lifetime.

3.5   Overview of the Method

Figure 3 shows the model architecture of our project where data was collected. We tested for the stationarity of the data and we moved forward by normalizing and performing standardization on the data after we implemented the clustering algorithm, we then performed the KNN algorithm on those clusters using the nodes of 2, 6, 4, and 4, 7, 10 and we checked for the performance of our prediction using LSTM model.

We use the neighboring sensor nodes to form clusters with the help of the correlation matrix, as stated in the problem formulation section.

Algorithm 1. Network Lifetime Algorithm

Input: S: the set of sensor nodes, C: the set of K clusters, the initial energy of nodes.
Output: the network lifetime L
1: Randomly select the base station;
2: Energy=[ ]
3: $Cluster_{Energy} = [\ ]$
4: **for** C_k **in** C **do**
5:      **for** E_i **in** $E(C_k)$ **do**
6:          Add E_i in Energy list
7:      **end for**
8:      Add $min(Energy)$ to $Cluster_{Energy}$ list
9: **end for**
10: $Total_{Energy} = sum(Cluster_{Energy})$
11: $L{=}\dfrac{K}{Total_{Energy}}$

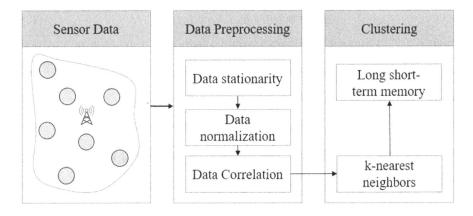

Fig. 3. Overview of the proposed method.

From Fig. 4, the model architecture was designed in such a way that, Clusters were done based on the closeness of nodes with the KNN model, and the correlation between the nodes was based on temperature and humidity and with a good prediction result where RNN model was used. Hence in each cluster instead of sending the whole nodes of data to the base station, we can send just a node from each cluster to the base station due to the good accuracy prediction and the correlation between the node.

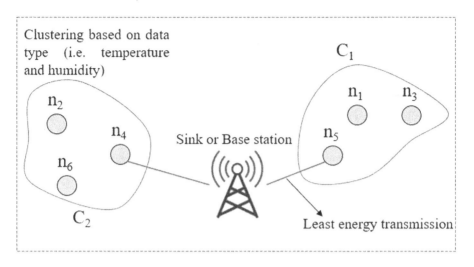

Fig. 4. Cluster organization. The node which consumes the least amount of energy to transfer data to the base station or sink is used.

3.6   Test Data Set

Data Description

Between February 28th and April 5th, 2004, data were collected from 54 sensors installed in the Intel Berkeley Research lab. Once every 31 s, Mica2Dot sensors with weatherboards collected timestamped topology information, as well as humidity, temperature, light, and voltage values. The TinyDB in-network query processing system, which is based on the TinyOS platform, was used to collect data. In the lab, the sensors were arranged as shown in the diagram below: Peter Bodik, Wei Hong, Carlos Guestrin, Sam Madden, Mark Paskin, and Romain Thibaux were the first to collect this information. Hardware was provided by Intel Berkeley. From observation, some nodes seem to be very close to one another in locations. Example nodes (4, 3, 2) or nodes (4, 7, 10), with the hypothesis being that closer nodes collect similar information (data redundancy).

Data Pre-processing

Because sensory data has a wide range of values, the data values are normalized and re-scaled using the min-max scalar function defined in an equation to ensure accurate and smooth model training.

$$min - max(x) = \frac{x - x_{min}}{x_{max} - x_{min}}. \tag{16}$$

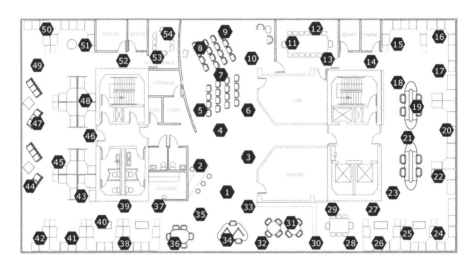

Fig. 5. Intel Berkeley lab sensor dataset. Spatial distribution of the sensor nodes across the working space [8].

where x, represents the data points, x_{min} and x_{max} denote the minimum and maximum of the raw data respectively. The advantage of data normalization is that it eases feature extraction to perform better data correlation. Correlation is a statistical procedure that shows the extent to which two variables are linearly related [25]. The study of the correlation between data points of two or more different sensor nodes as presented on Tables 2, 3 and 4 below are an argument for the choice of nodes.

$$\rho = \frac{1 - \sum 6d_i^2}{n(n^2 - 1)}. \tag{17}$$

where, d_i is the difference between the x and Y for each pair of data ρ is the strength of the rank correlation between variables. n is the number of samples, $\sum d_i^2$ is the difference between x and y variable ranks. n is the sample size. For example, computing the Pearson coefficient of temperature and humidity using Eq. 17, We have $\rho = -0.92$ the table below represents the correlation matrix of sensor node2 from the observation, there is a strong negative correlation between humidity and temperature.

To study the spatial-temporal distribution of the data, an investigation of the correlation between different nodes was performed to get clusters of nodes based on temperature and humidity. For example, the cluster of nodes 2, 3 and 4 gave a correlation of temperature and humidity as:

Table 2. Correlation matrix of sensor node 2

Correlation	Temperature	Humidity
Temperature	1.00	−0.92
Humidity	−0.92	1.00

Table 3. Correlation matrix of sensor node (2, 4, 6)

Correlation	Temperature 2	Temperature 4	Temperature 6
Temperature 2	1.00	−0.71	+0.87
Temperature 4	−0.71	1.00	−0.55
Temperature 6	+0.87	−0.55	1.00

From Table 3, we can see that there is a strong positive correlation between node 2 and node 6 and there is a strong negative correlation between node4 and node 2 hence are clustered as one cluster due to the similarity between the nodes based on temperature and humidity. And this is also due to the closeness of the nodes in terms of spatial distribution.

Let us consider another cluster of nodes (4, 7, 10).

Table 4. Correlation matrix of sensor node (4, 7, 10)

Correlation	Temperature 4	Temperature 7	Temperature 10
Temperature 4	1.00	0.41	0.43
Temperature 7	0.41	1.00	0.92
Temperature 10	0.43	0.92	1.00

It is observed that there is a positive strong correlation between node 10 and node 7 and there is another strong correlation between node 7 and 4 this is also due to the closeness of the nodes.

Figure 5 shows the 54 distribution of sensor nodes and their fixed position which are the same as in the Intel Berkeley Research Lab Sensor Data. From Table, we can see that nodes 2, 4, and 6 are closer and their correlation coefficient between the temperature and humidity was very high as well as other clusters of nodes.

4   Performance Evaluation

We present and analyze in this section the simulation results of the proposed model of data transmission reduction. We begin by describing the hyper-parameters required for training the k-NN model. In addition, we describe the variable selection process, which accounts for the model's best fit. We then represent the predicted output graphically and compare it to actual observations for a subset of nodes described in the Intel data set. In order to measure how far the predicted values are from the observed values, we use the Root Mean Squared Error(RMSE). Finally, we evaluate our proposed model in terms of performance and the amount of energy required for data transmission.

4.1 Model Training

After developing our model, we go over the fixed hyper-parameters required for training in this section. The data set is divided into 1000 observations for prediction and 20000 observations for training. The set standards are as follows:

- Epoch: In the training phase, the epoch specifies how frequently the entire data set is passed through the model. The number of epochs used to train the model is equal to 10.
- Batch Size: It considers all observations that have been processed following one training iteration. The model utilizes a batch size of 128 during the learning phase.
- Optimizer: We used the Adam Optimizer due to its smooth and fast convergence rate.

Table 5. Hyper-parameters values

look-back	Epochs	Batch-size	RMSE
300	33	160	0.02
280	30	140	0.01
250	25	130	0.01
200	20	128	0.01
150	15	120	0.05

As previously mentioned, in order to forecast the unavailable temperature value for node 4, we use historical data for nodes 4, 2, and 6. As a result, many different parameters can be acquired. The group of refined parameters used during the training process is shown in Table 5. The RMSE defines the average error of the overall 20000 prediction. From Table 5, we find that the first look back-back used during training gave a minimum error of 0.02. The look-back of 250 has a better error of 0.01 as well as 200. Looking at this performance base on the size and the epoch, the look-back of 200 performed better because it gave a lesser error during the prediction of node 4 and node 2.We further compare our model, with two proposed models. One auto-regressive model and a bi-directional long-short term recurrent neural network.

4.2   Node Selection

The Spearman correlation defined in Eq. 17, revealed a good coefficient score for node 2, 6, 4, as presented in Fig. 3 and Table 6 reports from the data prediction result of node 4, for the temperature values. For a clear visualization, we present the first 100 predicted values. The green line represents the predicted data points while the red-crossed line represents the actual observed values. Despite the proximity of the three sensor nodes, there may be some abnormality in the prediction because of additional noise present in the historical data. Erroneous data points may also be explained by how the nodes were distributed around nearby obstacles.

The RMSE recorded during the training and testing process for temperature data are 0.17 and 0.07 respectively. As for the humidity data, it was measured an RMSE of 16.78 for the training and 10.23 for the test. As the lower the RMSE, the better a given model is able to fit a dataset, it simply gives the ordering of the sensor nodes to perform prediction as we have to see with the results using node 2. Based on the results obtained in Tables 3 and 4, we can conclude that, sensor nodes with high correlation coefficient turn to have a low prediction error. Indeed, Table 3 showcases the correlation matrix of the set of nodes 2, 6, and 4.

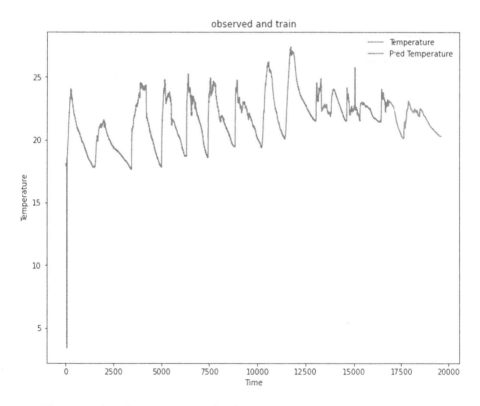

Fig. 6. Predicted temperature value for node 2 aided by node 4 and node 6.

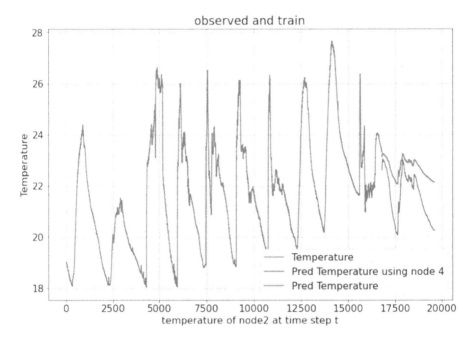

Fig. 7. Node used in predicting node node2 and compared to the previous predicted node2 of Fig. 6.

From Fig. 6, we use node 4 to predict node 2 since they are all in the same cluster. Thereafter, we compare the predicted value to that of the actual value of node 2 and hence we see that they all have the same distribution. We observe a few errors due to some failure of nodes and incorrect readings (Fig. 7).

4.3   Energy Consumption Analysis

The energy graph in Fig. 8 shows the total minimum energy of the network of the clusters. Thus, with respect to the energy, we calculated the minimum energy of each node in each cluster and we calculated the distance between each cluster using the Energy-radio model. With respect to that, we only transfer nodes with minimum energy to the base station and hence the lifetime of the node prolongs since energy is inversely proportional to the lifetime of the node.

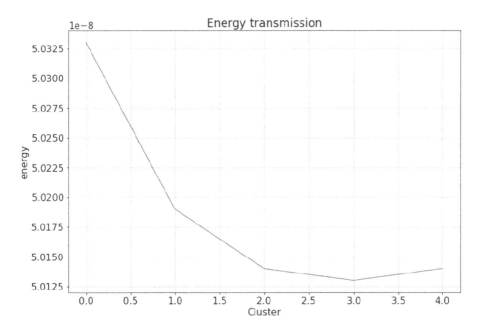

Fig. 8. Minimum energy of the entire network based on their clusters.

5   Conclusion

Sensor nodes in wireless networks gather various types of sensing data. In order
to transmit data to the base station, we attempted to investigate the variability
and correlation among the various sensor nodes in our work. By building clusters,
applying k-NN to those clusters, and using an RNN model for prediction, we were
able to complete the aforementioned task. The theory behind this method is that
by predicting the error performance, massive data transfer in wireless networks
will be significantly reduced, directly leading to a reduction in the energy needed
for data transmission. To avoid over-fitting during our model's learning phase,
the Intel indoor data set for the use case was first processed and re-scaled using
a min-max scaling function. The process of lagging was then used to transform
the data prediction problem into a supervised machine learning task. The set of
nodes 4, 6, 2, 7, and 10 show a strong positive correlation with one another in the
inter-correlation study between the sensor nodes, which we used as a benchmark
to implement the data prediction problem. The experimental results showed that,
after a rigorous set of parameter tuning, our proposed model performs extremely
well during the prediction phase with a noticeably low root mean square error in
comparison to the earlier related work. The spatial and temporal characteristics
of the sensing data can thus be captured by the KNN model. Using the radio-
energy transmission model, we finally quantified the performance of our model in
terms of the energy needed to transmit the sensing data and concluded that the
proposed architecture is ultimately capable of conserving more energy than the

model architectures currently in use. Furthering the study of data transmission can rely on the data aggregation approach which eliminates redundant data and conserve the energy of sensors and hence reducing the size and number of data transmissions.

References

1. Ari, A.A.A., Labraoui, N., Yenké, B.O., Gueroui, A.: Clustering algorithm for wireless sensor networks: the honeybee swarms nest-sites selection process based approach. Int. J. Sens. Netw. **27**(1), 1–13 (2018)
2. Carvalho, C., Gomes, D.G., Agoulmine, N., De Souza, J.N.: Improving prediction accuracy for WSN data reduction by applying multivariate spatio-temporal correlation. Sensors **11**(11), 10010–10037 (2011)
3. Elshrkawey, M., Elsherif, S.M., Wahed, M.E.: An enhancement approach for reducing the energy consumption in wireless sensor networks. J. King Saud Univ. Comput. Inf. Sci. **30**(2), 259–267 (2018)
4. Farooq, M.U., Waseem, M., Mazhar, S., Khairi, A., Kamal, T.: A review on internet of things (IoT). Int. J. Comput. Appl. **113**(1), 1–7 (2015)
5. Feng, W., Guan, N., Li, Y., Zhang, X., Luo, Z.: Audio visual speech recognition with multimodal recurrent neural networks. In: 2017 International Joint Conference on Neural Networks (IJCNN), pp. 681–688. IEEE (2017)
6. Gama, J., Gaber, M.M.: Learning from Data Streams: Processing Techniques in Sensor Networks. Springer, Berlin, Heidelberg (2007). https://doi.org/10.1007/3-540-73679-4
7. Gbadouissa, J.E.Z., Ari, A.A.A., Titouna, C., Gueroui, A.M., Thiare, O.: HGC: hypergraph based clustering scheme for power aware wireless sensor networks. Future Gener. Comput. Syst. **105**, 175–183 (2020)
8. Intel: Intel Berkeley lab sensor data (2004). http://db.csail.mit.edu/labdata/labdata.html. Accessed 15 May 2021
9. Liu, S., Liu, Y., Chen, X., Fan, X.: A new scheme for evaluating energy efficiency of data compression in wireless sensor networks. Int. J. Distrib. Sens. Netw. **14**(5), 1550147718776926 (2018)
10. Liu, X.: A deployment strategy for multiple types of requirements in wireless sensor networks. IEEE Trans. Cybern. **45**(10), 2364–2376 (2015)
11. Luo, X., Zhang, D., Yang, L.T., Liu, J., Chang, X., Ning, H.: A kernel machine-based secure data sensing and fusion scheme in wireless sensor networks for the cyber-physical systems. Future Gener. Comput. Syst. **61**, 85–96 (2016)
12. Matos, T.B., Brayner, A., Maia, J.E.B.: Towards in-network data prediction in wireless sensor networks. In: Proceedings of the 2010 ACM Symposium on Applied Computing, pp. 592–596 (2010)
13. Nian, Y., Wu, L., He, S.: A new video coding based on 3D wavelet transform and motion compensation. In: Wavelet Analysis and Active Media Technology: (In 3 Volumes), pp. 1307–1313. World Scientific (2005)
14. Njoya, A.N., et al.: Hybrid wireless sensors deployment scheme with connectivity and coverage maintaining in wireless sensor networks. Wirel. Pers. Commun. **112**(3), 1893–1917 (2020)
15. Njoya, A.N., Thron, C., Awa, M.N., Ari, A.A.A., Gueroui, A.M.: Lifetime optimization of dense wireless sensor networks using continuous ring-sector model. Future Gener. Comput. Syst. **129**, 212–224 (2022)

16. Njoya, A.N., Thron, C., Awa, M.N., Ari, A.A.A., Gueroui, A.M.: Power-saving system designs for hexagonal cell based wireless sensor networks with directional transmission. J. King Saud Univ. Comput. Inf. Sci. 1–12 (2022). https://doi.org/10.1016/j.jksuci.2022.07

17. Rahhal, J.S., Abualnadi, D.: IoT based predictive maintenance using LSTM RNN estimator. In: 2020 International Conference on Electrical, Communication, and Computer Engineering (ICECCE), pp. 1–5. IEEE (2020)

18. Razzaque, M.A., Bleakley, C., Dobson, S.: Compression in wireless sensor networks: a survey and comparative evaluation. ACM Trans. Sens. Netw. (TOSN) $10(1)$, 1–44 (2013)

19. Sezer, O.B., Gudelek, M.U., Ozbayoglu, A.M.: Financial time series forecasting with deep learning: a systematic literature review: 2005–2019. Appl. Soft Comput. 90, 106181 (2020)

20. Tahir, M., Farrell, R.: Optimal communication-computation tradeoff for wireless multimedia sensor network lifetime maximization. In: 2009 IEEE Wireless Communications and Networking Conference, pp. 1–6. IEEE (2009)

21. Tan, L., Wang, N.: Future internet: the internet of things. In: 2010 3rd International Conference on Advanced Computer Theory and Engineering (ICACTE), vol. 5, pp. V5–376. IEEE (2010)

22. Titouna, C., Ari, A.A.A., Moumen, H.: FDRA: fault detection and recovery algorithm for wireless sensor networks. In: Younas, M., Awan, I., Ghinea, G., Catalan Cid, M. (eds.) MobiWIS 2018. LNCS, vol. 10995, pp. 72–85. Springer, Cham (2018). https://doi.org/10.1007/978-3-319-97163-6_7

23. Titouna, C., Gueroui, M., Aliouat, M., Ari, A.A.A., Amine, A.: Distributed fault-tolerant algorithm for wireless sensor network. Int. J. Commun. Netw. Inf. Secur. $9(2)$, 241 (2017)

24. Wu, J., Guo, S., Li, J., Zeng, D.: Big data meet green challenges: greening big data. IEEE Syst. J. $10(3)$, 873–887 (2016)

25. Zar, J.H.: Significance testing of the spearman rank correlation coefficient. J. Am. Stat. Assoc. $67(339)$, 578–580 (1972)

26. Zhao, W., et al.: A human-centered activity tracking system: toward a healthier workplace. IEEE Trans. Hum. Mach. Syst. $47(3)$, 343–355 (2016)

Special Topics of African Interest

A Comparative Study of Regressors and Stacked Ensemble Model for Daily Temperature Forecasting: A Case Study of Senegal

Chimango Nyasulu[1]([✉])[iD], Awa Diattara[1][iD], Assitan Traore[2],
Abdoulaye Deme[3][iD], and Cheikh Ba[1][iD]

[1] LANI (Laboratoire d'Analyse Numérique et Informatique),
University of Gaston Berger, Saint-Louis, Senegal
{nyasulu.chimango,awa.diattara,cheikh2.ba}@ugb.edu.sn
[2] Business & Decision, Grenoble, France
assitan.traore@businessdecision.com
[3] Laboratoire des Sciences de l'Atmosphère et de l'Océan, Unité de Formation et de
Recherche de Sciences Appliquées et de Technologie, University of Gaston Berger,
Saint-Louis, Senegal
abdoulaye.deme@ugb.edu.sn

Abstract. Over the Sahel region, air temperature is anticipated to rise by 2.0 to 4.3 °C by 2080. This increase is likely to affect human life. Thus, air temperature forecasting is an important research topic. This study compares the performance of stacked Ensemble Model and three regressors: Gradient Boosting, CatBoost and Light Gradient Boosting Machine for daily Maximum Temperature and Minimum Temperature forecasting based on the five lagged values. Results obtained demonstrate that the Ensemble Model outperformed the regressors as follows for each parameter; Maximum Temperature: MSE 2.8038, RMSE 1.6591 and R^2 0.8205. For Minimum Temperature: MSE 1.1329, RMSE 1.0515 and R^2 0.9018. Considering these results, Ensemble Model is observed to be feasible for daily Maximum and Minimum Temperature forecasting.

Keywords: Machine learning · Regressors · Ensemble model · Temperature forecasting · Sahel region · Senegal

1 Introduction

Humanity has been challenged with issues of climate change and draws interest of different stakeholders: governments, public, decision makers, industry, planners and many more. Climate change possess a huge threat on human security and entire well-being. The West Africa Sahel region is not exempted from the aggravated negative effects of climate change. The West Africa Sahel region (between 12°N and 20°N) is a "semi-arid area that runs from the Atlantic Ocean eastward

T. M. Ngatched Nkouatchah et al. (Eds.): PAAISS 2022, LNICST 459, pp. 61–77, 2023.
https://doi.org/10.1007/978-3-031-25271-6_4

to Chad, separating the Sahara Desert to the north and the Sudanian Savana to the south" [1].

In terms of climate summary, West Africa Sahel region is characterized by generally high temperatures all the year with the dry season starting from the month of October to May. Rainy season start from the month of June to mid of October. Average temperatures vary from 21.9 °C–36.4 °C. Average annual rainfall differs from year to year, usually increases from north to south [2].

Agriculture happens to be a major source of food and income in the region. Agriculture is the main source of employment. For example agriculture accounts for more than 60% of the labor force. The region is regarded as more susceptible to climate change due to too much reliance on rain-fed agricultural production.

1.1 Projected Climate Changes

There is an increasing worry about the future climate of the region. Over the Sahel, air temperature is anticipated to rise by 2.0 to 4.3 °C by 2080, the yearly number of days with maximum temperature above 35 °C are anticipated to increase. Amount of available surface water for agricultural production is likely to reduce due to higher evapotranspiration. By 2080, annual mean soil moisture for a soil depth of up to one meter is projected to decrease by 0.8% [2,3].

Projected increasing temperatures and more extreme weather conditions are likely to cause continued food insecurity and slowed economic development in the region. Thus, this study is set out to compare three Machine Learning (ML) models and stacked Ensemble Model for daily forecasting of Maximum Temperature and Minimum Temperature for selected locations in Senegal.

1.2 Brief Review of Similar Studies

A study by [4] was conducted to compare 36 ML models to forecast room temperature for three successive hours using every 10 min data obtained from a smart building and a weather station. Some of the models used includes Random Forest (RF), Extra Trees (ET) and Gradient Boosting Machine. The ET regressor obtained a higher correlation coefficient and lower Root Mean Squared Error (RMSE) of 0.97 and 0.058 respectively.

[5] conducted a study to predict the endpoint temperature of molten steel in a converter using Catboost, Extreme Gradient Boosting, Linear Support Vector Regressor, Linear Regression, Light Gradient Boosting Machine and Ensemble model. Results for Mean Absolute Error (MAE) are as follows: Linear Regression 6.7367, Linear Support Vector Regressor 6.0612, Random Forest 6.1312, Extreme Gradient Boosting 5.2317, Catboost 5.3098 and Ensemble model 5.1937. From these results Ensemble model outperformed other models with a lower MAE score.

1.3 Study Location and Source of Data

Senegal is located in the West Africa Sahel region between latitudes and longitudes of 12°N - 17°N and 18°W - 11°W respectively. Rainfall is very variable and temperature has risen by 0.9 °C since 1975. Agriculture is predominantly rain-fed and is the major source of food and income. Agriculture remains a major source of employment and contribute about 12.4% to the gross domestic product [6].

As presented in Fig. 1, the dataset for this study is from ten stations found in the three geographical regions: south, center and north. Selected stations are: Rosso, Saint-Louis, Linguere, Matam, Diourbel, Kaolack, Tambacounda, Cap-Skirring, Kolda and Kedougou. The dataset is from 1982 to 2020 and was accessed on 26 July 2021 from the NASA Langley Research Center' POWER Project (https://power.larc.nasa.gov/data-access-viewer/). Features are Month, Day, Year, Maximum Temperature observed at two meters in °C and Minimum Temperature observed at two meters in °C.

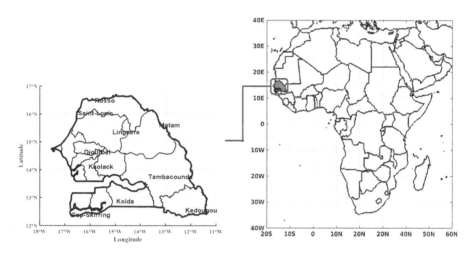

Fig. 1. Map of Africa and Senegal showing dataset locations.

1.4   Exploratory Data Analysis

In the study, we selected one location from the north (Matam), center (Diourbel) and south (Kedougou) for spatial temperature distribution and annual temperature cycle comparison.

Generally, the northern part of Senegal experiences a warm desert climate. As such, temperatures are warm to very hot in the north. Figure 2 and Fig. 3 summarizes daily Maximum Temperature and Minimum Temperature respectively.

Temperatures begin to increase from the month of February with the peak anticipated in the month of May in the center and north, and in April in the south. In the north there are noticeable heat spikes of over 40 °C [7,8]. Figure 4 and Fig. 5 summarizes monthly average Maximum Temperature and Minimum Temperature respectively.

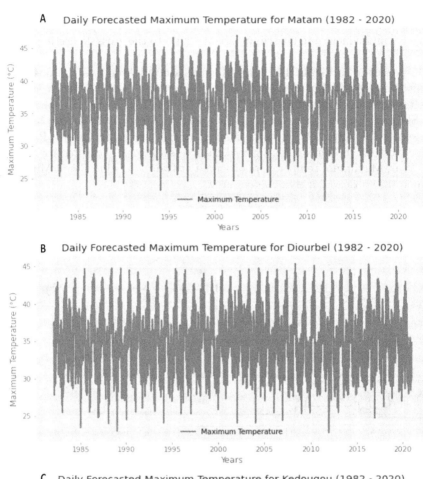

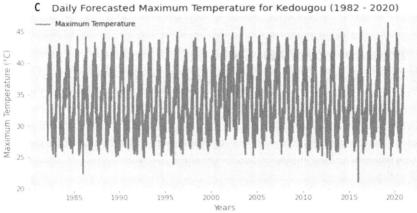

Fig. 2. Daily Maximum Temperature for Matam, Diourbel and Kedougou (1982–2020).

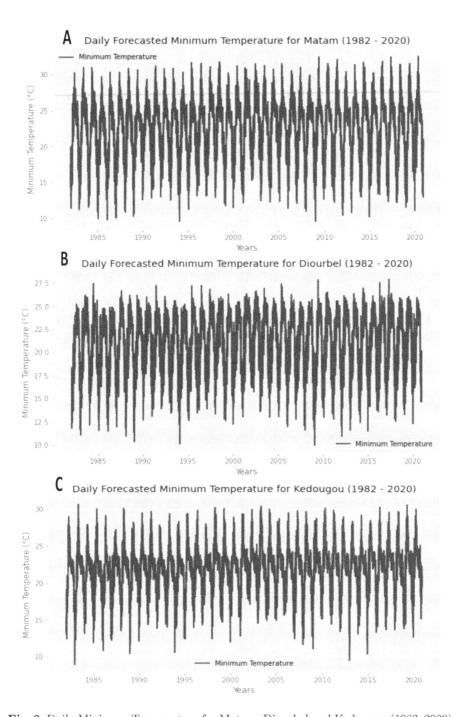

Fig. 3. Daily Minimum Temperature for Matam, Diourbel and Kedougou (1982–2020).

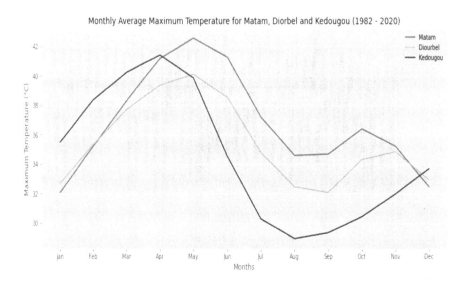

Fig. 4. Maximum Temperature monthly average for Matam, Diourbel and Kedougou (1982–2020).

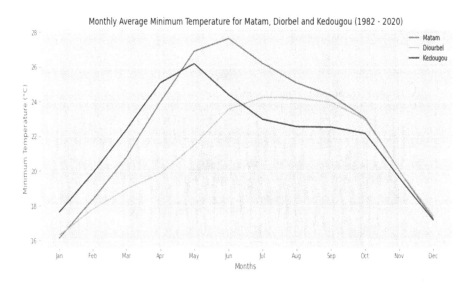

Fig. 5. Minimum Temperature monthly average for Matam, Diourbel and Kedougou (1982–2020).

2   Materials and Methods

Knowledge Discovery in Databases (KDD) process was used to conduct the entire study. The KDD process is defined as "an iterative multi-stage process, for extracting meaningful patterns from data" [12]. The KDD process uses methods from different fields such as Machine Learning. Data Selection, Data Preprocessing and Transformation, Data Mining, Pattern Evaluation and Interpretation are the major steps in KDD process [12].

2.1   Machine Learning Models

We compared three ML regressors (Gradient Boosting, Light Gradient Boosting Machine and CatBoost) with our Ensemble Model in this study. We stacked Light Gradient Boosting Machine, Gradient Boosting and CatBoost to develop the Ensemble Model. Pycaret [11] Python library was used to implement the study.

In this study, we used random search to find the optimal hyperparameter combination of ML models. Random search "defines a search space as a bounded domain of hyperparameter values and randomly samples points in that domain" [13]. Random search is perceived to be more efficient than grid search [13]. Therefore, the best configuration is considered to obtain the lowest MAE, Mean Squared Error (MSE) and RMSE and higher Coefficient of Determination (R^2).

For training the models we used dataset from 1982 to 2008 and from 2009 to 2020 for testing the models.

2.2   Dataset Restructuring

For each parameter, the lagged values of five days were used as an input to forecast the next day. This method is called sliding window with one-step forecasting in time series forecasting. Figure 6 summarizes how sliding window with one-step forecasting technique was used to restructure the dataset.

2.3   Model Evaluation Metrics

In this study, we used MSE, RMSE and R^2 to assess performance of the models. These metrics are frequently used for evaluation of model performance in time series forecasting.

Basically, MSE is the "average of the squared differences between predicted and expected target values in a dataset" [9]. The MSE is expressed as:

$$MSE = \frac{1}{N} \sum_{i=1}^{N} (y_i - \hat{y})^2 \tag{1}$$

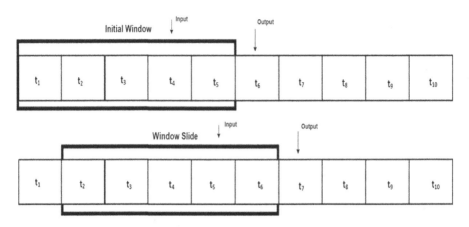

Fig. 6. Summary of dataset restructuring technique using sliding window with one-step forecasting.

While RMSE is the "square root of the average of squared errors" [9]. The RMSE is expressed as:

$$RMSE = \sqrt{\frac{1}{N} \sum_{i=1}^{N} (y_i - \hat{y})^2} \tag{2}$$

where N is the number of samples, y_i is the ith observed value in the dataset and $\hat{y}$ is the predicted value.

The R^2 is defined as the "proportion of the variance in the dependent variable that is predictable from the independent variables" [10]. The R^2 is expressed as:

$$R^2 = \frac{RSS}{TSS} \tag{3}$$

where RSS is the Residuals Sum of Squares and TSS is the Total Sum of Squares.

3   Results and Discussion

The presented results are ten folds cross validation average scores for R^2, MSE and RMSE.

3.1   Maximum Temperature

As presented in Table 1, Ensemble Model is the best model based on ten-fold cross-validated MSE, RMSE and R^2 with scores of 2.8038, 1.6591 and 0.8205 respectively. Table 1 summarizes performance of models.

Table 1. Performance of regressors and ensemble model for Maximum Temperature forecasting.

Parameter	Model	MSE	RMSE	R^2
Maximum temperature	Ensemble model	2.8038	1.6591	0.8205
	Light gradient boosting machine	2.8418	1.6694	0.8176
	Gradient boosting regressor	2.8478	1.6725	0.8175
	CatBoost regressor	2.8501	1.6716	0.8171

We evaluate the performance of the models as presented in Fig. 7 by considering the residuals on the training and test dataset. In summary, residual is considered to be the difference between the true value of y and predicted value of y. Figure 7A shows the residuals of the Ensemble Model on y axis and the predicted Maximum Temperature on the x axis, Fig. 7B shows the residuals of the Light Gradient Boosting Machine on y axis and the predicted Maximum Temperature on the x axis, Fig. 7C shows the residuals of the Gradient Boosting Regressor on y axis and the predicted Maximum Temperature on the x axis and Fig. 7D shows the residuals of the CatBoost Regressor on y axis and the predicted Maximum Temperature on the x axis. In all the figures, it is seen that there is no heteroskedasticity as the residuals are proportionately spread along the zero axis. This signifies lower errors. Heteroskedasticity refers to the unequal scatter of residuals. Further, we note that the models slightly struggled predicting the extreme temperatures (too low and too high). The histogram validates that model training was well done. This affirms that models generalizes well. Figure 7 shows the residuals of the training and test set.

3.2 Minimum Temperature

As seen in Table 2, Ensemble Model is the best model based on ten-fold cross-validated MSE, RMSE and R^2 with scores of 1.1329, 1.0515 and 0.9018 respectively. A summary performance of models is presented in Table 2.

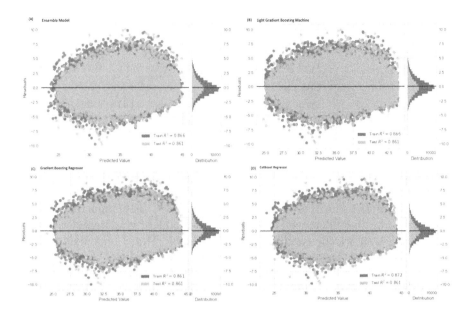

Fig. 7. Training and test set model residuals for Maximum Temperature.

Table 2. Ensemble model and regressors performance for Minimum Temperature forecasting.

Parameter	Model	MSE	RMSE	R^2
Minimum Temperature	Ensemble Model	1.1329	1.0515	0.9018
	Gradient Boosting Regressor	1.1481	1.0582	0.9006
	Light Gradient Boosting Machine	1.1508	1.0595	0.9004
	CatBoost Regressor	1.1554	1.0614	0.9001

Figure 8A shows the residuals of the Ensemble Model on y axis and the predicted Minimum Temperature on the x axis, Fig. 8B shows the residuals of the Gradient Boosting Regressor on y axis and the predicted Minimum Temperature on the x axis, Fig. 8C shows the residuals of the Catboost Regressor on y axis and the predicted Minimum Temperature on the x axis and Fig. 8D shows the residuals of the Light Gradient Boosting Machine on y axis and the predicted Minimum Temperature on the x axis. The residuals are proportionately spread along the zero axis which is a sign of lower errors and there is no sign of heteroskedasticity. In principle, the residuals do not form any pattern. Generally, the histogram validates that model training was well done in view of the residual dispersal of the forecasts on the training and testing set. Figure 8 shows the residuals of the training and test set.

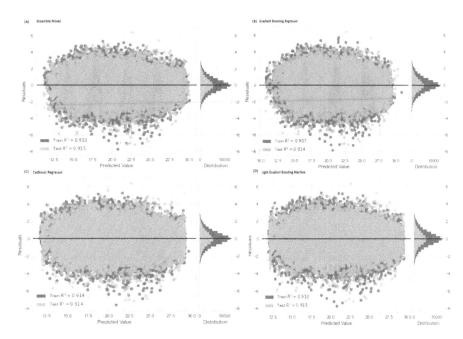

Fig. 8. Training and test set model residuals for Minimum Temperature.

3.3   Forecasts on the Test Dataset

We present the Ensemble Model forecasts based on the test dataset. In terms of spatial distribution, temperatures are warm to very hot moving from the south going to north as seen in Fig. 9A, Fig. 9B and Fig. 9C for the observed Maximum Temperature. The forecast of the model has followed the same spatial distribution as presented in Fig. 9A, Fig. 9B and Fig. 9C for the forecasted Maximum Temperature. Figure 9 and Fig. 10 summarizes daily actual and predicted Maximum Temperature and Minimum Temperature respectively.

In terms of annual cycle, temperatures begin to increase from the month of February with the maximum anticipated in the month of May in the center and north and April in the south as seen in Fig. 11A, Fig. 11B and Fig. 11C for the actual monthly average Maximum Temperature. Comparatively, the model forecast has followed the same annual cycle for Matam, Diourbel and Kedougou as seen in Fig. 11A, Fig. 11B and Fig. 11C for the forecasted monthly average Maximum Temperature. Figure 11 and Fig. 12 summarizes actual and predicted monthly average Maximum Temperature and Minimum Temperature respectively.

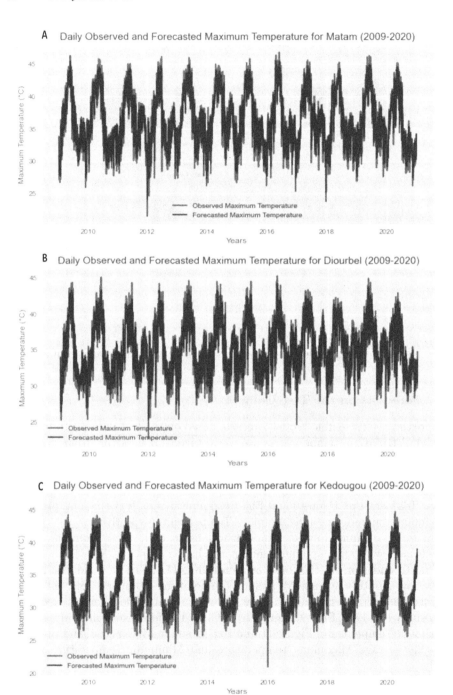

Fig. 9. Actual and predicted daily Maximum Temperature for Matam, Diourbel and Kedougou (2009–2020).

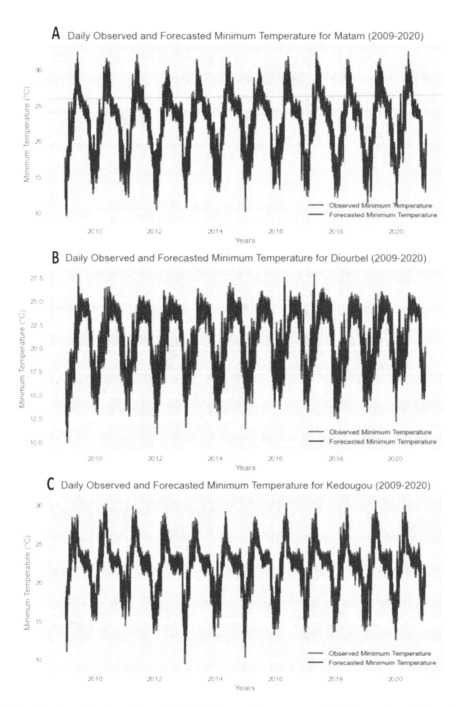

Fig. 10. Actual and predicted daily Minimum Temperature for Matam, Diourbel and Kedougou (2009–2020).

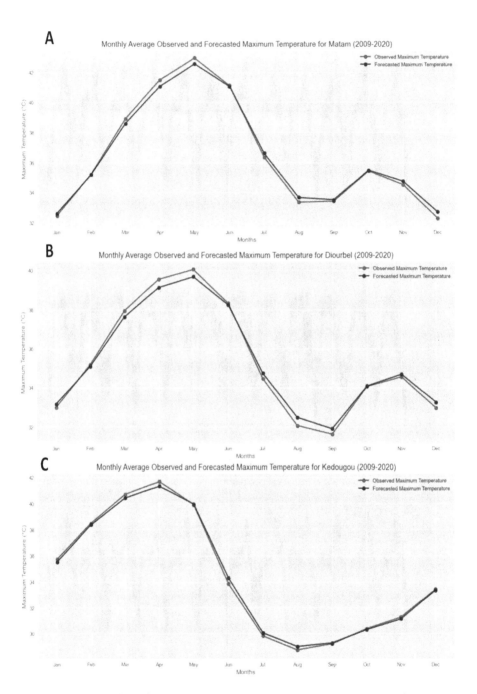

Fig. 11. Actual and predicted monthly average Maximum Temperature for Matam, Diourbel and Kedougou (2009–2020).

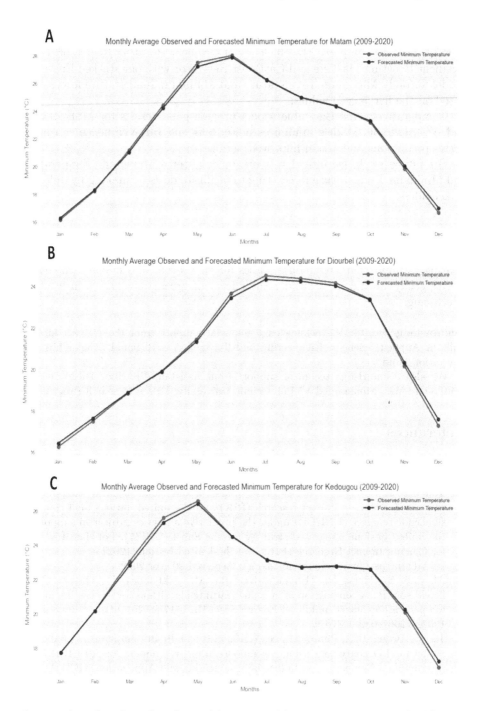

Fig. 12. Actual and predicted monthly average Minimum Temperature for Matam, Diourbel and Kedougou (2009–2020).

3.4   Conclusion

In this study, we compared the efficiency of Gradient Boosting Regressor, Light Gradient Boosting Machine and CatBoost Regressor with our stacked Ensemble Model for daily Maximum Temperature and Minimum Temperature forecasting based on the five lagged values.

Comparatively, the Ensemble Model provide good results for MSE, RMSE and R^2. Ensemble Models minimizes noise, bias and variance hence can make better predictions and attain improved performance.

For future work, we intend to work on long-term Maximum Temperature and Minimum Temperature forecasting to facilitate decision making by different stakeholders.

4   Limitation of the Study

Bearing in mind that greenhouse gasses affect weather and climate processes, in this study we did not consider the effects of greenhouse gasses in weather forecasting.

Acknowledgements. We acknowledge financial support from the Partnership for skills in Applied Sciences, Engineering and Technology - Regional Scholarship and Innovation Fund.

We also acknowledge technical support from Assistant Professor Diego Hernán Peluffo-Ordóñez, Mohammed VI Polytechnic University, MSDA Research Program.

References

1. Lewis, K., Buontempo, C.: Climate impacts in the Sahel and West Africa: the role of climate science in policy making. OECD (2016)
2. Tomalka, J., et al.: Climate risk profile: Sahel. a joint publication by the potsdam institute for climate impact research (PIK) and the united nations high commissioner for refugees (UNHCR) under the predictive analytics project in support of the united nations integrated strategy for the Sahel (UNISS). Potsdam Institute for Climate Impact Research (PIK) and the United Nations (2021)
3. USAID. https://www.climatelinks.org/. Accessed 20 Apr 2022
4. Alawadi, S., Mera, D., Fernández-Delgado, M., Alkhabbas, F., Olsson, C.M., Davidsson, P.: A comparison of machine learning algorithms for forecasting indoor temperature in smart buildings. Energy Syst. **13**, 1–17 (2020). https://doi.org/10.1007/s12667-020-00376-x
5. Jo, H., Hwang, H.J., Phan, D., Lee, Y., Jang, H.: Endpoint temperature prediction model for LD converters using machine-learning techniques. In: 2019 IEEE 6th International Conference on Industrial Engineering and Applications (ICIEA), pp. 22–26 (2019)
6. Salack, S., Muller, B., Gaye, A.T.: Rain-based factors of high agricultural impacts over Senegal. Part I: integration of local to sub-regional trends and variability. Theor. Appl. Climatol. **106**(1), 1–22 (2011)

7. Koudahe, K., et al.: Trend analysis in rainfall, reference evapotranspiration and aridity index in Southern Senegal: adaptation to the vulnerability of rainfed rice cultivation to climate change (2017)
8. World Bank Group. https://documents1.worldbank.org/curated/en/336611539873310474/pdf/. Accessed 20 Apr 2022
9. Shalev-Shwartz, S., Ben-David, S.: Understanding Machine Learning: From Theory to Algorithms. Cambridge University Press, Cambridge (2014)
10. Chicco, D., Warrens, M.J., Jurman, G.: The coefficient of determination R-squared is more informative than SMAPE, MAE, MAPE, MSE and RMSE in regression analysis evaluation. Peer J. Comput. Sci. **7**, e623 (2021)
11. Ali, M.: An open source, low-code machine learning library in Python. PyCaret version 1.0.0. https://www.pycaret.org. Accessed 20 Apr 2022
12. Fayyad, U., Stolorz, P.: Data mining and KDD: promise and challenges. Futur. Gener. Comput. Syst. **13**(2–3), 99–115 (1997)
13. Yang, L., Shami, A.: On hyperparameter optimization of machine learning algorithms: theory and practice. Neurocomputing **415**, 295–316 (2020)

Exploring Use of Machine Learning Regressors for Daily Rainfall Prediction in the Sahel Region: A Case Study of Matam, Senegal

Chimango Nyasulu[1]([📧])[iD], Awa Diattara[1][iD], Assitan Traore[2],
Abdoulaye Deme[3][iD], and Cheikh Ba[1][iD]

[1] LANI (Laboratoire d'Analyse Numérique et Informatique),
University of Gaston Berger, Saint-Louis, Senegal
{nyasulu.chimango,awa.diattara,cheikh2.ba}@ugb.edu.sn
[2] Business & Decision, Grenoble, France
assitan.traore@businessdecision.com
[3] Laboratoire des Sciences de l'Atmosphère et de l'Océan, Unité de Formation et de
Recherche de Sciences Appliquées et de Technologie, University of Gaston Berger,
Saint-Louis, Senegal
abdoulaye.deme@ugb.edu.sn

Abstract. Rainfall is the major source of water for rain-fed agricultural production in Sub-Saharan Africa. Overdependency on rain-fed agriculture renders Sub-Saharan Africa more prone to adverse climate change effects. Consequently, timely and correct long-term daily rainfall forecasting is fundamental for planning and management of rainwater to ensure maximum production. In this study, we explored use of regressors: Gradient Boosting, CatBoost, Random Forest and Ridge Regression to forecast daily rainfall for Matam in the northern geographical part of Senegal. Gradient Boosting model is therefore considered a better model with smaller values of Mean Absolute Error, Mean Squared Error and Root Mean Squared Error of 0.1873, 0.1369 and 0.3671 respectively. Further, Gradient Boosting model produced a higher score of 0.69 for Coefficient of Determination. Relative Humidity is perceived to highly influence rainfall prediction.

Keywords: Machine learning · Regressors · Gradient Boosting Regressor · Random Forest Regressor · CatBoost Regressor · Ridge Regression · Rainfall forecasting · Sub-Saharan Africa

1 Introduction

Attaining food security as required remains a major global challenge. Food insecurity is more visible in Sub-Saharan Africa (SSA). Food security is a condition in which all people, at all times, have access to adequate, harmless, and healthful food that ensures active and healthy life [1]. Globally, agriculture is considered

T. M. Ngatched Nkouatchah et al. (Eds.): PAAISS 2022, LNICST 459, pp. 78–92, 2023.
https://doi.org/10.1007/978-3-031-25271-6_5

to be a major source of food and income. Smallholder rain-fed agriculture is the major source of agricultural production in SSA. For instance, about 95% of food in SSA is produced under rain-fed agriculture [2]. Due to climate change effects, too much reliance on smallholder rain-fed agriculture renders SSA more prone to adverse weather conditions. Other notable challenges include: loss of soil fertility, environmental degradation, and pre-harvest and post-harvest crop loss.

1.1 Effects of Climate Change on Rainfall in Senegal

Like other SSA countries, climate change is among the major challenges facing the agriculture sector in Senegal. As a result of climate change, in Senegal there has been declining and highly unreliable rainfall, rampant water scarcity, intense and prolonged droughts. For instance, the previous three decades drought has been recurring [3]. The hostile effects of climate change have resulted into acute food insecurity due to reduced agricultural production [3].

1.2 Weather Forecasting

Weather forecasting is using technology, statistics, principles of physics and empirical techniques to predict the state of the atmosphere for a particular time and location [4]. Weather forecasting requires analysis of huge amounts of data (big data) to unearth hidden features which may provide leads for impending natural disasters such as drought and heavy rainfall before its occurrence. The term big data is used to define the enormous amount of data from several sources which can either be structured or unstructured [5]. Weather prediction in Africa has constantly been a huge challenge. In addition to the challenges of big data management, weather stations in Africa are generally rare, the observation network is poor, data is not of good quality and many more [6].

1.3 Weather Prediction Using Machine Learning

Several researchers have reported about use of Machine Learning (ML) for weather forecasting. Machine Learning method is considered to be the most robust method for weather forecasting [7,8]. Machine Learning is reported to be a subdivision of Artificial Intelligence [7,8].

1.4 Significance and Objective of the Study

Weather information and services are more vital for farmers to effectively manage agricultural resources and survive climate change effects. To ensure maximum crop yield, among other things, there is need to properly manage rainwater. Knowing when it will rain and the amount of rain expected, smallholder farmers can well anticipate how to react to extreme incidences of rainfall (little or too much rainfall).

In this study, the objective was to explore use of ML regressors to forecast daily rainfall for Matam based on meteorological features. Additionally, the study was meant to determine the influencing variables that affect rainfall prediction in this area.

1.5   Study Area Geographical Characteristics and Data Source

Senegal is found in the West Africa, sharing boarders with Mauritania, Mali, Gambia, Guinea-Bissau and Guinea-Conakry. Senegal covers an area of about 196,722 square kilometers. Senegal lies in the semi-arid region called Sahel. Rainfall is very variable. Rainfall is between May or June to October. Warmer climate has amplified incidence of droughts hence reduced crop harvest. Agriculture is considered to be a major source of food and income. For example, over 70% of the populace is employed in the agricultural sector. Largely, agriculture is rain-fed [3].

Matam is located in the northern geographical part of Senegal. The north experiences a hot desert climate. The rainy season falls from June to October and dry season falls from November to May. Rainy season is characterized by high temperatures, dampness and storms. Dry season is characterized by dust from harmattan winds. The expected average yearly cumulative rainfall is between 400–600 mm. It should be known that in Senegal rainfall is more scarce in the north compared to other regions. Figure 1 below shows the map of Senegal and location of the study area.

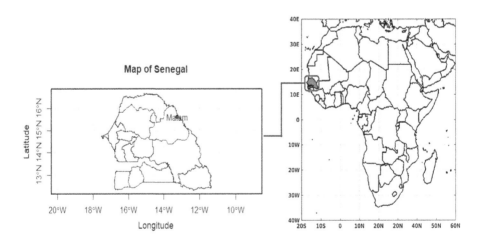

Fig. 1. Map of the study area.

The dataset used in this study was obtained from the NASA Langley Research Center POWER Project (https://power.larc.nasa.gov/data-access-viewer/), accessed on 21 July 2021.

The dataset is for the daily averaged data for Matam, Senegal, covering a period of 38 years starting from 01/01/1982 through 12/31/2020. Parameters observed are Day, Month, Year, Relative Humidity (%), Minimum Wind Speed (m/s), Rainfall (mm day-1), Minimum Temperature (°C), Maximum Wind Speed (m/s) and Maximum Temperature (°C).

1.6   Exploratory Data Analysis for Rainfall

Typically, exploratory data analysis is conducted to have a well understanding of the dataset by summarizing the major characteristics of the data. Exploratory data analysis enables quick interpretation of the data and selection of useful features for further analysis. As presented in Fig. 2, it is observed that precipitation varies considerably from year to year. The year 2020 was the peak and 1983 was the lowest. For the annual rainfall cycle as presented in Fig. 3, the rainy season falls from the month of June to the month of October and maximum rainfall is expected in the month of August.

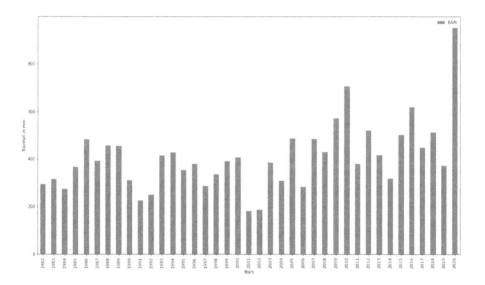

Fig. 2. Annual rainfall for Matam from 1982 to 2020.

The rest of the paper is presented as follows. In Sect. 2, we presents a review of literature. In Sect. 3, we introduces materials and methods. In Sects. 4, we present results and discussion. Lastly, in Sect. 5, we present the conclusions.

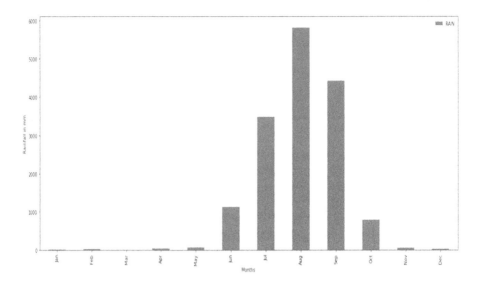

Fig. 3. Monthly average rainfall for Matam from 1982 to 2020.

2 Review of Related Work

Researchers have used ML models for rainfall forecasting. [9] predicted daily rainfall using gradient descent XGBoost, Multivariate Linear Regression (MLR) and Random Forest (RF) based on humidity, evaporation, minimum temperature, wind speed, maximum temperature, year, month, date and sunshine. The gradient descent XGBoost outperformed other models with scores for Mean Absolute Error (MAE) and Root Mean Squared Error (RMSE) of 3.58 and 7.85 respectively.

Another study by [10] was conducted to predict the rainfall intensity of Coonoor in India using Decision Tree (DT), RF and Support Vector Machine Regression (SVR) based on wind direction, humidity, wind speed, daily temperature and cloud speed. Coefficient of Determination (R^2) results for SVR are 0.814 and adjusted R^2 0.806, DT are R^2 0.904 and adjusted R^2 0.900 and RF are R^2 0.981 and adjusted R^2 0.980.

In this work by [11], ML regressors were used to predict several weather parameters including rainfall for Bangladesh. Five years data was collected from Bangladesh Meteorological Division which includes features such as rainfall, wind speed, temperature and humidity. Several ML regressors were used such as XGBoost, CatBoost, AdaBoost and Bayesian Ridge. Notable results for rainfall prediction are that of CatBoost: MAE 67.49 and Mean Squared Error (MSE) 11657.74.

3 Materials and Methods

We used Knowledge Discovery in Databases (KDD) process to implement the study. The KDD process is comprised of several steps which are performed iteratively for discovering useful patterns from data [5]. Knowledge Discovery in Databases process uses approaches from different fields like Artificial Intelligence, Database Management, Machine Learning and many more. General steps in KDD process are Data Selection and Integration, Data Cleaning and Pre-processing, Data Transformation, Data Mining and Pattern Evaluation/Interpretation [5].

3.1 Data Pre-processing, Transformation and Feature Engineering

Data pre-processing was done to identify and address missing values, normalize parameters within a specific interval and ensure that all features were converted to their data types and format. Data normalization was done using min max scaler. Normalization transforms features by scaling each feature to a given range. An observed value is normalized as follows:

$$y = (x - min)/(max - min) \tag{1}$$

where y is the new value, x is the observed value, min is the minimum value of the column and max is the maximum value of the column.

Rainfall was transformed by performing Log Transformation. The Log Transformation is one of the techniques used to change a skewed distribution to a normal or less skewed distribution. Feature engineering was done to derive Day of the Year from Year, Month and Day.

3.2 Correlation of Features

We used a heatmap in Fig. 4 to observe correlation of features. Correlation shows positive or negative (between -1 and $+1$) relationship between two variables. With respect to correlation with Rainfall, Maximum Wind Speed has the highest negative correlation of -0.42 and Relative Humidity has the highest positive correlation of 0.73.

3.3 Predictors and Splitting of the Dataset

In this study, Relative Humidity, Maximum Wind Speed, Minimum Wind Speed, Minimum Temperature, Maximum Temperature and Day of the Year were used to predict Rainfall. Several studies [9–11] have used similar weather variables to predict rainfall. Two thirds (1982 to 2008) of the dataset was used for training the ML models and one third (2009 to 2020) was used for testing the ML models.

3.4 Machine Learning Models

In this study we used the following regressors: Gradient Boosting, Random Forest, CatBoost and Ridge Regression. The study was implemented using Pycaret [12] Python library.

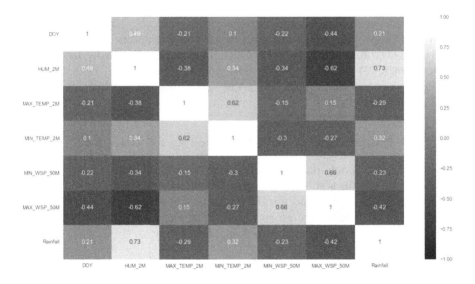

Fig. 4. Correlation of features.

3.5   Model Configuration and Performance Improvement

To develop a ML model with optimum performance, a set of hyperparameters configuration has to be explored [13]. Machine Learning model's performance is directly influenced by the best hyperparameters configuration. Hyperparameters are the parameters which are set before training a ML model to get the best fit. Hyperparameters are used to configure the architecture of the ML model. Basically, hyperparameter tuning is a search for a collection of hyperparameters that yields the best performance of a model on a dataset [13]. Searching for the best combination of hyperparameters can be challenging, thus search algorithms such as grid search and random search are used. In this study, we used random search to search for the hyperparameters of ML models. Generally, random search "defines a search space as a bounded domain of hyperparameter values and randomly samples points in that domain" [13]. Random search is perceived to be more efficient than grid search [13]. In this regard, the best configuration is considered to obtain the lowest MAE, MSE and RMSE and higher R^2. Table 1 summarizes the selected parameters for each model.

3.6   Model Evaluation

In this study, models were evaluated using MAE, MSE, RMSE and R^2 performance metrics.

The MAE is the "average of the absolute difference between the actual and predicted values in the dataset. In essence it measures the average of the residuals in the dataset" [14]. The Mean Absolute Error is expressed as:

Table 1. Parameter setting.

Model	Parameters
Gradient Boosting Regressor	alpha=0.9, ccp_alpha=0.0, criterion='friedman_mse', init=None, learning_rate=0.1, loss='squared_error', max_depth=3, max_features=None, max_leaf_nodes=None, min_impurity_decrease=0.0, min_samples_leaf=1, min_samples_split=2, min_weight_fraction_leaf=0.0, n_estimators=100, n_iter_no_change=None, random_state=123, subsample=1.0, tol=0.0001, validation_fraction=0.1, verbose=0, warm_start=False
Random Forest Regressor	bootstrap=True, ccp_alpha=0.0, criterion='squared_error' max_depth=None, max_features='auto', max_leaf_nodes=None, max_samples=None, min_impurity_decrease=0.0, min_samples_leaf=1, min_samples_split=2, min_weight_fraction_leaf=0.0, n_estimators=100, n_jobs=-1, oob_score=False, random_state=123, verbose=0,warm_start=False
CatBoost Regressor	nan_mode = Min, eval_metric = RMSE, iterations = 1000, sampling_frequency = PerTree,leaf_estimation_method = Newton, penalties_coefficient = 1, boosting_type = Plain, model_shrink_mode = Constant, feature_border_type = GreedyLogSum, force_unit_auto_pair_weights = False, l2_leaf_reg = 3, random_strength = 1, rsm = 1,boost_from_average = True, model_size_reg = 0.5,subsample = 0.800000011920929, use_best_model = False, random_seed = 123, depth = 6, posterior_sampling = False, border_count = 254, classes_count = 0,auto_class_weights = None, sparse_features_conflict_fraction = 0, l, best_model_min_trees = 1, model_shrink_rate = 0, min_data_in_leaf = 1, loss_function = RMSE, learning_rate = 0.0587799996137619, score_function = Cosine, task_type = CPU, leaf_estimation_iterations = 1, bootstrap_type = MVS, max_leaves = 64
Ridge Regression	alpha=1.0, copy_X=True, fit_intercept=True, max_iter=None, normalize='deprecated', positive=False, random_state=123, solver='auto',tol=0.001

$$MAE = \frac{1}{N} \sum_{i=1}^{N} |y_i - \hat{y}| \qquad (2)$$

where as MSE is the "average of the squared differences between predicted and expected target values in a dataset. The squaring has the effect of inflating large errors". Generally, the smaller the MSE, the better the forecast [14]. The Mean Squared Error is expressed as:

$$MSE = \frac{1}{N} \sum_{i=1}^{N} (y_i - \hat{y})^2 \qquad (3)$$

While RMSE is the "square root of the average of squared errors. The effect of each error on RMSE is proportional to the size of the squared error; consequently, larger errors have a disproportionately large effect on RMSE. Thus, RMSE is sensitive to outliers" [14]. The Root Mean Squared Error is expressed as:

$$RMSE = \sqrt{\frac{1}{N} \sum_{i=1}^{N} (y_i - \hat{y})^2} \tag{4}$$

where N is the number of samples, y_i is the ith observed value in the dataset and $\hat{y}$ is the predicted value.

The R^2 is defined as the "proportion of the variance in the dependent variable that is predictable from the independent variables". The R^2 is expressed as:

$$R^2 = \frac{RSS}{TSS} \tag{5}$$

where RSS is the Residuals Sum of Squares and TSS is the Total Sum of Squares.

4   Results and Discussion

Using the features and method of splitting the dataset into training and testing set as explained in Subsect. 3.3, we trained and tested the models. Presented are results of average scores across the 10-fold cross validation.

4.1   Gradient Boosting Regressor Results

After training and evaluation of the model, the following metric values were obtained: MAE 0.1873, MSE 0.1369, RMSE 0.3671 and R^2 0.6904. Generally, considering MAE value of 0.1873 it is perceived to be a good prediction. In addition, we present Fig. 5 with prediction error in Fig. 5(A), feature importance in Fig. 5(B) and feature selection in Fig. 5(C) to better understand performance of the model. It is common for a regression model to have some degree of error, meaning that randomness and unpredictability are always a part of the regression model. In Fig. 5(A), we plot the observed rainfall (y) on the x axis and what the model predicted (ŷ) on the y axis. Also, we compare our model's best fit line with the identity line to observe the degree of variance in the model. In this way, we inspect the model's good and bad predictions. Generally, we observe that the model made some good predictions with several points close to the identity line. We observe a high density of errors (forming like a vertical line) on the point zero of the x axis which shows that the model predicted rain on a wrong day. A conceivable clarification for that is that there is no strong correlation of the predictors with rainfall hence the false alarms of rainfall by the model. Secondly, in general, weather and rainfall are highly non-linear.

In terms of feature importance, Fig. 5(B) shows that Relative Humidity is of high importance to the prediction of the model with a score of above 0.8. Maximum Wind Speed and Minimum Wind Speed are the least important features with a score of 0.0. In this regard, the least important features can be removed. As seen in Fig. 5(C), the optimal accuracy (69%) was achieved with five features. Figure 5 summarizes the model's prediction error, feature importance and selection.

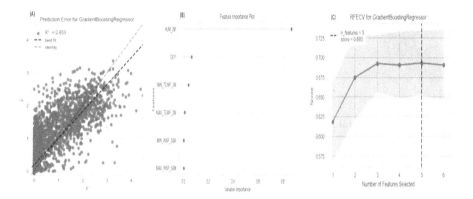

Fig. 5. Summary of Gradient Boosting Regressor prediction error, feature importance and selection.

4.2   Random Forest Regressor Results

As a result of the training and evaluation of the model, the calculated metrics were the following: MAE 0.1881, MSE 0.1429, RMSE 0.3764 and R^2 0.674. To better understand the model performance, we consider model's prediction error, feature importance and selection as presented in Fig. 6(A), Fig. 6(B) and Fig. 6(C) respectively. To observe the degree of variance of the model, in Fig. 6(A), we plot the observed rainfall (y) on the x axis and what the model predicted (ŷ) on the y axis. Further, we compare our model's best fit line with the identity line to observe the degree of variance in the model. In this way, we inspect the model's good and bad predictions. Generally, we observe that the model made some good predictions with several points close to the identity line. We note a high presence of errors on the point zero of the x axis which shows that the model predicted rain on a wrong day. A possible explanation for that is that there is no strong correlation of the predictors with rainfall hence the false alarms of rainfall by the model and generally weather and rainfall are highly non-linear.

Figure 6(B) shows that Relative Humidity is of high importance to the prediction of the model with a score of 0.7. Maximum Wind Speed is the least important feature with a score of slightly above 0.0. As seen in Fig. 6(C), the optimal accuracy (67%) was achieved with five features. Figure 6 summarizes the model's prediction error, feature importance and selection.

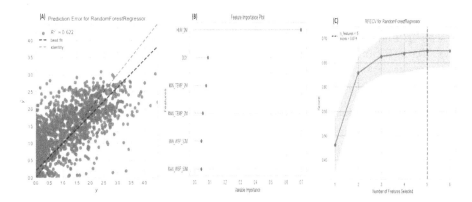

Fig. 6. Summary of Random Forest Regressor prediction error, feature importance and selection.

4.3 CatBoost Regressor Results

Training and evaluation of the model based on the performance metrics produced the following results: MAE 0.1898, MSE 0.144, RMSE 0.3774 and R^2 0.6727. Model's prediction error, feature importance and selection were considered to understand the model performance. As presented in Fig. 7(A) we plot the observed rainfall (y) on the x axis and what the model predicted ($\hat{y}$) on the y axis to observe the degree of variance of the model. Additionally, we compare our model's best fit line with the identity line to observe the degree of variance in the model. In this way, we inspect the model's good and bad predictions. Generally, we observe that the model made some good predictions with several points close to the identity line. We note a high presence of errors on the point zero of the x axis which shows that the model predicted rain on a wrong day. This is attributed to moderate to weak correlation of the predictors with rainfall which impacted the prediction of the model. Secondly, in general, weather and rainfall are highly non-linear.

Figure 7(B) shows that Relative Humidity is of high importance to the prediction of the model. Maximum Wind Speed is the least important feature. As seen in Fig. 7(C), the optimal accuracy (67%) was achieved with six features. Figure 7 summarizes the model's prediction error, feature importance and selection.

4.4 Ridge Regression Results

Training and evaluation of the model based on the performance metrics produced the following results: MAE 0.2987, MSE 0.1787, RMSE 0.4215 and R^2 0.5906. Looking at Fig. 8, the model's prediction error, feature importance and selection, it is evident that the model least performed. A possible explanation for the comparative poor performance is attributed to the choice of features as seen in Fig. 8(B). Contrary to other models, Minimum Temperature is of high importance to the prediction of the model and Day of the Year is the least

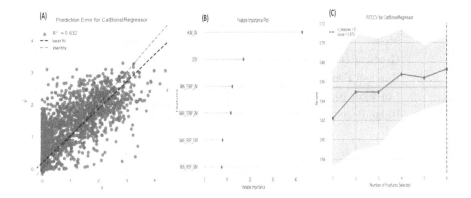

Fig. 7. Summary of CatBoost Regressor prediction error, feature importance and selection.

important feature. However, considering the correlation of features with rainfall, Relative Humidity has the higher correlation of 0.73 compared to 0.32 for Minimum Temperature. Another factor could be that predictor variables shows a correlation among themselves. As seen in Fig. 8(C), the optimal accuracy (59%) was achieved with six features. Figure 8 summarizes the model's prediction error, feature importance and selection.

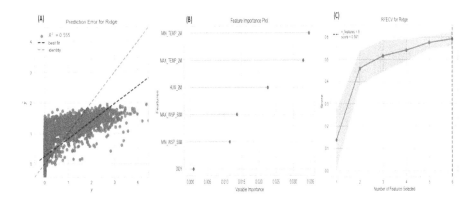

Fig. 8. Summary of Ridge Regression prediction error, feature importance and selection.

In summary, comparatively, Gradient Boosting model is therefore considered a best model with smaller values of MAE, MSE and RMSE 0.1873, 0.1369 and 0.3671 respectively. Further, it is seen to have a higher score of R^2 of 0.6904 as summarized in Table 2. This is attributed to the fact that Gradient Boosting trees are capable of correcting each other's errors. Additionally, it is able enough to find any nonlinear relationship between the model target and features.

Table 2. Summary of model performance.

Model	MAE	MSE	RMSE	R^2
Gradient Boosting Regressor	0.1873	0.1369	0.3671	0.6904
Random Forest Regressor	0.1881	0.1429	0.3764	0.674
CatBoost Regressor	0.1898	0.144	0.3774	0.6727
Ridge Regression	0.2987	0.1787	0.4215	0.5906

4.5   Forecasting on the Test Dataset

We present the models forecasts based on the test dataset by considering annual rainfall and monthly average rainfall. Figure 9 presents a graph that shows the comparison between the total annual observed rainfall and predicted rainfall from all models. In Fig. 9 it is seen that the models followed the annual variability of rainfall in Matam. Figure 10 presents the rainfall annual cycle of observed and predicted rainfall from all the models. It is seen that the models predicted well in terms of rainfall annual cycle. The models predicted substantial rainfall from June to October. This is in accordance with the rainfall annual cycle.

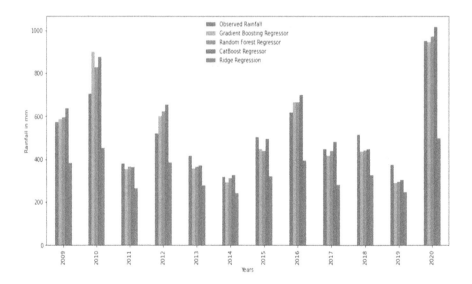

Fig. 9. Total annual observed and forecasted rainfall for Matam (2009–2020).

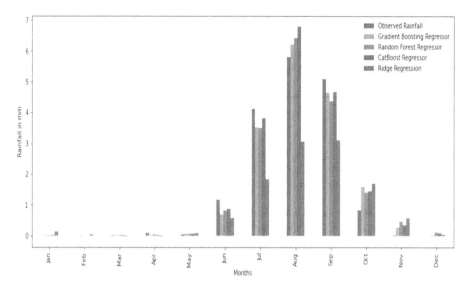

Fig. 10. Observed and forecasted monthly average rainfall for Matam (2009–2020).

5   Conclusion

In this study, we explored use of regressors (Gradient Boosting, Random Forest, CatBoost and Ridge Regression) to forecast daily rainfall for Matam in the northern geographical part of Senegal. The prediction was made based on the following features: Relative Humidity, Maximum Temperature, Minimum Temperature, Maximum Wind Speed, Minimum Wind Speed and Day of Year. Relative Humidity was observed to highly influence rainfall prediction. Generally, feature engineering and data transformation slightly improved the correlation of features with the target variable. The study has established that rainfall varies from year to year and has no specific pattern. Generally, Gradient Boosting Regressor model yielded a better performance with lower MAE, MSE and RMSE and higher R^2 comparatively.

6   Our Future Work

Due to climate change, timely and accurate weather forecasting is required to help farmers make comprehensive plans for their farming endeavors in advance. To prevent loss of quality and quantity of crop yield due to climate change, farmers need to consider precautionary procedures in case of hostile weather conditions. Therefore, our future work will focus on forecasting more weather variables that influences agricultural production.

Acknowledgements. This work is supported by the Partnership for skills in Applied Sciences, Engineering and Technology - Regional Scholarship and Innovation Fund.

We acknowledge technical support from Assistant Professor Diego Hernán Peluffo-Ordóñez, Mohammed VI Polytechnic University, Modeling, Simulation and Data Analysis Research Program.

References

1. Russell, J., Flood, V., Yeatman, H., Mitchell, P.: Food security in older Australians. J. Nutr. Educ. Behav. **43**(2), e1 (2011)
2. Sharp, G.: Food production and consumption. Capital. Nat. Social. **27**(7), 117–124 (2016)
3. Tall, M., et al.: Projected impact of climate change in the hydroclimatology of Senegal with a focus over the Lake of Guiers for the twenty-first century. Theoret. Appl. Climatol. **129**(1), 655–665 (2017). https://doi.org/10.1007/s00704-016-1805-y
4. Nyasulu, C., Diattara, A., Traore, A., Ba, C.: Enhancing farmers productivity through IoT and machine learning: a state-of-the-art review of recent trends in Africa. In: Faye, Y., Gueye, A., Gueye, B., Diongue, D., Nguer, E.H.M., Ba, M. (eds.) CNRIA 2021. LNICST, vol. 400, pp. 113–124. Springer, Cham (2021). https://doi.org/10.1007/978-3-030-90556-9_10
5. Fayyad, U., Stolorz, P.: Data mining and KDD: promise and challenges. Futur. Gener. Comput. Syst. **13**(2–3), 99–115 (1997)
6. Wichitarapongsakun, P., Sarin, C., Klomjek, P., Chuenchooklin, S.: Rainfall prediction and meteorological drought analysis in the Sakae Krang River basin of Thailand. Agric. Nat. Res. **50**(6), 490–498 (2016)
7. Ahuna, M.N., Afullo, T.J., Alonge, A.A.: Rain attenuation prediction using artificial neural network for dynamic rain fade mitigation. SAIEE Afr. Res. J. **110**(1), 11–18 (2019)
8. Bello, A.A., et al.: Monthly rainfall prediction using artificial neural network: a case study of Kano, Nigeria. Environ. Earth Sci. Res. J. **5**(2), 37–41 (2018)
9. Liyew, C.M., Melese, H.A.: Machine learning techniques to predict daily rainfall amount. J. Big Data **8**(1), 1–11 (2021). https://doi.org/10.1186/s40537-021-00545-4
10. Tharun, V.P., Prakash, R., Devi, S.R.: 2018 2nd International Conference on Inventive Communication and Computational Technologies (ICICCT), pp. 1507–1512. IEEE (2018)
11. Mahabub, A., Habib, A.B.: An overview of weather forecasting for Bangladesh using machine learning techniques (2019)
12. Ali, M.: An open source, low-code machine learning library in Python. PyCaret version 1.0.0, https://www.pycaret.org. Accessed 20 Apr 2022
13. Yang, L., Shami, A.: On hyperparameter optimization of machine learning algorithms: theory and practice. Neurocomputing **415**, 295–316 (2020)
14. Botchkarev, A.: Performance metrics (error measures) in machine learning regression, forecasting and prognostics: properties and typology. arXiv preprint. arXiv:1809.03006 (2021)

Artificial Intelligence Theory
and Methods

Dynamic Pre-trained Models Layer Selection Using Filter-Weights Cosine Similarity

Raphael Wanjiku[✉], Lawrence Nderu, and Michael Kimwele

Jomo Kenyatta University of Agriculture and Technology, Nairobi, Kenya
phaelgi@gmail.com

Abstract. Selecting fine-tuning layers in a pre-trained model is vital to adapting the target data in transfer learning. The selection process is mainly manual and or based on the last k layers of the network. So far, these methods have not yielded the best adaptation for various datasets. Therefore, it is a trial and error selection of the suitable layers for the ever-increasing pre-trained models. This paper looks at the effect of the weights based on the cosine similarity at the various layers leading to the omission or selection in the fine-tuning process. We experiment on four primary publicly available datasets utilizing four pre-trained models, and the results show better performance than the traditional approaches. Furthermore, a chest cancer imaging dataset is an application extension of the proposed approach. The results show improvements from the new methods between 0.65% in VGG16 to 39.01% for the InceptionV3 models compared to the standard fine-tuning baselines.

Keywords: Transfer learning · Cosine similarity · Dynamic layer selection

1 Introduction

With advances in deep learning, more pre-trained models are being published for use in transfer learning [1]. Transfer learning involves reusing knowledge previously learnt in one domain (datasets) in another domain (datasets). It works very well in closely related tasks [2, 3]. Transfer learning reduces datasets bias, reduces training time and is very suitable in cases of data insufficiency [4, 5]. In transfer learning of a classification task $\{P(X), Y, P(Y|X)\}$ whose features space is X, the outcome space Y is given by the objective function $P(Y|X)$ where $y \in Y$ and $p(X)$ is the probability distribution of the features space X. The outcomes space Y is normally different but related to X space [6].

Among transfer learning methods, fine-tuning is the most common method. The standard procedure involves freezing specific last layers of the pre-trained model or optimizing pre-trained model parameters. The freezing of the network layers enables the addition of the classification layer for the target task [7]. In using convolutional neural network (CNN) pre-trained models, the target task takes advantage of the learnt knowledge involving the low-level characteristics of the images (primarily textural features).

The use of transfer learning is slowly but steadily being used in many industries. In the medical field of medical imaging, convolutional neural networks transfer learning

© ICST Institute for Computer Sciences, Social Informatics and Telecommunications Engineering 2023
Published by Springer Nature Switzerland AG 2023. All Rights Reserved
T. M. Ngatched Nkouatchah et al. (Eds.): PAAISS 2022, LNICST 459, pp. 95–108, 2023.
https://doi.org/10.1007/978-3-031-25271-6_6

models are used in cancer type classification on computerized tomography (CT) and magnetic resonance imaging (MRI) images and classification of thoracic diseases from X-ray images [8], among others. Traditionally, the use of CNN needs large amounts of data that must be expert annotated; transfer learning can reduce the costs and the need for the large datasets needed for classification [9, 10]. In this work, the application of the proposed model is additionally tested on chest cancer tissue images classified into four types: adenocarcinoma, large cell carcinoma, squamous cell carcinoma and normal cells [27].

This paper addresses the dynamic selection of the pre-trained model layers as fine-tuning layers while freezing the non-selected layers. The process of layer selection has been a manual process [11]. With deeper models emerging, choosing the suitable layers is a trial and error process that renders the models inefficient [5] and cumbersome for effective transfer learning. Some researchers have recommended the selection of the last layers, while others have adopted the middle layers of the networks. It has therefore become an optimization problem. This work evaluates this problem from the weight perspective using filter-based weight cosine similarity among the network layers.

1.1 Contributions

In addressing the dynamic selection of layers, this work's contributions are as follows:

1. We propose using cosine similarity on filter weights to identify fine-tunable layers for effective transfer learning.
2. We conduct fine-tuning on four publicly available datasets on four ImageNet pre-trained models and a further concept application on the chest cancer dataset. The proposed method improves accuracy between 0.01% and 10.04%.
3. We analyse the impacts of positive and negative weights in a model and their effects on the standard fine-tuning methods of transfer learning.

The rest of the document is organized as follows: Sect. 2 discusses the existing literature on the dynamic selection of fine-tunable layers. Section 3 introduces the proposed approach outlining the methodology used in executing the proposed approach. Section 4 presents and discusses the results, while section five gives the conclusion and the expected future work.

2 Literature Review

The following literature highlights the various dynamic layers' selection methods for transfer learning pre-trained models.

The adaptive approach is introduced in a study by Guo et al. [12]. The method involves using Gumbel softmax sampling using a decision policy on discrete distribution that is passed through a lightweight neural network that determines the layers to fine-tune based on the samples from the distribution. The approach is tested on ResNet-50 and ResNet-26 architectures with ten datasets for standard fine-tuning, feature extraction and stochastic fine-tuning. This approach only utilizes the ResNet architectures, and its selection is based on discrete distribution. The proposed approach works with four pre-trained models. It can also be extended to other convolutional pre-trained models to address dynamic layer selection in CNNs better.

In the AdaFilter approach, Guo et al. [5] address the number of parameters of each sample in the target task. The researchers use a recurrent neural network (RNN) that decides which filters of the layers to use [13]. The approach is tested on Stanford dogs, Caltech 256, Aircraft and MIT Indoors datasets on the ResNet50 pre-trained model. This approach uses only one pre-trained model, which limits its generalisation for use in other pre-trained models. The proposed approach's use of four pre-trained models gives a better generalization and proof of the dynamic selection of layers. The proposed approach uses the standard k-layers method, one of the easiest fine-tuning methods; this has not been used in the AdaFilter approach.

Lampert and Royer [21] introduce the Flex-tuning approach that selects the best adopting layers units to select the best architecture in the transfer process. The method was tested on large Inception 2 architecture on the MNIST, PACS, CIFAR and ImageNet 2012 datasets. The early and immediate layers of the model give better performance than the final layers. This approach uses the training data to evaluate the performance of the validation data and compares the performance only by selecting the layers with the best performance. The proposed approach is different since it uses the weights in the filters to determine which layers to select. Furthermore, the proposed approach uses more pre-trained models to prove its superiority in dynamic layer selection.

In further efforts to address the dynamic selection of layers, Nagae, Nobuhara and Kawai introduce PathNet [20], which utilizes genetic algorithms with a layer's weights acting as the genotypes and the layers with the highest validation accuracies are used as the best layers for fine-tuning. This method is tested on the InceptionV3 and utilizes the CIFAR100 dataset. They further explore the concept using the tournament selection algorithm testing on the SVHN21 and Food-101 datasets. This approach is limited to one pre-trained model, which limits its generalization. Both the proposed approach and this approach use weights to determine the layers. However, the proposed approach looks at the difference in weights distributions, whereas this approach focuses on the highest validation accuracies in the layers, similarly to Flex-tuning.

Grega and Vili [7] introduce differential evolution based fine-tuning (DEFT), which determines how to select and which layers to select for fine-tuning. The selected layers are identified through a predictive performance of binary array values, ones with the least cross-entropy loss values. This approach is based on the layers' predictive performance, unlike the proposed approach. The proposed approach gives a direct influencing variable of weight which acts on the input. Furthermore, the DEFT uses only one pre-trained model, which limits its generalisation.

In a study by Sarhan, Lauri and Frintrop [25], a multi-phase fine-tuning approach for sign language is proposed. In this approach, weights are used in fine-tuning in several phases, starting with the topmost layers and adding more layers to the previous phases for joint fine-tuning. This approach uses GoogLeNet as the evaluation pre-trained model. Unlike this approach, the proposed approach uses weights from a distribution perspective and three extra pre-trained models to generalize its suitability in dynamic layer selection. It is also noted that the multi-phase approach gives accuracies below 80%, which is not good enough despite its low complexity for the RWTH-PHOENIX-Weather Multisigner 2014 dataset.

From the literature, most of the dynamic layer selection methods evaluated only single pre-trained models, making it difficult to generalize their findings in dynamic layer selection in CNN pre-trained models. The proposed model provides a more straightforward method that can be applied to any CNN pre-trained model.

3   Methodology

In convolutional neural network operation, the input is convolved, passed through the activation functions and pooled iteratively depending on the depth of the network. Finally, the final pooling layer output is fed to a fully connected layer when the best possible outcome classification of the input is determined [14]. Throughout the network operations, weights are updated until the model can learn features from the unseen input in the validation and testing stages. Therefore, it is crucial to understand how these weights correlate in a given filter, layer and between the layers and how they affect the performance of the models. This work evaluates the cosine similarity due to its lower complexity than other metrics [15].

3.1   Cosine Similarity

Cosine similarity (Cos) is a measure of similarity between two given vectors j and k, with lower values giving better similarity, as expressed in Eq. 1.

$$\cos(j, k) = \frac{|j||k|}{\|j\|\|k\|} \tag{1}$$

Cosine similarity has been widely used in various machine learning applications, including measuring similarity between neurons as reported by Pieterse and Mocanu [22] and expression of outputs between layers as reported by Luo et al. [16]. Further use of cosine similarity has been reported in measuring similarity between picture library footprint's features, as Chen et al. [17] reported.

A closer use of cosine similarity in regards to weights was done by Jin et al. [18] when they expressed how weights in a network affect the model's generalization using the probably approximately correct Bayesian Framework (PAC) as expressed in Eq. 2.

$$\text{Cos}(w_l) = \frac{1}{N_{l-1}\left(N_l^2 - N_l\right)} \sum_{\substack{i,j=1 \\ i \neq j}}^{N_l} \sum_{z=1}^{N_l} \frac{\left|w'^{T}_{li,z} w'_{lj,z}\right|}{\|w'_{li,z}\|\|w'_{lj,z}\|} \tag{2}$$

where $\text{Cos}(w_l)$ is the cosine similarities between the filters, N is the number of neurons and $w'_{li,z}$ and $w'_{lj,z}$ is the zth columns of the i and j filter matrices. This work forms the basis of using weights in identifying fine-tunable layers.

3.2 Proposed Approach

This study builds further on Eqs. 1 and 2 by evaluating the cosine similarities between the cumulative cosine similarities of the layers' weights as expressed in Definitions 1 and 2.

Definition 1 (Convolutional Layers Weight Correlation).
Given a weight matrix(filter) $w_l^f \in \mathbb{R}^{n \times n}$ of the lth layer, where $n \times n$ is the size of the kernel. $w_{lx}^f \in \mathbb{R}^{n \times n}$ And $w_{ly}^f \in \mathbb{R}^{n \times n}$ are the xth and y^{th} filters, respectively, in the tensor. Reshaping the $w_{lx}^f \in \mathbb{R}^{n \times n}$ and $w_{ly}^f \in \mathbb{R}^{n \times n}$ as $w_{lx}^{f'}$ and $w_{ly}^{f'}$, into one dimensional tensors respectively. The weight correlation of the layer filters is defined in Eq. 3 by:

$$\mathrm{Cos}\left(w_l^f\right) = \sum_{x,y=1}^{N_l} \left(\frac{\left| w_{lx,k}^{f'} w_{ly,k}^{f'} \right|}{\left\| w_{lx,k}^{f'} \right\| \left\| w_{ly,k}^{f'} \right\|} \right) \tag{3}$$

where N_l is the number of filters in the network on the kth column, and $\mathrm{Cos}\left(w_l^f\right)$ is the cosine similarity between the layer filter matrices.

Definition 2 (Signed Convolutional Layers' Weight Correlation). Given the lth layer with reshaped filters $w_{l1}^f \in \mathbb{R}^{n \times n}$, $w_{l2}^f \in \mathbb{R}^{n \times n}$, $w_{l3}^f \in \mathbb{R}^{n \times n}$, ..., $w_{ln}^f \in \mathbb{R}^{n \times n}$ with $w_{lx}^{f+ve} \in \mathbb{R}^{n \times n}$ and $w_{lx}^{f-ve} \in \mathbb{R}^{n \times n}$ as the positive weights and negative elements respectively in the layer tensor filters; the weight values cosine correlation can be defined by;

$$\mathrm{Cos}\left(w_l^{f\pm}\right) = \sum_{x,y=1}^{N_l} \left(\frac{\left| w_{lx,k}^{f+ve'} w_{ly,k}^{f-ve'} \right|}{\left\| w_{lx,k}^{f'} \right\| \left\| w_{ly,k}^{f'} \right\|} \right) \tag{4}$$

where $\mathrm{Cos}\left(w_l^{f\pm}\right)$ is the cosine similarity of the positive and negative weights between the filter matrices of a layer.

In this approach, the convolutional layers in the pre-trained models are identified, followed by identifying the weights from ImageNet. These layers are identified using the keyword "*conv*" among the other layers, as expressed in Eq. 5.

$$l^c = \begin{cases} Model_l, if \ l^N = \text{``conv''} \\ \qquad otherwise \end{cases} \tag{5}$$

where l^c is the model convolutional layer while l^N is the layer name.
The weights in the convolutional layers are then identified, starting with the weights in the filters and then grouped into the layers as expressed in Eq. 6.

$$Z^C = \left\{ L_1^C, L_2^C, L_3^C, \dots, L_n^C \right\} \tag{6}$$

where Z^C represents the weights of the layers.

The cosine similarities of the weights are then evaluated in the filter iteratively for the entire layer following Eq. 4. The similarity is evaluated based on positive to positive weights, negative to negative weights, and negative and positive weights. After that, the layers with the highest cosine similarity are selected for use. The number of the selected layers is determined by the layers whose value is greater than the arithmetic mean [28].

3.3   Experiments

Datasets
This work utilised five publicly datasets as outlined in Table 1.

Table 1. Datasets distribution

Dataset	Training	Validation	Classes
Cifar10	50000	10000	10
Cifar100	50000	10000	100
MNIST	60000	10000	10
Fashion-MNIST	60000	10000	10
Chest Cancer	700	300	4

The images were normalized to 224×224 pixels and batched in 64 samples for every training iteration. Cifar10, Cifar100, MNIST and Fashion-MNIST are available in Keras [26] with training and validation sets as specified in Table 1 with their classes (image categories). The Chest Cancer dataset is a subset of the larger dataset with about 10000 images [27]. From the subset, it contains 613 images and combines the samples from test and validation into one validation set: the validation data is set to 30%.

Pre-trained Models
The experiments were performed on four pre-trained architectures: ResNet50, VGG16, DenseNet169 and InceptionV3. The models were selected due to their development on ImageNet weights.

Experimental Settings
The experiments were performed on the PaperSpace platform (Quadro P4000 8CPU 30 GB RAM GPU) using Tensor flow 2.8. The Adam optimizer was used with a learning rate of 0.0001. The training was iterated to 100 epochs in each of the datasets. The softmax function was used in the classification, and Batch normalization and dropout at 0.5 were used to regularize the models [23].

Experimental Methods
In this study, cosine similarity is evaluated on three bases: positive weights cosine similarity (PCS), negative weights cosine similarity (NCS) and positive-negative weights cosine similarity (PNCS).

Positive weights cosine similarity evaluates the cosine similarly between two positive weights in a layer filter. Negative weights cosine similarity evaluates the cosine similarity between any two negative weights in a layer filter. The positive-negative cosine similarity evaluates oppositely signed weights in the layer filter. The positive or negative value of weight is dependent on its signed value.

Experiments Conventional Baselines

The fine-tuning processes followed in this work were analysed with respect to three standard fine-tuning baselines:

- Standard fine-tuning: this involves using all the pre-trained model parameters.
- Fine-tuning of k-last layers: this baseline involves using the last three convolutional layers (k–1, k–2 and k–3) while other layers remain frozen.
- Feature extraction: this involves the addition of a classification layer to the pretrained model, changing the work of the extracted features of the utilised pre-trained model.

4 Results and Discussion

The results from the experiments are presented in two sections: performance on the introduced methods and comparison of introduced methods against the standard fine-tuning baselines.

4.1 Comparison Between the Selected Methods

The results of the four introduced methods are presented in Tables 2, 3, 4, 5, and 6, listing the validation accuracy performance of the five datasets against the four selected pretrained models. The validation accuracy is used as the comparative performance metric due to its evaluation of unseen datasets.

Table 2. Accuracy comparison of Fashion-MNIST dataset

Model	Fashion-MNIST		
	Cosine similarity		
	Positive	*Negative*	*Positive-negative*
ResNet50	**87.14**	87.16	86.55
VGG16	89.47	89.68	**89.80**
InceptionV3	**86.57**	86.41	85.83
DenseNet169	88.35	88.41	**88.59**

The positive cosine similarity method performed better than the negative cosine similarity method in the accuracies presented in many instances. The positive-negative cosine similarity followed while the negative cosine similarity gave the least accuracies.

Table 3. Accuracy comparison of MNIST dataset

Model	MNIST		
	Cosine similarity		
	Positive	*Negative*	*Positive-negative*
ResNet50	**97.96**	97.77	97.71
VGG16	99.09	**99.12**	99.07
InceptionV3	**97.75**	97.69	**97.91**
DenseNet169	**98.60**	98.14	**98.35**

Table 4. Accuracy comparison of CIFAR10 dataset

Model	CIFAR10		
	Cosine similarity		
	Positive	*Negative*	*Positive-negative*
ResNet50	**38.89**	35.90	**37.90**
VGG16	**69.39**	69.38	**69.91**
InceptionV3	**49.39**	49.24	48.91
DenseNet169	**62.44**	59.89	59.92

Table 5. Accuracy comparison of CIFAR100 dataset

Model	CIFAR100		
	Cosine similarity		
	Positive	*Negative*	*Positive-negative*
ResNet50	**2.90**	2.75	2.65
VGG16	25.55	**27.63**	24.97
InceptionV3	**19.23**	14.25	**14.58**
DenseNet169	**10.59**	9.98	**10.73**

The positives gave better accuracy margins than the negatives in the chest cancer and CIFAR10 datasets. The positive-negative cosine similarity methods performed better than the negatives in CIFAR10 and the chest cancer datasets.

Table 6. Accuracy comparison of Chest Cancer dataset

Model	Chest Cancer		
	Cosine similarity		
	Positive	*Negative*	*Positive-negative*
ResNet50	**88.00**	85.82	**85.38**
VGG16	**97.25**	94.71	**96.43**
InceptionV3	**97.42**	96.61	**98.43**
DenseNet169	**95.57**	95.42	**96.67**

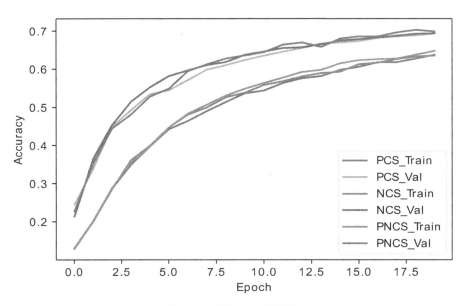

Fig. 1. VGG16 on CIFAR10

The CIFAR datasets were noted to give lower accuracy than the MNISTs, as seen in Figs. 1 and 2, even with higher training epochs, as highlighted in the ResNet50 performance on the four datasets in Tables 2, 3, 4 and 5. This trend is also reported by [5, 19] and could result from the size of the datasets, like the case of CIFAR100. The size of the architecture also influenced the performance in ResNet50, with many layers performing worse than the VGG16 model. This behaviour is highlighted in the chest cancer dataset in Table 6. The influence of the model depth is also reported by Kawai, Nobuhara and Nagae [20].

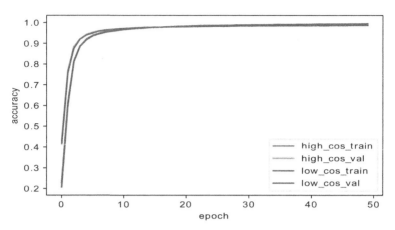

Fig. 2. InceptionV3 on MNIST dataset

4.2 Comparison of Selection Methods and the Baselines

Tables 6, 7, 8 and 9 show the selected methods' performance against the baselines on the four pre-trained models. These baseline methods perform lower than the selected methods in only performing better in 16/140 instances.

Table 7. Accuracy comparison of Cosine Similarity using selected fine-tuning methods on InceptionV3 model

Method	Datasets				
	Cifar10	Cifar100	MNIST	Fashion-MNIST	Chest
PCS	**49.39**	**19.23**	97.75	**86.57**	97.42
NCS	49.24	14.25	97.69	86.41	96.61
PNCS	48.91	14.58	97.91	85.63	98.48
1st layer	23.85	2.930	**98.12**	68.89	56.56
2nd layer	22.49	2.970	**97.83**	68.55	**59.27**
3rd layer	21.79	3.020	**98.79**	69.09	56.30
Feature extraction	23.04	2.700	91.97	68.04	**56.92**

In Tables 7, 8, 9 and 10, thes introduced methods give better accuracy results for positive and positive-negative cosine similarity methods than negative cosine similarity and perform much better than the standard fine-tuning methods, as seen in Fig. 3. The InceptionV3 model gives lower values due to the size of the network, and it would need either a lot more data or more epochs for its convergence. The better accuracies given by the positive weights can be attributed to the positive effects on the model accuracy, as stated by Thomas et al. [24] and that positive cosine similarity yields closeness of

Table 8. Accuracy comparison of Cosine Similarity using selected fine-tuning methods on ResNet50 model

Method	Datasets				
	Cifar10	Cifar100	MNIST	Fashion-MNIST	Chest
PCS	38.89	2.90	97.96	87.14	88.00
NCS	35.90	2.75	97.77	87.16	85.82
PNCS	37.90	2.65	97.71	86.55	85.38
1st layer	37.18	1.80	81.44	70.77	54.17
2nd layer	**38.01**	1.75	73.20	68.83	56.07
3rd layer	36.91	**2.95**	**90.12**	**77.28**	**56.97**
Feature extraction	**44.65**	**2.92**	**90.76**	**77.05**	**64.06**

Table 9. Accuracy comparison of Cosine Similarity using selected fine-tuning methods on VGG16 model

Method	Datasets				
	Cifar10	Cifar100	MNIST	Fashion-MNIST	Chest
PCS	69.39	25.55	99.09	89.47	97.25
NCS	69.38	27.63	99.12	89.68	94.71
PNCS	69.91	24.97	99.07	89.80	96.43
1st layer	**70.59**	14.04	96.63	82.41	69.30
2nd layer	69.58	18.35	97.35	84.90	84.39
3rd layer	70.29	**20.21**	**98.13**	**86.45**	**87.76**
Feature extraction	**73.76**	**22.73**	**98.48**	**87.23**	**95.19**

the weights in the layers. Farzaneh et al. [29] note that positive weights are excitatory, stimulating the features more and leading to faster gradient descent. This behaviour is further noted by Siti, Ashraf and Citra [30], who argue that weight is among the components that control the gradient descent during training. In layers with higher values or more weights, there is a likelihood of better descent, as described by Sidani [31], leading to better model transfer.

It could also be noted that the accuracies given by the introduced methods come from a combination of various layers within the model, unlike the case of the k-layers that advocate for the last 3 layers of the pre-trained model [7] as highlighted in the DEFT algorithm. This shows that the lower layers of the model that extract the low-level characteristics of the inputs (images) are not the only ones that can give higher accuracies when using pre-trained models.

Table 10. Accuracy comparison of Cosine Similarity using selected fine-tuning methods on DenseNet169 model

Method	Datasets				
	Cifar10	Cifar100	MNIST	Fashion-MNIST	Chest
PCS	62.44	10.59	98.60	88.35	95.57
NCS	59.89	9.980	98.14	88.41	95.42
PNCS	59.32	10.73	98.35	88.59	96.67
1st layer	36.09	**3.140**	98.52	72.68	58.42
2nd layer	34.03	2.890	99.07	72.08	**60.02**
3rd layer	**38.12**	**3.590**	**99.65**	**75.78**	57.53
Feature extraction	**36.66**	3.020	**99.36**	**75.56**	**62.49**

Among the standard fine-tuning methods, the k–3 layers method seems to perform followed by feature extractor in many instances. In contrast, the k–1 layer gives the least accuracy performance as highlighted in Tables 7, 8, 9 and 10.

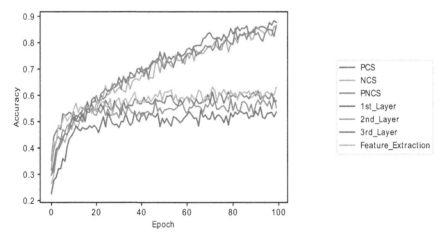

Fig. 3. ResNet50 on chest cancer dataset

However, one of the drawbacks of the new methods is time complexity: the methods take more computational time than the standard fine-tuning methods. This happens for all the datasets, with the DenseNet169 model taking the most time (150 s per epoch) and the VGG16 taking the least time (101 s) when using the CIFAR100 dataset. In terms of datasets, the CIFAR 100 takes the most time; a situation also noted in the DEFT algorithm owing to its size.

5 Conclusion

This work introduces three methods that evaluate the selection of fine-tuning layers based on the weights' cosine similarity. They are compared with the standard fine-tuning methods, performing marginally well using the accuracy metric on the validation data. A further application of the methods is used on a small chest cancer image dataset, giving similar results to that of the four publicly available datasets. Therefore, these methods provide an alternative method of dynamic layer selection using weights cosine similarity in fine-tuning pre-trained models, which improves classification accuracy in transfer learning. However, the methods have been noted to have slightly higher time computational complexity than the standard methods. In a field like medical imaging, accuracy to classification has more value than the introduced complexity, which makes these methods valuable techniques for adoption.

Data Availability Statement. All the datasets are available via Keras, and the source code can be found in https://github.com/geekhack/paaiss_Dynamic_Transfer_selection.

References

1. Towards Fast and Accurate Neural Networks for Image Recognition. https://ai.googleblog.com/2021/09/toward-fast-and-accurate-neural.html. Accessed 30 May 2022
2. Stergios, C., Lukas, E., Andreas, C., Stavroula, M.: Multisource transfer learning with convolutional neural networks for lung pattern analysis. IEEE J. Biomed. Health Inform. **2017**, 76–84 (2017)
3. Chopra, S., Balakrishnan, S., Gopalan, R.: DLID: deep learning for domain adaptation by interpolating between domains. In: ICML Workshop on Challenges in Representation Learning, Atlanta (2013)
4. Ross, G., Jeff, D., Trevor, D., Jitendra, M.: Rich feature hierarchies for accurate object detection and semantic segmentation. In: 2014 IEEE Conference on Computer Vision and Pattern Recognitio, Ohio (2014)
5. Yunhui, G., Yandong, L., Liqiang, W., Tajana, R.: AdaFilter: adaptive filter fine-tuning for deep transfer learning. AAAI 202, New York (2020)
6. Zhang, J., Li, W., Ogunbona, P., Xu, D.: Recent advances in transfer learning for cross-dataset visual recognition: a problem-oriented perspective. ACM Comput. Surv. **52**(1), 1–38 (2019)
7. Grega, V., Vili, P.: Transfer learning with adaptive fine-tuning. IEEE Access. **2020**, 196197–196211 (2020)
8. Islam, N., et al.: Thoracic imaging tests for the diagnosis of COVID-19. The Cochrane Database of Systematic Reviews, 11, CD013639 (2020). https://doi.org/10.1002/14651858.CD013639.pub3
9. Kim, H.E., Cosa-Linan, A., Santhanam, N., et al.: Transfer learning for medical image classification: a literature review. BMC Med Imaging **22**(69), 2022 (2022). https://doi.org/10.1186/s12880-022-00793-7
10. Alzubaidi, L., et al.: Novel transfer learning approach for medical imaging with limited labeled data. Cancers, **13**(7), 1590 (2021) https://doi.org/10.3390/cancers13071590
11. Satsuki, N., Daigo, K., Shin, K., Hajime, N.: Automatic layer selection for transfer learning and quantitative evaluation of layer effectiveness. Neurocomputing **2022**(469), 151–162 (2022)
12. Yang, C., Jieming, M., Cheng, C., Xuefeng, X., Run, Z., Zhiming, C.: An ensemble deep neural network for footprint image retrieval based on transfer learning. J. Sens. **2021**, 1–9 (2021)

13. Brenden, M.L., Ruslan, S., Joahua, B.T.B.T.: Human-level concept learning through probabilistic program induction. Science **2015**, 1332–1338 (2015)
14. Christian, S., Vincent, V., Sergey, I.: Rethinking the inception architecture for computer vision. In: 2016 IEEE Conference on Computer Vision and Pattern Recognition (CVPR), Las Vegas (2016)
15. Gaojie, J., Xinping, Y., Liang, Z., Lijun, Z., Sven, S., Xiaowei, H.: How does weight correlation affect generalisation ability of deep neural networks? In: NeurIPS 2020, Virtual (2020)
16. Kaiming, H., Xiangyu, Z., Shaoqing, R., Jian, S.: Deep residual learning for image recognition. In: 2016 IEEE Conference on Computer Vision and Pattern Recognition (CVPR), Las Vegas (2016)
17. Hakan, B., Basura, F., Efstratios, G., Andrea, V., Stephen, G.: Dynamic image networks for action recognition. In: 2016 IEEE Conference on Computer Vision and Pattern Recognition (CVPR), Las Vegas (2016)
18. Jindong, W., Yiqiang, C., Wenjie, F., Han, Y., Meiyu, H., Qiang, Y.: Transfer learning with dynamic distribution adaptation. ACM Trans. Intell. Syst. Technol. **11**(1), 1–25 (2020)
19. Yunhui, G., Honghui, S., Abhishek, K., Kristen, G., Tajana, R., Rogerio, F.: SpotTune: transfer learning through adaptive fine-tuning. In: 2019 IEEE/CVF Conference on Computer Vision and Pattern Recognition (CVPR), Long Beach, California (2019)
20. Andreas, V., Serge, B.: Convolutional networks with adaptive inference graphs. Int. J. Comput. Vis. 730–741 (2019)
21. Royer, A., Lampert, C.: A flexible selection scheme for minimum-effort transfer learning. In: 2020 IEEE Winter Conference on Applications of Computer Vision, Colorado (2020)
22. Pieterse, J., Mocanu, D.: Evolving and understanding sparse deep neural networks using cosine similarity. arXiv. [1903.07138v1] (2019)
23. Rusiecki, A.: Batch normalization and dropout regularization in training deep neural networks with label noise. In: Abraham, A., Gandhi, N., Hanne, T., Hong, T.-P., Nogueira Rios, T., Ding, W. (eds.) ISDA 2021. LNNS, vol. 418, pp. 57–66. Springer, Cham (2022). https://doi.org/10.1007/978-3-030-96308-8_6
24. Thomas, U., Daniel, K., Sylvain, G., Olivier, B., Ilya, T.: Predicting neural network accuracy from weights. arXiv preprint. arXiv:2002.11448 (2020)
25. Sarhan, N., Lauri, M., Frintrop, S.: Multi-phase fine-tuning: a new fine-tuning approach for sign language recognition. Künstl. Intell. **36**, 91–98 (2022). https://doi.org/10.1007/s13218-021-00746-2
26. Team, K.: Keras Documentation: Datasets. Keras. https://keras.io/api/datasets/. Retrieved 2 Sept 2022
27. Hany, M.: Chest CT-scan images dataset. Kaggle. https://www.kaggle.com/datasets/mohamedhanyyy/chest-ctscan-images. Retrieved 2 Sept 2022
28. Brownlee, J.: Arithmetic, geometric, and harmonic means for machine learning. Machine Learning Mastery. https://machinelearningmastery.com/arithmetic-geometric-and-harmonic-means-for-machine-learning/. Retrieved 2 Sept 2022
29. Najafi, F., Elsayed, G.F., Cao, R., et al.: Excitatory and inhibitory subnetworks are equally selective during decision-making and emerge simultaneously during learning. Neuron **105**(1), 165–179 (2020)
30. Shamsuddin, S.M., Ibrahim, A.O., Ramadhena, C.: Weight changes for learning mechanisms in two-term back-propagation network. In: Suzuki, K., (ed.) Artificial Neural Networks (2013)
31. Sidani, S.A.: Comprehensive study of the back propagation algorithm and modifications. In: Proceedings of the 1994 Southcon Conference, Orlando, Florida (1994)

Learning Approximate Invariance Requires Far Fewer Data

Jean-Michel A. Sarr[1,2]([✉]), Alassane Bah[1], and Christophe Cambier[2]

[1] UMI UMMISCO Université Cheikh Anta Diop Dakar, Dakar, Senegal
`jeanmichelamath.sarr@ucad.edu.sn`
[2] UMI UMMISCO Sorbonne Université, IRD, 75006 Paris, France

Abstract. Efficient learning, that is, learning with small datasets is difficult for current deep learning models. Invariance has been conjectured to be the key for its generalization potential. One of the most used procedure to learn invariant models is data augmentation (DA). Data augmentation can be performed offline by augmenting the data before any training, or it can be performed online during training. However, applying those technique won't yield better generalization gains every time. We frame this problem as the stability of generalization gains made by invariance inducing techniques. In this study we introduced a new algorithm to train an approximate invariant priors before posterior training of Bayesian Neural Network (BNN). Furthermore, we compared the generalization stability of our invariance inducing algorithm with online DA and offline DA on MNIST and Fashion MNIST with three perturbation processes: rotation, noise, and rotation+noise. Results showed that learning approximate invariant priors requires less exposure to the perturbation process, but it leads BNN to more stable generalization gains during posterior training. Finally, we also show that invariance inducing techniques enhance uncertainty in Bayesian Neural Networks.

Keywords: Learning approximate invariance · Dataset · Bayesian neural network · Algorithm

1 Introduction

The current success of deep supervised learning has been largely attributed to the advent of powerful computer infrastructure and big datasets [18]. Yet when it comes to small datasets the current paradigm falls short when compared to human learning. Hence, one of the remaining challenges of machine learning is to be able to learn with fewer data. It has been conjectured that the key to learning with few examples is invariance [1], the authors argued that most of the complexity in computer vision classification tasks is due to viewpoint or illumination nuisances that swaps the intrinsic characteristics of objects. This suggests that if an oracle could factor out all the transformations concerning viewpoint, scale, position, etc, the problem of categorization would become easy and could be

© ICST Institute for Computer Sciences, Social Informatics and Telecommunications Engineering 2023
Published by Springer Nature Switzerland AG 2023. All Rights Reserved
T. M. Ngatched Nkouatchah et al. (Eds.): PAAISS 2022, LNICST 459, pp. 109–123, 2023.
https://doi.org/10.1007/978-3-031-25271-6_7

done with very few labeled examples. The nuisances as described by Anselmi [1] are also called uninformative factors of variation by Bengio [3] who view the factor of variations in two categories: the factor of variations that are uninformative and informative to the task at hand. An ideal model would be sensitive to informative factors of variations and invariant to uninformative factors of variations. Informative factors of variation can affect the label predicted. For instance, in a classification setting, cats and dogs have two eyes, varying the number of eyes tells a lot in the object to identify, hence the number of eyes is informative. Uninformative factors of variation are label preserving, for instance, we could apply rotations, blurs, or translations on a cat image, the resulting images would still represent a cat for human perception but could fool a model that is not invariant to such transformations, therefore invariance is a highly desired property. Two ways to learn invariant models are considered: using data augmentation (DA) [9,13], or learning approximate invariant features [32]. There are various ways to learn invariant features directly, for instance Simard et al. [41] added a regularization term ensuring that the model has a zero derivative in the direction of the transformation. Another alternative is to take advantage of the topology of the data [22,37]. Recently, Dao et al. [9] have shown a correspondence between applying augmentation on the data space and the feature space of a model. The authors have shown that the effect of DA during training can be transferred by perturbing the weight of the model in a specific manner and keeping the data without augmentation. This links to the work of Nalisnick and Smyth [32] who have developed a general method to learn approximate invariant priors in Bayesian neural networks (BNNs), Indeed, DA applied directly onto the weights of a neural network create a weight distribution, this is typical of BNNs which are designed to involve a distribution over its weights. The Bayesian framework allows naturally formulating the technique of DA because it allows to treat uninformative factors of variation as prior knowledge and let the posterior learn only informative factor of variation. This factorization of factors of variation allows us to naturally regularize the model by learning representations that are only compatible with the invariances. Indeed, the prior can be seen as a regularization term in BNNs, for instance, there is a direct mapping between weight decay and Gaussian priors [29]. Furthermore, DA has been shown to regularize models [9,23]. It means that we can compare the generalization effects of approximate invariant prior and DA as both techniques induce invariance and regularization. However, in the case the modeler train a BNN with DA, posterior learning would require to decipher informative and uninformative factors of variation at the same time. Our main contribution in Sect. 3.4 is to propose an algorithm in the framework of Nalisnick and Smyth [32] that requires only a small fraction of the whole dataset to learn approximate invariant priors. Furthermore, we compared its stability with two flavors of DA in Sect. 4.2. Stability as in perturbation analysis refers to the variability of the learning outcome obtained by a change in the learning procedure [5]. This research varies the invariance inducing technique and studies how it impacts generalization gains. Moreover, we also show that invariance inducing techniques enhance uncertainty in posterior learning in Sect. 4.3.

2   Related Works

2.1   Data Augmentation Research

DA has been widely used to improve the generalization performance of deep learning models [9], it has allowed getting state of the art results in numerous domain such as computer vision [39] and speech processing [21,34] and natural language processing [15]. Several theoretical approaches have been provided about DA. The first who coined the term DA [43] used it to simulate the posterior distribution in Bayesian inference. Their interpretation was to use augmented data as latent variables and provided an iterative MCMC algorithm. As remarked by Van Dyk and Meng [46], the term evolved in the physics literature and was further referred to as the method of auxiliary variable, it has been used for instance to sample from the Ising and Post models [42]. However, the technique of DA as it is used today in the machine learning literature has been well formulated by Dao et al. [9] who have described its regularization effect with task invariance and model complexity penalization. Another line of research focuses on finding good or optimal augmentation schemes with the data at hand. Those augmentation policies rely on generative models [24,40,44] or reinforcement learning [8,25]. Searching good augmentation policies is similar to searching for uninformative factors of variation within the data. This can be seen as an orthogonal task to the extraction of informative factors of variation via semi-supervised learning. Furthermore, the combination of both approaches was successfully used to obtain state-of-the-art results in text classification and computer vision [49]. Data augmentation is also increasingly used for domain generalization [50].

2.2   Posterior Training

Bayesian neural networks can model uncertainty by learning a posterior distribution of the weights given the data. However the true posterior is often intractable, this has led to much technical development, Markov Chain Monte Carlo techniques (MCMC) afford the best theoretical guarantees to find the true posterior distribution, but are often impractical with big data as they need the full dataset to learn [2,6]. Variational Inference is another method for Bayesian inference, the core idea is to use a parametric probability distribution, and to optimize the KL between the posterior and the variational approximation. This technique has attracted a lot of attention recently, and variational approximation has been used in the context of BNNs. The first approaches used fully factorized Gaussian [4,19]. However, more sophisticated approximation distribution have been developed for variational posterior learning for instance using a full covariance matrix [27], but some authors have also used other variational approximation like a Bernoulli distribution with Dropout [17]. Later, other authors used Normalizing flows [28] to allow for an even more flexible posterior approximation. Recently other authors Mescheder et al. [30] have argued that implicit methods might offer more flexible approximation than invertible methods such as Normalizing Flows. This trend was followed by Pawlowski et al [36] with a Hypernetwork to model the posterior, similarly, Shi et al. [38] introduced a more efficient algorithm called Matrix Multiplication Neural Network (MMNN) to sample large matrix to model the posterior. Another perspective is to see deep ensembles as an approximation to the real posterior [47]. In summary, there are many other approximation distributions that one could use (1) to learn approximate invariant priors and (2) for posterior learning. In this work we sticked to the most basic one fully factorised Gaussian.

2.3   Encoding Prior Knowledge

One of the advantages of BNNs is their ability to leverage small datasets by incorporating prior knowledge. Prior knowledge can express a range of hypotheses about the data generating function. Moreover, several hypotheses have found a proper encoding directly into neural networks' weights, these include inducing compression: with sparsity over the weights [31,33], quantization [45] or a mix of both [14,26].This paper focused on incorporating invariance to improve generalization following the work of Nalisnick and Smyth [32]. As the prior induce a regularization term in the expression of the ELBO, we see a link between prior learning and unsupervised pre-training [12] as a form of semi-supervised learning in the non-Bayesian context. Both methods are applied before training and induce regularization. Unsupervised pre-training regularize by selecting initialization parameters taking into account the data distribution before the classification task. In other words, unsupervised pre-training initialize deep architectures in regions from which better basins of attraction can be reached, in terms of generalization improvements. Unsupervised pre-training favors hidden units that better explain informative factors of variation within the data X, and those factors of variation are useful in the task of predicting Y.

3   Methodology

3.1   Online and Offline Data Augmentation

When the dataset at hand is small, DA is often applied offline, it means that one or multiple transformations are applied to the original dataset multiple times to augment the dataset size. The amount of augmentation is referred to as the augmentation factor, for instance when the total size of the dataset is made 16 times larger, the augmentation factor is 16. The caveat with this approach is its memory consumption, for instance, a big dataset like Imagenet [10] could hardly be augmented by a factor of 64, because it would take too much place into the memory of personal laptops. When the dataset is large an alternative is to apply DA online, meaning that each batch of data is augmented 'on the fly' before being fed into the model. As a result, online DA is memory efficient, but it takes longer to train as it adds a sampling operation in the training loop and often reads data from the disk. Also, online augmentation results in a noisier data distribution than offline augmentation, because of the constant change during training. To the best of our knowledge, we have not yet seen any comparison of online and offline DA.

3.2   Bayesian Neural Networks

One way to picture how BNNs work is by comparing them with standard neural networks. The first difference is that BNNs involve two neural networks with the same architecture, one for the prior and one for the posterior. They are related by the Bayes formula:

$$p(\theta|X) = \frac{p(X|\theta)p(\theta)}{p(X)}$$

Where X is a dataset, $p(X)$ is the evidence, θ are the parameters of the network, $p(X|\theta)$ is the likelihood, finally $p(\theta)$ and $p(\theta|X)$ are respectively the prior and the posterior. The second difference is that each weight is represented by a probability distribution instead of a single unit. They are many ways to select a distribution for a learning problem, the reader interested might refer to Sect. 2. Often the prior is chosen with heuristics and does not involve learning, and only posterior learning is considered. The algorithm presented in Sect. 3.4 is focused on learning the prior and is typically done before learning the posterior. In the next subsection we describe the approach to learn approximate invariant priors.

3.3   Learning Approximate Invariant Priors

Most augmentation schemes can be cast as perturbation processes (PP) that are parametrized by a given magnitude, for instance, an image could be perturbed by a rotation between $-20°C$ to $20°C$ to get a new image. More generally, if x is an example, a transformation $\hat{x}$ can be sampled from a parametrized perturbation process q_η and can be written as follow: $\hat{x} \sim q(\hat{x}; x, \eta)$, where η parametrize the PP. Supervised learning focuses on learning functions, mapping high dimensional input data $x \in \mathbb{R}^d$ coming from an unknwown distribution $p_\mathcal{D}$ to output labels y. In that setting, parametric models can often be framed as probabilistic ones to easily compute their likelihood $p(y|x, \theta)$, where θ the parameters of the model typically depends on the architecture of the model. Such models can be described as invariant to a perturbation process q_η if and only if $p(y|x) = p(y|\hat{x}) \forall \hat{x} \in \mathcal{X}_{q_\eta}(x)$, with $\mathcal{X}_{q_\eta}(x)$ the set of all transformed examples from q_η. However this constraint might be too strong, and can be weakened with an approximate invariance constraint by ensuring $p(y|x) = \mathbb{E}_{\hat{x} \sim q_\eta}[p(y|\hat{x})]$. Thus an optimization objective might be to minimize the Kullback-Leibler (KL) divergence between those two terms. The KL divergence is well known to measure the discrepancy between probability distributions in generative models [20] or in BNNs [4,19]. It is defined as follows for two probability distribution p, q defined on a domain $\mathcal{X}$: $KL(p||q) = \int_\mathcal{X} p(x) \log(\frac{p(x)}{q(x)})dx$. Furthermore the prior can be exposed by expressing a model prediction as a marginalized likelihood $p(y|x) =$

$\mathbb{E}_{\theta \sim p_\lambda}[p(y|x, \theta)]$, where p_λ is the parametrized prior distribution. For instance in case the prior distribution is a Gaussian $\mathcal{N}(\mu, \sigma^2)$, then $\lambda = \{\mu, \sigma^2\}$. Finally, the approximate invariance constraint can be formulated with an upper bound thanks to the Jensen inequality and the convexity of the KL divergence:

$$KL(p(y|x)||\mathbb{E}_{\hat{x} \sim q_\eta}[p(y|\hat{x})]) \leq \mathbb{E}_{\hat{x} \sim q_\eta} \mathbb{E}_{\theta \sim p_\lambda} KL(p(y|x, \theta)||p(y|\hat{x}, \theta)) \qquad (1)$$

Minimizing this upper bound will result in learning approximate invariant priors, however directly optimizing this criterion would result in priors learning spurious solutions, in other words, solutions that would not be helpful in the second stage of Bayesian inference during posterior learning. This has been shown analytically by Nalisnick [32]. Thus, the proper optimization objective should be enhanced by referring to the maximum entropy principle: the appropriate distribution for representing prior beliefs is one that obeys known constraints and has maximum entropy otherwise [32]. Hence, the following formulation of the objective function:

$$\mathcal{J}(\lambda, x) = \mathbb{H}_\lambda[\theta] - \mathbb{E}_{\hat{x} \sim q_\eta} \mathbb{E}_{\theta \sim p_\lambda} KL(p(y|x, \theta)||p(y|\hat{x}, \theta))$$

With $\mathbb{H}_\lambda[\theta] = - \int_\theta p_\lambda(\theta) \log(p_\lambda(\theta))d\theta$ the entropy of the prior. Hence, the optimisation objective is to maximize the objective function for each example from the data distribution $p_\mathcal{D}$, which we write as an expectation in the following optimisation problem:

$$p_{\lambda^*}(\theta) = \arg \max_\lambda \mathbb{E}_{x \sim p_\mathcal{D}} \mathcal{J}(\lambda, x)$$

This optimization problem makes sense with respect to the goal of finding high entropy priors that obeys to the approximate invariance constraint because minimizing the upper bound to the approximate invariance objective is equivalent to maximizing its opposite. Finally, unbiased estimates of gradients with respect to the expectation are found using the reparametrization trick [20].

3.4   A Lightweight Formulation

A new approximate invariant learning technique is presented in algorithm 1 extending the work of Nalisnick and Smyth [32]. The algorithm uses only a small fraction of the full dataset and only a finite set of augmentation (or augmentation factor) for the whole learning process. Furthermore, we only sample as many weights from the prior as there are augmentations in the finite set. In the end, the process requires only $O(N)$ samples and $O(MN)$ operations at each epoch, with M the dataset size and N the augmentation factor. Also, we added an annealing term to the entropy, as we found that the optimization could easily favor maximizing the entropy to a point where the expected KL would increase. While, the paper of Nalisnick and Smyth [32] presents a novel and elegant mathematical framework to learn approximate invariant priors, it still involves the calculation of a complex expectation i.e.: $\mathbb{E}_{x \sim p_\mathcal{D}} \mathbb{E}_{\hat{x} \sim q_\eta} \mathbb{E}_{\theta \sim p_\lambda} KL(p(y|x, \theta)||p(y|\hat{x}, \theta))$. The authors used nested Monte Carlo to estimate it. The dataset is always fixed,

---

Algorithm 1. Lightweight approximate invariant prior

Input: data distribution $p_{\mathcal{D}}$, prior p_λ, perturbation process q_η, sample size M, augmentation factor N

Sample $\{x^{(1)}, \cdots, x^{(M)}\}$ from $p_{\mathcal{D}}$

for $i = 1$ **to** M **do**
    Sample $\{\hat{x}_1^{(i)}, \cdots, \hat{x}_N^{(i)}\}$ from q_η
end for
repeat
    Sample $\{\theta_1, \cdots, \theta_N\}$ from p_λ
    div $\leftarrow \frac{1}{MN} \sum_{m=1}^{M} \sum_{n=1}^{K}$
                $KL(p(y^{(m)}|x^{(m)}, \theta_n)||p(y^{(m)}|\hat{x}_n^{(m)}, \theta_n))$
    $\mathcal{L}(\lambda) \leftarrow \beta \cdot \mathbb{H}_\lambda[\theta] -$ div
    Compute $\nabla_\lambda \mathcal{L}(\lambda)$
    $\lambda \leftarrow \lambda + \alpha \nabla_\lambda \mathcal{L}(\lambda)$
until convergence

---

so we cannot sample indefinitely from the data distribution $p_{\mathcal{D}}$. However, it is possible to sample indefinitely from the perturbation process and the prior. The original formulation used the whole dataset and sampled new perturbations and new prior weights for each example at each epoch. So if the dataset has size M, and the nested Monte Carlo estimation requires N sample from the prior p_λ and N sample from the perturbation process q_η, then, the KL estimate would require $O(MN)$ samples and $O(M \cdot N^2)$ operations at each epoch.

4 Experiments

In all the experiments described below, we used the same architecture, a Bayesian neural network with one hidden layer of 512 neurons. The optimization algorithm Adam with a learning rate of 0.001 was used for all training purposes. The experiment described in sub-sect. 4.1 investigated different scenarios to learn invariant priors, all of them were fully factorized Gaussian. Then, in sub-sect. 4.2, we compared the effect of online, offline augmentation on posterior learning of Bayesian Neural Networks. Posterior learning was done using variational inference with fully factorized Gaussian as approximation distribution [4]. Finally, an experiment has been conducted to evaluate the uncertainty gains by each invariance inducing technique after posterior learning. It is described in 4.3. All the experiments were conducted with Pytorch [35][1].

4.1 Sample Size and Augmentation Factor

This experiment investigated the importance of the sample size and the augmentation factor (M and N in algorithm 1) when learning approximate invariant

---

[1] The code is available at https://github.com/jmamath/learning-approximate-invariance-requires-far-fewer-data.

priors. Intuitively we sample M data point from the original data, and augment them N times with the perturbation process. We used three sample sizes (256, 512, 1024) along with three augmentation factors (16, 32, 64). The augmentations were respectively: rotation, uniform noise, and rotation + uniform noise on the original MNIST training set. The rotation of the image was sample between $[-20°, 20°]$; uniform noise between $[0, 255]$ was added to the image. The last augmentation was simply a composition of rotation and noise. The models were trained for 2000 epochs with an early stopping after 500 epochs without progress. Finally, the annealing term for the entropy was $\frac{i}{2000}$, where i was the current epoch. It means that the weight of the entropy term grew with training. To evaluate learning, we used the whole 60,000 examples from the original MNIST training set and implemented a loader that sampled a batch of data X and the same batch augmented $\hat{X} \sim q(\hat{X}, X, \eta)$, with one set of weights from the learned prior $\theta \sim p_\lambda$ to compute the Expected KL (upper bound in Eq. 1). This procedure was performed on the whole dataset and iterated 10 times to have descriptive statistics. The goal was to witness the right combination of sample size and augmentation factor to get an approximate invariant prior (small or null expected KL) on an unseen dataset. The results of the experiment are summarized in Fig. 1. There is a clear pattern, for noise and rotation+noise. Augmenting the sample size and the augmentation factor leads to more invariant priors. However, what is surprising in this experiment, is that the network does not need the full dataset, nor infinite variation of the perturbation process to learn invariant representations. Indeed, only sampling 1024 examples from the original dataset and applying an augmentation factor of 64 is enough to learn an approximately invariant prior. This suggests that augmenting the full dataset might not be necessary to get the generalization improvement from DA. Note however, that this pattern does not hold in the case for rotation. We hypothesize that the architecture is not complex enough to learn the invariance with so few information ($M = 1024, N = 64$). An additional question is: do these approximate invariant priors lead to a better generalization when learning posteriors? This is what was considered in Sect. 4.2.

4.2 Stability of Invariance Inducing Techniques on Generalization Gains

In this experiment, we investigated the generalization gains and stability of posterior learning under three invariance inducing techniques: invariant prior, online, and offline DA. To evaluate the effect of the different forms of augmentation, four BNNs were used. The first three BNNs involved a fully factorized standard Gaussian as a prior $\mathcal{N}(0, 1)$ and the posteriors were trained respectively with: no augmentation (vanilla), offline augmentation with an augmentation factor of 8, and online augmentation respectively. The last BNN used an approximate invariant prior and its posterior was trained with no augmentation at all. The approximate invariant prior was learned for 2000 epochs with an early stopping after 500 epochs without progress. The sample size was set to 1024, and the augmentation factor to 64. Finally, the annealing term for the entropy was

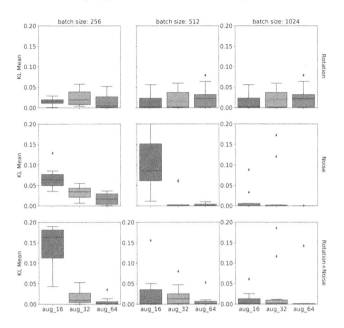

Fig. 1. Comparison of different choices for the nested Monte Carlo approximation. Each column denotes a different sample size between 256, 512, and 1024. Each row refers to a different augmentation scheme: rotation, noise, and rotation+noise. Finally each plot as the same structure, different augmentation factors are compared between 16, 32, and 64. The y-axis has the same scale and computed the expected KL divergence.

$\frac{i}{2000}$, where i was the current epoch. The four Bayesian neural networks were compared on the MNIST and Fashion MNIST datasets [11,48]. Moreover, to have a basis of comparison we fixed the amount of computation available for each model in terms of mini-batch processed. Therefore, 800 epochs were used for each model except for offline DA that was trained with only 100 epochs, because its dataset was 8 times larger. The batch size for every model was set to 1024, and we computed 30 Monte Carlo pass per batch of data to compute the expected lower bound (ELBO). Finally, each model was tested with the respective test set of the MNIST and Fashion MNIST datasets. To get the prediction on the test set, 100 passes per batch of data were made, and we ran the evaluation 10 times to get the mean and standard deviation for each model. The results are summarized in Table 1. We observe that using approximate invariant priors never performed worse than the control Vanilla BNN. Overall it yielded the best generalization improvements. Also, it takes roughly as long to train as it takes for the vanilla BNN. Online augmentation takes the longest to train and is the least stable method, for instance, it failed multiple times: noise on Fashion MNIST, rotation+noise on MNIST, and Fashion MNIST. We explain that online augmentation dramatically shifts the data distribution because much more noise is added to the learning process, which leads the optimizer to more

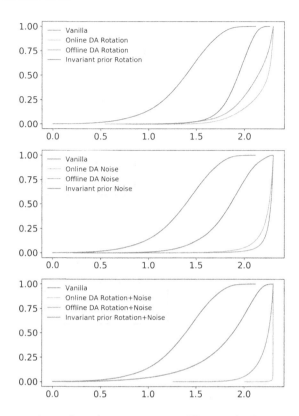

Fig. 2. CDF comparison of predictive entropies. The graphs from up to bottom represent models trained on MNIST respectively with rotation, noise and mix of rotation and noise.

likely be trapped in local minima. Hence online DA might require a more careful optimization strategy to yield good results. Yet it got the best generalization accuracy for noise on Fashion MNIST. Offline learning is faster to train and more stable when compared to online learning, it achieves the best result for rotation MNIST.

4.3   Effect of Invariance Inducing Technique on Uncertainty

One weakness of neural networks is that they cannot model uncertainty, and this can lead to overconfident prediction even when they are wrong, this is known as overfitting. Uncertainty is critical if neural networks are deployed in applications such as medicine, autonomous vehicles, nuclear power plant, or high-frequency trading [16]. BNNs can model uncertainty by learning a posterior distribution of the weights given the data, in the following experiment we evaluate the effect of approximate invariant priors, online and offline DA on posterior uncertainty after learning. What is typically done to evaluate uncertainty, is to train a model on a

Table 1. Comparison of the different settings for posterior learning. N.A means no data augmentation when learning the posterior.

Rotation - MNIST

Prior	DA	Accuracy (%)	Time (s)
$\mathcal{N}(0,1)$	Online	96.7 ± 0.2	11726
$\mathcal{N}(0,1)$	Offline	$\mathbf{96.9 \pm 0.1}$	7649
$\mathcal{N}(0,1)$	N.A	96.8 ± 0.1	10483
Invariant	N.A	96.8 ± 0.1	10715

Noise - MNIST

Prior	DA	Accuracy (%)	Time (s)
$\mathcal{N}(0,1)$	Online	95.3 ± 0.1	17276
$\mathcal{N}(0,1)$	Offline	79.5 ± 0.1	7660
$\mathcal{N}(0,1)$	N.A	96.8 ± 0.1	10483
Invariant	N.A	$\mathbf{97.0 \pm 0.1}$	10411

Rotation+Noise - MNIST

Prior	DA	Accuracy (%)	Time (s)
$\mathcal{N}(0,1)$	Online	19.8 ± 0.6	18934
$\mathcal{N}(0,1)$	Offline	82.2 ± 0.2	7643
$\mathcal{N}(0,1)$	N.A	96.8 ± 0.1	10483
Invariant	N.A	$\mathbf{97.0 \pm 0.1}$	10431

Rotation - Fashion MNIST

Prior	DA	Accuracy (%)	Time (s)
$\mathcal{N}(0,1)$	Online	$\mathbf{77.5 \pm 0.3}$	11529
$\mathcal{N}(0,1)$	Offline	76.4 ± 0.5	7554
$\mathcal{N}(0,1)$	N.A	44.3 ± 0.2	10476
Invariant	N.A	74.7 ± 0.2	10659

Noise - Fashion MNIST

Prior	DA	Accuracy (%)	Time (s)
$\mathcal{N}(0,1)$	Online	26.5 ± 0.3	16951
$\mathcal{N}(0,1)$	Offline	78.4 ± 0.3	7593
$\mathcal{N}(0,1)$	N.A	44.3 ± 0.2	10476
Invariant	N.A	$\mathbf{83.3 \pm 0.3}$	10221

Rotation+Noise - Fashion MNIST

Prior	DA	Accuracy (%)	Time (s)
$\mathcal{N}(0,1)$	Online	21.1 ± 0.3	18600
$\mathcal{N}(0,1)$	Offline	70.6 ± 0.6	7570
$\mathcal{N}(0,1)$	N.A	44.3 ± 0.2	10476
Invariant	N.A	$\mathbf{83.8 \pm 0.2}$	10290

given dataset and evaluate its predictive entropies on another dataset involving different classes [28]. Indeed, a model able to know when an example does not come from the original dataset is useful. The predictive entropy allow to measure it as follows, when an item has a high predictive entropy, it means that the model has outputted a rather uniform distribution giving each class equal weight. In other words, the model acknowledges that it does not know how to classify the item. To evaluate the effect of invariance on uncertainty we used the networks trained in experiment 4.2 as in all cases except online DA with rotation+noise, the models have learned reasonably well on MNIST (see Table 1). Furthermore, we evaluate them on the EMNIST dataset [7] which involves letters instead of digits. The first ten letters of the alphabet: a-j were selected to emulate a ten class classification problem. The dataset has 4,800 examples per class which leads to a total of 48,000 examples for the ten classes. To evaluate the uncertainty in the prediction, the empirical cumulative distribution function (CDF) of the predictive entropy was used as by Louizos et al. [28]. The results are displayed in Fig. 2. To interpret these graph it is helpful to notice that the CDF of the predictive entropy is a global measure of uncertainty because it displays the proportion of items with high entropy within a given bound. For instance, in the case of the upper graph, all items from vanilla have entropy less or equal than 2, whereas only 25% of items have entropy less or equal than 2 in the case of online DA rotation. It means that 75% of items classified with the online DA rotation have entropy higher than 2. In other words, the network does not know how to classify the items from an unknown dataset, thus its output is close to a uniform distribution. Overall, online and offline DA have the greater effect on the uncertainty of the trained posterior than the invariant prior, whatever the augmentation type considered, as most of items have an entropy around 2 which is around the highest computed value of entropy. Moreover, all invariant inducing techniques display higher uncertainty than the vanilla BNN. Another detail to notice is that items which display the minimal amount of entropy depend not only on the invariance inducing technique but also on the augmentation type. For instance, if we consider offline DA, its minimal entropy is around 0.5 on the rotation perturbed dataset but is around 1.25 on the rotation+noise perturbed dataset. The same phenomenon is observed for online DA, which suggests that combining multiple augmentations directly on data increases the uncertainty of the model, yet this phenomenon is not observed for the BNN trained with an approximate invariant prior. Moreover, the only model that failed to learn MNIST: online DA trained with rotation+noise exhibit maximum uncertainty, it displays a uniform distribution for every item of EMNIST. To conclude, all invariant inducing techniques enhance the ability of a model to be uncertain, also, DA has a greater effect on model uncertainty than approximate invariant priors.

5   Conclusion

This paper support evidences that approximate invariant priors learned with only a fraction of the full dataset can get stable generalization improvements when learning the posterior of BNNs. Furthermore, posterior training with invariant prior is faster than posterior learning with online DA, and do not require to inflate the memory as with offline DA. Moreover, it is reported that offline DA is more stable than online DA. It should be pointed out that the approximation distribution used for prior and posterior learning is very rudimentary, indeed fully factorized Gaussians are among the simpler approximation distributions one could choose. So, future work might include more complex variational inference techniques.

Aknowledgment. We would like to thank the PDI-MSC (Programme Doctoral International Modélisation des Systèmes Complexes) and the Google PhD Fellowship to have supported this research.

References

1. Anselmi, F., Leibo, J.Z., Rosasco, L., Mutch, J., Tacchetti, A., Poggio, T.: Unsupervised learning of invariant representations with low sample complexity: the magic of sensory cortex or a new framework for machine learning? (2014). Publisher: Center for Brains, Minds and Machines (CBMM), arXiv
2. Balan, A.K., Rathod, V., Murphy, K.P., Welling, M.: Bayesian dark knowledge. In: Advances in Neural Information Processing Systems, pp. 3438–3446 (2015)
3. Bengio, Y., Courville, A., Vincent, P.: Representation learning: a review and new perspectives. IEEE Trans. Pattern Anal. Mach. Intell. **35**(8), 1798–1828 (2013)
4. Blundell, C., Cornebise, J., Kavukcuoglu, K., Wierstra, D.: Weight uncertainty in neural networks. arXiv preprint arXiv:1505.05424 (2015)
5. Bousquet, O., Elisseeff, A.: Stability and generalization. J. Mach. Learning Res. **2**, 499–526 (2002)
6. Chen, T., Fox, E., Guestrin, C.: Stochastic gradient Hamiltonian monte carlo. In: International Conference on Machine Learning, pp. 1683–1691 (2014)
7. Cohen, G., Afshar, S., Tapson, J., Van Schaik, A.: EMNIST: extending MNIST to handwritten letters. In: 2017 International Joint Conference on Neural Networks (IJCNN), pp. 2921–2926. IEEE (2017)
8. Cubuk, E.D., Zoph, B., Mane, D., Vasudevan, V., Le, Q.V.: Autoaugment: learning augmentation strategies from data. In: Proceedings of the IEEE Conference on Computer Vision and Pattern Recognition, pp. 113–123 (2019)
9. Dao, T., Gu, A., Ratner, A.J., Smith, V., De Sa, C., Ré, C.: A kernel theory of modern data augmentation. In: Proceedings of Machine Learning Research, vol. 97, pp. 1528–1537 (2019). NIH Public Access
10. Deng, J., Dong, W., Socher, R., Li, L.J., Li, K., Fei-Fei, L.: ImageNet: a large-scale hierarchical image database. In: 2009 IEEE Conference on Computer Vision and Pattern Recognition, pp. 248–255. IEEE (2009)
11. Deng, L.: The MNIST database of handwritten digit images for machine learning research [best of the web]. IEEE Sig. Process. Mag. **29**(6), 141–142 (2012)
12. Erhan, D., Bengio, Y., Courville, A., Manzagol, P.A., Vincent, P., Bengio, S.: Why does unsupervised pre-training help deep learning? J. Mach. Learn. Res. **11**, 625–660 (2010)
13. Fawzi, A., Frossard, P.: Manitest: Are classifiers really invariant? arXiv preprint arXiv:1507.06535 (2015)

14. Federici, M., Ullrich, K., Welling, M.: Improved Bayesian compression. arXiv preprint arXiv:1711.06494 (2017)
15. Feng, S.Y., et al.: A survey of data augmentation approaches for NLP. arXiv preprint arXiv:2105.03075 (2021)
16. Gal, Y.: Uncertainty in deep learning. Univ. Camb. **1**, 3 (2016)
17. Gal, Y., Ghahramani, Z.: Dropout as a Bayesian approximation: representing model uncertainty in deep learning. In: International Conference on Machine Learning, pp. 1050–1059 (2016)
18. Goodfellow, I., Bengio, Y., Courville, A.: Deep Learning. MIT Press, Cambridge (2016)
19. Graves, A.: Practical variational inference for neural networks. In: Advances in Neural Information Processing Systems, pp. 2348–2356 (2011)
20. Kingma, D.P., Welling, M.: Auto-encoding variational Bayes. arXiv preprint arXiv:1312.6114 (2013)
21. Ko, T., Peddinti, V., Povey, D., Khudanpur, S.: Audio augmentation for speech recognition. In: Sixteenth Annual Conference of the International Speech Communication Association (2015)
22. LeCun, Y.: Learning invariant feature hierarchies. In: Fusiello, A., Murino, V., Cucchiara, R. (eds.) ECCV 2012. LNCS, vol. 7583, pp. 496–505. Springer, Heidelberg (2012). https://doi.org/10.1007/978-3-642-33863-2_51
23. Leen, T.K.: From data distributions to regularization in invariant learning. In: Advances in Neural information processing systems, pp. 223–230 (1995)
24. Lemley, J., Bazrafkan, S., Corcoran, P.: Smart augmentation learning an optimal data augmentation strategy. IEEE Access **5**, 5858–5869 (2017)
25. Lim, S., Kim, I., Kim, T., Kim, C., Kim, S.: Fast autoaugment. In: Advances in Neural Information Processing Systems, pp. 6662–6672 (2019)
26. Louizos, C., Ullrich, K., Welling, M.: Bayesian compression for deep learning. In: Advances in Neural Information Processing Systems, pp. 3288–3298 (2017)
27. Louizos, C., Welling, M.: Structured and efficient variational deep learning with matrix gaussian posteriors. In: International Conference on Machine Learning, pp. 1708–1716 (2016)
28. Louizos, C., Welling, M.: Multiplicative normalizing flows for variational Bayesian neural networks. In: Proceedings of the 34th International Conference on Machine Learning, vol. 70, pp. 2218–2227. JMLR (2017)
29. MacKay, D.J.: Bayesian methods for adaptive models. PhD Thesis, California Institute of Technology (1992)
30. Mescheder, L., Nowozin, S., Geiger, A.: Adversarial variational Bayes: unifying variational autoencoders and generative adversarial networks. In: Proceedings of the 34th International Conference on Machine Learning, vol. 70, pp. 2391–2400. JMLR (2017)
31. Molchanov, D., Ashukha, A., Vetrov, D.: Variational dropout sparsifies deep neural networks. In: Proceedings of the 34th International Conference on Machine Learning, vol. 70, pp. 2498–2507. JMLR (2017)
32. Nalisnick, E., Smyth, P.: Learning priors for invariance. In: International Conference on Artificial Intelligence and Statistics, pp. 366–375 (2018)
33. Neklyudov, K., Molchanov, D., Ashukha, A., Vetrov, D.P.: Structured Bayesian pruning via log-normal multiplicative noise. In: Advances in Neural Information Processing Systems, pp. 6775–6784 (2017)
34. Park, D.S., et al.: Specaugment: A simple data augmentation method for automatic speech recognition. arXiv preprint arXiv:1904.08779 (2019)

35. Paszke, A., et al.: PyTorch: an imperative style, high-performance deep learning library. In: Advances in Neural Information Processing Systems, pp. 8024–8035 (2019)
36. Pawlowski, N., Brock, A., Lee, M.C., Rajchl, M., Glocker, B.: Implicit weight uncertainty in neural networks. arXiv preprint arXiv:1711.01297 (2017)
37. Ranzato, M., Huang, F.J., Boureau, Y.L., LeCun, Y.: Unsupervised learning of invariant feature hierarchies with applications to object recognition. In: 2007 IEEE Conference on Computer Vision and Pattern Recognition, pp. 1–8. IEEE (2007)
38. Shi, J., Sun, S., Zhu, J.: Kernel implicit variational inference. arXiv preprint arXiv:1705.10119 (2017)
39. Shorten, C., Khoshgoftaar, T.M.: A survey on image data augmentation for deep learning. J. Big Data **6**(1), 60 (2019). https://doi.org/10.1186/s40537-019-0197-0/
40. Shrivastava, A., Pfister, T., Tuzel, O., Susskind, J., Wang, W., Webb, R.: Learning from simulated and unsupervised images through adversarial training. In: Proceedings of the IEEE Conference on Computer Vision and Pattern Recognition, pp. 2107–2116 (2017)
41. Simard, P., Victorri, B., LeCun, Y., Denker, J.: Tangent prop-a formalism for specifying selected invariances in an adaptive network. In: Advances in Neural Information Processing Systems, pp. 895–903 (1992)
42. Swendsen, R.H., Wang, J.S.: Nonuniversal critical dynamics in Monte Carlo simulations. Phys. Rev. Lett. **58**(2), 86 (1987)
43. Tanner, M.A., Wong, W.H.: The calculation of posterior distributions by data augmentation. J. Am. Stat. Assoc. **82**(398), 528–540 (1987)
44. Tran, T., Pham, T., Carneiro, G., Palmer, L., Reid, I.: A Bayesian data augmentation approach for learning deep models. In: Advances in Neural Information Processing Systems, pp. 2797–2806 (2017)
45. Ullrich, K., Meeds, E., Welling, M.: Soft weight-sharing for neural network compression. arXiv preprint arXiv:1702.04008 (2017)
46. Van Dyk, D.A., Meng, X.L.: The art of data augmentation. J. Comput. Graph. Stat. **10**(1), 1–50 (2001)
47. Wilson, A.G., Izmailov, P.: Bayesian deep learning and a probabilistic perspective of generalization. Adv. Neural. Inf. Process. Syst. **33**, 4697–4708 (2020)
48. Xiao, H., Rasul, K., Vollgraf, R.: Fashion-MNIST: a novel image dataset for benchmarking machine learning algorithms. arXiv preprint arXiv:1708.07747 (2017)
49. Xie, Q., Dai, Z., Hovy, E., Luong, M.T., Le, Q.V.: Unsupervised data augmentation. arXiv preprint arXiv:1904.12848 (2019)
50. Zhou, K., Liu, Z., Qiao, Y., Xiang, T., Loy, C.C.: Domain generalization in vision: A survey. arXiv preprint arXiv:2103.02503 (2021)

Deep Matrix Factorization for Multi-view Clustering Using Density-Based Preprocessing

Raphael K. M. Ahiaklo-Kuz[1], Charles Jnr. Asiedu[1],
Telex M. N. Ngatched[2(✉)], and Isaac Woungang[3]

[1] Huzhou University, Zhejiang, China
[2] Department of Electrical and Computer Engineering, Memorial University,
St. John's, NL, Canada
tngatched@grenfell.mun.ca
[3] Department of Computer Science, Toronto Metropolitan University,
Toronto, ON, Canada
iwoungan@ryerson.ca

Abstract. Using algebraic tools to advance autonomous data mining is difficult because the best clustering techniques do not scale with the dataset's modulo/cardinality, especially in this era of data surge. This paper suggested a pre-processing strategy based on density to compact primary data through a collection of representative points while maintaining the original data's density and distribution. This study used data compression to preserve the dataset's density distribution and features. Most multiview clustering approaches use a single-layer formulation. Since the mapping between the new presentation and the primary data contains intricate hierarchical details, it's more efficient to investigate hidden structures hierarchically. The emphasis is on learning the complementary information to solve the clustering problem. This study presented a deep matrix factorization framework that made use of multi-view clustering (MVC). Semi-nonnegative matrix factorization (NMF) learns multi-view data hierarchies layer-by-layer. To effectively mine shared information from each view, the output layer must be identical. Graph regularizers combine deep structure layer representations to maintain geometry across views. Benchmark results show the model's effectiveness.

Keywords: Multi-view clustering · Factorization · Datasets · Feature extraction · Optimization

1 Introduction

1.1 Overview

Clustering is an orthodox issue that has been around for years. In view of the fact that the amount of data is increasing exponentially in the era of technology,

Supported by organization x.

it is much more important than ever to logically categorize similar things to limit the level of data confusion, which allows researchers to more readily detect its fundamental logic [1]. Under certain intriguing practical areas, instances are characterized by qualities that may be naturally divided into two categories, both of which are sufficient for learning. Web pages, for example, can be categorized based on their anchor texts of inbound hyperlinks as well as their content; additional examples are collections of academic articles. If a few unlabeled data and labeled examples are available, the co-training approach and other multi-view clustering (MVC) techniques can significantly enhance classification accuracy [2, 4, 7].

Even before the data is clustered and processed, there is the need for the data to be properly mined and cleaned in a quest to make the clustering process more efficient. In the current settings, due to the proliferation and digitization of everyday processes, data comes in more complex and huge forms which leads to the need for processing arrangements to be made for big data scenarios. Traditional clustering techniques were not intended for processing big and complex data.

The vast majority of the most advanced clustering techniques are not immediately applicable to big data, often known as massive data volumes. In light of these constraints, parallelized and new distributed algorithms based on the traditional centralized ones have been developed and put into practice in an effort to address the scalability issue. While K-Means and other simple clustering algorithms have been used in a parallelized approach on large data frameworks, only a small subset of the complicated but vastly precise clustering techniques exist that can be easily parallelized. Several research, for instance, have been devoted to the scalability of Density-Based Spatial Clustering of Applications with Noise (DBSCAN) across a variety of devices. Nevertheless, when dealing with specific data distributions or high-dimensional data, these methods still have issues with scalability.

Machine learning and data mining experts generally agree that clustering is a crucial technique. It's been used extensively in the realms of research and data analysis, and it is regarded as one of the most important unsupervised learning approaches to date Examples of fields that apply clustering extensively include market analysis, heterogeneous data analysis, gene expression analysis, and social network analysis. Clustering is a technique for organizing data by creating smaller groups of records that share characteristics [9, 11].

1.2   Problems Introduction

The three key problems identified in this paper are: (i) the inability of most traditional clustering algorithms to scale input data without compromising the characteristic integrity of the data, (ii) the inability of existing MVC techniques to uncover and maintain the inherent geometric form of the multi-view data, and (iii) the relevance of each view is not appropriately measured. As a result, very important attributes or features are either overlooked or get lost in the clustering process.

The first problem can be tackled by introducing a density based preprocessing techniques that uses sets of representative points to compress the size of the original data while preserving its density information and data distribution. The other two problems can be solved by introducing an algorithm whose primary focus is on constructing a deep structure by means of semi non-negative matrix factorization, with the secondary aim of discovering a common feature representation with much more consistent data in order to improve the process of clustering. The proposed framework is expected to possess the following key contributions in order to mitigate these challenges; (i) in order to extract the hidden information, the deep semi-NMF framework was developed. This was accomplished by capitalising on the significance of the Semi-interpretability NMF's and the deep structure's capacity for efficient feature learning. Through the utilisation of a deep matrix factorization framework, the insignificant factors are disassembled in a layer-by-layer manner in order to generate an efficient harmonious depiction in the MVC's final layer, (ii) by using graph regularizers to supervise mutual/concurrent feature learning in every perspective/view, the inherent geometric relationship within data samples is preserved. Using this method, the consensus function in the final layer can be relied upon to preserve the vast majority of the shared characteristics across various graphs. As such, it may be seen as a fusion system that improves the whole MVC's functionality, (iii) to check the viability of this research, the clustering results are compared against that of benchmark techniques on prominent datasets. These benchmark techniques and performance indicators are widely used and are of high credibility.

The paper is organized as follows. In Sect. 2, the proposed approach, which consists of clustering techniques, is presented. In Sect. 4, the considered datasets are presented and a comparison of the proposed algorithm with some benchmark schemes using MATLAB is provided. Finally, Sect. 5 concludes the paper.

2 Proposed Approach

This study introduces and tests the use of a density- based preprocessing technique on multi-view data. It also involves mathematical works to validate the proposed framework which is then stipulated in an algorithm. The algorithm is then coded into a MATLAB program to run and evaluate the proposed system. Then, it is tested and weighed against existing algorithms or techniques. The results obtained are used in analysis and conclusions. Henceforth, in this research study, the proposed algorithm or framework is referred to as DMF_4_MVC which stands for Deep Matrix Factorization Framework for Multi-View Clustering. As seen below, Fig. 1 demonstrates the entire workflow process of the algorithm from the data preprocessing stage, through the Semi-non negative matrix factorization (Semi-NMF) feature extraction phase and finally to the optimization phase. Firstly, multiple base partition matrices are obtained by deep semi-NMF. Then, a consensus partition matrix is learned by optimizing these matrices with uniformly weighted base matrices via optimal permutations. Next, the deep matrix decomposition stage and late reconstruction stages are alternately boosted until convergence.

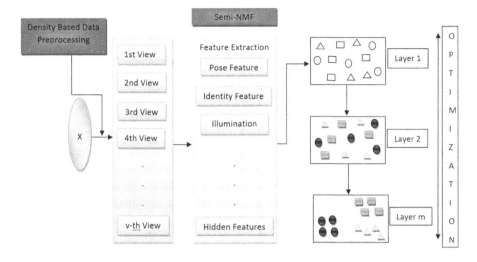

Fig. 1. Illustration of the proposed DMF_4_MVC framework.

2.1 Density-Based Data Preprocessing

Traditional algorithms of clustering are not well tailored for the management of complicated and large datasets. This research therefore makes use of a density-based preprocessing approach which, enhances the elimination of traditional clustering techniques while still conserving clustering quality. Condensing the raw data into a more manageable format is the key to successfully implementing the pinpoint notion in data aggregation. When doing data reduction, an approximation of the original data is converted into a compressed form. This is done while maintaining the information on the density and distribution of the original data. Aggregating results in a reduction in the amount of volume used by the original/initial data. The raw compressed/condensed data are then used as the input for the algorithm that clusters the data. In this case, the amount of data reduction that may be achieved can be controlled by adjusting how the algorithm compresses the data. The amount of compression has an effect not only on the output of the algorithm but also on the quality or accuracy of the clustering. Therefore, a clustering of less accurate result may be achieved if the level is set too high, which implies that a low compression may elevate the amount of computation time required for clustering.

Figure 2 uses the two-moon data set to present an understanding into the driving principle of the density preprocessing procedure and outlines its focused stages. Using the input data, as shown in Fig. 2(a), the entire attribute

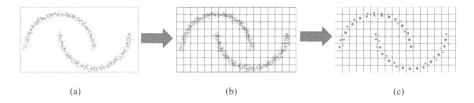

Fig. 2. Illustration of the steps for the density point aggregation method.

area/space has been split into a non-overlapping square cells matrix as shown in Fig. 2(b), where the size of each cell is the normal/typical size and is designated as the subsequent step across all dimensions. There is just one input parameter, and that is a step. To keep things as simple as possible, it is presumed dimensions are characterized by the same measurement unit, implying that they are comparable. Every single data point is mapped to the cell that it corresponds to. After that, the centroid and density of each cell are calculated. After that, the data from each cell is condensed into a format termed as a micro-point, as shown in Fig. 2(c) defined by the location of its cell centroid and a weight/mass that is determined by the density of the cell. In Fig. 2(c) the size of the correlating centroid is what determines the macro-point density. Now the clustering algorithm may take as input the densely referenced macro-points from the original feature space. Take note of the fact that every single macro-point has a weight, which is determined by the density of the point. As a result, not all of the micro-points have the same level of significance. Therefore, the modified data set uses an observation-weighted methodology.

Algorithm 1 illustrates the pseudocode of the density-based data preprocessing phase, where $points = s_1, s_2, s_3, ..., s_i, ..., s_n$ denote a set of n points.

2.2 Semi-Non-Negative Matrix Factorization

This study uses Semi-NMF, which is a variation of NMF in extending the application of traditional NMF from a non-negative input to a mix-sign input, despite the fact that it is still conserving the strong interpretability concurrently. The key Semi-NMF function is obtained as:

$$\min_{Z, H \geq 0} \|X - ZH\|_F^2, \tag{1}$$

where $X \in R^{d \times n}$ represents the input data containing n samples each having a $d - dimensional$ feature. Equation (1) presents an enhanced absolute value variant of NMF [5]–[7]. Ding et al. presented this version of the non-negative matrix factorization (NMF) which transformed the operation of the conventional NMF from a strict non-negative input to a more general mix-sign input, meanwhile still maintaining the significance of interpretability [8]. Given that the sample dataset is represented as $X = \{X^{(1)}, \cdots, X^{(v)}, \cdots, X^{(V)}\}$, and where V is the

Algorithm 1. Density-based data preprocessing technique.

1: **Input**$\{points, steps\}$
2: $gridCells = \{\}$
3: $macro - points = \{\}$
4: Grid definition: compute min for each dimension
5: $minsmaxs = getMinMaxDimensions(points)$
6: Assign each point s to the corresponding cell
7: **for** s in points **do**
8:     $cellIds = computeCellId(s, minsmaxs, mins, step)$
9:     $gridCells = updateGrid(cellId, s)$
10: **end for**
11: **for** cell in gridCells **do**
12:     $centroid = computeCentroid(cell)$
13:     $weight = |\text{points in cell}|$
14:     $macro - points \cdot add(centroid, weight)$
15: **end for**
16: return $macro - points$
17: **Output** Macro-Points

number of views of the model, $X^{(v)} \in R^{d_v \times n}$, where d_v represents the dimensionality of the $v - view$ data and n denotes the total number of data samples. Based on these parameters, the framework can be modeled as:

$$\min_{\substack{C_m^{(v)}, H_m^{(v)} \\ H_m^{(v)}, (\alpha^{(v)}}} \sum_{v=1}^{V} (\alpha^{(v)})^{\gamma} \left(\left(\|X^{(v)} - C_1^{(v)} C_2^{(v)} C_3^{(v)}, \cdots, C_m^{(v)} H_m\|_F^2 \right) + \beta tr \left(H_m L^{(v)} H_m^T \right) \right)$$

$$\text{s.t. } H_1^{(v)} \geq 0, H_m \geq 0, \sum_{v=1}^{V} (\alpha^{(v)} = 1, (\alpha^{(v)} \geq 0,$$

$$(2)$$

where $X^{(v)}$ denotes the given data for the $v - th$ view, $C_i^{(v)}, i \in \{1, 2, 3, \cdots, m\}$, denotes the $i - th$ mapping for the view v, m denotes the number of layers, H_m denotes the consensus latent illustration for all views, $\alpha^{(v)}$ denotes the weighting coefficient for the $v - th$ view, γ denotes the parameter which controls the weight distribution, and $L^{(v)}$ represents the graph Laplacian of the graph for view v, in which every graph is constructed in $k - nearest$ neighbor $(k - NN)$ manner. The weight matrix of the graph for view v is $A^{(v)}$ and $L^{(v)} = A^{(v)} - D^{(v)}$, where $D_{ii}^{(v)} = \sum_l A_{ij}^{(v)}$.

2.3 Optimization Algorithm

The optimization procedure is described in Algorithm 2.

Algorithm 2. Weight Matrices Optimization.

1: **Input**{Multi-view data $X^{(v)}$, tuning parameters γ, β, layer size pi, the number of nearest neighbors k}
2: **Initialization**
3: **for** all layers in each view **do**
4:      $\left(C_i^{(v)}, H_i^{(v)}\right) \leftarrow SemiNMF\left(H_{i-1}^{(v)}, d_i\right)$
5:      $\alpha^{(v)} \leftarrow \frac{1}{V}$
6:      $P^{(v)} \leftarrow k - NN$ graph construction of $X^{(v)}$
7: **end for**
8: **while** not converged **do**
9:      **for** all layers in each view **do**
10:          $\tilde{H}_i^{(v)} \leftarrow \begin{cases} H_m, & \text{if } i = m \\ C_{i+1}^{(v)}\tilde{H}_{i+1}^{(v)} & \text{otherwise} \end{cases}$
11:          $\Phi \leftarrow \prod_{\tau=1}^{i-1} C_\tau$
12:          $C_i \leftarrow \Phi^\dagger X^{(v)}\tilde{H}_i^{(v)}$
13:          $H_i^{(v)} \leftarrow$ update to optimized value
14:          $\alpha_i^{(v)} \leftarrow$ update to optimized value
15:      **end for**
16: **end while**
17: **Output**Weighted matrices $Z_i^{(v)}$, feature matrices $H_i^{(v)}(i < m)$ and H_m in the final layer

---

3   Experimentation

In this section, the considered datasets are presented and a comparison of the proposed algorithm with some benchmark schemes using MATLAB is provided, along with the obtained results.

3.1   Datasets

Since face data includes great structural information that appears to be advantageous in the process of exhibiting the quality of the deep NMF structure, two face/image benchmarks have been selected for the purpose of experimenting with this framework (Table 1).

Table 1. Overview of datasets used.

Dataset	No. of Subjects	No. of Images per Subject
Yale	15	11
Extended YaleB	38	64

3.2   Benchmarks

For the baseline comparison, the experimental results of this framework were compared with the results obtained from the benchmark algorithms described in Table 2.

Table 2. Baseline functions used.

Function	Role
BestSV	Typical spectral clustering is implemented on the features in each and every view. The utmost results are logged
ConcatFea	After concatenating every one of the features, a standard spectral clusteringis applied
ConcatPCA	All of the attributes are concatenated, and then, using Principal Component Analysis (PCA), the original features are presented in a lower-dimensional subspace. The projected feature representation is subjected to spectral clustering
Co-Reg (SPC)	Clustering theories are co-regularized so that memberships from different views are imposed to agree with each other
CoTraining (SPC)	Adopts the strategy of co-training in order to alter the graph structure of each view by making use of the information provided by other views
Min-D (disagreement)	Forms a bipartite graph driven by the idea of "minimizing disagreement"
MultiNMF	This method uses NMF to send data about both views to a shared latent space. Our proposed method and this system may both be thought of as variations on a single-layer theme
NaMSC	The data from each view is first evaluated using feature extraction, then the learned depictions are integrated and fed into a spectral clustering algorithm
DiMSC	Uses a diversity term to analyze the complementary information included in multi-view representations of structures

To conduct a fully complete assessment, six different evaluation metrics including Normalized Mutual Information (NMI), Accuracy (ACC), Adjusted Rand Index (AR), F-score, Precision and Recall are used.

4   Results and Analysis

4.1   Results Using Yale Dataset

From Table 3, it is evident that the results from this research show an improved performance by about 7.58% in NMI, 5.09% in ACC, 8.24% in AR, 6.57% in F-score, 10.14% in Precision, and 4.62% in Recall. On average, this framework improves the state-of-the-art DiMSC by about 8%.

Table 3. Results using Yale dataset.

Method	NMI	ACC	AR	F-score	Precision	Recall
BestSV	0.654 ± 0.011	0.618 ± 0.030	0.440 ± 0.011	0.475 ± 0.011	0.457 ± 0.011	0.495 ± 0.010
ConcatFea	0.641 ± 0.006	0.544 ± 0.038	0.394 ± 0.009	0.431 ± 0.008	0.415 ± 0.007	0.448 ± 0.008
ConcatPCA	0.665 ± 0.037	0.578 ± 0.038	0.396 ± 0.011	0.434 ± 0.011	0.419 ± 0.012	0.452 ± 0.009
Co-Reg	0.648 ± 0.002	0.564 ± 0.000	0.438 ± 0.002	0.466 ± 0.000	0.455 ± 0.004	0.491 ± 0.003
Co-Train	0.672 ± 0.006	0.630 ± 0.001	0.452 ± 0.010	0.487 ± 0.009	0.470 ± 0.010	0.507 ± 0.007
Min-D	0.645 ± 0.005	0.616 ± 0.043	0.433 ± 0.006	0.472 ± 0.006	0.446 ± 0.005	0.496 ± 0.006
MultiNMF	0.690 ± 0.001	0.673 ± 0.001	0.495 ± 0.001	0.527 ± 0.000	0.512 ± 0.000	0.545 ± 0.000
NaMSC	0.673 ± 0.011	0.636 ± 0.000	0.475 ± 0.004	0.508 ± 0.007	0.492 ± 0.003	0.524 ± 0.004
DiMSC	0.727 ± 0.010	0.709 ± 0.003	0.535 ± 0.001	0.564 ± 0.002	0.543 ± 0.001	0.586 ± 0.003
DMF_4_MVC	0.782 ± 0.010	0.745 ± 0.011	0.579 ± 0.002	0.601 ± 0.002	0.598 ± 0.001	0.613 ± 0.002

4.2   Results using Extended YaleB Dataset

Table 4. Results using Extended YaleB dataset.

Method	NMI	ACC	AR	F-score	Precision	Recall
BestSV	0.360 ± 0.016	0.366 ± 0.059	0.225 ± 0.018	0.303 ± 0.011	0.296 ± 0.010	0.310 ± 0.012
ConcatFea	0.147 ± 0.005	0.224 ± 0.012	0.064 ± 0.003	0.159 ± 0.002	0.155 ± 0.002	0.162 ± 0.002
ConcatPCA	0.152 ± 0.003	0.232 ± 0.005	0.069 ± 0.002	0.161 ± 0.002	0.158 ± 0.001	0.164 ± 0.002
Co-Reg	0.151 ± 0.001	0.224 ± 0.000	0.066 ± 0.001	0.160 ± 0.000	0.157 ± 0.001	0.162 ± 0.000
Co-Train	0.302 ± 0.007	0.186 ± 0.001	0.043 ± 0.001	0.140 ± 0.001	0.137 ± 0.001	0.143 ± 0.002
Min-D	0.186 ± 0.003	0.242 ± 0.018	0.088 ± 0.001	0.181 ± 0.001	0.174 ± 0.001	0.189 ± 0.002
MultiNMF	0.377 ± 0.006	0.428 ± 0.002	0.231 ± 0.001	0.329 ± 0.001	0.298 ± 0.001	0.372 ± 0.002
NaMSC	0.594 ± 0.004	0.581 ± 0.013	0.380 ± 0.002	0.446 ± 0.004	0.411 ± 0.002	0.486 ± 0.001
DiMSC	0.635 ± 0.002	0.615 ± 0.003	0.453 ± 0.000	0.504 ± 0.006	0.481 ± 0.002	0.534 ± 0.001
DMF_4_MVC	0.651 ± 0.002	0.765 ± 0.001	0.513 ± 0.002	0.565 ± 0.001	0.526 ± 0.001	0.610 ± 0.001

From Table 4, it is evident that the method also improves the performance by about 7.57% in NMI, 5.08% in ACC, 8.22% in AR, 6.56% in F-score, 10.13% in Precision and 4.61% in Recall. On average, it improves the state-of-the-art DiMSC by about 7%.

4.3   Covergence Analysis

The objective value curve is plotted in Fig. 3. It is observed that the objective value reduces continuously, and then casually meets the convergence after about 100 iterations.

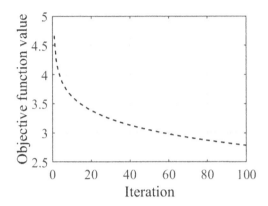

Fig. 3. Objective function value with respect to iteration time.

5   Conclusion

This study has extended a preprocessing method based on density to facilitate large-scale clustering. While maintaining the original density and spatial information, the original/primary dataset was minimized by condensing/combining the sets of points into macro-points. After that, a multi-view clustering method was used to effectively group the macro-points into a small, efficient cluster. The experimental result reveals the impact of the density-based preprocessing technique, while ensuring that the quality of the generated clusters is maintained. It was shown that the proposed framework outperforms some benchmark techniques. This study also demonstrated the use of a deep matrix factorization technique for the MVC problem, and has shown that introducing the density parameter in the preprocessing stage can be effective in maintaining the uniqueness of the data features. In addition, the obtained results demonstrate the efficiency of the proposed framework for deep matrix factorization.

When the dimension of the dataset changes arbitarily, the *Curse of Dimensionality* phenomenon, which is usually experienced in K-means clustering, occurs. Further research can be conducted to produce an algorithm that adjusts the parameter step in an automated manner when the dimensionality changes to ensure that the complete enumeration of all subspaces remains tractable with increasing dimensionality.

References

1. Fu, L., Lin, P., Vasilakos, A.V., Wang, S.: An overview of recent multi-view clustering. Neurocomputing **402**, 148–161 (2020)
2. Fan, J., Cheng, J.: Matrix completion by deep matrix factorization. Neural Netw. **98**, 34–41 (2018)
3. Xu, C., Tao, D., Li, Y., Xu, C.: Large-margin multi-view Gaussian process. Multimed. Syst. **21**(2), 147–157 (2014). https://doi.org/10.1007/s00530-014-0389-6
4. De Handschutter, P., Gillis, N., Siebert, X.: A survey on deep matrix factorizations. Comput. Sci. Rev. **42**, 100423 (2021)
5. Yang, Y., Wang, H.: Multi-view clustering: a survey. Big Data Min. Anal. **1**(2), 83–107 (2018)
6. Zhao, J., Xie, X., Xu, X., Sun, S.: Multi-view learning overview: recent progress and new challenges. Inf. Fusion **38**, 43–54 (2017)
7. Trigeorgis, G., Bousmalis, K., Zafeiriou, S., Schuller, B.W.: A deep matrix factorization method for learning attribute representations. IEEE Trans. Pattern Anal. Mach. Intell. **39**(3), 417–429 (2017)
8. Ren, Y., Huang, S., Zhao, P., Han, M., Xu, Z.: Self-paced and auto-weighted multi-view clustering. Neurocomputing **383**, 248–256 (2020)
9. Liu, S., Ding, C., Jiang, F., Wang, Y., Yin, B.: Auto-weighted multi-view learning for semi-supervised graph clustering. Neurocomputing **362**, 19–32 (2019)
10. Nie, F., Cai, G., Li, J., Li, X.: Auto-weighted multi-view learning for image clustering and semi-supervised classification. IEEE Trans. Image Process. **27**(3), 1501–1511 (2018)
11. Chen, C., Ng, M.K., Zhang, S.: Block spectral clustering methods for multiple graphs. Numer. Linear Algebra Appl. **24**(1), e2075 (2016)
12. Zong, L., Zhang, X., Liu, X.: Multi-view clustering on unmapped data via constrained non-negative matrix factorization. Neural Netw. **108**, 155–171 (2018)
13. Gong, X., Huang, X.: A probabilistic matrix factorization recommendation method based on deep learning. J. Phys: Conf. Ser. **1176**, 022–043 (2019)
14. Li, Z., Tang, J.: Weakly supervised deep matrix factorization for social image understanding. IEEE Trans. Image Process. **26**(1), 276–288 (2017)
15. Qiu, Y.C., Sun, W.J., Zhang, Yu., Gu, X.B., Zhou, G.X.: Approximately orthogonal nonnegative Tucker decomposition for flexible multiway clustering. Sci. Chin. Technol. Sci. **64**(9), 1872–1880 (2021). https://doi.org/10.1007/s11431-020-1827-0
16. Allab, K., Labiod, L., Nadif, M.: A semi-NMF-PCA unified framework for data clustering. IEEE Trans. Knowl. Data Eng. **29**(1), 2–16 (2017)

Application of Genetic Algorithm for Complexity Metrics-Based Classification of Ontologies with ELECTRE Tri

Ameeth Sooklall(iD) and Jean Vincent Fonou-Dombeu$^{(\boxtimes)}$(iD)

School of Mathematics, Statistics and Computer Science,
University of KwaZulu-Natal, Pietermaritzburg, South Africa
fonoudombeu@gmail.com

Abstract. The selection of suitable ontologies for reuse remains a challenging task. Although there have been attempts to cluster and classify ontologies using machine learning techniques, little or no studies have applied Multi-Criteria Decision Making (MCDM) techniques to classify ontologies. This study applies a MCDM model known as ELECTRE Tri to classify 200 ontologies using a Genetic Algorithm. The classes were defined *a priori* according to four ontology quality dimensions, namely, Accuracy, Understandability, Cohesion, and Conciseness. These dimensions were measured with 13 complexity metrics of ontology. The parameters for the ELECTRE Tri model were inferred from a set of assignments by taking a metaheuristic approach with the Genetic Algorithm. The experimental results show that the ELECTRE Tri model has successfully classified the ontologies in the dataset into the 3 classes with ratios of 21.5%, 24% and 54.5%, respectively. These results constitute interesting insights for the selection and reuse of the ontologies.

Keywords: Ontology classification · ELECTRE Tri · Genetic algorithm · Complexity metrics · BioPortal

1 Introduction

The field of Artificial Intelligence (AI) is expanding at a rapid pace [1]. AI is proving to be beneficial to a multitude of areas and domains. Knowledge is essential for any AI technology or system, and accordingly it must be represented in a form that enables reasoning and problem solving. Furthermore, the myriad semantics associated with knowledge should be comprehended and also differentiable by different systems, technologies, and agents. A crucial technology that provides a rich representation of knowledge and existence is ontology.

An ontology is defined as a formal and explicit specification of a shared conceptualization [2]. It is essentially a form of representing knowledge pertaining to a domain, comprising vocabulary in the form of classes, properties, and instances.

© ICST Institute for Computer Sciences, Social Informatics and Telecommunications Engineering 2023
Published by Springer Nature Switzerland AG 2023. All Rights Reserved
T. M. Ngatched Nkouatchah et al. (Eds.): PAAISS 2022, LNICST 459, pp. 135–146, 2023.
https://doi.org/10.1007/978-3-031-25271-6_9

The use of ontologies is growing, with their applications spanning across various domains worldwide. However, the complexity associated with the engineering and development of ontologies is high. To create and validate an ontology is often a complex process, requiring many experts from multiple domains. Therefore, it is often more appropriate to reuse existing ontologies rather than creating ontologies *de novo*. Furthermore, in recent years there has been an increase in the number of ontologies available online. The emergence of ontology repositories, such as the AgroPortal Library[1] and the BioPortal Repository[2], enable and stimulate the applications of ontology engineering. Nonetheless, there is still a substantial issue that knowledge engineers are faced with. Due to the large number of available ontologies as well as their inherent complexity, it becomes increasingly difficult to select appropriate ontologies for reuse. Accordingly, it is of utmost importance that techniques be developed to enable efficient and effective evaluation and selection of ontologies. Whilst there are studies that focus on selecting and ranking ontologies [3–7], most of the studies focus on matching the ontologies to the user's search queries. Little research has been done regarding ontology selection according to the quality and characteristics of ontologies. Classifying ontologies that portray similarity between their attributes is an excellent way of allowing engineers to choose ontologies with desired qualities and characteristics.

There already exists metrics, known as complexity metrics [8], that provide insights pertaining to the characteristics of ontologies. These metrics are relatively easy to comprehend and compute, and they are well documented and widely used in order to better understand an ontology. Classification of ontologies according to their complexity metrics is therefore a suitable technique for eliciting ontology selection for reuse. Although there has been a small number of studies that have clustered ontologies according to their complexity metrics using machine learning techniques [9,10], there has been no studies that have applied Multi-Criteria Decision Making (MCDM) to classify ontologies based on their complexity metrics. MCDM enables a decision-maker to define categories *a priori* as opposed to machine learning techniques wherein the categories are usually generated from some analysis of the data.

In this study ELECTRE Tri is used to classify 200 biomedical ontologies into 3 categories. The classes are differentiated according to the complexity metrics, and each class signifies a different level of performances of the ontologies in light of 4 dimensions of ontology quality. The parameters and boundaries for the ELECTRE Tri model were inferred from a set of assignments with the aid of a Genetic Algorithm. After inferring the profiles and parameters, the classification was performed. The experimental results show that the ELECTRE Tri model has successfully classified the ontologies in the dataset into the 3 classes with ratios of 54.5%, 24% and 21.5%, respectively, based on their degree of accuracy, understandability, cohesion and conciseness. These results constitute interesting insights for the selection and reuse of the ontologies.

---

[1] http://agroportal.lirmm.fr/.
[2] https://bioportal.bioontology.org/.

The rest of the paper is structured as follows. Section 2 reviews related studies. The methods and materials, and the model specifications are provided in Sect. 3. Section 4 presents and discusses the results obtained and the paper is concluded in Sect. 5.

2 Related Work

In recent years, a number of studies have addressed the "classification of ontology" or "ontology classification" [11–14], to mean different things. For authors [12,13], ontology classification is the measurement of the consistency and satisfiability of ontology with reasoner systems. In molecular biology [11], ontology classification related to the classification of proteins. Classification of ontology pertained to the manual grouping of ontologies related to the software engineering domain, into various categories based on criteria such as the scope of application, information content and the corresponding software engineering phase [14]. In this study, the classification of ontology is also treated as the task of grouping ontologies that display the same characteristics or properties into various categories to aid their selection for reuse. In recent studies the authors applied k-means clustering method to partition ontologies into clusters [9] and k-nearest neighbors to classify ontologies [10], based on their degree of complexity.

There has been a substantial amount of research related to ranking and selecting ontologies [3–7]. These studies mainly focused on the matching of users queries with the ontologies to rank them according to their degree of similarity with the query terms. In recent years, authors have applied various MCDM algorithms in ontology ranking [15–17]. However, the MCDM experimented did not address the task of classifying ontologies into categories for selection. The ELimination Et. Choix Traduisant la REalité (ELECTRE) is a popular MCDM model that has 5 main versions, I, II, III, IV and Tri [28]. The first four versions of ELECTRE perform the selection and ranking based on the pairwise comparisons of the different choices. The fifth version, ELECTRE Tri, classifies alternatives based on predetermined intervals. The ELECTRE Tri method was developed to address classification problems. No previous study has attempted to apply ELECTRE Tri in the classification of ontology. However, the ELECTRE Tri model has been applied to various fields and domains, such as finance [19], supply chain [20], education [21], and healthcare [22]. Furthermore, there has been an interest in inferring the thresholds of the ELECTRE Tri method with the use of assignment examples. Two main approaches have been considered, the first comprises mathematical optimization methods such as linear programming. The second involves metaheuristic approaches such as evolutionary techniques.

A study [23], applied a non-linear optimization program to infer the ELECTRE Tri thresholds from assignment examples. The authors excluded the veto thresholds due to the computational complexity. Another study [24] applied a linear optimization model to infer the thresholds and profiles for the ELECTRE Tri model, and a non-linear optimization model to infer the cut-off level and the weights. One of the first attempts to incorporate metaheuristic approaches for threshold inference was by Doumpos et al. [25] where the differential evolution optimization method was applied to infer thresholds based on assignment examples. A recent study [26] applied the genetic algorithm to infer the thresholds for the ELECTRE Tri method.

In light of the above, there has been an interest in applying the ELECTRE Tri method together with threshold inference support to solve a range of problems. To the best of our knowledge, no previous study has attempted to apply the ELECTRE Tri method to classify ontologies into various categories/classes based on their degree of complexity like it is done in this study.

3   Materials and Methods

3.1   Ontology Quality Dimensions

Ontology is inherently complex due to the expert knowledge and the underlying logic required for its design. Therefore, ontology is difficult to analyse and comprehend. To solve this problem researchers have proposed various metrics and measures [8] to enable users or knowledge engineers to better understand the complexity of the design of an ontology. In this study, 13 metrics that measure the design complexity of ontology are used to classify ontology based on four quality dimensions of accuracy, understandability, cohesion, and conciseness. These complexity metrics are [8]: Average Population (AP), Average Number of Paths (ANP), Average Breadth (AB), Maximal Breadth (MB), Average Depth (AD), Maximal Depth (MD), Attribute Richness (AR), Class Richness (CR), Relationship Richness (RR), Inheritance Richness (IR), Absolute Root Cardinality (ARC), Absolute Leaf Cardinality (ALC), and Equivalence Ratio (ER). The four quality dimensions are elaborated on as follows [27].

Accuracy expresses to what extent an ontology is representative of a real world domain. The metrics that measure this quality dimension are ANP, AD, AB, MD, MB, ER, RR, AR, and IR. *Understandability* is an indicator of the comprehensiveness of the ontology's constituents such as the concepts and relations. The ALC metric can be used to measure this dimension. The *Cohesion* quality dimension measures how related the constituents of the ontology are, and can be quantified with the ALC and ARC metrics. The *Conciseness* quality dimension measures how useful the knowledge in the ontology is to the domain it represents. The CR and AP metrics are indicators of this quality dimension.

3.2   ELECTRE Tri

The ELECTRE Tri method [18] is one of the most widely-applied MCDM classification methods. It performs alternative assignments to predefined categories by comparing an alternative with the boundaries of all classes. Due to space constraints, only a short description of ELECTRE TRI is provided in this study. Interested readers may find more information on ELECTRE Tri in [18,28]. The ELECTRE Tri procedure is elaborated on as follows.

Expression of Decision Problem. The decision-maker must specify the decision problem, comprising m alternatives, denoted by $A = \{a_1, a_2, \ldots, a_m\}$, and a set of n criteria, $g_1, g_2, \ldots, g_n$. Thereafter, a decision matrix $D_{m \times n}$ can be formed to represent the decision-problem, where $g_n(a_m)$ represents the performance of the mth alternative at the nth criterion.

Definition of Categories and Thresholds. The decision-maker defines a set of classes, $C = C_1, C_2, \ldots, C_p, C_{(p+1)}$, with $p+1$ classes bounded by lower and upper class boundaries, b_i and b_{i+1}, where $g_j(b_i) \leq g_j(b_{(i+1)})$. The decision-maker must also define three thresholds, the indifference q_j, preference p_j, and veto thresholds v_j, where $v_j \geq p_j \geq q_j$. A set of importance weights must also be specified, denoted as $W = \{w_1, w_2, \ldots, w_n\}$.

Calculation of Concordance and Discordance Values. The concordance values are determined for comparing alternatives a_i with boundaries b_h as $c(a_i, b_h) = \sum_{j=1}^{n} w_j c_j(a_i, b_h) / \sum_{j=1}^{n} w_j$, where $c_j(a_i, b_h)$ is given by Eq. (1). The discordance values are determined for comparing a_i and b_h at each criterion j, as $d_j(a_i, b_h)$ in Eq. (2).

$$c_j(a_i, b_h) = \begin{cases} 0, & \text{if } g_j(b_h) - g_j(a_i) \geq p_j \\ 1, & \text{if } g_j(b_h) - g_j(a_i) < q_j \\ \frac{p_j + g_j(a_i) - g_j(b_h)}{p_j - q_j}, & \text{otherwise} \end{cases} \quad (1)$$

$$d_j(a_i, b_h) = \begin{cases} 0, & \text{if } g_j(b_h) - g_j(a_i) < p_j \\ 1, & \text{if } g_j(b_h) - g_j(a_i) \geq v_j \\ \frac{-p_j - g_j(a_i) + g_j(b_h)}{v_j - p_j}, & \text{otherwise} \end{cases} \quad (2)$$

Exploitation of Credibility Indices. The credibility index is then determined for comparing the alternatives and boundaries, using Eq. (3). A cut-off level λ is specified to determine the relations between the alternatives and boundaries. Thereafter, to classify the alternatives, the *optimistic procedure* is applied. This begins by comparing alternative a to boundary b_h, where $h = 1, 2, \ldots, p-1, p$. The first profile b_h where $b_h > a$, is used to assign the alternative, $a \to C_h$.

$$\sigma(a_i, b_h) = c(a_i, b_h) \prod_{\forall j \in n:\, d_j(a_i, b_h) > c(a_i, b_h)} \frac{1 - d_j(a_i, b_h)}{1 - c(a_i, b_h)}, \quad (3)$$

3.3   Threshold Inference with the Genetic Algorithm

ELECTRE Tri has a large number of thresholds that are required to be specified. In general, there are two approaches a decision-maker can take to define these thresholds, a *direct* or an *indirect* approach. The direct approach is when the decision-maker must specify the threshold values directly. This is generally difficult and requires the decision-maker to have a deep understanding of the subject domain. The indirect approach is when the users preferences are inferred through a subset of example assignments. There have been different models applied to learn these thresholds, many of which were based on some form of mathematical programming [23,24]. In recent years, there has been an interest in applying metaheuristic approaches [25,26] to learn these thresholds. The genetic algorithm is able to represent the solutions to the threshold inference problem effectively with the use of chromosomes and genes. It also has the ability to explore a vast range of candidate values, as well as exploit these values with its selection and combination procedures, allowing the decision-maker a large amount of flexibility. It is for these reasons the genetic algorithm is applied in this study to infer an appropriate set of thresholds for the ELECTRE Tri model. The architecture of the genetic algorithm is discussed as follows.

The genetic algorithm [29] is a population-based, nature-inspired, meta-heuristic optimization algorithm. It is based on the concept of biological evolution and begins by the definition of a population of candidate solutions. The candidate solutions are then evaluated according to a pre-defined fitness function and if the accepted performance is not realized in any candidate then a new population is created. This is done by selecting parent solutions from the current population and combining them to create new child solutions. The new population is then evaluated and further populations are developed until a satisfactory solution is identified within a population.

In order to infer a set of thresholds, a set of assignments are required. A denotes the set of all ontologies and $\tilde{A}$ represents the set of assignments, $\tilde{A} \subset A$. Since there are m ontologies, n criteria, and t classes, then $(1 + 3n)$ thresholds have to be inferred, specifically, n veto thresholds v_j, n preference thresholds p_j, n indifference thresholds q_j, and 1 cut-off level λ. Accordingly, each chromosome representing a candidate solution has $(1 + 3n)$ individual genes. The diagram in Fig. 1 depicts an individual chromosome. The values that a chromosome can take are constrained by $0.5 \leq \lambda \leq 1$, and $q_j \leq p_j \leq v_j, \forall j \in n$.

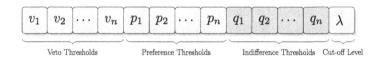

Fig. 1. A chromosome representation of a solution with $1 + 3n$ genes

The fitness function for evaluating the solutions is given by $\mathcal{F}(X) = \mathcal{C}(X, \tilde{A})/|\tilde{A}|$, where $\mathcal{F}(X)$ represents the fitness score for chromosome X, and $\mathcal{C}(X, \tilde{A})$ represents the number of assignments in $\tilde{A}$ that were correctly classified.

Each population is composed of 3 aspects. Elitism is first applied to keep the best solutions, allowing for the carry over of well-performing solutions. The second aspect applies arithmetic crossover to generate offspring from selected parents. The last aspect involves creating new random solutions, allowing for further exploration of possible solutions. These three techniques together make up a new population, and different proportions of the new population can be composed from each of the three techniques as desired.

4 Experimental Results and Discussion

4.1 Dataset

The dataset used in this study was obtained from the BioPortal ontology repository and consisted of 200 ontologies. Due to space constraints the dataset was not included in this paper, but it can be accessed in this location[3]. The ontologies in the dataset included various types of knowledge related to the biological and biomedical domains. The thirteen complexity metrics for measuring the quality of the ontologies in the dataset were calculated with the use of the OntoMetrics[4] platform.

4.2 Computer and Software Environment

This study was performed using a 64-bit Microsoft® Windows® 10 device with 12 GB of RAM and a 1 TB HDD. The device had an Intel® Core™ i-5 processor with a speed of 2.30 GHz. The software for the ELECTRE Tri algorithm and the genetic algorithm was implemented using the Java 8 programming language, together with the JetBrains IntelliJ IDEA Community Edition 2019.1.3 development environment.

4.3 Class Definition

Three classes were defined for the ELECTRE Tri model. The classes were representative of varying levels of quality of the ontologies in respect to the four dimensions, i.e., accuracy, understandability, cohesion, and conciseness defined in Subsect. 3.2. The characteristics and implications of these three classes are discussed as follows.

Class 1 represents those ontologies that have a high level of accuracy indicating that the ontologies are strongly representative of a real-world domain. The ontologies in this class have a high level of understandability, signifying a vastly comprehensive set of concepts, relations, and properties. These ontologies also have a high level of cohesion and conciseness, which means that the ontologies are highly relevant in the domain they are representative of.

Class 2 represents those ontologies that have a moderate level of accuracy indicating that the ontologies are moderately representative of a real-world domain. The ontologies in this class have a fairly comprehensive set of concepts, relations, and properties. These ontologies also have a moderate level of cohesion and conciseness, which means that they have a considerable amount of importance in relation to their domains.

---

[3] https://bit.ly/3xySKCr.
[4] https://ontometrics.informatik.uni-rostock.de/ontologymetrics/.

Class 3 represents the ontologies that have a low level of accuracy, which indicates that the ontologies are only somewhat representative of a real-world domain. The ontologies also have low understandability, meaning that they have a set of concepts, relations, and properties that are not very comprehensive. Ontologies in this class have a minor level of cohesion and conciseness, which means that the ontologies are of lower importance in relation to the domain they are representative of.

4.4   Ontology Classification

After analyzing the ontologies along with their classes, properties, and relations, an assignment of 27 ontologies was made. Nine ontologies were assigned to each of the three classes, as shown in Table 1, where O_i represents the ith ontology in the dataset, and $1 \leq i \leq 200$.

Table 1. Assignment examples for each class

Class 1	O_{14}	O_{36}	O_{60}	O_{78}	O_{136}	O_{153}	O_{179}	O_{184}	O_{195}
Class 2	O_{13}	O_{16}	O_{20}	O_{80}	O_{102}	O_{151}	O_{157}	O_{159}	O_{173}
Class 3	O_4	O_{26}	O_{30}	O_{49}	O_{58}	O_{59}	O_{72}	O_{140}	O_{152}

The class boundaries were defined as shown in Table 2 in the rows b_2 and b_1. The genetic algorithm was then applied to infer the thresholds according to the assignments in Table 1. The weights were set as follows: $AR = 0.06$, $IR = 0.08$, $RR = 0.14$, $ER = 0.07$, $AP = 0.07$, $CR = 0.10$, $ARC = 0.05$, $ALC = 0.08$, $AD = 0.12$, $MD = 0.07$, $AB = 0.04$, $MB = 0.07$, and $ANP = 0.05$.

Table 2. Inferred thresholds by the genetic algorithm

	g_1	g_2	g_3	g_4	g_5	g_6	g_7	g_8	g_9	g_{10}	g_{11}	g_{12}	g_{13}
q	0.01	0.01	0.02	0.04	0.01	0.01	0.01	0.03	0.03	0.01	0.01	0.02	0.02
p	0.01	0.02	0.02	0.06	0.01	0.02	0.01	0.06	0.05	0.01	0.01	0.05	0.04
v	0.02	0.05	0.03	0.09	0.03	0.02	0.10	0.10	0.07	0.02	0.01	0.08	0.09
b_2	0.02	0.06	0.04	0.07	0.05	0.03	0.03	0.10	0.11	0.03	0.04	0.07	0.05
b_1	0.06	0.12	0.08	0.16	0.09	0.07	0.05	0.25	0.23	0.08	0.06	0.18	0.18

The parameters for the genetic algorithm are shown in Table 3. The algorithm yielded a set of thresholds with $\mathcal{F}(X) = 1$, as displayed in Table 2, and a cut-off level of 0.72. These thresholds were then applied to the ELECTRE Tri model and the ontologies were classified accordingly. The optimistic assignment procedure was applied and each ontology was classified into one of the three classes.

Figure 2 shows the classification of the ontologies. Each numbered block represents an ontology, where the ith block represents the ith ontology in the dataset. The orange blocks were assigned to the 3rd class, the blue blocks were assigned to the 2nd class, and the blocks colored in white were assigned to the 1st class.

Table 3. Parameters of the genetic algorithm

Population size	Selection	Crossover	Generations
100	Tournament	Arithmetic	1000
Random candidates	Mutation rate (λ)	No. of elites	Tournament size
10	0.04	4	2

All assignments in $\tilde{A}$ were assigned correctly by the inferred thresholds, as can be observed in Fig. 2. Most of the ontologies were classified to the third class, denoting lower levels of the four quality dimensions. About one fifth of the dataset was classified to the second class, and about one quarter was classified to the first class. Out of 200 ontologies, 109 (54.5%) were assigned to class 3, 43 (21.5%) were assigned to the class 2, and 48 (24%) were assigned to class 1.

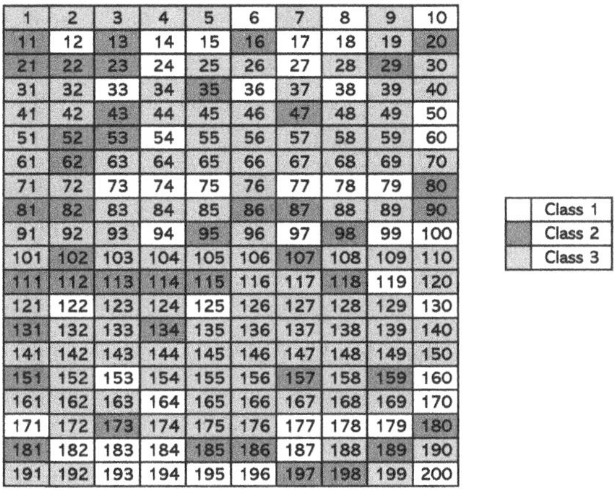

Fig. 2. Diagram showing classification of ontologies.

Table 4 shows the names of some ontologies as per the classes they were assigned to, along with their indices O_i. Only 20 ontologies are displayed per class due to space constraints, but the full classification results for each ontology are shown in Fig. 2. The indices of the ontologies in Table 4 correspond to the indices in Fig. 2, depicting their respective classes. All of the ontologies that were assigned to class 1 (examples in the left column of Table 4) have high level of accuracy indicating that the ontologies are strongly representative of a real-world domain. They also have high level of understandability, that is, the structure of their concepts, relations, and properties are easy to understand. These ontologies also have a high level of cohesion and conciseness, which means that the ontologies are highly relevant in the domain they are representative of. The ontologies in class 2 (examples in the middle column of Table 4) have a moderate level of accuracy, understandability, cohesion, and conciseness. This indicates that these ontologies are moderately representative of a real-world domain, have a fairly comprehensive set of concepts, relations, and properties, and are relatively important in their domains of use.

Table 4. Names of ontologies and their assigned classes

O_i	Class 1	O_i	Class 2	O_i	Class 3
O_{14}	STO_v4.0.owl	O_{11}	Hsapdv.owl	O_2	Ceph.owl
O_{17}	MaHCO.owl	O_{21}	Omp.owl	O_{19}	DLORO.owl
O_{27}	Ontología_V3.owl	O_{23}	Mmusdv.owl	O_{26}	PhylOnt.owl
O_{33}	Pco.owl	O_{29}	eCP.owl	O_{28}	root-ontology.owl
O_{36}	Pav.owl	O_{35}	Sopharm2.2.owl	O_{30}	CSOontology.owl
O_{38}	chem2bio2rdf.owl	O_{43}	CBO.owl	O_{31}	Zeco.owl
O_{50}	OntoFood.owl	O_{53}	saude_mental.owl	O_{39}	SCIO_51.owl
O_{54}	Ocmr-merged.owl	O_{80}	Caro.owl	O_{42}	Atoll_v6.owl
O_{75}	Rvo.owl	O_{86}	ONSTR.owl	O_{44}	Carelex.owl
O_{79}	SAO.owl	O_{87}	Vico_merged.owl	O_{46}	HPI.owl
O_{94}	DIAB_v90rb.owl	O_{95}	bim_beta.owl	O_{48}	CAO.owl
O_{97}	BRIDG.owl	O_{107}	ohmi_merged.owl	O_{58}	Antoneo.owl
O_{99}	VO.owl	O_{111}	ohpi_merged.owl	O_{63}	PDO_ver0.7.owl
O_{122}	ido.owl	O_{113}	webService.owl	O_{69}	Genepio.owl
O_{125}	BCGO.owl	O_{114}	oae.owl	O_{83}	Emo.owl
O_{153}	cogat.owl	O_{134}	foodon.owl	O_{117}	chmo.owl
O_{170}	lifestyle.owl	O_{186}	System.owl	O_{135}	genomics-cds.owl
O_{179}	oboe.owl	O_{189}	ccon0.9.3-rdf.owl	O_{145}	vdot_core.owl
O_{182}	sse-p.owl	O_{197}	cdao.owl	O_{166}	omrse.owl
O_{193}	cio.owl	O_{198}	ogsf-merged.owl	O_{169}	PreMedOnto.owl

Lastly, the ontologies in class 3 (examples in the right column of Table 4) have a low level of accuracy, understandability, cohesion and conciseness. This means that these ontologies are very generic and do not represent a real-world domain, the structure of their concepts, relations, and properties are not easy to understand and they are of low importance to the domain of use. The classification results achieved are useful insights that may assist users or knowledge engineers in the choice of the suitable ontologies for reuse.

5 Conclusion

This study applied the ELECTRE Tri model to classify a set of 200 biomedical ontologies into three classes. A subset of the dataset was initially assigned and thereafter a genetic algorithm was applied to infer the thresholds from the assignment examples. The classification was performed according to four quality dimensions of ontology, namely, accuracy, understandability, cohesion, and conciseness. These four dimensions were measured by using 13 complexity metrics, and these metrics were used as criteria in the ELECTRE Tri method. The results portrayed that all 200 ontologies were classified into one of three classes. The results achieved provide useful insights that may assist users or knowledge engineers in the selection of the ontologies for reuse. This study demonstrated the successful application of the genetic algorithm in inferring thresholds for ontology classification with the ELECTRE Tri model. The future direction of research may involve an analysis of the scalability of the model applied in this study. Larger datasets of ontologies may be classified, and a larger number of dimensions and complexity metrics can be applied to gain insights regarding the scalability of the techniques.

References

1. Tang, X., Li, X., Ding, Y., Song, M., Bu, Y.: The pace of artificial intelligence innovations: speed, talent, and trial-and-error. J. Informetrics **14**(4), 101094 (2020)
2. Gruber, T.: A translation approach to portable ontology specifications. Knowl. Acquis. **5**(2), 199–220 (1993)
3. Alani, H., Brewster, C.: Ontology ranking based on the analysis of concept structures. In: Proceedings of the 3rd International Conference on Knowledge Capture, K-CAP 2005 (2005)
4. Yu, W., et al.: A novel approach for ranking ontologies on the semantic web. In: 2006 First International Symposium on Pervasive Computing and Applications (2006)
5. Yu, W., Li, Q., Chen, J., Cao, J.: OS_RANK: structure analysis for ontology ranking. In: 2007 IEEE 23rd International Conference on Data Engineering (2007)
6. Alipanah, N., Srivastava, P., Parveen, P., Thuraisingham, B.: Ranking ontologies using verified entities to facilitate federated queries. In: 2010 IEEE International Conference on Web Intelligence & Intelligent Agent Technology (2010)
7. Butt, A., Haller, A., Xie, L.: DWRank: learning concept ranking for ontology search. Semant. Web **7**(4), 447–461 (2016)
8. Gangemi, A., Catenacci, C., Ciaramita, M., Lehmann, J.: Ontology evaluation and validation: an integrated formal model for the quality diagnostic task (2005)
9. Koech, G., Fonou-Dombeu, J.: K-means clustering of ontologies based on graph metrics. In: 2019 International Multidisciplinary Information Technology and Engineering Conference (IMITEC) (2019)
10. Koech, G., Fonou-Dombeu, J.V.: K-nearest neighbors classification of semantic web ontologies. In: Attiogbé, C., Ben Yahia, S. (eds.) MEDI 2021. LNCS, vol. 12732, pp. 241–248. Springer, Cham (2021). https://doi.org/10.1007/978-3-030-78428-7_19
11. Wolstencroft, K., Lord, P., Tabernero, L., Brass, A., Stevens, R.: Protein classification using ontology classification. Bioinformatics **22**, e530–e538 (2006)

12. Glimm, B., Horrocks, I., Motik, B., Shearer, R., Stoilos, G.: A novel approach to ontology classification. J. Semant. Web **14**, 84–101 (2012)
13. Wang, C., Feng, Z., Zhang, X., Wang, X., Rao, G., Fu, D.: ComR: a combined OWL reasoner for ontology classification. Front. Comp. Sci. **13**(1), 139–156 (2019). https://doi.org/10.1007/s11704-016-6397-2
14. Zhao, Y., Dong, J., Peng, T.: Ontology classification for semantic-web-based software engineering. IEEE Trans. Serv. Comput. **2**, 303–317 (2009)
15. Fonou-Dombeu, J.V., Viriri, S.: CRank: a novel framework for ranking semantic web ontologies. In: Abdelwahed, E.H., Bellatreche, L., Golfarelli, M., Méry, D., Ordonez, C. (eds.) MEDI 2018. LNCS, vol. 11163, pp. 107–121. Springer, Cham (2018). https://doi.org/10.1007/978-3-030-00856-7_7
16. Fonou-Dombeu, J.V.: A comparative application of multi-criteria decision making in ontology ranking. In: Abramowicz, W., Corchuelo, R. (eds.) BIS 2019. LNBIP, vol. 353, pp. 55–69. Springer, Cham (2019). https://doi.org/10.1007/978-3-030-20485-3_5
17. Fonou-Dombeu, J.: Ranking semantic web ontologies with ELECTRE. In: 2019 International Conference on Advances in Big Data, Computing and Data Communication Systems (icABCD) (2019)
18. Yu, W.: ELECTRE TRI - Aspects Méthodologiques et Manuel d'utilisation. Document - Université de Paris-Dauphine, LAMSADE (1992). (in French)
19. Schotten, P., Pereira, L., Morais, D.: Credit granting sorting model for financial organizations. Financ. Innov. **8**(1), 1–24 (2022)
20. Gonçalves, A., Araújo, M., Mol, A., Rocha, F.: Application of the ELECTRE Tri method for supplier classification in supply chains. Pesquisa Operacional **41** (2021)
21. Şahin, M., Ulucan, A., Yurdugül, H.: Learner classification based on interaction data in E-learning environments: the ELECTRE TRI method. Educ. Inf. Technol. **26**(2), 2309–2326 (2020). https://doi.org/10.1007/s10639-020-10358-2
22. Rocha, A., Costa, A., Figueira, J., Ferreira, D., Marques, R.: Quality assessment of the Portuguese public hospitals: a multiple criteria approach. Omega **105**, 102505 (2021)
23. Mousseau, V., Słowiński, R.: Inferring an ELECTRE TRI model from assignment examples. J. Glob. Optim. **12**(2), 157–174 (1998)
24. De Leone, R., Minnetti, V.: The estimation of the parameters in multi-criteria classification problem: the case of the Electre Tri method. In: Vicari, D., Okada, A., Ragozini, G., Weihs, C. (eds.) Analysis and Modeling of Complex Data in Behavioral and Social Sciences. SCDAKO, pp. 93–101. Springer, Cham (2014). https://doi.org/10.1007/978-3-319-06692-9_11
25. Doumpos, M., Marinakis, Y., Marinaki, M., Zopounidis, C.: An evolutionary approach to construction of outranking models for multicriteria classification: the case of the ELECTRE TRI method. Eur. J. Oper. Res. **199**(2), 496–505 (2009)
26. Fernández, E., Figueira, J., Navarro, J.: An indirect elicitation method for the parameters of the ELECTRE TRI-nB model using genetic algorithms. Appl. Soft Comput. **77**, 723–733 (2019)
27. Fonou-Dombeu, J.V., Viriri, S.: OntoMetrics evaluation of quality of e-Government ontologies. In: Kő, A., Francesconi, E., Anderst-Kotsis, G., Tjoa, A.M., Khalil, I. (eds.) EGOVIS 2019. LNCS, vol. 11709, pp. 189–203. Springer, Cham (2019). https://doi.org/10.1007/978-3-030-27523-5_14
28. Rogers, M., Bruen, M., Maystre, L.: ELECTRE and Decision Support: Methods and Applications in Engineering and Infrastructure Investment (2000)
29. Mitchell, M.: An Introduction to Genetic Algorithms. MIT Press, Cambridge (2002)

Local Features Based Spectral Clustering for Defect Detection

Gael Dimitri Tekam Fongouo[2], Berthine Nyunga Mpinda[2],
and Jules-Raymond Tapamo[1(✉)] (iD)

[1] University of KwaZulu-Natal, Durban 4041, South Africa
tapamoj@ukzn.ac.za
[2] African Institute for Mathematical Sciences (AIMS), AIMS-Cameroon,
Crystal Garden, Limbe, Cameroon
dimitri.tekam@aims-cameroon.org, bmpinda@aimsammi.org

Abstract. Metallurgical industries want to be able to effectively control the quality of their products in order to maintain their prestige and increase their customer base. Therefore, the design and implementation of an optimal technical scheme to detect metal defects would be a solution to this problem. In this work, two methods to extract local characteristics from images of metal products have been presented. These methods are the Local Binary Pattern (LBP) and the Grey Level Co-occurrence Matrix (GLCM). After extracting the specific characteristics describing each image, the information is grouped into a matrix on which the spectral clustering technique is applied in order to classify images according to their similarities. Experiments were carried out and results have shown that defectuous metal surface classification is more accurate when spectral clustering is used in combination with LBP than with GLCM.

Keywords: Local Binary Pattern · Grey Level Co-occurrence Matrix · Spectral clustering

1 Introduction

Numerous studies have been carried out to automate the process of detecting and eliminating defective products during the manufacturing process. The development of Machine Learning algorithms to produce more accurate systems is an activity that is rapidly expanding. Computer vision progress has enabled engineers to equip machines with the ability to sense their environment, perform industrial quality control, help in medical diagnosis and understand human actions, amongst many other applications. It has been established that texture plays a crucial role in the characterization of surface images. Many texture analysis techniques have been proposed in the literature, but most of them are either not very efficient for natural textures and/or are computationally very expensive to be used in real time applications. Nowadays, many discriminative and computationally efficient local feature descriptors have been developed such as

T. M. Ngatched Nkouatchah et al. (Eds.): PAAISS 2022, LNICST 459, pp. 147–165, 2023.
https://doi.org/10.1007/978-3-031-25271-6_10

Local Binary Pattern (LBP), Local Directional Pattern (LDP) and Grey-level Co-occurrence matrix (GLCM). The LBP method as feature descriptor was combined to Support Vector Machine (SVM) as classifier by Hadid et al. for face detection. Experiments showed a recognition rate of 82% [6]. In the work proposed in [3], it has been shown that a good choice of the Grey level quantization would help having good co-occurrence statistics from the GLCM, which will then improve the accuracy of the classification. The diversification of defects encountered on steel surfaces motivated researchers to think about Deep Learning. Some of the most prominent algorithms are Region-based Convolutional Neural Network (R-CNN), fast R-CNN and faster R-CNN [19]. But these algorithms are therefore computationally expensive. Estimates of the testing time of the R-CNN algorithm for one image is about 50s, which indicates that this process could not be adopted in Industry 4.0 to provide defect detection and classification of objects due to its poor performance execution [8]. Most previous detection methods use a supervised learning classification algorithm, which is not a great advantage, as the learning process is subjective and sensitive to human error. Therefore, methods based on a learning process are fundamentally flawed. Selecting and labeling the samples is an error-prone process that limits system detection accuracy.

To address these concerns, defect detection methods based on unsupervised learning have been developed. Bartova and Bina [2] proposed a method of detecting the potential cause or area of the production process where the majority of defects occur during the production using clustering algorithms. They demonstrated that the combination of the hierarchical clustering and K-means algorithms is an effective and efficient method of identification and classification of defects in a manufacturing process [2]. Mosorov et al. [10] used Principle Component Analysis (PCA) technique to calculate the features and also the fuzzy c-means algorithm to classify the sample as defective or non-defective. However, the drawback of these clustering methods is that they are very sensitive to the initialization; moreover, they need multiple restarts to get high quality clusters and they make assumptions on the shapes and the number of clusters.

A more efficient classification method called Spectral clustering has been developed. In [16] an improved spectral clustering algorithm based on a random walk approach to deal with the Gaussian kernel similarity matrix gave excellent classification results when applied to real world problems. Authors assumed that the pairwise similarity between two points is not only related to these latter but also to their neighborhood. Shen et Ye have presented a new spectral clustering algorithm using the spectrum of the pairwise distance matrix [15,16]. In this paper, we investigated LBP and GLCM as feature extractors and Spectral Clustering as classifier to propose a framework to detect defects on flat steel surfaces.

2   Materials and Methods

2.1   Local Binary Patterns

LBP is a popular technique used for gray level image feature extraction and classification because it is an efficient texture descriptor. This feature extractor algorithm has been used by Li and Xuan to detect defects in fabrics [8]. The most important properties of LBP are its tolerance to monotonic illumination changes and its computational simplicity. LBP extracts local structures of image efficiently by comparing each pixel with its neighboring pixels. The generation of the LBP code is done by subtracting the grey level of central pixel from that of each of its eight equidistant nearest neighbours as shown in Fig. 1. Indeed, if the difference gives a negative number, we encode it as 0 and if it is positive, we encode it as 1. For each central pixel considered, the binary number consisting of 0 and 1 is obtained by simple concatenation clockwise of all the individual binary values obtained, starting with the binary number placed at the top of the left side of the central pixel we want to encode [6,8].

Given an image I with pixels $\{P_0, .., P_{np-1}\}$ where np is the number of pixels. To produce the LBP code of each pixel P_j, we consider its 3×3 local neighborhood as shown in Fig. 1, where g_c is the grey level of P_j and g_i, $i = 0, \ldots, 7$, are the grey levels of the neighboring pixels. The following steps will enable us to compute the LBP code of each pixel P_j of the image:

– *Step 1*: For each pixel P_j, compute the following eight dimensional vector:

$$T_{P_j} = (g_0, g_1, g_2, g_3, g_4, g_5, g_6, g_7) - (g_c, g_c, g_c, g_c, g_c, g_c, g_c, g_c)$$
$$= (g_0 - g_c, g_1 - g_c, g_2 - g_c, g_3 - g_c, g_4 - g_c, g_5 - g_c, g_6 - g_c, g_7 - g_c,)$$

g_0	g_1	g_2
g_7	g_c	g_3
g_6	g_5	g_4

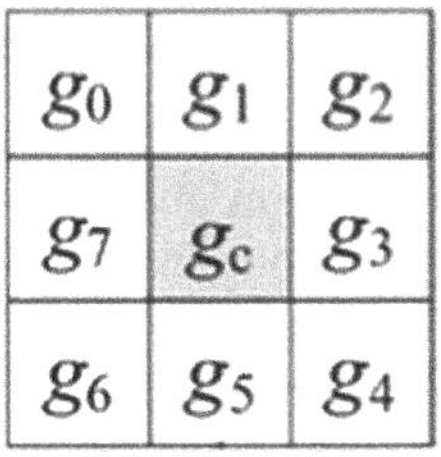

Fig. 1. 3×3 neighborhood [17].

At this level, to get the texture's characteristic, the key information is only on the signed difference of $g_i - g_c$ but not the amplitude of the differences $|g_i - g_c|$. It is from this relationship that the invariance of LBPs to monotonic illuminations originates. Because, when applying a monotonic illumination on the image, all pixels vary in the same way so that the differences are preserved.

– *Step 2*: For each pixel P_j, compute $LBP_{8,R}$ as follows:

$$I_j = LBP_{8,R}(T_{P_j}) = \sum_{p=0}^{7} s(g_p - g_c)2^p. \tag{1}$$

with $s(x)$ the signed difference function defined as:

$$s(x) = \begin{cases} 1 & \text{if } x < 0 \\ 0 & \text{if } x \geq 0 \end{cases} \tag{2}$$

The description of a texture is approximately done with 2^P bins of LBP codes:

$$H \approx f(LBP_{8,R}(T_{P_0}), LBP_{8,R}(T_{P_1}), \dots, LBP_{8,R}(T_{p_{np-1}})) \tag{3}$$

where f is the function computing the histogram of the image $(I_0, \dots, I_{np-1})$

In the set of 2^p binary patterns of a neighborhood consisting of P pixels, it has been proven that some patterns contain more information than others, and therefore, it is possible to use a subset of the initial 2^p binary patterns to describe the texture of the image. These patterns have been called uniform patterns by Ojala et al. [4]. The $LBP_{(P,R)}^{U2}$ notation is commonly used to characterize them. The uniformity measure of a pattern refers to the number of bitwise transitions from 0 to 1 or conversely when the bit pattern is considered circular [2]. Therefore, a local binary pattern is called uniform if it contains at most two bitwise transitions from 0 to 1 or reciprocally. This also means that if the uniformity measure of this pattern is at most equals to 2. For example, patterns 00000000 (zero transitions), 00001111 (one transition), 11101111 (two transitions) are uniform while the patterns 10101011 (six transitions) and 11001100 (three transitions) are not uniform. In uniform LBP mapping, there is a separate output labels for each uniform pattern and all the non uniform patterns are assigned to a single label.

The number of different output labels for mapping for patterns of P bits is $P(P-1)+3$. Then, for the case of eight neighborhood pixels, there are 58 labels for uniform patterns and 1 label for non uniform patterns, which means we have 59 output labels. Ojala et al. pointed out that the main reason why we need to be interested in uniform patterns for image texture description is that the majority of local binary patterns present in natural images are uniforms. It was found in [6] that for the experiments on facial images that 90.6% of the patterns in the (8, 1) neighborhood are uniform. Another reason to consider uniform patterns is their statistical robustness. Indeed, the use of uniform patterns has given quite good results when applied to recognition problems. Uniform patterns are more stable and more resistant to noise.

Texture image rotations lead to the translation of LBP patterns to a different location, from the initial location to a rotation around the central pixel. Considering a uniform LBP pattern $U_P(n, r)$ where n is the number of $1-$ bits in the pattern, corresponding to the row number in the Fig. 2 and r the rotation of the pattern which corresponds to the column number. For the case where the

Fig. 2. 58 possible uniform patterns of p-r-8-r [11].

neighborhood is formed by P sampling points, the number n belongs to the set $\{0, \ldots, P\}$, moreover, when $1 \leq n \leq P - 1$, this also means that $0 \leq r \leq P - 1$. Let, $I(x, y)$ and $I^{\alpha}(x, y)$ be the image and its rotation by α degrees respectively; every point of coordinates (x, y) is rotated to the new location (x', y') as we can see on Fig. 3. In the case where the chosen rotation angles correspond to integer multiples of the angle between two points, i.e. $\alpha = k\frac{360}{P}$, with $k = 0, 1, \ldots, P - 1$; then, the uniform pattern $U_P(n, r)$ at point (x, y) is replaced by uniform pattern $U_P(n, r + k \bmod P)$ at point (x', y') of the rotated image [12].

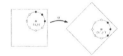

Fig. 3. Effect of image rotation on points in circular neighborhood [11].

To ensure translation and rotation invariance in the computation of LBP code, a rotation-invariant LBP is proposed. Each LBP binary code is circularly rotated into its minimum value [7] by:

$$LBP_{P,R}^{ri} = min\{ROR(LBP_{P,R}, i) | \; i = 0, 1, \ldots, P - 1\} \qquad (4)$$

where $ROR(x, i)$ performs a circular bitwise right rotation of bit sequence x by i steps. For example, the 8-bit LBP codes 10000010, 00101000, and 00000101 all map to the minimum code 00000101. Indeed, the $LBP_{P,R}^{ri}$ codes is invariant only to rotations of input image by angles $\alpha = k\frac{360}{P}$, $k = 0, 1, \ldots, P - 1$. It has been shown that this descriptor is very robust to in-plane rotations of images by any angle.

2.2   Grey Level Co-occurrence Matrix (GLCM)

GLCM is a method used for texture characterization. It is a second-order statistical measures since it considers the relationship between groups of two pixels in the original image. Features obtained are based on the assumption that the texture information in an image is contained in the overall spatial relationship that each grey levels of pixel and its neighbouring have together. The GLCM is simply a tabulation of how often different combinations of grey levels co-occur in an image or in a section of an image.

The co-occurrence probability between grey levels i and j is defined as:

$$C_{ij} = \frac{P_{ij}}{\sum_{i,j=1}^{G} P_{ij}} \tag{5}$$

with P_{ij} being the number of occurrences of grey levels i and j within a precise window characterized by the parameters (δ, θ) or more precisely, $P_{\theta,d}(i,j)$ is the number of times that grey level j occurs at distance d away from pixel with grey level i in the direction θ. Here, G is the quantization number and the denominator represents the total number of grey pairs (i, j) within the predefined window [7]. Smaller values of G increase the speed computation of the co-occurrence matrix, then the co-occurrence texture features and reduce noise, but the problem is that, this leads to the reduction of information [4]. The GLCM is a square matrix and can be calculated at any angle and at any offset. The most directions considered to calculate the GLCM are those given by $\theta = 0°, 45°, 90°, 135°, 180°, 225°, 270°, 315°$ [5]. We can see these orientations in Fig. 4.

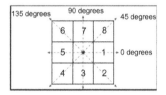

Fig. 4. Angular relationships with nearest neighbours [14].

Computing the GLCM at $0°$ for a considered pixel, simply means to count the frequency of appearance of this pixel and its nearest neighbor at the right hand side. The distance chosen is also a very important factor in determining the occurrences. In 1991, Barber and LeDrew [1] demonstrated statistically that the choice of $\delta = 1$ gives a significant higher classification accuracy than the higher values of $\delta = 5$ and $\delta = 9$. In 1992, Nystuen et al. used multiples distances between one to ten and concluded that the features are consistent for distances greater than four [5]. Figure 5 presents an example of the Co-occurrence Matrix (CM) computed from a part of an original image (Fig. 5 (a)) for $\delta = 1$. As we can see from the original image, pixel values are in the set$\{1, 2, 3, 4, 5, 6, 7, 8\}$ so the CM will be of size 8×8. Generally, before having a good accuracy during statistical analysis, it is recommended to make the CM symmetric. This is done by a simple algebraic process. The CM contained many information, the diagonal of the GLCM matrix gives how many times each grey level reappears at the given

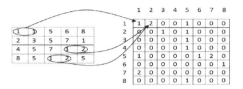

Fig. 5. Example of gray level co-occurrence matrix [18].

distance (d) and direction (θ); it then represents the homogeneous area of our image, and when we go away from the diagonal the heterogeneity increases.

The characterization of the different textures is then obtained by computing the second order statistics from the GLCM. In general, more than 22 features can be derived from the CM, but five are considered as parameters of importance as reported in [3,4]. These are Homogeneity, Dissimilarity, Energy and Entropy, Contrast. Considering $P(i,j)$ to be the $(i,j)^{th}$ of the normalized symmetrical GLCM. N_g, the number of distinct grey levels specified during the quantization and μ_x, μ_y, σ_x, σ_y the means and standard deviations of P_x and P_y of the $GLCM$ where $P_x(i)$ is the ith entry in the marginal probability matrix obtained by summing the rows of P(i, j). The value of P_x is given by:

$$P_x(i) = \sum_{j=1}^{N_g} P(i,j).$$

(6)

Using Eq. (6), the computation of Contrast, Dissimilarity, Homogeneity, Entropy, Energy is given in the following sections.

2.2.1 Contrast

The contrast is defined as a local grey level variation in the grey level co-occurrence matrix. When an image has a low contrast, it is difficult to identify the details present in it compared to the one with higher contrast. To compare the contrast of images, an easy way is to compute their histograms. The Contrast, CON, can be computed as:

$$CON = \sum_{n=0}^{N_g-1} n^2 \sum_{i=1}^{N_g} \sum_{j=1}^{N_g} p(i,j)$$

(7)

2.2.2 Homogeneity

Homogeneity which is also known as Inverse Difference Moment, measures image homogeneity as it assumes larger values for smaller grey tones differences in pair elements [4]. It is more sensitive to the presence of near diagonal elements in GLCM. It has maximum value when all elements in the image are the same. Homogeneity, HOM, decreases if contrast increases, and it is given by:

$$HOM = \sum_i \sum_j \frac{1}{1-(i-j)^2} P(i,j)$$

(8)

2.2.3   Entropy

Entropy measures how stochastic co-occurrence matrix or the image is [4]. An image with a very random texture will have a big Entropy, while smooth texture will have a low Entropy. The Entropy, ENT, can be computed as

$$ENT = -\sum_i \sum_j P(i,j) log(p(i,j)) \tag{9}$$

2.2.4   Energy

Energy of an image measures the localized change in this image. It is the measure of color/brightness of the pixels over local areas [4,5]. Energy, ENR, is expressed by:

$$ENR = \sum_i \sum_j P(i,j)^2 \tag{10}$$

2.2.5   Correlation

Correlation, COR, is a measure used to study a grey level linear dependence between the pixels located at specified positions [12] and it is defined as:

$$COR = \frac{\sum_i \sum_j P(i,j) - \mu_x \mu_y}{\sigma_x \sigma_y} \tag{11}$$

These methods allow us to have a particular characteristic of the texture of images. We present the formalism of the spectral clustering method which is used to classify images according to information received from their textures.

2.3   Spectral Clustering

2.3.1   Similarity Graph

Given data points $x_1, \ldots, x_n$. In the case where we don't have a sufficient information, it is good to represent the data by similarity graph denoted by $G(V, E)$. Where V is the set of data points (vertices) and E the set edges. In the graph, each vertex represents a data point x_i. The similarity between data points x_i and x_j is defined by S_{ij}. Two vertices x_i and x_j are connected if S_{ij} is positive or greater than a certain threshold value [9]. The clustering problem is formulated as follows: Clustering is the process of finding a partition of the graph such that the edges between different groups have low weights (points are dissimilar) and the edges within a group have high weights. There exists several ways to construct a graph representing the relationships between data points. These graphs help to transform a given set $\{x_1, x_2, \ldots, x_n\}$ with a pairwise similarity function S_{ij} into a graph. The ϵ-neighborhood graph, the K-nearest neighbors graphs, the Gaussian similarity graph are different possibilities to represent relationship between data points. In this paper we used the Gaussian similarity graph obtained from the function [13]:

$$S_{ij} = exp(\sum_{j=1}^{d} \frac{(x_{ik} - x_{jk})^2}{\sigma^2}) \tag{12}$$

Definitions [13]: Given $G(V, E)$ an undirected weighted graph, with w_{ij} denoting weight of the edge between vertices v_i and v_j, the adjacency matrix of the graph is a square matrix defined as:

$$W = (w_{ij})_{i,j=1,\dots,n} = (w_{ji})_{i,j=1,\dots,n} \tag{13}$$

For a given vector v_i, its degree is defined as

$$d_i = \sum_{j=1}^{n} w_{ij} \tag{14}$$

where n is the cardinality of $V(|V|)$. In fact, the degree d_i of the node i is the sum of edges weights incident in i [14]. The diagonal matrix D containing the degrees of the vertices is called the degree matrix.

Let $A \subset V$ a subset of vertices and $\bar{A} = V \setminus A$ the complement of A. For two clusters $A, B \subset V$, the following expressions are defined.

Definition 1. *The sum of weight connections between two clusters:*

$$Cut(A, B) = \sum_{x_i \in A, x_j \in B}^{n} w_{ij} \tag{15}$$

Definition 2. *The sum of weight connections within cluster A:*

$$Cut(A, A) = \sum_{x_i \in A, x_j \in A}^{n} w_{ij} \tag{16}$$

Definition 3. *The total weights of edges originating from cluster A:*

$$Vol(A) = \sum_{x_i \in A}^{n} d_i = \sum_{x_i \in A}^{n} \sum_{x_j \in B}^{n} w_{ij}. \tag{17}$$

Any two subgraphs A and B are said to be connected if any two vertices in each of them can be joined by a path such that all intermediates points also belong to any of them [15].

2.3.2 Laplacian Matrix

Graph Laplacian matrices are the main tools for spectral clustering. Considering that we have an undirected weighted graph with weight matrix W such that $(w_{ij} = w_{ji} \geq 0)$, there are two main matrices considered as normalized graph Laplacians, and denoted by: L_{sym} and L_{rw} where 'sym' stands for symmetric and 'rw' for random walk. But there is also the unnormalized version denoted by L. They are defined as follows:

$$L_{sym} = D^{-1/2} L D^{-1/2} \tag{18}$$

and

$$L_{rw} = D^{-1}L \tag{19}$$

where

$$L = D - W$$

Properties of the Normalized Laplacian matrices [8, 13].

Property 1. For every vector $f \in \mathbb{R}^n$, we have:

$$f^T L f = \frac{1}{2} \sum_{ij}^{n} w_{ij} \left(\frac{f_i}{\sqrt{d_i}} - \frac{f_j}{\sqrt{d_j}} \right)^2 \tag{20}$$

λ is an eigenvalue of L_{rw} with eigenvector v if and only if $Lv = \lambda D u$.

Property 2. 0 is an eigenvalue of L_{rw} with the constant vector of 1 as elements and 0 is also an eigenvalue of L_{sym} with eigenvector $D^{1/2}(1, \ldots, 1)^T$.

Property 3. L_{sym} and L_{rw} are positive semi-definite with n non-negative real eigenvalues such that $0 = \lambda_1 \leq, \ldots, \leq \lambda_n$.

Property 4. The eigenspace of the eigenvalue 0 is spanned by the indicator vectors. For the matrix L_{sym}, the eigenspace of 0 is spanned by the vectors $D^{1/2}(1, \ldots, 1)^T$.

The aim of the spectral clustering is to assemble data points based on their similarities. When doing a cut to split a graph in two or more subgraphs, the set of edges chosen to cut has to be such that the summation of weights of these is as smallest as possible. This means mathematically that considering a subgraph A and its complements $\bar{A}$, we need to have:

$$Cut(A, \bar{A}) \; minimal \tag{21}$$

which simply means to minimize:

$$\sum_{x_i \in A, x_j \in \bar{A}}^{n} w_{ij} \tag{22}$$

where $A \cup \bar{A} = V$, is the set of vertices of the graph. This is a good idea, but it has some limitations for certain complex graphs. Then to mitigate these imperfections, the approach has been revised a little. A and $\bar{A}$ being sets of nodes in these respective subgraphs. The idea is to minimize what is called the Ratio-Cut [14] defined by:

$$Ratio - Cut(A, \bar{A}) = \frac{cut(A, \bar{A})}{|A|} + \frac{cut(\bar{A}, A)}{|A|} \tag{23}$$

The following example explains why this formulation is more convenient than the previous one.

Example 1. Let's take Fig. 6. Considering the first formulation in order to cut the graph, this will be done by cutting the edge with weight w_{kh}. It is true that w_{kh} is the edge having the smallest weight but as we can see, this cut is not optimal and we cannot have a good partition, since the two data points in the sub-graph located at the right hand side of the edge w_{kh} can be considered as outliers. That is, it is convenient to consider the density of sub-graphs.

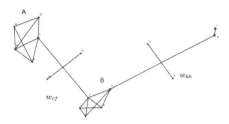

Fig. 6. Graph.

Considering a vector $f \in \mathbb{R}^n$ such that [13]:

$$f_i = \begin{cases} \sqrt{\frac{|\bar{A}|}{|A|}} & \text{if } x_i \in A \\ -\sqrt{\frac{|A|}{|\bar{A}|}} & if \ x_i \in \bar{A} \end{cases} \tag{24}$$

and L the un-normalized Laplacian matrix, we have [13]:

$$f^T L f = \frac{1}{2} \sum_{ij}^{n} w_{ij}(f_i - f_j)^2 \tag{25}$$

Again in [13] It is shown that Minimizing $\sum_{i,j} w_{ij}(f_i - f_j)^2$ is equivalent to minimizing the Ratio-Cut. Thus the solution of the minimization becomes the problem of finding a vector f such that $f^T L f$ is minimal, defined as:

$$\min_f \sum_{i,j} w_{ij}(f_i - f_j)^2 = \min_f f^T L f \tag{26}$$

Given L an $n \times n$ matrix. The Rayleigh Quotient sometimes denoted as $\mathbb{R}_L(f)$ [13] of a vector $f \in \mathbb{R}^n$ with respect to the matrix L is defined to be $\frac{f^T L f}{f^T f}$. For any symmetric matrix $L \in M_n(\mathbb{R})$ with eigenvalues $\lambda_1 \le \lambda_2 \le, \ldots, \le \lambda_n$, we have [8,13]:

$$\lambda_1 = \min_{f \in \mathbb{R}^n} \mathbb{R}_L(f) \tag{27}$$

Hence:

$$\min f^T L f = \min \frac{f^T L f}{f^T f} = \lambda_1 \tag{28}$$

In conclusion, for answering our clustering problems, we have to cluster based on the eigenvector given by the second smallest eigenvalue of the Laplacian matrix, since the first one is equal to zero. This method is very efficient for the case of two cluster's classification. For $k \geq 2$ clusters as we will see in this work, we cluster by using multiples eigenvectors as Shi-Malik proposed in [15]. Algorithm 1, proposed by Ng et al. [15], presents the normalized spectral clustering.

2.3.3 Experimental and Set Up Data Preparation

The results presented in this section have been performed using Python 3 and R programming languages. Data available are images of tabulators extracted from a radiator similar to that of Fig. 7. These images have been divided into three basic classes. The first class is that of tabulators assumed to be well manufactured (Good tabulator), the second class is that of tabulators for which the component has been omitted during the manufacturing process (Empty tabulator) and the third class is that of tabulators poorly made during the manufacturing process (defectuous tabulator). The distinction between good and bad tabulators has been made by experts.

Algorithm 1 The Spectral Clustering algorithm

1: **Input**: Similarity matrix $S \in \mathbb{R}^{n \times n}$, number k of clusters to construct.

2: Construct a similarity graph.

3: Let W be its weighted adjacency matrix.

4: Compute the normalized Laplacian L_{sym}.

5: Compute the first k eigenvectors $u_1, ..., u_k$ of L_{sym}

6: Form the matrix $T \in \mathbb{R}^{n \times k}$ from U by normalizing the rows to norm 1 such as $t_{ij} = \frac{u_{ij}}{\sum_k (U_{ik}^2)^{1/2}}$

7: For $i = 1, ..., n$, $y_i \in \mathbb{R}^k$ the vector corresponding to i^{th} row of T:

8:    Cluster the points $(y_i)_{i=1,...,n}$ with the $k - means$ algorithm into clusters $C_1, ..., C_k$

9: **Output**: Clusters $A_1, ..., A_k$ with $A_i = \{j | y_j \in C_i\}$.

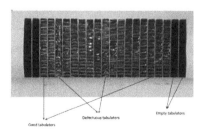

Fig. 7. Image of a manufactured radiator.

After converting each of these images to grey scale, we filtered each of them using the median filter to remove noise. Using LBP, the extraction of uniform and rotationally invariant features has been made with a radius $r = 2$ and a neighborhood consisting of 8 pixels. These parameters will produce for each image 58 uniform patterns and one set containing all other non-uniform patterns, hence, a total of 59 patterns. Because of the rotational invariance, each image will become perfectly described by giving 10 uniform and rotationally stable patterns. We were interested in the number of occurrences of each uniform pattern in each image. Figure 8 represents the different histograms obtained from one image chosen among each of the three different categories of tabulators. Since we face a detection problem, we first took separately the set consisting of good images and extracted the uniform features of each of them, this process was repeated on the sets containing the empty and bad images. Figures 9, 10 and 11 give an overview of what has been done.

Using GLCM, we computed the co-occurrence matrices of each image. The features we have extracted from these matrices were energy, homogeneity, contrast, correlation and entropy. The inter-peak distances taken are $1, 2$ and the orientations considered are $0°, 45° 90° 135°$. However, each of images was described by 40 features.

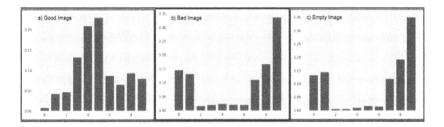

Fig. 8. Different Histograms obtained from the images after applying LBP.

	f1	f2	f3	f4	f5	f6	f7	f8	f9	f10
g	0.006067	0.030269	0.044393	0.104740	0.153295	0.262197	0.087861	0.072370	0.150751	0.089017
g	0.005688	0.023749	0.032997	0.067542	0.156736	0.275636	0.102354	0.071409	0.100673	0.143968
g	0.008106	0.043035	0.047909	0.132540	0.211227	0.231393	0.087110	0.065073	0.093858	0.080249

Fig. 9. Good tabulators images.

	f1	f2	f3	f4	f5	f6	f7	f8	f9	f10
b	0.146206	0.127902	0.021429	0.025893	0.023651	0.039509	0.024107	0.124107	0.126339	0.340848
b	0.146283	0.125188	0.024417	0.017934	0.031115	0.035436	0.026577	0.121003	0.129213	0.341832
b	0.147215	0.131963	0.016578	0.020115	0.024757	0.022325	0.021220	0.111188	0.167551	0.337091

Fig. 10. Bad tabulators images.

	f1	f2	f3	f4	f5	f6	f7	f8	f9	f10
e	0.150208	0.151875	0.012708	0.009167	0.012708	0.022917	0.018125	0.133333	0.180000	0.308958
e	0.136199	0.174434	0.007892	0.009656	0.009656	0.016515	0.013601	0.130090	0.177149	0.332805
e	0.136149	0.150307	0.006135	0.009438	0.024540	0.019565	0.022180	0.133554	0.157857	0.340256

Fig. 11. Empty tabulators images.

3   Results and Discussion

3.1   Combination LBP and Spectral Clustering

Case 1. We applied spectral clustering on all the features extracted by using the LBP. The objective was to know if with the features extracted using Local Binary pattern, the spectral clustering method would optimally distinguish the three categories of tabulators. We therefore want to obtain three distinct classes at the end of the algorithm. We chose a control parameter $\sigma = 1$. We compute the eigenvalues of our Laplacian matrix, represent them in ascending order by zooming in on the first 10 eigenvalues, as shown on Fig. 12. We used the second and the third eigenvectors v_2 and v_3 obtained from the second and the third smallest eigenvalues, thus, they became the vectors based on which we have applied the last step of the classification algorithm. The results are presented in the Table 1 and Fig. 13.

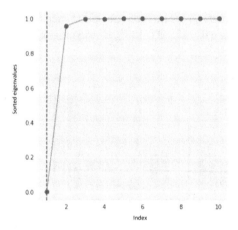

Fig. 12. Sorted-eigenvalues.

Table 1. Results of 3 class clustering of the 160 tabulator using LBP and GLCM.

LBP and Spectral Clustering			
Quality	True positive	False positive	Accuracy
Bad	52	1	98.11%
Empty	55	0	100%
Good	52	0	100%
GLCM and Spectral Clustering			
Quality	True positive	False positive	Accuracy
Bad	6	47	11.32
Empty	16	39	29.1
Good	35	17	67.31

Remark 1. Among the 53 bad tabulators, 52 were correctly predicted as really bad and only one could not be accurately classify, but considered as an empty tabulator. On the other hand, all 55 empty tabulators and 52 good ones were perfectly detected. The detection accuracy obtained by combining the Local Binary pattern and Spectral Clustering is of 99.375%.

Case 2. We cluster all the data in two groups. The maximum grouping is obtained thanks to the eigenvector provided by the second smallest eigenvalue of the Laplacian matrix. These results are presented in Fig. 14 and Table 2.

Case 3. Figure 15 is another way to perceive the density of each of our clusters. Other experiments were carried out not on combinations of pairs, good and empty tabulators, bad and empty tabulators. The respective results of these experiments have been reported in the Tables 4 and 3. The accuracy of detection for the pair (Good Empty) is 99.09% of 97% accuracy for (Bad, Empty) tabulators. Figure 16 represents the clusters obtained when we performed the experiment on the Good and Empty images.

Remark 2. From the clustering of all tabulators into two classes, it has been noticed that, bad tabulators and empty ones have been grouped together in the

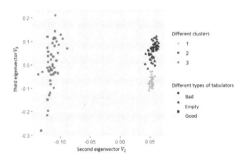

Fig. 13. Results of 3 class clustering of the 160 tabulator images.

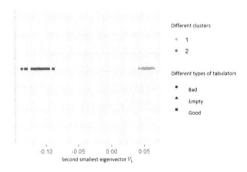

Fig. 14. Presentation of the two clusters.

Table 2. Results of the clustering LBP and GLCM: Components of each cluster when using two clusters.

LBP and Spectral Clustering			
Clusters	Bad	Empty	Good
1	53	55	0
2	0	1	51
GLCM and Spectral Clustering			
Clusters	Bad	Empty	Good
1	3	54	1
2	50	1	51

first cluster and the good tabulators have been grouped in the other cluster. Only one good tabulator was found to be wrongly classified and it was considered as an empty tabulator. Initially, due to the similarity between the histograms of the empty and faulty tabulators, it was hypothesized that they could be grouped together in the case where the target is to have two classes.

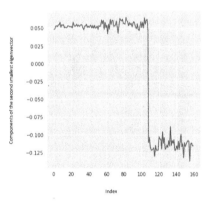

Fig. 15. Ranked elements of the second smallest eigenvector.

Fig. 16. LBP:Clustering of Good and Empty images

Table 3. Results of the detection obtained from Good and Empty tabulators.

LBP and Spectral Clustering			
Quality	True positive	False positive	Accuracy
Good	52	0	100
Empty	54	1	98.18
GLCM and Spectral Clustering			
Quality	True positive	False positive	Accuracy
Good	51	1	98.07
Empty	51	4	92.73

3.2 Combination GLCM and Spectral Clustering

Case 4. We applied the algorithm with a similar aim as in *Case 3*. From Table 1, we realized that Spectral clustering fails to correctly group the tabulators when we are using the features extracted from the co-occurrence matrices. While looking for two classes as presented in Table 2. It is observed that good and bad tabulators were clustered together and empty tabulators grouped in the other cluster. That is, the spectral algorithm was not able to differentiate the good tabulators from the bad ones but able to distinguish these two types of tabulators from the empty ones.

Table 4. Accuracy Results of the detection obtained from Bad and Empty tabulators using both LBP and GLCM.

LBP and Spectral Clustering			
Quality	True positive	False positive	Accuracy
Bad	52	1	98.11
Empty	53	2	96.36
GLCM and Spectral Clustering			
Quality	True positive	False positive	Accuracy
Bad	51	2	96.13
Empty	53	2	96.36

Case 5. In this case we applied the algorithm on the Bad Empty and tabulators with objective to get two classes. Results in Table 4 and Fig. 17 show that spectral clustering is performing well for the detection of bad and empty tabulators. It means that, features obtained from the co-occurrence matrices can be used under certain conditions in order to effectively address defect detection problems. The last experiment was done on the Good and Empty tabulators. As presented in that Table 3, the accuracy of detection of Good tabulators is bitter compared to that of Empty tabulators. Also the detection accuracy of 99.09% when using

Fig. 17. GLCM: Clustering of bad and Empty images.

LBP as feature extractor is greater than the accuracy of 95.4% when we use GLCM.

4   Conclusion

It has been shown that LBP gives more accurate results for defectuous items detection when combined with spectral clustering compared to GLCM. The main limitation of this work is the small size of the data available. For future work it is planned to explore the effectiveness of the proposed framework on a larger dataset. It is reported in the literature that, Local Directional Pattern performs better than LBP. It is also worth exploring the accuracy of the framework by replacing LBP by Local Directional Pattern.

References

1. Clausi, D.: An analysis of co-occurrence texture statistics as a function of grey level quantization. Can. J. Remote Sens. **28**, 45–62 (2002). https://doi.org/10. 5589/m02-004
2. Bartova, B., Bına, V., et al.: Early defect detection using clustering algorithms. Acta Oeconomica Pragensia **2019**(1), 3–20 (2019)
3. Clausi, D.: An analysis of co-occurrence texture statistics as a function of grey level quantization. Can. J. Remote Sens. **28**, 45–62 (2002)
4. Gebejes, A., Huertas, R.: Texture characterization based on grey-level co-occurrence matrix. Databases **9**(10), 375–378 (2013)
5. Huang, D., Shan, C., Ardabilian, M., Wang, Y., Chen, L.: Local binary patterns and its application to facial image analysis: a survey. IEEE Trans. Syst. Man Cybern. Part C (Appl. Rev.) **41**(6), 765–781 (2011)
6. Tabid, T., Kabir, M.H., Chae, O.: Facial expression recognition using local directional pattern (LDP). In: 2010 IEEE International Conference on Image Processing, pp. 1605–1608 (2010)
7. Lee, J.R., Gharan, S.O., Trevisan, L.: Multi-way spectral partitioning and higher-order Cheeger inequalities (2014)
8. Meila, M.: Spectral clustering: a tutorial for the 2010's (2016)
9. Mosorov, V., Tomczak, L.: Image texture defect detection method using fuzzy c-means clustering for visual inspection systems. Arab. J. Sci. Eng. **39**(4), 3013–3022 (2014)

10. Ojala, T., Pietikäinen, M., Mäenpää, T.: Gray scale and rotation invariant texture classification with local binary patterns. In: Vernon, D. (ed.) ECCV 2000. LNCS, vol. 1842, pp. 404–420. Springer, Heidelberg (2000). https://doi.org/10.1007/3-540-45054-8_27

11. Pietikainen, M., Hadid, A., Zhao, G., Ahonen, T.: Computer Vision Using Local Binary Patterns, vol. 40. Springer, Heidelberg (2011)

12. Prats-Montalbán, J.M., de Juan, A., Ferrer, A.: Multivariate image analysis: a review with applications. Chemometrics Intell. Lab. Syst. **107**(1), 1–23 (2011)

13. Von Luxburg, U.: A tutorial on spectral clustering. CoRR, abs/0711.0189 (2007)

14. Wang, S.: Image-based road terrain classification. In: Wang, S. (ed.) Road Terrain Classification Technology for Autonomous Vehicle. UST, pp. 55–68. Springer, Singapore (2019). https://doi.org/10.1007/978-981-13-6155-5_4

15. Yen, L., Fouss, F., Decaestecker, C., Francq, P., Saerens, M.: Graph nodes clustering with the sigmoid commute-time kernel: a comparative study. Data Knowl. Eng. **68**(3), 338–361 (2009)

16. Hang, X., You, Q.: An improved spectral clustering algorithm based on random walk. Front. Comput. Sci. China **5**, 268–278 (2011)

17. He, C., Zhang, Q., Qu, T., Wang, D., Liao, M.: Remote sensing and texture image classification network based on deep learning integrated with binary coding and Sinkhorn distance. J. Remote Sens. **11**, 2870 (2019). https://doi.org/10.3390/rs11232870

18. Singh, S., Srivastava, D., Agarwal, S.: GLCM and its application in pattern recognition, pp. 20–25 (2017). https://doi.org/10.1109/ISCBI.2017.8053537

19. Ren, S., He, K., Girshick, R., Sun, J.: Faster R-CNN: Towards Real-Time Object Detection with Region Proposal Networks. MIT Press, Cambridge (2015)

Artificial Intelligence Applications in Medicine

Help in the Early Diagnosis of Liver Cirrhosis Using a Learning Transfer Method

Ndeye Penda Diagne[1,2,3,4,5], Mamadou Lamine Mboup[1,2,3,4,5],
Mamadou Bousso[1,2,3,4,5(✉)], Boucar Ndong[1,2,3,4,5], Ousmane Sall[1,2,3,4,5],
and Marie Louise Bassene Dieme[1,2,3,4,5]

[1] Iba Der Thiam University, Thies, Senegal
{tgueye,mbousso}@univ-thies.sn, {rectorat,rectorat}@ucad.edu.sn,
eno.dakar@uvs.edu.sn
[2] Biophysical and Nuclear Medicine Laboratory, Cheikh Anta Diop University, Dakar-Liberté,
Senegal
[3] Gastro-Enterology Department, Aristide Le Dantec National University Hospital, Dakar,
Senegal
[4] Faculty of Science and Technics, Cheikh Anta Diop University, Dakar, Senegal
[5] Scientific, Technological and Digital Pole, Virtual University of Senegal – VUS, Diamniadio,
Senegal

Abstract. Liver cirrhosis is a disease that has a fairly high prevalence, affecting many people around the world. It's a silent disease. It progresses without symptoms to a stage of decompensated cirrhosis. Therefore, many patients are dying more and more because of this disease. It is therefore important to use data science and more particularly artificial intelligence in the diagnosis and identification of liver fibrosis for the rapid management of the patient thus improving his chances of survival.

In this perspective, this study proposes a tool to assist in the diagnosis of liver cirrhosis. To do this, an automatic transfer learning model was set up, which takes as input ultrasound images of the liver and gives as output the corresponding level of fibrosis or liver cirrhosis.

The solution provided uses convolutional neural networks. It is based on the ResNet50 model pre-trained on ImageNet data. We calculated the accuracy, the f1-score, the recall, the precision and the AUC.

The results obtained on the test set give an accuracy of 84%. The ROC curve shows an AUC of 0.85.

Keywords: Machine learning · Echography · Liver cirrhosis · Hepatitis · Deep learning · Diagnosis

1 Introduction

Hepatitis B is a viral infection that attacks the liver and can cause liver fibrosis if not treated effectively. According to the World Health Organization (WHO), 296 million

T. M. Ngatched Nkouatchah et al. (Eds.): PAAISS 2022, LNICST 459, pp. 169–180, 2023.
https://doi.org/10.1007/978-3-031-25271-6_11

people were living with chronic hepatitis B in 2019 and 1.5million people are infected with the virus each year. Also according to the WHO, in 2019, hepatitis B caused about 820000 deaths, mainly from cirrhosis or hepatocellular carcinoma (i.e., primary liver cancer).The diagnosis of liver cirrhosis due hepatitis B is a public health problem. It is very often diagnosed late.

The identification of cirrhosis of the liver was done, until now, by histology, the biopsy, which is an invasive examination. It is performed by inserting a needle into the patient's liver to collect a portion that is analyzed by pathologists.

In recent years, non-invasive markers to detect the level of fibrosis or cirrhosis of the liver have been developed. In addition, we can mention the Fibrotest which is a blood marker and the Fibroscan which measures the hardness of the liver or elasticity by sending shear waves. These tests are alternatives to biopsy, but they are not available to the overwhelming majority of the population.

In patients with Hepatitis B virus who are followed in the Gastroenterology Department, an abdominal ultrasound examination is prescribed periodically to monitor the liver for cirrhosis of the liver. The ultrasound examination is relatively accessible to the population. However, the resolution of ultrasound does not allow for early detection of the occurrence of cirrhosis. Thanks to an artificial intelligence application using machine learning, it is possible to work on improving the contribution of ultrasound in the diagnosis of liver cirrhosis.

The aim of this study was to set up a Deep Learning method allowing the classification of liver images according to the level of hepatic fibrosis (Fig. 1).

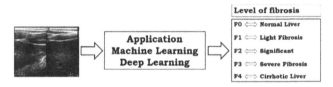

Fig. 1. Detection of fibrosis level by machine learning.

The proposed solution uses convolutional neural networks. They are widely used in the field of data science, for the classification of images obtained from ultrasound of patients' liver. Thus, we apply on our images the pre-trained ResNet-50 model on the ImageNet data. To measure the performance of our model on our data, we calculated accuracy, f1-score, recall, accuracy, and AUC. Afterwards, our results will be compared with those of the articles that dealt with similar subjects.

2 Methodologies

2.1 Presentation of the Data

Our data were collected in the gastroenterology department of Le Dantec Hospital with the permission of the department head and the consent of the patients. The physicians gave us the ultrasound, fibroscan and fibrotest examinations of the patients. Then the images of these examinations were scanned and stored in a database. Then, a pre-processing was performed on the data in order to recover the liver part. After that, the images were labeled and anonymized (removal of patient information). Then, with the filter class of the PIL library, a filter was applied to our images to reduce the noise present on them. In the end, we obtain a dataset composed of 118 liver images. As the images have different sizes, we resized them to 329 × 375 by cutting the part of the image that is not part of the liver (the skin). These data are then classified into five levels of fibrosis (F0: no fibrosis, F1: minimal fibrosis, F2: moderate fibrosis, F3: severe fibrosis and F4: cirrhosis). The following figure shows a sample image before and after processing (Fig. 2).

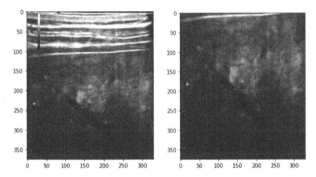

Fig. 2. Resized liver image (329 × 375) by cutting out the part that is not part of the liver

Since we are going to perform a binary classification, the data have been grouped into two classes (0 and 1). Class 0 corresponds to the non-diseased and class 1 to the patients with a significant level of fibrosis. Since the fibrosis images F1 and F2 are negligible compared to the F0 and F4 images, we grouped the F0 and F1 images into a single class (class 0). Thus, images F2 to F4 form class 1. The images of class 1 are thus seventy-one (approximately 60% of our data set) and the images of class 0 represent the remaining 40% (47 images). The following table presents a sample image of each class (Table 1).

Table 1. Sample of one image from each class

Image of the class 0	Image of the class 1
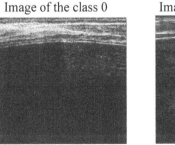	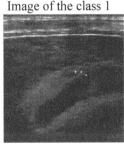

After labeling the data to classes 0 and 1 we mix and split them with the pytorch random_split function into three sets:

- The train set: 60%
- The validation set: 20% of the data
- The test set: 20%.

The training set will be used to train the model, the validation set will be used to set the parameters and hyper parameters and the test set will be used to evaluate the final model on data it has never seen.

The DataLoader class is then applied to each of our datasets to:

- Split the dataset by batch with the batch_size option. This specifies the number of data samples to use in an iteration and uses the iter() function to traverse each batch.
- Shuffle the data during batch loading with the shuffle option
- Load the data on the gpu with cuda to allow pytorch to work with the data on the gpu.

2.2 Deep Learning and Transfer Learning in Liver Image Classification

Deep learning is one of the most widely used branches of artificial intelligence in medical image classification. Indeed, image classification has seen a major advance in terms of performance thanks to the rise of convolutional neural networks. Thanks to these networks, the machine learns to recognize and classify images in a precise manner.

A convolutional neural network is a connection of artificial neurons inspired by biological neurons. It is generally composed of several layers, one part of which is used for convolution and another for classification.

Convolution is a technique that consists in applying a filter of size (x, x) on an image with a shift from left to right called "step".

A neural network consists of alternating blocks containing:

- Convolution layers in which a value of weight W_{ij} and bias b are associated with a pixel of the input image with the formula
  $W_{ij}*A_{ij} + b$.
- An activation in which an activation function that can be RELU, Sigmoid… is applied to the result of the convolution layer. The activation functions determine the output of the neural network.
- Pooling layers that reduce the size of the image to minimize the risk of overlearning.

The output of a block is then passed to a fully connected layer for classification. The classification error is calculated from a loss function (cross entropy, NLLLoss etc.). Neural networks work in an iterative way thanks to back-propagation and gradient descent. Back-propagation is the validation phase of the model, where the parameters are updated according to the error value (Fig. 3).

Thus, for our study, which aims to partition images of livers according to their fibrosis level, convolutional neural networks will be used.

Fig. 3. Convolutional neural network

To do this, we will perform transfer learning using the Resnet 50 model pretrained on ImageNet data. Deep residual networks or the popular ResNet-50 model is a convolutional neural network (CNN) of 50 layers deep. A residual neural network (ResNet) is a connection of artificial neurons (ANN) that stacks residual blocks on top of each other to form a network.

The architecture of the model is composed of:

- A convolution kernel size (7 × 7.64) and a stripe of size 2
- A max pooling layer of size 3 × 3
- 9 layers: three convolution layers with three alternating kernels of size (1 × 1, 64), (3 × 3, 64) and (1 × 1, 256) respectively
- 12 layers: four convolution layers composed of an alternation of three kernels respectively of size (1 × 1, 128), (3 × 3, 128) and (1 × 1, 512)
- 18 layers: six convolution layers each with three kernels of size (1 × 1, 256), (3 × 3, 256) and (1 × 1, 1024) respectively
- 9 layers: three convolution layers each with three alternating kernels of size (1 × 1, 512), (3 × 3, 512) and (1 × 1, 2048) respectively
- A fully connected layer containing 1000 nodes and at the end a softmax function.

To avoid a possible overlearning of our model, we used regularization techniques such as dropout, data augmentation, hyperparameters adjustment such as learning rate…

The dropout consists in randomly eliminating nodes from the network in order to reduce the over learning of the model. Data augmentation encompasses a suite of techniques that improve the size and quality of the training datasets so that better learning models can be created.

The learning rate is a hyper parameter which is usually between 0 and 1. It controls the speed of the descent of the error gradient. The lower the value, the slower we move along the downward slope.

To reduce the learning error and thus obtain an optimal model, we used the Adam optimizer.

Our model is progressively optimized by adjusting hyper-parameters such as learning rate, optimizer (adam, rmsprop, adamax etc.), batch size…

For this, the python library Tune was used. Tune allows, thanks to search algorithms, to find the best combination of hyper parameters for a given model. It relies on its *config* parameter which is a structure containing a list of values for each hyper parameter to select the best of them.

The functions of the transforms module of torchvision(Resize, RandomHorizontalFlip, RandomVerticalFlip, ToTensor, Normalize) are also used on our images in order to resize them, to apply a rotation to them, to convert them into tensor and to normalize them.

2.3   Statistical Analysis

Statistical methods were used to evaluate the performance of the learning model. Indeed, we calculated the accuracy, the sensitivity and the specificity in order to measure the efficiency of our model.

The accuracy represents an indicator of performance of a model which is obtained by taking the ratio between the well predicted data (true positives and true negatives) on the whole data. The precision is the ratio between the correctly predicted positive observations (true positives) and the total of the predicted positive observations (true positives and false positives).

Recall is the ratio between the correctly predicted positive observations (true positives) and all the observations of the real class (true positives and false negatives).

The f1-score represents the weighted average of precision and recall as the average is the average of precision and recall.

Other no less important performance indicators are sensitivity and specificity. Sensitivity is the probability that the model can visualize pathological signs in a confirmed patient. It is the ratio of patients with significant fibrosis who are well predicted (truly predicted) to all patients with significant fibrosis in reality. Specificity is the probability of concluding that there are no pathological signs in a healthy individual. It is the complement of the ratio of patients without significant fibrosis and incorrectly predicted (falsely predicted) on all patients without significant fibrosis. In addition, the area under the receiver operating characteristic curve (AUC) was used as an index of accuracy to assess the diagnostic performance of the model on test data.

3   Results

3.1   Results of the Classification

The application of deep learning methods on our dataset allowed us to set up a learning model for the classification of liver images. Thus, the model is now able, thanks to the training phase, to recognize the corresponding level of liver fibrosis. The results of classification are detailed in the following Table 2.

Table 2. Results of the classification of some images

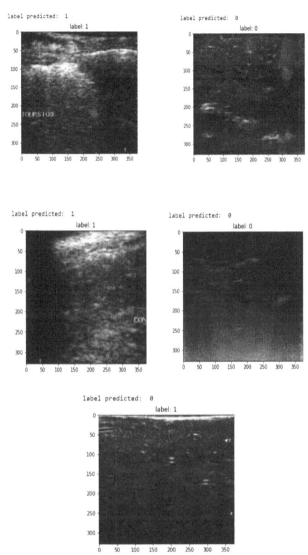

Above we have examples of classification results of liver images by our learning model. We have well predicted labels for classes 0 and 1 and poorly predicted labels. We can also see below the table that groups the set of predicted labels against the true labels for our test set (Table 3).

To get an overall view of the learning quality of the model, we plotted the evolution of the error on the train and validation data as a function of time (Fig. 4).

Table 3. Labels predicted in relation to real labels

Test Accuracy of the model: 84.0 %

	labels	predicted
0	1	1
1	0	0
2	1	1
3	0	1
4	1	1
5	0	0
6	1	1
7	0	0
8	1	0
9	1	1
10	1	1
11	1	0
12	0	0
13	1	1
14	1	0
15	1	1
16	1	1
17	0	0
18	1	1
19	1	1
20	0	0
21	0	0
22	1	1
23	1	1
24	0	0

The curve shows that, on both data sets, the learning error decreases until it reaches a certain threshold (about 0.001). This decrease in error shows that the model is learning well to classify our data.

After calculating the performance metrics, we had an accuracy of 84%, 73% accuracy of the model on class 0 and 93% accuracy on class 1, for the recall we obtain 0.89 for class 0 and 0.81 for class 1. Class 0 and 0.81 for class 1 and finally concerning the F1-score we have respectively 0.8 and 0.87 for classes 0 and 1 (Table 4).

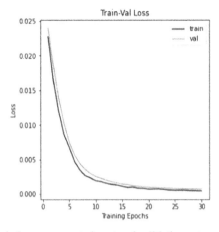

Fig. 4. Error evolution curve on train set and validation set according to epochs

Table 4. Model performance indicators on test data

	precision	recall	f1-score	support
0	0.73	0.89	0.80	9
1	0.93	0.81	0.87	16
accuracy			0.84	25
macro avg	0.83	0.85	0.83	25
weighted avg	0.86	0.84	0.84	25

3.2 Confusion Matrix

The confusion matrix or contingency table is a tool for measuring the performance of a model. It is obtained by comparing predicted classes to real classes and thus measures the accuracy of model predictions.

In our case, we obtained the following confusion matrix (Table 5):

Table 5. Confusion matrix

	Real Significant Fibrosis	Real Not Significant Fibrosis
Predicted Significant Fibrosis	**13** *True Positives*	**3** *False Positives*
Predicted Non Significant Fibrosis	**1** *False Negatives*	**8** *True Negatives*

Class 0 corresponds to the non-diseased and class 1 to the patients with a significant level of fibrosis.

Through the confusion or contingency matrix, we can see that we have 8 true negatives (i.e., images of class 0 well predicted), 1 false negative (an image of class 0 badly predicted), 3 false positives (images predicted as being part of class 1 which are not) and 13 true positives (images of class 1 well predicted).

3.3 ROC Curve

The ROC curve is a graph showing the performance of a classification model at all classification thresholds. It allows us to evaluate the accuracy of the predictions of a model by plotting the probability curve of true positives versus false positives at various threshold values.

For our study the ROC curve obtained allows us to have an AUC (Area Under the Curve) equal to 0.85. The area under the curve (AUC) is the measure of the ability of a classifier to distinguish classes. The higher the AUC, the better the performance of the model in distinguishing classes. Thus, we can say that our model classifies our test images well at 85% (Fig. 5).

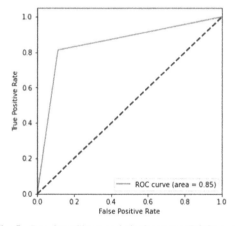

Fig. 5. Receiver Characteristic Operator (ROC) curve

4 Discussion

4.1 Discussion Following the Results of Other Models (VGG16, AlexNet, GoogleNet)

Convolutional neural network models differ due to their complexity and the size of the filters, which means that the accuracy on the same data can change from one model to another. Therefore, in order to detect the best model, it is necessary to train our dataset with other models and to compare the results obtained with those of the Resnet50 model.

- Vgg16: This model is made of convolutional neural networks with a depth of sixteen layers. It uses a filter of size 3 × 3 with a stride equal to 1. Using this model on our images gave an accuracy of 80%.
- AlexNet: The Alexnet model proposes an eight-layer network (five convolution layers and three fully connected layers) and uses a filter of size 11x11 in its first layer. This model classifies our liver images with an accuracy of 76%.
- GoogleNet or inception v1 is a convolutional neural network model of twenty-two layers deep. The main difference in this architecture is that it does not use multiple dense layers but rather uses clustering layers with small filters. It has filters ranging from 1 × 1 to 5 × 5. The classification of our images from this model is 84% accurate with an AUC equal to 0.83.

The results of the application of these models on our dataset show us that the Resnet50 model offers a better accuracy on the classification of liver images. Indeed, the latter has a higher accuracy than the models mentioned above except for the Googlenet model which offers the same accuracy but with a lower AUC.

4.2   Discussion Following the Results of the Literature Articles

In this section, we will compare our results with those obtained in the literature. Indeed, Lee et al. [1] aimed to set up a deep convolutional neural network for predicting the level of fibrosis from liver ultrasound images. Their data was composed of four classes (F0, F1, F2.3, F4). The diagnostic performance of the algorithm is validated on a set of internal tests carried out on 266 patients with 300 images and a set of external tests on 572 patients with 1232 images. The Precision of the model obtained is 83.5% and 76.4% respectively on the set of internal and external tests. The area under the data curve is between 0.857 and 0.90.

Studies by Roi Anteby et al. [2] evaluating the application of deep learning to the classification of liver fibrosis using non-invasive imaging methods used sixteen articles published between 2017 and 2020. In total, 40,405 radiological images were analysed in 15 853 patients. All 10 articles use ultrasound images with AUROCs of 0.85 to 0.97 for classification of significant fibrosis, 0.93 to 0.98 for advanced fibrosis, and 0.93 to 0.97 for cirrhosis. Three studies had a precision that ranged from 63% to 100%.

Huang et al. [3], Yasaka et al. [4], and Hectors et al. [5] worked on the classification of hepatic fibrosis using magnetic resonance (MR) images and had as results the AUROCs for fibrosis stages F2, F3 and F4 of 0.85, 0.84 and 0.84, respectively. These results are also comparable to ours.

Still in the same vein, Kagadis et al. [6] carried out similar work and aimed to propose appropriate deep learning schemes for the diagnosis and evaluation of the progress of chronic liver diseases. In this work, they used five learning models (AlexNET, GoogleNET, VGG16, ResNET50 and DensNET221). All gratings achieved maximum average precisions ranging from 87.2% to 97.4% and area under receiver operating characteristic curves (AUC) ranging from 0.979 to 0.990. The ResNet50 and DenseNet201 models have the best average performance compared to other networks.

Their results show that the best overall precision performances are estimated at 91.25% and 94.65% for fibrosis for the combinations F0 or F1/F2/F3 or F4 and F0 or F1/F2/F3/F4 (F $\geq$ F1) were performed by ResNet50-FT. Then, DenseNet201-FT achieved the best performance with an accuracy of 87.2% for all classifications (F0 or F1 or F2 or F3 or F4) using augmentation. For the combinations F0/F1/F2 or F3/F4 (F $\geq$ F3) and F0/F1/F2/F3 or F4 (F $=$ F4), the most significant results were achieved by GoogLeNet-FT (95.5%) and VGG16-FT (97.4%). On the other hand, the best AUC (Area Under the Curve) are obtained through the ResNET50 and DenseNet201 models.

These results show that the studies [2] and [6], confirm the similarity of our results with those found in the literature, to a certain extent, despite a relatively low amount of data. They also show that Resnet50 residual networks performed very well. So, a larger data set would help achieve better results.

5   Conclusion

In this article, we have proposed a solution to help with the early diagnosis of cirrhosis of the liver. As cirrhosis is a dangerous disease that is often identified late, it becomes important to find a way to detect this liver anomaly quickly. To do this, artificial intelligence methods, more precisely convolutional neural networks, have been used for the identification of livers affected by fibrosis from ultrasound images. In our study, we have liver images divided into two classes (0 and 1). To classify these images, we used a transfer learning model, ResNET50, pre-trained on the data from imageNET data. The error rate, when trained, decreased with time, which shows that the model learned well to classify the images according to their fibrosis levels. This model, despite the small number of our data set, showed its performance with an accuracy of 84% and an AUC of 0.85. To confirm the efficiency of our model, we compared it with those of some articles dealing with the same subject. This comparison showed us that the results of our learning model were good but that they would be better if we had a larger data set. In this perspective, a data collection would be necessary to feed our database and thus improve our learning model. It would also be relevant to detect precisely the localization of fibrosis in the liver image to allow medical specialists to have a global view of the affected areas and thus be able to treat the disease efficiently.

References

1. Lee, J.H., et al.: Deep learning with ultrasonography: automated classification of liver fibrosis using a deep convolutional neural network. Eur. Radiol. **30**(2), 1264–1273 (2020)
2. Anteby, R., et al.: Deep learning for noninvasive liver fibrosis classification: a systematic review. Liver Int. **41**, 2269–2278 (2021)
3. Huang, Q., Zhang, F., Li, X.: Machine learning in ultrasound computer-aided diagnostic systems: a survey. BioMed Res. Int. **2018** (2018)
4. Yasaka, K., Akai, H., Kunimatsu, A., Abe, O., Kiryu, S.: Liver fibrosis: deep convolutional neural network for staging by using gadoxetic acid–enhanced hepatobiliary phase MR images. Radiology **287**(1), 146–155 (2018)
5. Hectors, S.J., et al.: Fully automated prediction of liver fibrosis using deep learning analysis of gadoxetic acid–enhanced MRI. Eur. Radiol. **31**(6), 3805–3814 (2020). https://doi.org/10.1007/s00330-020-07475-4
6. Kagadis, G.C., et al.: Deep learning networks on chronic liver disease assessment with fine-tuning of shear wave elastography image sequences. Phys. Med. Biol. **65**(21), 215027 (2020)

Automatic Detection of COVID-19 Using Ensemble Transfer Learning Based on Lung CT Scans

Ricardo Pillay[1], Serestina Viriri[1,2(✉)] , and Reolyn Heymann[2]

[1] School of Mathematics, Statistics and Computer Science,
University of KwaZulu-Natal, Durban, South Africa
[2] Department of Electrical and Electronic Engineering Science,
University of Johannesburg, Johannesburg, South Africa
viriris@ukzn.ac.za, rheymann@uj.ac.za

Abstract. In order to curb the rapid spread of COVID-19, early and accurate detection is required. Computer Tomography (CT) scans of the lungs can be utilized for accurate COVID-19 detection because these medical images highlight COVID-19 infection with high sensitivity. Transfer learning was implemented on six state-of-the-art Convolutional Neural Networks (CNNs). From these six CNNs, the three with the highest accuracies (based on empirical experiments) were selected and used as base learners to produce hard voting and soft voting ensemble classifiers. These three CNNs were identified as Vgg16, EfficientNetB0 and EfficientNetB5. This study concludes that the soft voting ensemble classifier, with base learners Vgg16 and EfficientNetB5, outperformed all other ensemble classifiers with different base learners and individual models that were investigated. The proposed classifier achieved a new state-of-the-art accuracy on the SARS-CoV-2 dataset. The accuracy obtained from this framework was 98.13%, the recall was 98.94%, the precision was 97.40%, the specificity was 97.30% and the F1 score was 98.16%.

Keywords: Deep learning · Convolutional neural network · Transfer learning · Hard voting · Soft voting

1 Introduction

The coronavirus disease 19 (COVID-19) is a highly transmittable and pathogenic viral infection caused by severe acute respiratory syndrome coronavirus 2 (SARS-CoV-2), which emerged in Wuhan, China and spread around the world [7]. It is a new strain of coronavirus that has never been identified in humans before [6] which has resulted in approximately 4 million deaths worldwide [8]. Besides being highly transmittable, this virus is also able to mutate and thus has resulted in many strains of the same virus. Such strains include, the alpha, beta and theta strain. A characteristic symptom of this disease in early stages is a dry cough.

© ICST Institute for Computer Sciences, Social Informatics and Telecommunications Engineering 2023
Published by Springer Nature Switzerland AG 2023. All Rights Reserved
T. M. Ngatched Nkouatchah et al. (Eds.): PAAISS 2022, LNICST 459, pp. 181–204, 2023.
https://doi.org/10.1007/978-3-031-25271-6_12

Additionally, this disease also has symptoms such as fever, headache, tiredness, sore throat etc. For this reason, it is easy to mistake COVID-19 for the common cold. Furthermore, it is also possible that certain people may be infected with COVID-19 and can spread it to others, but show no symptoms. They are known as "carriers" of the disease. In order to "flatten the curve" and reduce mortality rates, it is imperative for diagnosis to be done accurately and swiftly, as soon as an individual experiences symptoms of COVID-19, so they may self-isolate.

The "gold standard" for COVID-19 detection is the PCR (Polymerase chain reaction) swab test [11]. The standard PCR test involves obtaining respiratory samples, from a person, using a nasopharyngeal swab, however nasal swabs or sputum samples may also be used. A substance called DNA polymerase is added to these samples in a laboratory to replicate any viral mRNA that may be present. This allows for detection of the presence of the COVID-19 viral mRNA, which will be detectable in the body before antibodies form or symptoms of the disease are present. This means these tests show whether someone has the virus very early on in their illness. They, however, have a recall rate of 71% and can produce false negatives up to 30% of the time. A person must also wait for at least 24 h to get their test result.

In an attempt to alleviate such issues with the PCR test, radiologists make use of medical images such as X-rays and CT scans of the lungs, to provide a clinical diagnosis ahead of the actual PCR test or to perform a secondary check to confirm and validate results after the PCR test. X-rays are cheaper, but they have been shown to not be very suitable for early COVID-19 detection, since they show lesser sensitivity to areas that highlight COVID-19 infection [10]. CT scans, on the other hand, display areas that highlight COVID-19 infection of the lungs with high sensitivity and specificity [9]. When compared to a CT scan of a COVID-19 negative individual, a COVID-19 positive CT scan exhibits hazy increased ground-glass opacities, with preservation of bronchial and vascular margins [9]. This manual diagnosis of medical images, however, is time-consuming and is prone to human error.

Computer-vision and machine learning approaches may be used in order to automate and improve on the manual medical image diagnosis process. As of recently, there have been multiple studies carried out in this domain with promising results. In particular, deep learning methods [14] are being intensively investigated and considered, in order to develop a reliable and accurate framework for automatic detection of COVID-19. Due to the lack of available medical image data, researchers have employed transfer learning of state-of-the-art CNNs [15]. These CNNs are pre-trained on large datasets, such as "ImageNet" [24] and their knowledge obtained is transferred over into the domain of detecting COVID-19 from medical images. Although transfer learning methods in this domain has shown favourable results, there have been attempts where ensemble methods [12] have been used to further improve the predictive ability of transfer learning models.

In this paper, we consider 6 CNNs as candidate base learners to produce ensemble classifiers. These are Vgg16 [16], Vgg19 [16], EfficientNetB0 [17], EfficientNetB5 [17], DenseNet121 [18] and DenseNet201 [18]. After transfer learning and training is performed, it was found that Vgg16, EfficientNetB0 and EfficientNetB5 had the highest accuracies when applied to the test set. In order to further improve the accuracy obtained, these 3 CNN architectures are then used as base learners to produce a framework for COVID-19 detection from CT scans. Both soft voting and hard voting approaches are explored [13]. The aims are to determine which ensemble approach is more suitable, which base learners produce the best ensemble classifier, to show that ensemble can further improve the performance of the individual CNNs and to prove that these deep learning approaches are more accurate than manual laboratory tests (PCR). On the other hand, this investigation is being carried out primarily to validate results achieved by similar studies that used ensemble methods for COVID-19 detection and possibly improve on the results obtained.

The rest of this paper is organized as follows: Sect. 2 is a review of related works, Sect. 3 outlines the methods and techniques used in this study, Sect. 4 gives the final results of this investigation, Sect. 5 is the conclusion and the last section is the bibliography.

2   Related Works

The use of Computer Vision for medical image diagnosis and detection dates back to a study done in the 1960s [23]. There has been much progress and advancement over the years, with many researchers reporting better accuracies than manual approaches.

The investigations, carried out for computer-aided COVID-19 detection, use X-rays or CT-scans. X-rays have higher availability and are cheaper, however CT scans are more sensitive and specific within the domain of COVID-19 detection. Most of the recent studies published on COVID-19 detection make use of transfer learning of state-of-the-art CNNs and more recent works make use of ensemble to improve accuracy. An overview of related and recent studies is captured in this literature review.

Chowdhury, et al. [1] performed a study on ensemble of deep convolutional neural networks (CNN) based on their newly proposed EfficientNet, namely the ECOVNet, to detect COVID-19 using a large chest X-ray dataset. In addition, a visualization technique was used to highlight regions of interest, where COVID-19 effects on the lungs were evident. A challenge faced during this study was the need for massive amounts of X-ray samples for training of the transfer learning models in order to produce a truly accurate framework. This resulted in lengthy training times. The authors claimed that the ensemble method (especially soft ensemble) can greatly improve prediction performance with 97% accuracy, while the accuracy and recall rate of detecting COVID-19 was 100%.

A research article developed by Lawton and Viriri [2] suggests that COVID-19 could be detected from CT scans of lungs, using transfer learning. Pre-trained Convoluted Neural Networks would be retrained using a COVID-19 lung CT scan dataset and the best model would be chosen as a framework for COVID-19 detection. The major benefit is the production of very accurate, high-performance models, even though there is limited training data. Furthermore, this study investigated the effects of standard Histogram Equalization (HE) and Contrast Limited Adaptive Histogram Equalization (CLAHE), on the performance of transfer learning models, within the domain of COVID-19 detection from CT scans. The results of this study indicate that the VGG-19 model, which is retrained using a dataset of CLAHE CT scans, had the highest accuracy of 95.75%. The results of this study do not provide a definite answer whether histogram equalization techniques have an overall effect on the performance across all the transfer learning models used, as some show better performance with CLAHE while others perform better without CLAHE.

Gianchandani, et al. [3] proposed the rapid diagnosis of COVID-19 using ensemble of transfer learning models from chest radiographic images (X-rays). The 2 models VGG16 and ResNet152V2 are used to produce an ensemble model. This approach has the advantage of being able to differentiate between COVID-19, viral pneumonia and bacterial pneumonia. It achieved a 99.21% accuracy for classifying between COVID-19, bacterial pneumonia and viral pneumonia and a 95.15% accuracy for classifying if someone is COVID-19 positive or COVID-19 negative. An issue with this approach is a limited patient dataset was available, and it impacted the training and learning capacity of the models investigated, with regard to finding the optimal features to extract. This is due to the fact that X-rays are less sensitive to COVID-19-related visible features on the lungs.

Gifani, Shalbaf and Vafaeezadeh [4] have suggested an article detailing the automatic detection of COVID-19, using ensemble of transfer learning with deep convolutional neural networks based on CT scans. 15 existing and pre-trained (on the ImageNet dataset) transfer learning models were investigated and used in this study, namely: EfficientNets (0–5), Inception_resnet_v2, InceptionV3, NAS-NetLarge, NASNetMobile, ResNet50, Xception, DenseNet121, SesResnet50 and ResNext50. These 15 models were fine-tuned to the target task of detecting COVID-19 from CT scans, by only using the convolutional part of each model and adding a global average pooling layer, followed by the final classification layer, on top of the last convolutional layer. Data augmentation was also applied to increase the training dataset size, to prevent overfitting. Upon testing these 15 pre-trained models, EfficientNetB0 performed the best with 82% accuracy, 84.7% precision and 82.2% recall. 5 of these models (EfficientNetB0, EfficientNetB3, EfficientNetB5, Inception_resnet_v2 and Xception) were ensembled, based on majority voting. This ensembled framework has an accuracy of 85%, precision of 85.7% and recall of 85.2%. The accuracy of this approach could be far higher if the amount of training data is increased. This approach, however, does lend validity to the concept that an ensemble of models will result in better accuracy than if an individual model is used.

Kundu, et al. [19] proposed a new framework called "ET-NET", which is an ensemble of transfer learning models for prediction of COVID-19 through chest CT-scans. The CNNs used for transfer learning were Inception v3, ResNet34 and DenseNet201. A bagging soft voting ensemble method was used to create the framework, which produced an accuracy of 97.73%. 5-fold cross validation was used to measure the performance of the framework. This study emphasised that the use of a bagging ensemble over boosting was important because bagging helps reduce overfitting, while boosting increases overfitting. It is also important to note that the CNN models used for the ensemble, were pre-selected based on model quality and not by empirical experiments. This study concludes that their proposed ET-NET is better than the standard PCR testing. ET-NET has a few limitations, however, because a few poor quality and high contrast CT scans were classified incorrectly. It was also not able to predict an early COVID-19 positive case, since ground-glass opacities had not developed in the lungs as yet. The researchers of this paper aim to use more complicated ensemble techniques in the future to alleviate these minor errors in ET-NET's predictive ability.

Islam, et al. [20] proposed a Vgg19 and RNN hybrid model for predicting COVID-19 from chest X-rays. The classifier was able to classify an X-ray image as normal, COVID-19 or COVID-19 pneumonia. They also used a Grad-CAM technique to visualize specific regions of the X-rays that highlight COVID-19 infection. The dataset used in this study was put together by the authors because current datasets with X-rays for COVID-19 detection are unbalanced. They applied pre-processing techniques to the images as well to mitigate the inconsistency in these images. The extracted feature maps of an X-ray scan, from the convolutional layers of Vgg19, were fed into a single layer RNN which classified the X-ray into normal, COVID-19 or COVID-19 pneumonia. The results achieved in this study are outstanding with a 99.9% accuracy, 99.9% AUC, 99.8% recall and 99.8% F1-Score. The limitations of this approach are that the number of image samples was not large enough to properly validate the system. In addition, the system only works with the posterior-anterior view of the chest X-ray and no other views of the X-rays. Finally, the performance of the system is not compared with the performance of radiologists.

A study by Ardakani, et al. [21] investigated the performance of 10 different CNN architectures on the detection of COVID-19 from CT scans. The CT scans for all patients were converted to gray scale before training occurred. This study showed that ResNet101 was the best classifier for COVID-19 detection, from the all the 10 CNNs, since it had not only a 99.4% accuracy but also a recall of 100% (0% false negative rate). This study also introduced a comparison between the performance of the proposed classifier and the performance of an experienced radiologist on the same CT scan images. The machine classifier outperformed the moderate performance of the radiologist, who had an accuracy of 86.27% and an 89.21% recall. The study concluded that this approach is suitable as an additional method to diagnose COVID-19 from CT scans in radiology departments. The stated performance of this machine classifier in the real world is not guaranteed however because the number of CT scan images it is tested on only 102 (Fig. 1).

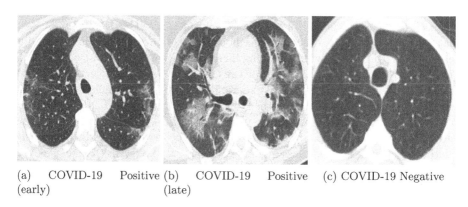

(a)   COVID-19   Positive (b)   COVID-19   Positive (c) COVID-19 Negative
(early)   (late)

Fig. 1. Examples of CT scan images from the SARs-CoV-2 CT Dataset [5]

3   Methods and Techniques

3.1   Dataset

The SARS-CoV-2 CT dataset was chosen for training and evaluating model performance. Examples of images from this dataset are shown in Fig. 2. This is a publicly available dataset which can be downloaded on Kaggle.com which was developed by Soares, et al. [5]. This dataset consists of, 2482 CT scan images of patient's lungs in Brazil. It has 1252 COVID-19 positive CT scan images and 1230 COVID-19 negative images. To combat the issue of overfitting, due to a relatively small dataset, it was initially proposed to use image augmentation. The images would have been rotated randomly, left or right, with an angle of $40°$, randomly translated horizontally or vertically by a factor of 0.2 or randomly flipped horizontally. However, it was found that image augmentation prevented the models from learning from the dataset and, as a result, the models were not able to converge to a global minimum loss. Thus, a decision was made to not use image augmentation. The dataset was split in the ratio of 70:15:15 for training, validating and testing, respectively. Initially, it was proposed to use a ratio of 60:20:20, however it was found that an extra 10% of training data greatly improved the individual model's performance and in turn improved the ensemble framework's results. The process of data set splitting was automated by utilizing the split_folder library.

3.2   Image Pre-processing

The CNNs used in this study were pre-trained on 224×224 resized images from the Imagenet dataset [24], and hence their weights have been adjusted to work optimally with 224×224 images. Therefore, every image in the SARS-CoV-2 dataset has been resized to a length and width of 224×224. Initially, it was proposed that Contrast Limited Adaptive Histogram Equalization (CLAHE) would be applied to the images before training. However, as the study in [2] states,

CLAHE is not proven to improve accuracy of detection of CT-scans by state-of-the-art CNNs. Through investigation, it was found that CLAHE negatively affected the performance of EfficientNetB0 and EfficientNetB5.

3.3   Training Process

Training of the individual CNN models were done as follows:

Batch Size. CT scan images from the training set were given as input to a model in batches of size 16.

Output Layer Activation Function. Each model produced 2 softmax probability outputs. Softmax outputs a probability value between 0 and 1 for each class in the prediction scenario. The class with the highest predicted probability is the predicted class of the model. Softmax is required for the soft voting ensemble technique as it makes use of probabilities for class predictions over a distinct, direct class prediction. This activation function works together with the categorical cross entropy loss function, since this loss function requires class probabilities as well. The softmax formula is given below.

$$softmax(x)_i = \frac{exp(x_i)}{\sum_j exp(x_j))}$$

Loss Function. The Categorical Cross Entropy loss function was used to determine the error. Categorical cross entropy is a loss function used for multi-class predictions. It returns a value that approaches 1 but never reaches 1. The higher the probability for a certain class prediction, the lower the loss that is produced. This means that correct classifications will have much lower loss than incorrect classifications. The formula for categorical cross entropy is given below. $y_{o,c}$ is a switch which is 0 if the class c is the correct classification for observation o. p is the predicted probability of observation o being in class c.

$$-\sum_{c=1}^{M} y_{o,c} log(p_{o,c})$$

Optimizer. The Adam optimizer used this error to update the neural network's weights through backpropagation, using a learning rate of 0.001. The Adam optimizer has the benefits of RMSprop and Stochastic Gradient Descent + Momentum. It allows for a smooth path to the global minimum loss while also being an efficient algorithm. It does not require tiny learning rates in order to converge to the global minimum. The weight update formulae are given below. β is the momentum, θ is the differential gradient for the current weight and N is the learning rate. w_t is the current weight, w_{t+1} is the updated weight, and Δw_t is the change in current weight.

$$v_t = \beta_1 v_{t-1} + (1 - \beta_1)\theta_t^2$$

$$s_t = \beta_2 s_{t-1} + (1 - \beta_2)\theta_t^2$$

$$\Delta w_t = -N(\frac{v_t}{\sqrt{s_t + \epsilon}})\theta_t$$

$$w_{t+1} = w_t + \Delta w_t$$

Number of Epochs. Training was performed over 50 epochs for each model.

Hyper-parameter Tuning. After each epoch, validation accuracy was calculated in order to determine if training needs to be stopped early, so hyperparameters can be adjusted. Learning rate reduction was carried out during training, where the learning rate was reduced by a rate of 0.2 if the validation loss was not improving every 2 epochs. Early stopping was also used to prevent the model from becoming worse and overfitting after it reached it's global minimum loss. This means that the model's training was stopped after 5 epochs if validation accuracy was not improving. The best weights obtained during training were retained and loaded when a model's training was stopped early. This was implemented via tensorflow.keras callbacks.

This process of training was implemented via the tensorflow libraries.

3.4   Transfer Learning

In order to fine-tune these models to the task of predicting COVID-19 from CT-scans, each of these models were used to produce 3 new transfer learning models as follows:

Convolutional Bases. Convolutional bases were retained and were made frozen (untrainable). This was done, so we could make use of the pre-trained weights of these CNNs.

Hidden Layer. A hidden layer of 256 neurons, using the ReLU activation function, was added on top of the convolutional bases to allow for the models to receive training as the top convolutional layers are frozen. The ReLU activation function is used because it has the benefit of lower computational overhead. The ReLU activation function is given below. z is the input given to the neuron.

$$ReLU(z) = max(0, z)$$

Dropout. A dropout with a probability of 0.3 was placed between this hidden layer and the output layer. This dropout randomly ignores certain neurons in the fully connected layer. These neurons are not considered on the forward pass through the neural network. They also receive no weight updates when back-propagation occurs. This assists with preventing overfitting to training data as well as speeds up training.

Softmax Output Layer. Finally, a softmax layer with 2 output neurons were added on top of this model.

This process of transfer learning was implemented via the tensorflow libraries.

3.5   Convolutional Neural Network Selection

VggNet [16], DenseNet [18] and EfficientNet [17] appear to be the most promising architectures for accurate prediction of COVID-19 from medical images. Two notably promising models from each CNN architecture were selected. These are Vgg16, Vgg19, EfficientNetB0, EfficientNetB5, DenseNet121 and DenseNet201. Each model was subjected to transfer learning (see Sect. 3.4) and then training (see Sect. 3.3). These trained transfer learning models were then individually tested on the test set. The accuracy results are recorded in Table 1 below.

Table 1. CNN accuracy comparisons from empirical experiments

Architecture type	CNN name	Test accuracy
VggNet	Vgg16	96,26%
VggNet	Vgg19	94,15%
EfficientNet	EfficientNetB0	95,45%
EfficientNet	EfficientNetB5	96,26%
DenseNet	DenseNet121	89,03%
DenseNet	DenseNet201	93,04%

From the table above, we see that Vgg16, EfficientNetB0 and EfficientNetB5 had the greatest test accuracies and thus were selected as base learners to create the ensemble framework. It is not desirable to use many models because having too many predictors can greatly increase the computational requirements for the ensemble predictor. The 3 CNN architectures selected will be discussed below,

Vgg16. This architecture consists of 16 convolutional layers of 3×3 filter with a stride of 1. In between every few convolutional layers, there is a max pooling layer of 2×2 filter with stride of 2. Finally, it has 2 fully connected layers at the end, which is followed by a softmax output layer. This architecture has a strong focus on convolution filtering over numerous hyperparameters. This means this architecture is primarily focused on extracting highly abstract features from images. This is important because it means this architecture will be able to differentiate between borderline class cases, such as differentiating between early COVID-19 positive cases and COVID-19 negative cases. The layered architecture for Vgg16 is shown in Fig. 2.

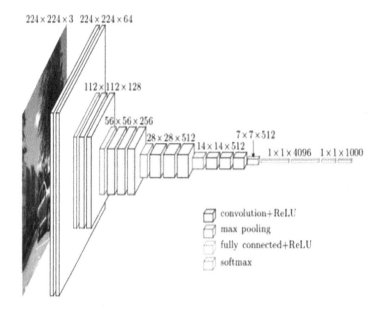

Fig. 2. Vgg16 architecture [16]

EfficientNetB0 and EfficientNetB5. EfficientNetB0 consists of an initial 3×3 convolutional layer, which is then followed by a series of MBConv blocks that outputs a final feature map. EfficientNetB5 follows the same structure, however, it has a far larger number of MBConv sub-blocks and trainable parameters. The use of MBConv blocks reduces the overall number of operations performed as well as the size of the entire model. The layered architecture for EfficientnetB0 and is shown in Fig. 3.

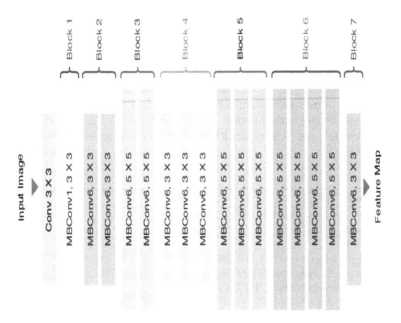

Fig. 3. EfficientNetB0 architecture [17]

EfficientNet architectures implement the process of model scaling, whereby model depth, width and image input resolution is scaled by a constant coefficient to improve the performance of the architecture. This process of scaling allows these architectures to adapt to different problem domains and still perform excellently. This means these architectures will perform well even in this problem domain of COVID-19 detection from CT scans. The equations for model scaling are given below. $\emptyset$ is the model scaling coefficient.

$$depth : d = \alpha^{\emptyset}$$

$$width : w = \beta^{\emptyset}$$

$$resolution : r = \gamma^{\emptyset}$$

$$s.t : \alpha.\beta^2.\gamma^2 \approx 2$$

$$\alpha \geq 1, \beta \geq 1, \gamma \geq 1$$

3.6 Ensemble

Each transfer learning model was used to independently predict the COVID-19 diagnosis of the CT scans in the test set. The softmax layer produced 2 probability outputs for each image - the first being the probability of a COVID-19 positive case and the second being the probability of a COVID-19 negative case.

Soft Voting. To determine the soft voting [22] prediction, the probabilities for a COVID-19 positive case were added for each model, and divided by the number of models used in the ensemble to get the average probability of a CT scan being classified as a positive case. A similar approach was taken to determine the average probability of a CT scan being classified as a negative case. These 2 average probabilities were compared, and the class that was the output of the ensemble, was the one with a higher average probability. This was done for each CT scan in the test set. Algorithm 1 below shows the process of determining the soft vote prediction.

Algorithm 1. Soft Voting for a single instance

$baseClassifierArr \leftarrow loadBaseClassifiers()$
$sumPos \leftarrow 0$
$sumNeg \leftarrow 0$
for $Model\ m$: $baseClassifierArr$ **do**
    $X \leftarrow m.getProbabilityCOVIDPos()$
    $Y \leftarrow m.getProbabilityCOVIDNeg()$
    $sumPos \leftarrow sumPos + X$
    $sumNeg \leftarrow sumNeg + Y$
end for
$avgPos \leftarrow sumPos/baseClassifierArr.size()$
$avgNeg \leftarrow sumNeg/baseClassifierArr.size()$
if $avgPos ¿= avgNeg$ **then**
    return COVID-19 Positive
else
    return COVID-19 Negative
end if

Hard Voting. To determine the hard voting [22] prediction, the predictions from each model for each CT scan were first determined. This was the class that had the highest probability output. The number of each class was counted and the class that was predicted the most, from all predictions, was selected as the ensemble framework prediction. In the case where the number of base classifiers are even, and the base classifiers produce an equal number of COVID-19 positive vote(s) and COVID-19 negative vote(s), then the ensemble prediction was selected as COVID-19 positive. In this case where the models have not come to majority decision, it is better to classify a person as COVID-19 positive than negative, since there is still a chance the person has the virus, according to the base classifiers. Algorithm 2 below shows the process for obtaining the hard vote prediction.

Figure 4 summarizes the entire methodology used to obtain the ensemble predictions.

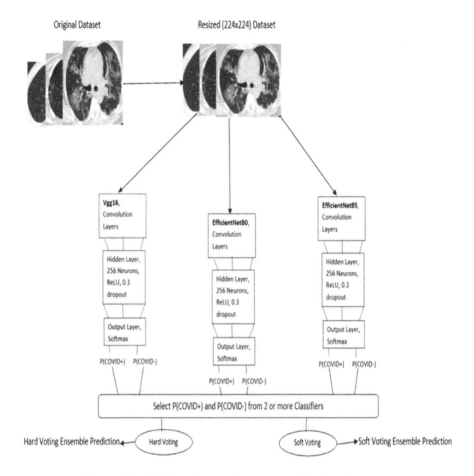

Fig. 4. Methodology for producing ensemble classifications

3.7   Hardware Specifications

Both a Google Colab and Kaggle were used for training purposes because the use of a GPU greatly improves training time for image classification systems. The testing was conducted on the PyCharm IDE on a 64-bit Windows 10 desktop machine, with 8 GB DDR4 RAM and Intel i5 processor, running at 3.60 GHz. All code was written in Python.

4   Results and Discussions

The performance of the classifiers used in this study are evaluated using metrics derived from a confusion matrix. These are accuracy, recall, specificity and F1-score. Here, the performance metrics for the 3 selected CNNs (Vgg16, Efficient-NetB0 and EfficientNetB5) as well as the hard voting and soft voting ensemble combinations of these 3 CNNs are compared.

Algorithm 2. Hard Voting for a single instance

$baseClassifierArr \leftarrow loadBaseClassifiers()$
$sumPos \leftarrow 0$
$sumNeg \leftarrow 0$
for $Model\ m: baseClassifierArr$ **do**
    $X \leftarrow m.getProbabilityCOVIDPos()$
    $Y \leftarrow m.getProbabilityCOVIDNeg()$
    if $X \geq Y$ **then**
        $sumPos \leftarrow sumPos + 1$
    else
        $sumNeg \leftarrow sumNeg + 1$
    end if
end for
if $sumPos \geq sumNeg$ **then**
    return COVID-19 Positive
else
    return COVID-19 Negative
end if

There are 4 values for a binary classification confusion matrix, namely True Positive (TP), True Negative (TN), False Positive (FP) and False Negative (FN). The True Positives are the number of CT scans that were correctly predicted as COVID-19 positive. The True Negatives are the number of CT scans that were correctly predicted as COVID-19 negative. The False Positives are the number of CT scans that were predicted as COVID-19 positive, but were in fact COVID-19 negative. The False Negatives are the number of CT scans that were predicted as COVID-19 negative, but were in fact COVID-19 positive. The confusion matrices for Vgg16, EfficientNetB0, EfficientNetB5, the hard voting and soft voting ensemble combination classifiers are shown in Fig. 5, 6, 7, 8, 9, 10, 11, 12, 13, 14 and 15.

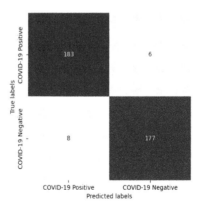

Fig. 5. Confusion matrix for Vgg16

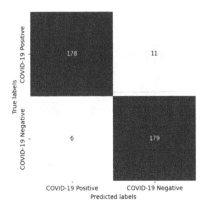

Fig. 6. Confusion matrix for EfficientNetB0

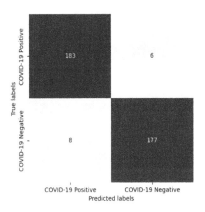

Fig. 7. Confusion matrix for EfficientNetB5

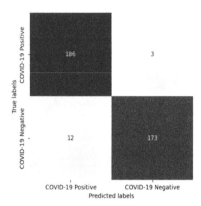

Fig. 8. Confusion matrix for Vgg16+EfficientNetB0 (hard voting)

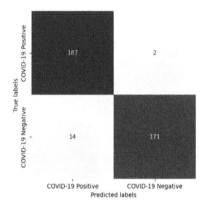

Fig. 9. Confusion matrix for Vgg16+EfficientNetB5 (hard voting)

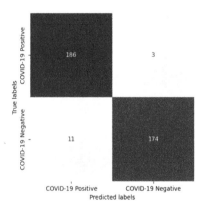

Fig. 10. Confusion matrix for EfficientNetB0+EfficientNetB5 (hard voting)

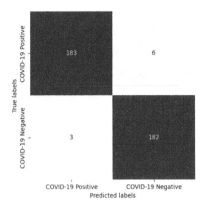

Fig. 11. Confusion matrix for Vgg16+EfficientNetB0+EfficientNetB5 (hard voting)

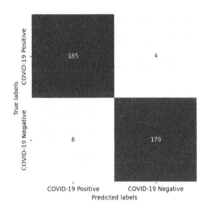

Fig. 12. Confusion matrix for Vgg16+EfficientNetB0 (soft voting)

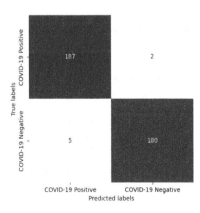

Fig. 13. Confusion matrix for Vgg16+EfficientNetB5 (soft voting)

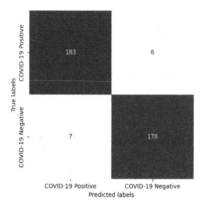

Fig. 14. Confusion matrix for EfficientNetB0+EfficientNetB5 (soft voting)

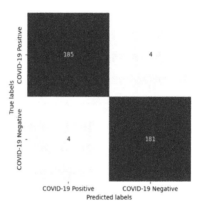

Fig. 15. Confusion matrix for Vgg16+EfficientNetB0+EfficientNetB5 (soft voting)

4.1 Evaluation Metrics

Accuracy. The accuracy of a classifier is the number of correctly predicted samples from the test set divided by the total number of samples. This is usually the main indicator of a classifier's performance. In the case where class distribution is uneven, accuracy may not be the best indicator of performance alone. Accuracy is given by the formula below.

$$Accuracy = \frac{TP + TN}{TP + TN + FP + FN}$$

Recall. Recall or sensitivity is the measure of a classifier's ability to correctly classify positive test samples. It is the number of true positives divided by the sum of the number of true positives and false negatives. A low Recall indicates that the classifier predicted many false negatives. The formula for Recall is given below.

$$Recall = \frac{TP}{TP + FN}$$

Precision. Precision is a measure of the number of true positives predicted out of all the correct predictions made (both true positives and true negatives). A low precision indicates that the classifier predicted many false positives. The formula is shown below.

$$Precision = \frac{TP}{TP + FP}$$

Specificity. Specificity is a classifier's ability to correctly classify negative test samples. It is the number of true negatives divided by the sum of the number of true negatives and the number of false positives. A low specificity can also indicate that the classifier predicted many false positives. The formula for specificity is shown below.

$$Specificity = \frac{TN}{TN + FP}$$

F1-Score. F1-score can be seen as an average of precision and recall. A high F1-score shows the ratios of precision and recall are balanced. A low F1-score can indicate that the values for precision and recall differ greatly. F1-score is calculated using the formula below:

$$F1 - Score = \frac{2xPrecisionxRecall}{Precision + Recall}$$

Table 2. Individual classifier performance metrics

Classifier	Accuracy	Recall	Precision	Specificity	F1-score
Vgg16	96,26%	96,83%	95,81%	95,68%	96,32%
EfficientNetB0	95,45%	94,18%	96,74%	96,76%	95,44%
EfficientNetB5	96,26%	96,83%	95,81%	95,68%	96,32%

Table 3. Hard voting ensemble classifier performance metrics

Hard voting ensemble classifier	Accuracy	Recall	Precision	Specificity	F1-score
Vgg16+EfficientNetB0	95,99%	98,41%	93,93%	93,51%	96,12%
Vgg16+EfficientNetB5	95,72%	98,94%	93,03%	92,43%	95,90%
EfficientNetB0+EfficientNetB5	96,26%	98,41%	94,42%	94,05%	96,37%
Vgg16+EfficientNetB0+EfficientNetB5	97,59%	96,82%	98,38%	98,37%	97,60%

Table 4. Soft voting ensemble classifier performance metrics

Soft voting ensemble classifier	Accuracy	Recall	Precision	Specificity	F1-score
Vgg16+EfficientNetB0	97,33%	97,88%	96,86%	96,76%	97,37%
Vgg16+EfficientNetB5	98,13%	98,94%	97,40%	97,30%	98,16%
EfficientNetB0+EfficientNetB5	96,52%	96,83%	96,32%	96,22%	95,60%
Vgg16+EfficientNetB0+EfficientNetB5	97,86%	97,88%	97,88%	97,83%	97,88%

4.2 Discussions

From the results in Tables 2, 3 and 4, the following deductions can be made. The Vgg16+EfficientNetB5 soft voting ensemble classifier produced the best accuracy, recall and F1-score. The Vgg16+EfficientNetB5 hard voting ensemble classifier had the highest recall as well. The Vgg16+EfficientNetB0+EfficientNetB5 hard voting ensemble classifier had the highest precision and specificity.

In the case of COVID-19 detection, a higher recall is considered to be very important, since a higher recall means fewer false negatives were predicted. A higher false negative rate (lower recall) means that people who are COVID-19 positive are more likely to be classified as COVID-19 negative by the classifier. This would result in greater spread of COVID-19 since it would cause more people with COVID-19 to carry on with their life as normal instead of self-isolating because they would believe that they are COVID-19 negative. Furthermore, these individuals will not be actively receiving treatment for COVID-19 and may die as a result. Hence, the most suitable classifier for automatic COVID-19 detection based on CT scans of the lungs is the Vgg16+EfficientNetB5 soft voting ensemble classifier.

Even though the Vgg16+EfficientNetB5 hard voting ensemble classifier and Vgg16+EfficientNetB5 soft voting classifier have the same and highest recall, the soft voting ensemble classifier has better performance, with regard to the other evaluation metrics. They both predict the same number of false negatives, but the soft voting ensemble classifier is able to predict fewer false positives and thus has a higher accuracy, precision, specificity and F1-score than the hard voting ensemble classifier. The soft voting ensemble classifier also has the highest F1-score, which indicates that it strikes the best balance between precision and recall. Therefore, **the proposed framework for automatic COVID-19 detection from CT scans is the Vgg16+EfficientNetB5 soft ensemble classifier.**

The performance of Vgg16 and EfficientNetB5 as individual classifiers is the same. It was assumed that a soft ensemble of these would predict the same results as the individual classifiers. However, upon experimentation, it was found that they produced the greatest performance when ensembled with soft voting. This highlights the main advantage of soft voting ensemble in that it takes into account more information, by using each of the model's uncertainty to produce the final decision [13].

4.3   Comparisons with Related Works

All the studies discussed in this section detect COVID-19 from CT-scans only.

The study done by Gifani et al. [4], proposed the use of 5 CNNs (Efficient-NetB0, Efficient- NetB3, EfficientNetB5, Inception_resnet_v2 and Xception) to create a majority (hard) voting classifier. This classifier outperformed the individual CNN's performances. The dataset used was a publicly available dataset, however there were only 447 images used for training, which resulted in a much lower accuracy rate for each CNN and in turn the hard voting classifier.

In the paper written by Kundu et al. [19], they propose a soft voting ensemble of Inception v3, ResNet34 and DenseNet201. They used a bagging ensemble, whereas this study used a stacking ensemble. The soft voting classifier outperforms the individual model performances on the publicly available SARS-CoV-2 dataset developed by Soares et al. [10]. This is the same dataset used in this paper as well. The accuracy (97.73%) reported in the paper by Kundu et al. [19] was the highest accuracy achieved on the SARS-CoV-2 dataset [5], but the proposed classifier in this paper achieved an even higher accuracy of 98.13%.

The paper written by Viriri and Lawton [2] describes that the best classifier in their study was Vgg19 trained on CLAHE CT scans. The reported accuracy was 95.75%. This study also made use of the publicly available SARS-CoV-2 dataset [5].

The study carried out by Ardakani et al. [21] reports that ResNet101 had the best performance when compared to the other 9 CNNs that were also experimented on. The study achieved a 100% recall rate and an accuracy of 99.51%. The impressive part is that this was achieved without ensemble techniques, and it has better performance than studies that use ensemble techniques for diagnosing COVID-19 from CT scans. However, the dataset used is not publicly available (custom dataset) and has a limited number of CT scans compared to the SARS-CoV-2 dataset [5].

Table 5 below summarizes the differences between results achieved in related studies and in this study.

Table 5. Comparison of accuracies of related works that used CT scans for COVID-19 detection

Models used	Ensemble technique	Accuracy
EfficientNetB0, EfficientNetB3, EfficientNetB5, Inception_resnet_v2, Xception [4]	Hard voting	85%
Inception v3, ResNet34 and DenseNet201 [19]	Soft voting	97,73%
Vgg19 on CLAHE dataset [2]	None	95,75%
ResNet101 [21]	None	99,51%
(Proposed) Vgg16, EfficientNetB5	**Soft voting**	**98,13%**

5   Conclusion

In this paper, an investigation was carried out to determine if an ensemble of transfer learning models can be used to accurately detect or diagnose the presence of COVID-19 from a CT scan of a person's lungs. Six state-of-the-art CNNs (Vgg16, Vgg19, EfficientNetB0, EfficientNetB5, DenseNet121 and DenseNet201) were selected as candidate base learners for ensemble classifiers and transfer learning was performed on each. The candidate base learners with the highest accuracies were Vgg16, EfficentNetB0 and EfficentNetB5. Thus, they were selected as the base learners for the ensemble classifiers. Two ensemble methods were investigated, namely, hard voting and soft voting. It was found that both hard voting and soft voting ensemble classifiers had better performance than the individual base classifier CNNs used to form the ensembles. The soft voting ensemble classifiers had higher accuracy and recall rates than hard voting ensemble classifiers with the same base classifiers. Furthermore, it was found that a soft voting ensemble of Vgg16 and EfficientNetB5 had the best overall performance with an accuracy of 98.13%, recall of 98.94%, precision of 97.40%, specificity of 97.30% and F1 score of 98.16%. This soft voting ensemble classifier is reliable enough to be used as a secondary check to validate PCR or to give a pre-diagnosis before the actual PCR test, since it is far more accurate than PCR with a much lower false negative rate. It should also be noted that the proposed classifier has achieved the highest performance, as compared to related works, on the publicly available SARS-CoV-2 dataset [5]. However, the proposed approach has a few issues. This framework is still capable of predicting false negative results (recall rate is not 100%), which means that there is room for improvement. This dataset was trained on very high-quality CT scans, and thus may not predict CT scans that are of poor quality correctly. Lastly, the proposed classifier is not trained to identify the differences between someone with COVID-19 and another person with some other lung disease like Tuberculosis or non-COVID caused pneumonia.

Future work can involve exploring a weighted soft ensemble technique where more weight is given to better classifiers and less weight to worse classifiers, in order to further improve the ensemble classifier's performance. In addition, more complex image pre-processing techniques can be explored to improve the quality and consistency of CT scans given to the classifier. Lastly, training data can be expanded to introduce COVID-19 negative CT scans that exhibit hazy-increased ground-glass opacities due to other lung diseases in order to improve the flexibility of the final classifier.

References

1. Chowdhury, N.K., Kabir, M.A., Rahman, M.M., Rezoana, N.: An ensemble of deep covolutional neural networks based on EfficientNet to detect COVID-19 from chest X-rays (2020). https://www.researchgate.net/publication/344372971
2. Lawton, S., Viriri, S.: Detection of COVID-19 from CT lung scans using transfer learning. Comput. Intell. Neurosci. **2021**(5527923) (2021). https://doi.org/10.1155/2021/5527923

3. Gianchandani, N., Jaiswal, A., Singh, D., Kumar, V., Kaur, M.: Rapid COVID-19 diagnosis using ensemble deep transfer learning models from chest radiographic images. J. Ambient Intell. Human. Comput. (2020). https://doi.org/10.1007/s12652-020-02669-6

4. gifani, P., Shalbaf, A., Vafaeezadeh, M.: Automated detection of COVID-19 using ensemble of transfer learning with deep convolutional neural network based on CT scans. Int. J. Comput. Assist. Radiol. Surg. **16**(1), 115–123 (2020). https://doi.org/10.1007/s11548-020-02286-w

5. Soares, E., Angelov, P., Biaso, S., Froes, M.H., Abe, D.K.: SARS-CoV-2 CT-scan dataset: a large dataset of real patients CT scans for SARS-CoV-2 identification. medRxiv (2020). https://doi.org/10.1101/2020.04.24.20078584

6. Government of the District of Columbia, DC Muriel Bowser, Mayor. What is COVID-19? https://coronavirus.dc.gov/page/what-covid-19

7. Shereen, M.A., Khan, S., Kazmi, A., Bashir, N., Siddiquea, R.: COVID-19 infection: origin, transmission, and characteristics of human coronaviruses. J. Adv. Res. How Sci. Improves Soc. **2020**, 91–98 (2020). https://www.ncbi.nlm.nih.gov/pmc/articles/PMC7113610/

8. Worldometer. COVID Live Update (2020). https://www.worldometers.info

9. Gaia, C., et al.: Chest CT for early detection and management of coronavirus disease (COVID-19): a report of 314 patients admitted to emergency department with suspected pneumonia. La Radiol. Med. **125**(10), 931–942 (2020). https://www.ncbi.nlm.nih.gov/pmc/articles/PMC7388438

10. Cleverley, J., Piper, J., Jones, M.M.: The role of chest radiography in confirming COVID-19 pneumonia (2020). https://www.bmj.com/content/370/bmj.m2426

11. Cleveland Clinic. PCR Test for COVID-19: What it is, How its done, What the results mean (2020). https://my.clevelandclinic.org

12. Kumar, V.: Hands-on guide to create ensemble of convolutional neural networks (2020). https://analyticsindiamag.com/hands-on-guide-to-create-ensemble-of-convolutional-neural-networks/

13. Stack Exchange. Hard Voting, Soft Voting in Ensemble based methods (2018). https://stats.stackexchange.com/questions/349540/hard-voting-soft-voting-in-ensemble-based-methods

14. Alzubaidi, L., Zhang, J., Humaidi, A.J., et al.: Review of deep learning: concepts, CNN architectures, challenges, applications, future directions. J. Big Data **8**, 53 (2021). https://doi.org/10.1186/s40537-021-00444-8

15. Towards Data Science. Illustrated: 10 CNN Architectures (2019). https://towardsdatascience.com/illustrated-10-cnn-architectures-95d78ace614d

16. Simonyan, K., Zisserman, A.: Very deep convolutional networks for large-scale image recognition arXiv:1409.1556 (2014)

17. Tan, M., Le, Q.: EfficientNet: rethinking model scaling for convolutional neural networks (2014)

18. Huang, G., Liu, Z., Van Der Maaten, L., Weinberger, K.Q.: Densely connected convolutional networks. In: 2017 IEEE Conference on Computer Vision and Pattern Recognition (CVPR), pp. 2261–2269 (2017). https://doi.org/10.1109/CVPR.2017.243

19. Kundu, R., Singh, P.K., Ferrara, M., Ahmadian, A., Sarkar, R.: ET-NET: an ensemble of transfer learning models for prediction of COVID-19 infection through chest CT-scan images. Multimed. Tools App. **81**(1), 31–50 (2021). https://doi.org/10.1007/s11042-021-11319-8

20. Islam, M., Al-Rakhami, M.S., Islam, Z., Azraf, A., Sodhro, A.H., Ding, W.: Diagnosis of COVID-19 from X-rays using combined CNN-RNN architecture with transfer learning. medRxiv (2021). https://doi.org/10.1101/2020.08.24.20181339
21. Ardakani, A.A., Kanafi, A.R., Acharya, U.R., Khadem, N., Mohammadi, A.: Application of deep learning technique to manage COVID-19 in routine clinical practice using CT images: results of 10 convolutional neural networks. Comput. Biol. Med. **121**, 103795 (2020). https://doi.org/10.1016/j.compbiomed.2020.103795
22. Geron, A.: Hands-On Machine Learning with Scikit-Learn and TensorFlow: Concepts, Tools, and Techniques to Build Intelligent Systems, 1st edn. O'Reilly Media, France (2017)
23. Horry, M.J., Chakraborty, S., Paul, M., et al.: COVID-19 detection through transfer learning using multimodal imaging data. IEEE Access **8**(2020), 149808–149824 (2020)
24. ImageNet. ImageNet. https://www.image-net.org/

Pancreas Instance Segmentation Using Deep Learning Techniques

Wilson Bakasa[ID] and Serestina Viriri[✉][ID]

School of Mathematics, Statistics and Computer Science,
University of KwaZulu-Natal, Durban, South Africa
viriris@ukzn.ac.za

Abstract. The segmentation of pancreatic ductal adenocarcinoma (PDAC) images facilitates computer vision applications. This paper proposes using UNet, a fully convolutional neural network based on a residual neural network (ResNet34), as an encoder and turning point for boundary class separation, designed for biomedical applications. Image segmentation separates one image into a number of smaller pieces. When doing PDAC image segmentation tasks, these resulting fragments or numerous segments are helpful. Another important requirement for image segmentation tasks is masks and edge classes. TensorFlow and Keras are deep learning frameworks used to build U-Net architectures. UNet aims to capture the characteristics of both context and localisation. The main idea of the implementation is to use a continuous shrink layer and immediately use the upsampling operator to get a higher resolution output on the input image. A total of 800 images were used, 0.2 for testing and 0.8 for training. When using the original UNet model, the accuracy was 0.86. With the help of masking and boundary classes, binary images consisting of null or non-zero values, we got an accuracy of 0.89 from the segmentation tasks.

Keywords: Segmentation · UNet · ResNet-34 · Watershed · Tensorflow · Border classes · PDAC medical images

1 Introduction

Computer vision [1] is an interdisciplinary branch of science that studies how to make computers grasp complex information from digital photos or movies. It aims to construct things that the human visual system can perform by automating them. In recent years, the discipline of computer vision [2] has advanced thanks to deep learning. By utilising boundary classes [3–5] of pancreatic ductal adenocarcinoma (PDAC) images, the authors will discuss a computer vision problem called instance segmentation via Semantic segmentation. Although, there are several approaches that academics have developed to address this issue. We will focus on one specific architecture called U-Net [6] that uses ResNet-34 [7] as its foundation and a Fully Convolutional Network (FCN) Model to perform segmentation.

© ICST Institute for Computer Sciences, Social Informatics and Telecommunications Engineering 2023
Published by Springer Nature Switzerland AG 2023. All Rights Reserved
T. M. Ngatched Nkouatchah et al. (Eds.): PAAISS 2022, LNICST 459, pp. 205–223, 2023.
https://doi.org/10.1007/978-3-031-25271-6_13

This paper looks at instance segmentation of the pancreas using deep learning techniques. In Sect. 2, the original UNet model first analyses how the encoder and decoder are used in deep learning. The proposed model is discussed in Sect. 3, implementing ResNet34 as an encoder to UNet, plus Watershed to form a hybrid model. The max pooling and convolution operations are discussed in Sect. 4 under methods and techniques used in this paper. In Sect. 5, we looked at the experiments done to generate the border classes and the implementation of UNetet plus Watershed, including the training. Results are discussed in Sect. 6, showing the batch normalisation and max pooling from implementing the original against the proposed model.

1.1 Semantic Segmentation

In the computer vision task of semantic segmentation [8,9], each pixel of an image frame is categorised or labelled according to the class to which it belongs. ResNet and UNet are two common Convolutional Neural Networks (CNNs) used for segmentation tasks. This study uses the UNet architecture to achieve multi-class segmentation on the PDAC images dataset. Semantic image segmentation aims to assign a class of what is represented to each image pixel.

1.2 Instance Segmentation

The time needed to perform diagnostic tests on PDAC patients can be drastically decreased using machines to supplement radiologists' analysis. Semantic image segmentation aims to assign a class of what is represented to each pixel of PDAC images [10]. This process is known as a dense prediction since we predict every pixel in the image. The result is a high-resolution image with each pixel assigned to a certain class. Thus, it is PDAC image classification at the pixel level.

2   UNet

In the original work, [11] created the UNet, an architecture for semantic segmentation for Biomedical Image Segmentation. Two paths are present in the architecture. The encoder used to record the context of the image is called the contraction path, which is the first path. The encoder is essentially a standard stack of max-pooling and convolutional layers. The second method is the symmetric expanding path, or decoder, which uses transposed convolutions to provide exact localisation. Therefore, it is an end-to-end, FCN [12–14]; it has no dense layers and solely has convolutional layers. Any size photograph can be accepted.

The feature map must be up-sampled before each step in the expansion route, which is then followed by a 2×2 up-convolution that reduces the number of feature channels in half. Cropping is necessary since each convolution loses boundary pixels. There are a total of 23 convolutional layers in the network [11].

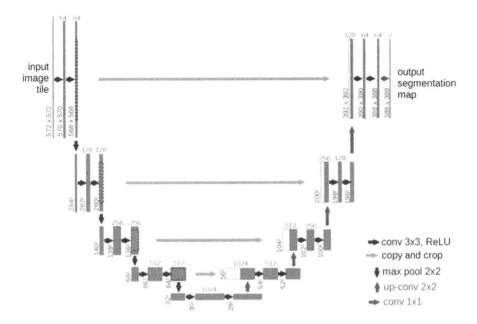

Fig. 1. 32 × 32 pixel original U-Net architecture.

According to the design Fig. 1, a model is applied to an input image before a few convolutional layers with the ReLU activation function are applied. The image size decreases from 572 × 572 to 570 × 570, then to 568 × 568. This reduction is because they used unpadded convolutions, which reduced the total dimensionality. We also see an encoder block on the left side, a decoder block on the right side, and the Convolution blocks [15,16].

The encoder block using the max-pooling layers of strides two continuously decreases the size of the image. The encoder architecture also includes recurrent convolutional layers with many filters. When we get to the decoder part, we see that the convolutional layers' number of filters starts to go down and that the subsequent layers gradually upsample the top layer [17].

2.1   Encoder

Because the encoder in this scenario has repetitive blocks as seen in Fig. 2, it is best to add functions to render the code modular. In these encoder blocks, ReLU will initiate the two 2D Convolution Layer (Conv2D) layers, which will be followed by the MaxPooling and Dropout layers. Each stage will include more filters due to the pooling layer, and the dimensionality of the features will decrease [18,19].

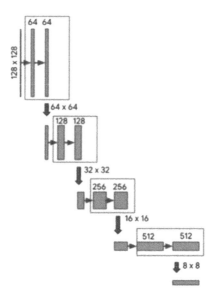

Fig. 2. Encoder left side

2.2 Decoder

The decoder Fig. 3 [20,21], which restores the features' original image size by upsampling, is the last component. We will concatenate the output of the relevant encoder block at each level of upsampling before passing it on to the following decoder block.

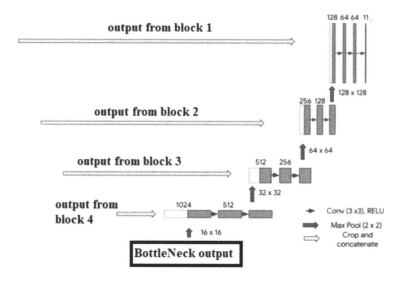

Fig. 3. Decoder right side

3   Proposed Model

This research suggests UNet [11] segmentation of PDAC images followed by object separation based on watersheds as in Fig. 4. In order to create boundary classes [5], the object properties will also be computed. The UNet backbone will be made of ResNet-34.

$$[Semantic segmentation(UNet) with ResNet34] + watershed$$
$$--> Instance segmentation$$

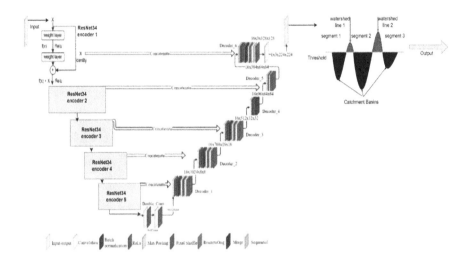

Fig. 4. The proposed model: ResNet-34 blocks as encoders 1–5. The decoder is the usual original UNet decoder. The output from the decoder is then fed onto Watershed for object separation using border classes.

3.1   Residual Networks (ResNet)

ResNet is a CNN architecture composed of numerous residual blocks (Res-Blocks), which are described below in Fig. 5. Skip connections are what set ResNets apart from other CNNs. ResNet is best used as the encoder because it addresses the vanishing gradient problem. Accuracy does not increase or degrade when additional layers have been added, but training grows slower as a result. Because of the network's skip connections, this is conceivable [22–24].

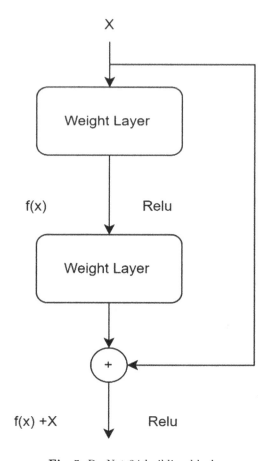

Fig. 5. ResNet-34 building block

Two connections from the input are present in each ResBlock, one of which passes across a series of linear functions, batch normalization, and convolutions. These convolutions and functions are bypassed by the identity when it crosses or skips connections [7].

The combined tensor outputs of the two connections are used. Adding cross-connections [25] between network layers enables vast areas to be bypassed if necessary, resulting in the lost surface. Making it much simpler to train the model with the right weights to minimise the loss.

3.2 Watershed

The image measure module, the "region props" function, extracts attributes of observed classes and produces relevant parameters for each item. Remove any backgrounds or areas that could be considered objects [26–28].

4   Methods and Techniques

Utilising the Keras API [29–31], the paper implemented UNet in Python. Convolution, max-pooling, down- and upsampling, and transposed convolution were all used in the implementation. The study covers UNet image segmentation followed by watershed-based object separation. Additionally, object properties will be computed. Uses a model trained on the common UNet framework based on ResNet-34 for semantic segmentation, implementing Watershed in border classes separation. Segmenting instances is the outcome of all this.

4.1   Max Pooling Operation

We have less parameters in the network because of the pooling function, Fig. 6, which shrinks the size of the feature map [32].

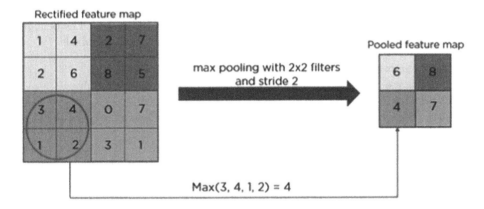

Fig. 6. Max pooling operations

In essence, we choose the highest pixel value from each 2×2 block of the input feature map to create a pooled feature map. Strides and filter size are two crucial [33] processes. The goal is to keep the pixels with the highest values from each region and discard the data that best fits the image's context. The fact that the convolution decreases the image size and, in particular, the pooling operation is crucial to keep in mind.

The term "downsampling" [34,35] refers to this method. In the illustration above, the image size was 4×4 *before and* 2×2 after pooling.

4.2   ResNet-34 Encoder

The encoder/downsampling portion of the UNet can utilise a ResNet-34 [22] (the left half of the U). ResNet-34, a 34-layer ResNet architecture, was employed in our models because it is more efficient, trains quicker than ResNet-50 [36], and requires less memory. Using a pre-trained model greatly reduces training time for an image generation/prediction model, which is necessary for the model to understand how to carry out its prediction. The features that need to be found and enhanced are then known to the model as a starting point. Model and weights already trained on PDAC images are used as input, which turns the ResNet-34 encoder into a UNet with cross-connections.

5   Experiments

The U-Net blocks are more akin to DenseBlocks than ResBlocks [19] since their outputs are concatenated. However, stride two convolutions shrink the grid size once more, preventing excessive memory consumption.

5.1   Generate Border Classes Steps

With binary masks, generate border pixels. When training a multi-class UNet semantic segmenter, these border pixels can be added as a new class. The benefit is that we can do watershed and segment "instances" using border pixels.

1. Call function to define the border.
2. Erode some pixels into objects and dilate to outside the objects.
3. This region would be the border. Replace border pixel value with something other than 255.
4. Start by eroding edge pixels.
5. Define the kernel size for dilation based on the desired border size, adding 1 to keep it odd.
6. Replace 255 values with 127 for all pixels. Eventually, we will only define border pixels with this value.
7. The above-dilated image converts the eroded object parts to pixel value 255.
8. What is remaining with a value of 127 would be the boundary pixels.

5.2   Implementing UNet Plus Watershed

Instance segmentation was done via semantic segmentation (U-Net) plus the Watershed. The steps are as follows:

1. Load the U-Net(ResNet-34 backbone) trained model and corresponding weights.
2. The test image, which needs to be segmented, should be loaded and processed.
3. Predict and threshold for probabilities that are greater than 0.5.
4. Binaries the U-Net result to create an image.

5. Utilizing OTSU, threshold image to binary. The value 255 will be applied to each thresholded pixel.
6. Morphological operations to eliminate small noise - opening. To get rid of holes, we can use closing.
7. Finding certain foreground areas using distance transform and thresholding.

Verify the total number of regions discovered before and after using the "Opening" function. We now understand that the areas in the middle of cells are unquestionably necessary. The distant region serves as the backdrop. We can utilise "erode" to extract specific regions that we need to. However, certain PDAC pictures feature regions that contact, making erosion alone ineffective.

The optimal strategy would be to threshold after distance transform to distinguish contacting items. Let us begin by determining a specific backdrop area and increasing the cell boundary to the background by distorting pixels a few times. In this manner, everything that is left will be history. Our ambiguous area is located between the foreground and the background. The watershed [26] should discover this location.

i The foreground points'intensities are adjusted to correspond to the distances between them and the nearest 0 value, which is the boundary.
ii Let's threshold the distance transform by beginning at its maximum value, $\frac{1}{2}$.
iii We now make a marker and give the inside sections labels. For some places, both the foreground and the backdrop will be given positive numbers. Regions that are unknown will be labeled 0. Let's use Connected Components as markers.
iv One issue is that all backdrop pixels have a value of 0, which indicates to the Watershed that this area is unknowable. For a specific backdrop to be 10 rather than 0, let us add 10 to all labels.
v Put a 0 marker in the area that is currently unknown.
vi Now we are ready for watershed filling.
vii Now that regions have been recognized, it is time to extract their properties; each object's valuable parameters are calculated using the "region props" function in the skimage measure module.

5.3   TensorFlow Implementation of UNet

We will implement TensorFlow to the UNet architecture for the computation of the model. We shall stick to the TensorFlow library for this model. We will import all necessary libraries to build our UNet architecture before starting from scratch. However, we will make a few important adjustments that will enhance the model's overall performance while making it a little less complicated [37,38].

Importing the Required Libraries. We will construct the UNet architecture using the TensorFlow deep learning framework. As a result, we will import the Keras framework and the TensorFlow library, which are now both part of the TensorFlow model structures. According to what we know, one of the primary imports for the UNet architecture is the activation function ReLU for the basic modelling structure, along with the convolutional layer, the max-pooling layer, an input layer, and the layer with the activation function. Then, we will conduct an upsampling for the decoder blocks we want to use by adding additional layers, such as the Conv2DTranspose layer. Additionally, we will stabilise the training process with batch normalisation layers and combine the required skip connections with concatenating layers [37, 39].

Building the Convolution Block. After importing the required libraries, we can move on to creating the UNet architecture. We may do this in a single class by correctly specifying each argument's value and executing the process until the end or a few iterative blocks. The latter strategy will be employed since, with the help of a few building pieces, most people can more easily understand the model architecture of U-Net. The three iterative blocks we will employ are the convolution operation block, the ResNet-34 (encoder block), and the decoder block, as shown in the architecture representation. By using these three construction blocks, we can create the U-Net architecture. Now that we have gone through and comprehended each of these function code sections [15, 16].

Constructing the Encoder and Decoder Blocks. Consecutive inputs from the top layer to the base layer will be used in the ResNet-34 encoder architecture. The convolutional block has two convolutional layers and corresponding batch normalisation and ReLU layers. The block will make up the ResNet-34 encoder function as stated [34, 35].

Construct the UNet Architecture. The U-Net architecture contains a high number of processing blocks. Thus the entire structure might be huge if we tried to create it from scratch in a single layer. By dividing our functions into the three independent code blocks of convolutional operation, ResNet-34 (encoder) structure, and decoder structure, we can easily develop the UNet architecture in a few lines of code. The input layer, which contains the various forms from our input image, will be used [11].

5.4   Training

Since there are two classes, the model is built using the Adam optimiser, and we utilise the binary cross-entropy loss function (salt and no salt). Keras callbacks are employed to implement:

i monitor if the validation loss remains unchanged for five consecutive epochs, the learning rate decays.

ii Early termination, if the validation loss does not decrease during ten consecutive epochs.

iii Only keep the weights if the validation loss improves. A batch size of 32 is
employed.

6   Results

The diagram below contrasts the segmented PDAC image and its markers with
the original PDAC image from the original dataset, shown in Fig. 8. The optimisation approach known as the local gradient is frequently used to train neural
networks and machine learning models. Using training data, these models learn
new things over time. In gradient descent, the cost function acts as a barometer
by evaluating the precision of each iteration of parameter changes. Until the
function is close to or equal to zero, the model will keep altering its parameters
to provide the least amount of error. Once their accuracy has been improved,
machine learning models can be useful tools for computer science and artificial
intelligence (AI) applications (Fig. 7).

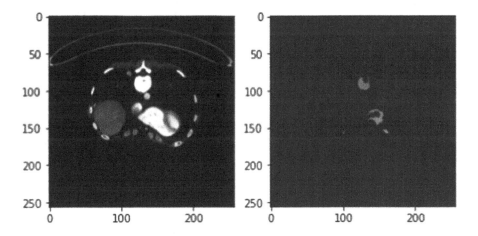

Fig. 7. Showing the original image and the testing label image.

The training of deep neural networks using batch normalisation [40], which
normalises the contributions to a layer for each mini-batch, is illustrated in Fig.
9. As a result, the learning process is stabilised, and a significant reduction in the
number of training epochs required to build deep neural networks. Between one
hidden layer and the subsequent hidden layer, there is just another network layer
called "Batch Norm". Before sending them on as the input of the next hidden
layer, it has the responsibility of normalising the outputs from the previously
hidden layer.

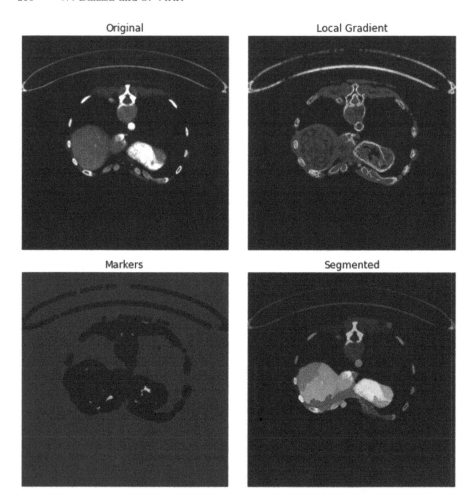

Fig. 8. Diagram for the segmented image

Additionally displayed are the total, trainable, and non-trainable model parameters. In the context of deep learning, they are the weight and bias characteristics of the training data that will be learned during the learning process. A parameter is frequently used to gauge a model's performance.

```
100%|███████████| 800/800 [00:15<00:00, 50.02it/s]
Model: "model"
```

Layer (type)	Output Shape	Param #
input_1 (InputLayer)	[(None, 256, 256, 3)]	0
conv2d (Conv2D)	(None, 256, 256, 64)	1792
batch_normalization (BatchN ormalization)	(None, 256, 256, 64)	256
activation (Activation)	(None, 256, 256, 64)	0
conv2d_1 (Conv2D)	(None, 256, 256, 64)	36928
batch_normalization_1 (Batc hNormalization)	(None, 256, 256, 64)	256
activation_1 (Activation)	(None, 256, 256, 64)	0
max_pooling2d (MaxPooling2D)	(None, 128, 128, 64)	0
conv2d_2 (Conv2D)	(None, 128, 128, 128)	73856
batch_normalization_2 (Batc hNormalization)	(None, 128, 128, 128)	512
activation_2 (Activation)	(None, 128, 128, 128)	0
conv2d_3 (Conv2D)	(None, 128, 128, 128)	147584
batch_normalization_3 (Batc hNormalization)	(None, 128, 128, 128)	512
activation_3 (Activation)	(None, 128, 128, 128)	0
max_pooling2d_1 (MaxPooling 2D)	(None, 64, 64, 128)	0

Fig. 9. Batch normalisation and max pooling from implementing UNet model.

Epochs are represented in Fig. 10 and refer to training the neural network using all training data for a single cycle.

Figure 11 depicts the reconstructed image. Deep learning-based picture reconstruction is an effective use of artificial intelligence and cutting-edge machine learning. Deep learning has been widely used in computer vision and image analysis, which deal with existing images, enhance them and derive features from them (Figs. 12 and 13).

We may plot the train and validation loss to see how the training went as in Fig. 14, which should show typically decreasing values per epoch. The training

```
=================================================================
Total params: 27,923,523
Trainable params: 27,911,747
Non-trainable params: 11,776
_____
None
Epoch 1/5
1/1 [==============================] - 110s 110s/step - loss: 0.2671 -
accuracy: 0.6961
Epoch 2/5
1/1 [==============================] - 103s 103s/step - loss: 0.1819 -
accuracy: 0.8558
Epoch 3/5
1/1 [==============================] - 101s 101s/step - loss: 0.1370 -
accuracy: 0.7828
Epoch 4/5
1/1 [==============================] - 101s 101s/step - loss: 0.1078 -
accuracy: 0.8763
Epoch 5/5
1/1 [==============================] - 101s 101s/step - loss: 0.0897 -
accuracy: 0.8623
```

Fig. 10. Loss and accuracy after 5 epochs obtained from implementing UNet model

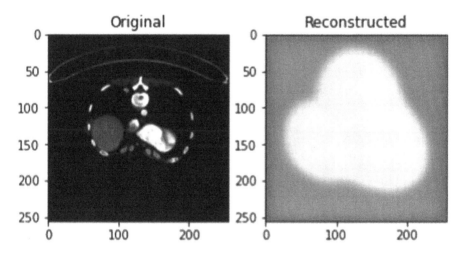

Fig. 11. The reconstruction of images

loss is the degree to which a deep learning model matches the training set of data. It assesses the model's variance on the training set, in other words. Keep in mind that the dataset utilised train the model was split up into the training set. The training loss is computed using the total mistakes for each sample in the training set.

Remember that each batch also concludes with a measurement of the training loss. A training loss curve is typically displayed to demonstrate this. On the other hand, a statistic known as validation loss is used to assess a deep learning

```
batch_normalization_30 (BatchN    (None, 256, 256, 12   512
['conv2d_31[0][0]']
ormalization)                     8)

activation_30 (Activation)        (None, 256, 256, 12   0
['batch_normalization_30[0][0]']
                                  8)

conv2d_32 (Conv2D)                (None, 256, 256, 12   147584
['activation_30[0][0]']
                                  8)

batch_normalization_31 (BatchN    (None, 256, 256, 12   512
['conv2d_32[0][0]']
ormalization)                     8)

activation_31 (Activation)        (None, 256, 256, 12   0
['batch_normalization_31[0][0]']
                                  8)

max_pooling2d_9 (MaxPooling2D)    (None, 128, 128, 12   0
['activation_31[0][0]']

::::::::::::::::::::::::::::::::::::::::::::::::::::::::::::::::::::

batch_normalization_45 (BatchN    (None, 512, 512, 64   256
['conv2d_46[0][0]']
ormalization)                     )

activation_45 (Activation)        (None, 512, 512, 64   0
['batch_normalization_45[0][0]']
                                  )

conv2d_47 (Conv2D)                (None, 512, 512, 1)   65
['activation_45[0]|[0]']
================================================================
Total params: 31,055,297
Trainable params: 31,043,521
Non-trainable params: 11,776
```

Fig. 12. Batch Normalisation and Max Pooling from implementing the proposed model of UNet (ResNet-34) plus Watershed.

model's performance on the validation set. The validation set is a portion of the dataset used to evaluate the model's performance. Similar to how we calculated the training loss, we calculated the validation loss by summing the mistakes for each sample in the validation set.

```
Epoch 1/5
25/25 [==============================] - 140s 6s/step - loss: 0.0211 -
accuracy: 0.4535
Epoch 2/5
25/25 [==============================] - 140s 6s/step - loss: 0.0092 -
accuracy: 0.5791
Epoch 3/5
25/25 [==============================] - 140s 6s/step - loss: 0.0071 -
accuracy: 0.8354
Epoch 4/5
25/25 [==============================] - 140s 6s/step - loss: 0.0060 -
accuracy: 0.8735
Epoch 5/5
25/25 [==============================] - 139s 6s/step - loss: 0.0052 -
accuracy: 0.8932
```

Fig. 13. Loss and accuracy after five epochs obtained from implementing the proposed model of UNet (ResNet-34) plus Watershed

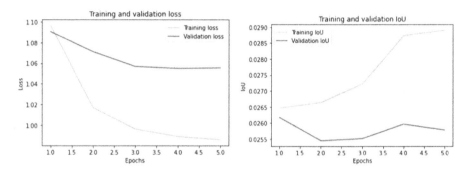

Fig. 14. Training against the Validation loss and IoU graph

7   Conclusion

Apart from a class label and a set of bounding box parameters, semantic segmentation generates further information, as was previously mentioned. The final product is a comprehensive, high-resolution PDAC image with labelled pixels. By widening the receptive field, Max Pooling facilitates understanding of "WHAT" in the visual. However, it frequently forgets the location of the objects. Semantic segmentation requires an understanding of "WHAT" in the image and "WHERE". Therefore, we must find a means to up-sample the image from low resolution to high resolution to recover the "WHERE" information. Backpropagation is used by transposed convolution to learn parameters. The preferred method for upsampling is to transform a low-resolution image into a high-resolution one.

Stride two convolutions gradually shrink the grid size, preventing excessive memory consumption. A modern GPU can quickly compute the segmentation of images with a size of 512×512 using this UNet architecture. However, the UNet (ResNet-34) plus watershed model's modern efficiency, speed, and simplicity will be enhanced PDAC image segmentation tasks. Using the value of convolution as "same" is one of the changes made to this structure because numerous subsequent research studies have demonstrated that this alteration had no detrimental effects on the construction of the building. Additionally, the original architecture did not use this feature because batch normalisation was only introduced in 2016. Nevertheless, batch normalisation will be a part of our model implementation because it typically produces the best outcomes. In subsequent publications, we will investigate the functionality of the PyTorch-based U-Net architecture and a few alternative model structures.

References

1. Wiley, V., Lucas, T.: Computer vision and image processing: a paper review. Int. J. Artif. Intell. Res. **2**(1), 29–36 (2018)
2. Thevenot, J., López, M.B., Hadid, A.: A survey on computer vision for assistive medical diagnosis from faces. IEEE J. Biomed. Health Inform. **22**(5), 1497–1511 (2017)
3. Wang, R., Chen, S., Ji, C., Fan, J., Li, Y.: Boundary-aware context neural network for medical image segmentation. Med. Image Anal. **78**, 102395 (2022)
4. Chen, X., Williams, B.M., Vallabhaneni, S.R., Czanner, G., Williams, R., Zheng, Y.: Learning active contour models for medical image segmentation. In: Proceedings of the IEEE/CVF Conference on Computer Vision and Pattern Recognition, pp. 11632–11640 (2019)
5. Asaturyan, H., Thomas, E.L., Fitzpatrick, J., Bell, J.D., Villarini, B.: Advancing pancreas segmentation in multi-protocol MRI volumes using Hausdorff-Sine loss function. In: Suk, H.-I., Liu, M., Yan, P., Lian, C. (eds.) MLMI 2019. LNCS, vol. 11861, pp. 27–35. Springer, Cham (2019). https://doi.org/10.1007/978-3-030-32692-0_4
6. Li, X., Chen, H., Qi, X., Dou, Q., Chi-Wing, F., Heng, P.-A.: H-DenseUNet: hybrid densely connected UNet for liver and tumor segmentation from CT volumes. IEEE Trans. Med. Imaging **37**(12), 2663–2674 (2018)
7. Koonce, B.: ResNet 34. In: Koonce, B. (ed.) Convolutional Neural Networks with Swift for Tensorflow, pp. 51–61. Springer, Heidelberg (2021). https://doi.org/10.1007/978-1-4842-6168-2_5
8. Guo, Y., Liu, Y., Georgiou, T., Lew, M.S.: A review of semantic segmentation using deep neural networks. Int. J. Multimed. Inf. Retrieval **7**(2), 87–93 (2018)
9. Garcia-Garcia, A., Orts-Escolano, S., Oprea, S., Villena-Martinez, V., Garcia-Rodriguez, J.: A review on deep learning techniques applied to semantic segmentation. arXiv preprint arXiv:1704.06857 (2017)
10. Bakasa, W., Viriri, S.: Pancreatic cancer survival prediction: a survey of the state-of-the-art. Comput. Math. Methods Med. **2021**, 1–17 (2021)
11. Ronneberger, O., Fischer, P., Brox, T.: U-net: convolutional networks for biomedical image segmentation. In: Navab, N., Hornegger, J., Wells, W.M., Frangi, A.F. (eds.) MICCAI 2015. LNCS, vol. 9351, pp. 234–241. Springer, Cham (2015). https://doi.org/10.1007/978-3-319-24574-4_28
12. Roth, H.R., et al.: An application of cascaded 3D fully convolutional networks for medical image segmentation. Computer. Med. Imaging Graph. **66**, 90–99 (2018)
13. Dolz, J., Desrosiers, C., Ayed, I.B.: 3D fully convolutional networks for subcortical segmentation in MRI: a large-scale study. NeuroImage **170**, 456–470 (2018)

14. Dai, J., He, K., Li, Y., Ren, S., Sun, J.: Instance-sensitive fully convolutional networks. In: Leibe, B., Matas, J., Sebe, N., Welling, M. (eds.) ECCV 2016. LNCS, vol. 9910, pp. 534–549. Springer, Cham (2016). https://doi.org/10.1007/978-3-319-46466-4_32

15. Teng, L., Li, H., Karim, S. DMCNN: a deep multiscale convolutional neural network model for medical image segmentation. J. Healthc. Eng. **2019**, 1–11 (2019)

16. Khanna, A., Londhe, N.D., Gupta, S., Semwal, A.: A deep residual U-net convolutional neural network for automated lung segmentation in computed tomography images. Biocybern. Biomed. Eng. **40**(3), 1314–1327 (2020)

17. Zongwei Zhou, Md., Siddiquee, M.R., Tajbakhsh, N., Liang, J.: UNet++: redesigning skip connections to exploit multiscale features in image segmentation. IEEE Trans. Med. Imaging **39**(6), 1856–1867 (2019)

18. Sathananthavathi, V., Indumathi, G.: Encoder enhanced atrous (EEA) UNet architecture for retinal blood vessel segmentation. Cogn. Syst. Res. **67**, 84–95 (2021)

19. Kiran, I., Raza, B., Ijaz, A., Khan, M.A.: DenseRes-Unet: segmentation of overlapped/clustered nuclei from multi organ histopathology images. Comput. Biol. Med. **143**, 105267 (2022)

20. Choi, S.: Utilizing Unet for the future traffic map prediction task traffic4cast challenge 2020. arXiv preprint arXiv:2012.00125 (2020)

21. Arrastia, J.L., et al.: Deeply supervised UNet for semantic segmentation to assist dermatopathological assessment of basal cell carcinoma. J. imaging **7**(4), 71 (2021)

22. Al-Moosawi, N.M.A.-M.M., Khudeyer, R.S., et al. Resnet-34/dr: A residual convolutional neural network for the diagnosis of diabetic retinopathy. Informatica **45**(7), 115–124 (2021)

23. Xue, Yu., Wang, Y., Liang, J., Slowik, A.: A self-adaptive mutation neural architecture search algorithm based on blocks. IEEE Comput. Intell. Mag. **16**(3), 67–78 (2021)

24. Zhou, S., Nie, D., Adeli, E., Yin, J., Lian, J., Shen, D.: High-resolution encoder-decoder networks for low-contrast medical image segmentation. IEEE Trans. Image Process. **29**, 461–475 (2019)

25. Chen, C., Dou, Q., Chen, H., Qin, J., Heng, P.A.: Unsupervised bidirectional cross-modality adaptation via deeply synergistic image and feature alignment for medical image segmentation. IEEE Trans. Med. Imaging **39**(7), 2494–2505 (2020)

26. Zanaty, E., Afifi, A.: A watershed approach for improving medical image segmentation. Comput. Methods Biomech. Biomed. Eng. **16**(12), 1262–1272 (2013)

27. Ramesh, K.K.D., Kiran Kumar, G., Swapna, K., Datta, D., Rajest, S.S.: A review of medical image segmentation algorithms. EAI Endors. Trans. Pervasive Health Technol. **7**(27), e6 (2021)

28. Shen, T., Wang, Y.: Medical image segmentation based on improved watershed algorithm. In: 2018 IEEE 3rd Advanced Information Technology, Electronic and Automation Control Conference (IAEAC), pp. 1695–1698. IEEE (2018)

29. Arnold, T.B.: kerasr: R interface to the keras deep learning library. J. Open Source Softw. **2**(14), 296 (2017)

30. Manaswi, N.K.: Understanding and working with Keras. In: Manaswi, N.V. (ed.) Deep Learning with Applications Using Python, pp. 31–43. Springer, Heidelberg (2018). https://doi.org/10.1007/978-1-4842-3516-4_2

31. Gulli, A., Kapoor, A., Pal, S.: Deep Learning with TensorFlow 2 and Keras: Regression, ConvNets, GANs, RNNs, NLP, and More with TensorFlow 2 and the Keras API. Packt Publishing Ltd. (2019)

32. Murray, N., Perronnin, F.: Generalized max pooling. In: Proceedings of the IEEE Conference on Computer Vision and Pattern Recognition, pp. 2473–2480 (2014)

33. Loussaief, S., Abdelkrim, A.: Convolutional neural network hyper-parameters optimization based on genetic algorithms. Int. J. Adv. Comput. Sci. Appl. **9**(10) (2018)
34. Chen, Q., Xu, J., Koltun, V.: Fast image processing with fully-convolutional networks. In: Proceedings of the IEEE International Conference on Computer Vision, pp. 2497–2506 (2017)
35. Zhang, Y., Zhao, D., Zhang, J., Xiong, R., Gao, W.: Interpolation-dependent image downsampling. IEEE Trans. Image Process. **20**(11), 3291–3296 (2011)
36. Wen, L., Li, X., Gao, L.: A transfer convolutional neural network for fault diagnosis based on ResNet-50. Neural Comput. Appl. **32**(10), 6111–6124 (2020)
37. Qamar, S., Jin, H., Zheng, R., Ahmad, P., Usama, M.: A variant form of 3D-UNet for infant brain segmentation. Futur. Gener. Comput. Syst. **108**, 613–623 (2020)
38. Cai, S., Tian, Y., Lui, H., Zeng, H., Yi, W., Chen, G.: Dense-UNet: a novel multiphoton in vivo cellular image segmentation model based on a convolutional neural network. Quant. Imaging Med. Surg. **10**(6), 1275 (2020)
39. Tuan, T.A., Tuan, T.A., Bao, P.T.: Brain tumor segmentation using bit-plane and UNET. In: Crimi, A., Bakas, S., Kuijf, H., Keyvan, F., Reyes, M., van Walsum, T. (eds.) BrainLes 2018. LNCS, vol. 11384, pp. 466–475. Springer, Cham (2019). https://doi.org/10.1007/978-3-030-11726-9_41
40. Daimary, D., Bora, M.B., Amitab, K., Kandar, D.: Brain tumor segmentation from MRI images using hybrid convolutional neural networks. Proc. Comput. Sci. **167**, 2419–2428 (2020)

Automating Sickle Cell Counting Using Object Detection Techniques

Souhoude Ouedraogo[1(✉)], Mamadou Bousso[1], Abdourahmane Balde[2], Ousmane Sall[2], Cheikh Sall[3], and Mamadou Soumboundou[3]

[1] Department of Management of Organizations, Scientific, Technological and Digital Pole, Iba Der Thiam University of Thies, Thies, Senegal
ouedraogosouhoude@gmail.com, mbousso@univ-thies.sn
[2] Virtual University of Senegal – VUS, Thies, Senegal
{abdourahmane.balde,ousmane1.sall}@uvs.edu.sn
[3] UMRED, Health Faculty Thies University, BP 967, Thies, Senegal
{cheikh.sall,mamadou.soumboundou}@univ-thies.sn

Abstract. Blood cell counting is an important part of the medico-clinical diagnostic process. However, counting sickle cells by manual visual inspection under the microscope is time intensive and subject to human error. In order to efficiently automate blood cell counting, we propose in this paper a detection method based on deep learning in this case YOLO, one of the most powerful object detection models in recent years. To perform our study, we collect and label a dataset of 223 images including about 6,012 cells (normal and sickle cell). We explored five YOLOV5 models version optimized by a pre-trained model on biological images, and the YOLOV5x one gives us better accuracy. We got a detection accuracy of 95% on the validation data. Deployed as a web application via Flask, this identification methodology can help healthcare professionals make faster and more efficient diagnoses.

Keywords: Sickle cell disease · Neural networks · YOLO · Flask

1 Introduction

Sickle cell disease, also known as sickle cell anemia, is an inherited genetic disorder affecting red blood cells. It is characterized by an alteration in hemoglobin, the main protein in red blood cells. Hemoglobin carries oxygen from the lungs to the tissues and helps to remove carbon dioxide. Normal hemoglobin has a round, elastic shape, which allows the blood to float normally in the blood vessels. When a person has sickle cell disease, the abnormal shape of this protein causes the red blood cells to become brittle and stiff. These abnormalities lead to anemia, painful vaso-occlusive crises and an increased risk of infections [1]. It is the most common genetic disease in the world with nearly 50 million people affected and each year 300,000 children are born with this condition. Between 5% and 20% of people with the disease are found in Africa and its

T. M. Ngatched Nkouatchah et al. (Eds.): PAAISS 2022, LNICST 459, pp. 224–236, 2023.
https://doi.org/10.1007/978-3-031-25271-6_14

dominance is more identified in sub-Saharan regions. Ten percent of people carry the sickle cell gene in Senegal [2]. Early identification of abnormal hemoglobin (sickle cell) in the patient allows physicians to propose diagnoses in order to reduce serious risks.

Detection of abnormal hemoglobin allows for a more efficient diagnosis of sickle cell disease, but the process of identification and manual counting is costly in terms of time and energy, and the expected results are not necessarily reliable. Christoph [3] and Maciaszek [4] have discussed the disadvantages of time-consuming microscopic results and manual inspection, which lead to incorrect diagnostic results.

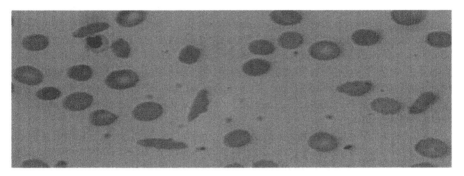

Fig. 1. Giemsa-stained blood smear.

To solve this problem, we propose a detection and counting method based on computer vision that will be deployed as a web application. This process starts by collecting and annotating blood smear images (see Fig. 1) of a person with sickle cell disease, then we will use YOLOv5 neural networks namely YOLOv5n, YOLOv5s, YOLOv5m, YOLOv5l, YOLOv5x and finally the flask Framework for deployment. In order to have better performances, image augmentation and transfer learning techniques have been applied.

In the rest of this article, we start with literature review, present methodology, experiences and results, and finally conclusion and future work.

2 Related Work

Blood smear image processing can be used to reduce observational fault in visual examination. In this paper, a method has been presented for the fast and accurate recognition of sickle cells in blood images. However, research has been conducted in the processing of biological images in general and sickle cell images in particular.

In 1976, S. A. Bentley and S. M. Lewis [5] and C. D. Ruberto [6] described a much faster method of processing blood smear images. All undesirable features of a blood smear image are removed by a precise algorithm. This also involves noise removal, normalization of the intensity of any particles in the image as well as the removal of reflections. The filtering of the image is a set of steps that are generally edge detection and zoom, linear and non-linear operations. Thanks to methods of refinement, the brightness and contrast of the image can be adjusted. The comparison of the filtered images after the application of the different filters highlights the median filter [7] as the most effective for the treatment of sickle cell disease.

Acharya and Kumar [8] advanced an image processing method to count RBC (red blood cells). They processed the blood smear image to count RBCs and identify normal and abnormal cells. They used the K-medoids algorithm to extract WBCs (white blood cells) from the image and particle size analysis to separate RBCs from WBCs, and then counted the number of cells using the labeling algorithm and a CHT (Hough circular transformation).

Sarrafzadeh et al. [9] proposed a Circlet transform to count RBCs on the grayscale image. They used an iterative soft thresholding method for identification and counting.

Kaur et al. [10] proposed a method to automatically count platelets by applying CHT in a microscopic image of blood cells. They used the size and shape characteristics of the platelets in the CHT in the counting process.

Bao et al. [11] proposed a method to classify normal and sickle cells using spatiotemporal analysis. With a compact and inexpensive 3D printed shear interferometer. The method aimed to study the morphology and mechanical properties of red blood cells to identify sickle cell cells.

Mohammad Mahmudul Alam et al. [12] present in 2018 a deep learning-based approach for the detection and counting of three types of blood cells using the Tiny YOLO computer vision algorithm. YOLO's architecture was trained with a configuration adapted to the blood smear image dataset to automatically locate and count red blood cells, white blood cells and platelets. Moreover, in this study other convolutional neural network algorithms like VGG-16, InceptionV3, ResNet50 and MobileNet have been implemented.

Ana Luiza Motta Gomes and Fernando de Almeida Coelho [13] use an approach to design a system capable of automatically detecting and counting sickle cells using methods such as image segmentation and ellipse fitting. The proposed work consists of building an automated system for the detection of sickle cells among red blood cells using the Conic Fitting method [14] and then counting the red blood cells in these images.

3   Methodology

3.1   Yolov5

YOLO uses a single neural network to make predictions. The network performs an integral analysis on the entire image and all objects in the image. The detection frames are predicted based on the features of the image. The network thus predicts bounding boxes in all classes for an image. The YOLO detection system divides the input image into square grids of dimension $S \times S$ (Fig. 2), each with class probabilities C, bounding box locations B and confidence scores. If the center of an object is in a grid cell, the cell is responsible for detecting that object. Each cell makes a prediction of the bounding boxes B and the confidence scores.

The confidence scores reflect the certainty of the model that the object is present in that cell and that the bounding box is accurate. The confidence score is generally defined as follows:

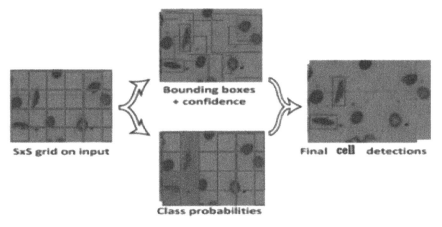

Fig. 2. Detection of YOLO.

$$score = Pr(Objet) * IoU_{pred}^{truth}, Pr(Objet) \in \{0, 1\}. \tag{1}$$

In Eq. (1), *Pr(Objet)* represents the probability that an object is inside the bounding box and IoU_{pred}^{truth} denotes the union between the ground truth (the actual bounding boxes) and the prediction. If no object is found in this cell, the confidence scores must be "0, 0". On the other hand, if the model makes a good prediction, the scores must be "1, 0". Note that "0.0" is the lowest level of prediction and "1.0" the highest. Each of these bounding boxes typically consists of 5 prediction numbers: x, y, w, h and the score. The coordinates (x, y) represent the location of the center of the predicted bounding box relative to the grid cell boundaries. W and h, respectively length and width are predicted relative to the size of the entire image. The score prediction represents the IoU between the predicted bounding box and the actual bounding box, the ground truth box. Each grid cell predicts the class of the object represented by a single vector length, over the number of classes in the data set.

Glenn Jocher [18] introduced YOLOv5 using the Pytorch framework, published by Ultralytics LLC team. Although the official website of the original author did not announce a recognized does not affect its usefulness compared to other YOLO series. YOLOV5 can reach 140 FPS (Frames per seconds) on Tesla P100, YOLOv4 [17] is only 50 FPS. YOLOV5 inherited the advantages of YOLOV4, the emphasis on new data enhancement methods, such as mosaic training, self-adversarial training (SAT), and Feature pyramid network (FPN) fusion with pixel aggregation network (PAN) to replace multi-channel features [19].

YOLOv5 consists of five different architectures, YOLOv5n, YOLOv5s, YOLOv5m, YOLOv5l and YOLOv5x. Each of these architectures differs in the number of layers of the neural network. We have experimented with these different architectures and we can see that the performance of the network improves as the number of layers increases, but with a loss in terms of prediction speed. YOLOv5x is the architecture we have chosen (607 layers). Our architecture, YOLOv5x (Fig. 3) consists of four main parts: input, backbone, neck, and output. The input endpoint mainly contains data preprocessing, including mosaic data augmentation and adaptive image filling [20]. The backbone network mainly uses a partial cross-stage network (CSP) [21] and spatial pyramid clustering (SPP) [21]. BottleneckCSP is not only factorizes the computational volume but increases the inference transmission. In the neck network, the pyramidal structures of FPN and PAN are used. The FPN structure [22] conveys strong semantic features from the higher features, at the same time, the PAN structure [23] conveys strong localization features from the lower feature maps to the higher feature maps. As the final detection step, the output is mainly used to predict targets.

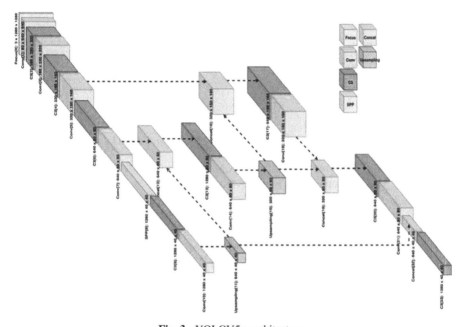

Fig. 3. YOLOV5x architecture.

3.2   Loss Function

The YOLOv5 loss is composed of three parts: class loss (cls), objectivity loss (coord), localization loss (IoU).

$$Loss = Loss_1 L_{coord} + Loss_2 L_{iou} + Loss_3 L_{cls}. \tag{2}$$

- Coordinate prediction error $Loss_{coord}$

    The coordinate prediction error $Loss_{coord}$ is defined as follows:

$$Loss_{coord} = \lambda_{coord} \, \Sigma_{i=1}^{s^2} \Sigma_{j=1}^{B} 1_{ij}^{obj} \left[(x_i - \hat{x}_i)^2 + (y_1 - \hat{y}_i)^2 \right]$$

$$+ \lambda_{\text{coord}} \sum_{i=1}^{S^2} \Sigma_{j=1}^{B} 1_{ij}^{obj} \left[\left(w_i - \hat{w}_i \right)^2 + \left(h_i - \hat{h}_i \right)^2 \right]. \qquad (3)$$

In Eq. (3), λ_{coord} is the weight of the coordinate error, S^2 is the number of grids in the input image, and B is the number of bounding boxes produced by each grid. $1_{ij}^{obj} = 1$ indicates that the object falls in the jth bounding box of grid i, otherwise $1_{ij}^{obj} = 0$. $\left(\hat{x}_i, \hat{y}_i, \hat{w}_1, \hat{h}_i \right)$ are the values of the center coordinate, height and width of the predicted bounding box, (x_i, y_i, w_i, h_i) are the actual values.

- IoU error $loss_{\text{iou}}$

The IoU is a standard for defining the accuracy with which target object detection is done. The IoU evaluates the performance of the model by calculating the rate of overlap between the actual and predicted bounding box, it is defined as follows

$$IoU = \frac{S_{\text{overlap}}}{S_{\text{union}}}. \qquad (4)$$

where S_{overlap} is the crossing area between the actual bounding box and the predicted one. S_{union} is the matching area of the two bounding boxes.

The IoU error $loss_{\text{iou}}$ is defined as follows:

$$loss_{\text{iou}} = \sum_{i=1}^{S^2} \sum_{j=1}^{B} 1_{ij}^{obj} \left(C_i - \hat{C}_i \right)^2$$
$$+ \lambda_{\text{noobbj}} \Sigma_{i=1}^{S^2} \Sigma_{j=1}^{B} 1_{ij}^{obj} \left(C_i - \hat{C}_i \right)^2. \qquad (5)$$

where the parameter λ_{mooby} is the weight of the error IoU. $\hat{C}_i$ is the predicted score, and C_i is the actual score.

- Classification error $loss_{cls}$

The classification error $loss_{cls}$ is defined as follows:

$$loss_{cls} = \Sigma_{i=1}^{S^2} \Sigma_{j=1}^{B} 1_{ij}^{obj} \Sigma_{c \in \text{classes}} \left(p_i(c) - \hat{p}_i(c) \right)^2 \qquad (6)$$

where c denotes the membership class of the detected target, $p_i(c)$ is the true probability that the object belonging to class c is in grid i. $\hat{p}_i(c)$ is the predicted value. The cls error for grid i is the sum of the classification errors for all objects in the grid.

3.3 Grid Sensitivity

When we decode the bounding box center coordinate, it is therefore difficult to predict the centers of bounding boxes that lie right on the grid boundary (Fig. 4).

We can solve this problem by removing the grid sensitivity, this makes it easier for the model to predict the exact box center located on the grid boundary. The FLOP

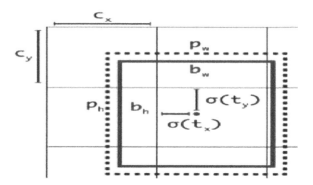

Fig. 4. Grid Sensitivity diagram.

(floating-point operations per second) added by Sensitivity of the grid is really small and can be reduced considerably. It is defined by these equations:

$$
\begin{aligned}
b_x &= (2 \cdot \sigma(t_x) - 0.5) + c_x \\
b_y &= \left(2 \cdot \sigma(t_y) - 0.5\right) + c_y \\
b_w &= p_w \cdot (2 \cdot \sigma(t_w))^2 \\
b_h &= p_h \cdot (2 \cdot \sigma(t_h))^2.
\end{aligned}
\tag{7}
$$

4 Experiments and Results

4.1 Datasets

4.1.1 Data Acquisition

Our data are in image format and are based on the EMMEL test, which is a test for the detection of hemoglobin S that identifies red blood cells that take a typical "sickle" shape after the application of Meta (metabisulfite). These experiments were carried out in the laboratory of UMRED, Health Faculty Thies University, BP 967 Thies following a well-defined protocol. First, we put the red blood cells of a sickle cell patient in a mixture with Meta in an apraxia medium created by kerosene oil. After 15 min, we took a drop of 10 μl of the SS blood + Meta 2% mixture to make a blood smear [15]. In order to improve the quality and the visibility of our images, we applied the Giemsa staining protocol [16], it consists in making a mixture of eosin and methylene blue. After staining with Giemsa for 20 min, the slides are read with an optical microscope at ×100 magnification with immersion oil. The reading fields are visualized on a screen and pictures are extracted for image processing.

4.1.2 Image Annotation

The recovered blood smear images contain two types of red blood cells: normal and abnormal. Thus, the main objective of the work is to detect abnormal red blood cells or sickle cells from a blood smear image. To identify the class of the abnormal red blood cell, we used an annotation tool to distinguish the coordinates of each sickle cell present in an image. We used the Computer Vision Annotation Tool (CVAT) platform because it is easy to use, open source and allows exporting data in several formats. For the annotation, we used the bounding box shape which allows to define the spatial location of the object in the image. It is used to determine the coordinates (the length and width of the box) of the annotated object in the image that serve as a reference for the computer vision algorithm to identify and classify the object. The class is identified by a name and also by a color. We had two classes: a falciform and a normal class (cells in the process of malformation are considered as falciform) identified respectively by the name's 'F', 'N' and the colors 'red' and 'green'.

4.1.3   Image Data Augmentation and Dataset Production

Before submitting the dataset to our algorithm, we made a number of pre-processing's in order to improve the quality of our model. For this, we used the ROBOFLOW platform. Our dataset contained 186 images (Table 1), we applied data augmentation with the aim of quantifying our images by 20%, the techniques used were cropping with a zoom of 0–26% and rotation with a variability between 8° and 8°. We also reduced the size of our images from 3,264 × 1,836 to 640 × 640 in order to fit the architecture of our model and at the same time reduce the training time. Finally, our dataset was divided into 70%, 20% and 10% for training, validation and testing respectively. The data was exported in yolov5 format and directly connected to the training model thanks to the Roboflow library available on python. The following table summarizes the set of collected and augmented images and the distribution of our dataset.

Table 1. Datasets statistics.

Raw images	Data augmentation	
186 images	223 images	
Train	Val	Test
156 images	45 images	22 images
Normal cell	Sickle cell	
5231 cells	Cells	

4.2   Training

A pre-trained model on images was used to improve the performance of our model. This is a blood cell dataset available on Roboflow, 364 images of three classes: WBC, RBC and platelets, with 4,888 labels. We performed our training on google colab pro with Tesla P100-PCIE-16 GB GPU, 16,280 MB RAM, and 56 multiprocessors. Our input image size was set to 640 × 640 and the batch size used was 16. We used the Adams optimizer and leaky ReLU as the activation function. The training rate was initialized to 0.01 and the momentum was 0.937. The training was done over 1000 epochs with an early stopping from 100 epochs.

4.3 Results

4.3.1 Evaluation Metrics

For object detection tasks, traditional evaluation measures include precision, recall, and mean precision (mAP), precision (P) and recall (R) can be expressed as follows:

$$P = \frac{TP}{TP + FP}, R = \frac{TP}{TP + FN}. \tag{8}$$

where TP, FP, and FN denote true positives, false positives, and false negatives, respectively. To calculate mAP, the average precision (AP) of each class must be measured, which can be calculated by an all-point interpolation approach to smooth the precision and recall curve. In addition, the mAP can be calculated by taking the average of the AP with respect to each class. The formulas can be expressed as follows:

$$AP = \sum_{i=1}^{n}(R_{i+1} - R_i) \max_{\tilde{R}:R \geq R_{i+1}} P(\tilde{R}), mAP = \frac{1}{N}\sum_{i=1}^{N} AP_i. \tag{9}$$

where i is the index value, P and R denote precision and recall respectively, N is the number of classes and AP_i is the average precision of the i-th class.

4.3.2 Evaluation

The different models of YOLOV5 have been implemented and the table below contains the results of these models on our validation data. YOLOV5x is the most satisfactory model (Table 2) with an accuracy of 0.95 and is used as the final model for deployment.

Table 2. Comparison of results.

Models	Accuracy	Recall	mAP
YOLOV5n	0,812	0,734	0,840
YOLOV5s	0,921	0,836	0,806
YOLOV5m	0,913	0,873	0,813
YOLOV5l	0,934	0,884	0,889
YOLOV5x	0,951	0,904	0,870

The performance of our model (YOLOV5x) allows us to rule out underfitting. Given the almost similar learning and loss curve (Fig. 5) on the training and validation data, we can also rule out overfitting. The early stopping occurred from epoch 396 onwards, but the saved weights are those obtained during the epoch that had the best performance.

The table above compares the accuracy of our model to other model techniques in our literature review (Table 3).

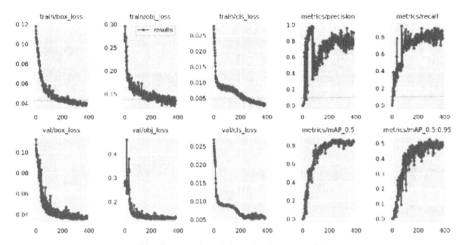

Fig. 5. Results of the YOLOV5x model.

Table 3. Comparison of our model with other models

Auteurs	Method	Accuracy
Acharya and Kumar	K-medoids	71%
Mohammad Mahmudul Alam et al	Tiny YOLO	96%
Our models	Yolov5x	95%

4.4 Deployment

The deployment was done locally with Flask, HTML\CSS were used for the frontend. To do this, we create a virtual environment in which we installed Flask and its dependencies in addition to the other libraries related to the model. The interface allows to load a blood smear image and to download the result (Fig. 6) afterwards.

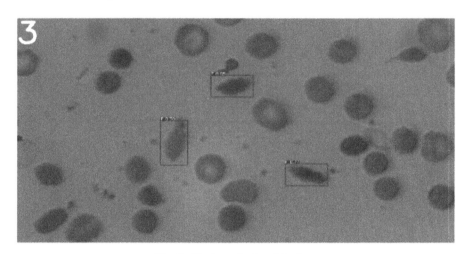

Fig. 6. Final result after detection.

5   Conclusion and Future Work

Accurate cell counting is very important in medical image analysis. In clinical applications, usually different types of cells are counted manually, which leads to a huge workload. In this paper, we have developed a YOLOV5-based identification and counting method that can help medical professionals to make a faster and efficient diagnosis of cells from a blood smear image.

Although our results are satisfactory, there is still a lot of room for improvement especially since we are in the medical field where accuracy is very fundamental. The YOLOV5 model thanks to its grid sensitivity method allowed us to reduce the FLOPs added by the sensitivity, but nevertheless, for some cases the model has difficulty in identifying overlapping cells and partial cells in the edges of the images.

The research work done in this paper highlights many perspectives to be explored. The development of a computer vision model requires a large amount of annotated data. In our model, the training set consists of only 156 images. We plan to acquire more data to improve the performance of the model.

Also, the experimentation of other algorithms can allow us to widen our field of research, so we plan to explore other models of object detection namely YOLOX, YOLOR, YOLOV6, Fast R-CNN, EfficientDet, etc.

In order to generalize our model, we intend to perform tests on samples prepared in another laboratory.

It would also be interesting to extend our research to other types of diseases such as malaria, hepatitis B.

Tests at the laboratory of UMRED over a long period of time could give us other perspectives for improvement.

References

1. Sherman, I.J.: The sickling phenomenon, with special reference to the differentiation of sickle cell anemia from the sickle cell trait. Bull. Johns Hopkins Hosp. **67**(309), 19 (1940)
2. Thiam, L., et al.: Epidemiological, clinical and hematological profiles of SS homozygous sickle cell disease in the inter critical phase in children in Ziguinchor, Senegal. Pan Afr. Med. J. **28**, 208 (2017)
3. Christoph, G.W., Hofrichter, J., Eaton, W.A.: Understanding the shape of sickled red cells. Biophys. J. **88**(2), 1371–1376 (2005)
4. Maciaszek, J.L., Andemariam, B., Lykotrafitis, G.: Micro-elasticity of red blood cells in sickle cell disease. J. Strain Anal. Eng. Des. **46**(5), 368–379 (2011)
5. Bentley, S.A., Lewis, S.M.: The morphological classification of red cells using an image analysing computer. Br. J. Haematol. **32**(2), 205–214 (1976)
6. Stuart, M.J., Nagel, R.L.: Sickle-cell disease. Lancet **364**(9442), 1343–1360 (2004)
7. Tomari, R., Zakaria, W.N.W., Jamil, M.M.A., Nor, F.M., Fuad, N.F.N.: Computer aided system for red blood cell classification in blood smear image. Procedia Comput. Sci. **42**, 206–213 (2014)
8. Acharya, V., Kumar, P.: Identification and red blood cell automated counting from blood smear images using computer-aided system. Med. Biol. Eng. Comput. **56**(3), 483–489 (2017). https://doi.org/10.1007/s11517-017-1708-9
9. Sarrafzadeh, O., Dehnavi, A.M., Rabbani, H., et al.: Circlet based framework for red blood cells segmentation and counting. In: IEEE Workshop on Signal Processing Systems, December 2015
10. Kaur, P., Sharma, V., Garg, N.: Platelet count using image processing. In: International Conference on Computing for Sustainable Global Development (INDIACom), March 2016
11. Bao, P., Zhang, L., Wu, X.: Canny edge detection enhancement by scale multiplication. IEEE Trans. Pattern Anal. Mach. Intell. **27**(9), 1485–1490 (2005)
12. Alam, M.M., Islam, M.T.: Machine learning approach of automatic identification and counting of blood cells. In: Healthcare Technology Letters, 20 October 2018 (2018)
13. Gomes, A.L.M., de Almeida Coelho, F.: Sickle cell identification in red blood cell images. In: Proseminar: Computer Vision and Human-Computer Interaction, CSCI 2014, 19 December 2014 (2014)
14. Fitzgibbon, A.W., Fisher, R.B.: A buyer's guide to conic fitting. DAI Research paper (1996)
15. Blood smear-realization-and-systematic-examination.pdf. https://vetodiag.fr/wpcontent/upl oads/2020/12/Frottis-sanguin-re%CC%81alisationet-examen syste%CC%81matique.pdf. Accessed 10 Mar 2022
16. MM-SOP-07a-eng.pdf. https://iris.wpro.who.int/bitstream/handle/10665.1/14374/MM-SOP-07a-fre.pdf. Accessed 10 Mar 2022
17. Bochkovskiy, A., Wang, C.-Y., Liao, H.-Y.M.: YOLOv4: optimal speed and accuracy of object, detection. Computer Science, 23 April 2020
18. https://github.com/ultralytics/yolov5. Accessed 13 Dec 2021
19. Liu, S., Qi, L., Qin, H., Shi, J., Jia, J.: Path aggregation network for instance segmentation. In: Proceedings of the IEEE Conference on Computer Vision and Pattern Recognition, pp. 8759–8768 (2018)
20. Wu, C., Wen, W., Afzal, T., Zhang, Y., Chen, Y.: A compact DNN: approaching GoogLeNet-level accuracy of classification and domain adaptation. In: Proceedings of the 2017 IEEE Conference on Computer Vision and Pattern Recognition (CVPR), Honolulu, HI, USA, 21–26 July 2017 (2017)
21. Kim, D., Park, S., Kang, D., Paik, J.: Improved center and scale prediction-based pedestrian detection using convolutional block. In: Proceedings of the 2019 IEEE 9th International

Conference on Consumer Electronics (ICCE-Berlin), Berlin, Germany, 8–11 September 2019, pp. 418–419 (2019)

22. Liu, Wei, Anguelov, Dragomir, Erhan, Dumitru, Szegedy, Christian, Reed, Scott, Fu, Cheng-Yang., Berg, Alexander C.: SSD: Single shot multibox detector. In: Leibe, Bastian, Matas, Jiri, Sebe, Nicu, Welling, Max (eds.) ECCV 2016. LNCS, vol. 9905, pp. 21–37. Springer, Cham (2016). https://doi.org/10.1007/978-3-319-46448-0_2

23. Wang, W., et al.: Efficient and accurate arbitrary-shaped text detection with pixel aggregation network. In: Proceedings of the IEEE/CVF International Conference on Computer Vision, Seoul, Korea, 27 October–2 November 2019, pp. 8440–8449. IEEE

Remote sensing and AI in Agriculture

Quaternionic Wavelets for Estimating Forest Biomass by Gradient Boosting Methods

Adamou Mfopou[1,2,4(✉)], Hippolyte Tapamo[1,2,5], and Justin Moskolai[3,4]

[1] LIRIMA, Equipe IDASCO, Yaoundé, Cameroon
mfopadamou@yahoo.fr
[2] IRD UMI 209 UMMISCO, Paris, France
[3] INP Toulouse, Toulouse, France
[4] University of Douala, Douala, Cameroon
[5] University of Yaounde, Yaoundé, Cameroon

Abstract. The AGB estimation is an vital issue inside the system of lessening Emissions from Deforestation and Forest Degradation (UNCCC REDD system). This question is even more troublesome for tropical area which endure from the deficiency of exact data from forest inventories on the ground and above all from the complexity of the forests. This problem can be addressed by satellite remote sensing as very high spatial resolution optical images giving data on forest structure through canopy grain texture analysis are becoming increasingly available. The FOTO (FOurier Texture Ordination) method has stood out for its relevance for predicting forest biomass in a few tropical regions. It employments PCA and linear regression, and in this work we propose a unused texture classifier based on the quaternionic wavelet transform (QWT). This recent transform isolates the data contained in an image more efficiently than previous methods and gives a multi-scale analysis whose coefficients are 2D analytic, with almost translationally invariant amplitude and phase, composed of three angles. The use and interpretation of QWT coefficients, in particular phase, are covered, and we show a texture classifier that uses both amplitude and phase. Thanks to the QWT, we get way better classification performance than with the classic FOTO method with a gain of around 30%.

Keywords: Quaternionic wavelet transform · Extrem gradient boosting · Aboveground biomass · FOTO method

1 Introduction

The 195 countries present at the COP21 climate conference held in Paris in 2015 agreed to restrain the increment in global temperature to $1.5\,°C$. This measure was taken for limit the affect of climate change within limits that man can tolerate. Due to the close relationship between the temperature of the terrestrial air

T. M. Ngatched Nkouatchah et al. (Eds.): PAAISS 2022, LNICST 459, pp. 239–250, 2023.
https://doi.org/10.1007/978-3-031-25271-6_15

and the quantity of CO_2 in the atmosphere, this objective cannot be achieved without a strong policy of limiting deforestation and the degradation of forests, which represent more than 10% of carbon emissions, more than the whole global transport sector and second only to the energy sector [9]. This is why a mechanism called REDD+ (Reducing Emissions from Deforestation and Forest Degradation) was developed by the Parties to the United Nations Framework Convention on Climate Change (UNFCCC). This framework makes financial value for carbon put away in forests by giving motivations for developing countries to reduce emissions from forest lands and contribute in low-carbon pathways to sustainable development. (ANNUAL REPORT OF THE UN-REDD PROGRAM FUND, www.unredd.net and www.un-redd.org). The follow-up to this initiative whose philosophy is to improve global knowledge to find solutions to deforestation and forest degradation as nature-based solutions to climate change can only be achieved by using innovative platforms and collaboratives that developed exact and vigorous strategies for assessing and monitoring aboveground and monitoring aboveground forest biomass (AGB) over expansive ranges in tropical regions [1]. The evaluation of forest biomass is the result of fieldwork during which researchers combine the estimates of biomass at the level of each tree generally obtained from allometric equations utilizing easy-to-measure explanatory variables such as the diameter from the trunk to chest height, with the sampling of huge domains to count trees and measure these variables [1]. These forest inventories require the mobilization of strong delegations thus leading to very high expenses. Despite this mobilization, we very often do not manage to cover huge testing ranges, nor to achieve a high temporal frequency of observations as required for monitoring purposes. It therefore becomes imperative to use remote sensing techniques to overcome this limitation. This will help to interpolate rare terrain information in space and time [1]. There are several remote sensing techniques, including optical satellite remote sensing. The latter is less expensive compared to airborne techniques and, thanks to the availability of high to very high spatial resolution (VHRS) images comprising pixels of size 1 m or less, its relevance with regard to the evaluation of biomass forestry has increased. VHRS imagery allows the texture to be linked to the shapes of the forest canopy, in particular the size of the crowns [1]. Several studies have found that there is a correlation between texture information on two-dimensional textural images and certain variables describing the 3D structure of forest stands. Which is used to indirectly predict stand biomass. Methods based on image texture analysis, such as the FOTO [2,7,8] method, have shown promising results for applications to biomass predictions in tropical rainforests, in particular because the indices of texture showed no signs of saturation at high biomass levels [2]. The FOTO method is a 3-step process. It starts with 2D fast Fourier transform by calculating r spectra on very high resolution images. After this step, it uses principal component analysis (PCA) for the ordination of the spectra r obtained. Finally, she builds a linear regression (LR) model that will be used to estimate biomass values or stand parameters from reference datasets (data or simulations derived from data). ACP and LR are the two mathematical models used to deduce the result of the method. The literature shows that FOTO relies on linear models [2,7,8,12,14–16] and cannot capture all angles of issues that are inalienably nonlinear. Over the past decades, a few machine learning strategies based on nonlinear models have risen to illuminate classification or estimation issues. In this study, we examine quaternion wavelet transform (QWT) and extreme gradient boosting (XGBOOST) strategies which will be valuable to way better address biomass estimation in tropical forests.

2   Aboveground Biomass Estimation

Strategies available for mapping forest biomass drop beneath two fundamental approaches. Within the to begin with approach, radiometric modelling strategies involve regression analysis to connect spectral values to measured or estimated biomass at comparing areas [10]. The spectral values can be the digital numbers or their radiometric transformation recorded in each image channel, as well as band proportions and vegetation indices. In the second class of methods, a supervised learning scheme is used to produce a conversion table for the thematic classification of windows of the image. The work presented here falls in the second category. Several methods have been proposed in this second category and we will now present one detail we well know FOTO Method.

2.1   FOTO Method

The FOTO method uses canopy grains to estimate forest biomass. It relies on these canopy grains because they depend on the spatial distribution of the trees, the shapes of the crowns and the dimensions of the crowns. The important element of the FOTO method is the estimation of the degree of repetitiveness in the grains of the canopy; it constitutes the most important characteristic of the texture. To obtain this, we use the two-dimensional Fourier transform which moves the grain of the canopy from the spatial domain to the frequency domain [15]. The fundamental steps of the FOTO method are shown in Fig. 1.

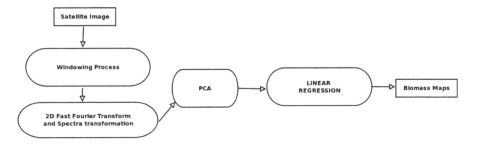

Fig. 1. The FOTO method

Windowing Process. The first step after the acquisition is to cut the image into thumbnails of size w and we store all in a directory on the disk. If the size of the image is not a multiple of w, we complete the image with white. We can then apply a preprocessing algorithm to the thumbnails exhibiting a texture that may distort the desired results. It can be a series of functions of mathematical morphology such as thresholding, opening, closing and erosion.

2D FFT and R-Spectra Computation. At this stage, we start by defining the size of the square window in which the 2D FFT will be calculated. The image is then cut into square windows in which the radial Fourier spectra will be calculated. The Fourier coefficients are thus obtained by a convolution between the value of the image, the waveform of variable directions and the spatial frequency is used to calculate the spectrum r [15]. This spectrum neglects orientation information and has been shown to be useful for summarizing textural properties in relation to coarseness/fitness, which are of great importance in the treatment of natural forest canopies [8].

The observation is that the r spectra produced by the coarse textured windows tend to be biased towards small spatial frequencies, whereas the spectra are more balanced on the fine textures.

Textural Ordination. The algorithm calculates the spectrum r of each window and saves it in a global table within which each line contains the corresponding values for a given window. The columns of this table present the parts of the variance of the luminance of the image explained by a given spatial frequency or wavenumber. We will then submit this table of spectra r to a standardized principal component analysis (PCA). The latter will make an analysis by eigenvectors of the correlation matrix between the spatial frequencies. We will therefore extract the most important components (generally three) that we will use as texture indices. This allows windows to be ordered along texture gradients. [15].

Texture Mapping and Biomass Prediction. The results of the PCA are used as texture indices. Such texture maps have a spatial resolution that is strongly related to the window size. An increase in the window size results in a decrease in the spatial resolution of the texture. In the FOTO Method, biomass prediction is made using a linear regression model that relates ground forest biomass and these texture indices.

2.2   FOTO+ Method

The FOTO+ method was introduced by Tapamo et al. [12] in 2014. The authors there modified the original FOTO method by exploring other nonlinear machine learning methods. The new algorithms obtained made it possible to estimate the biomass of tropical forest areas based on the texture of the images of the canopy.

In the absence of representative real data, images simulated on the models of three types of forests presenting diversified textures and forms of canopy (open or closed, fine or coarse) were used. Many situations indicate nonlinearity in the relationship between tree biomass and crown size as well as that between stand biomass and canopy texture characteristics. Classification methods such as k-NN (k-nearest neighbors), SVM (support vector machines) and Random Forests apply to texture descriptors extracted from images via Fourier spectra. Experiments were conducted on simulations images produced by the DART (Discrete Anisotropic Radiative Transfer) software [11] with reference to information (3D stand models) from forests in the DRC (Democratic Republic of Congo), CAR (Central African Republic) and Congo. The observation made here is that better results are obtained with the nonlinear methods applied to the texture indices than with the linear method based on PCA and linear regression. According to Tapamo et al. [12], the non-linear methods obtain a gain of 19.50% compared to the linear method. This non-linearity is then an important factor to take into account in the estimation of the biomass using the analysis of the texture of the images of the canopy. The FOTO method uses PCA to reduce the amount of useful information to get it the phenomen on under study, but very often this does not produce the most significant texture variables as one can obtain with the selection of attributes. Attribute selection ves more suitable variables to represent the texture.

3   Using Quaternionic Wavelets Transform for Descriptors Extraction

3.1   Classic Wavelet Transform

The classical DWT gives a space-scale analysis of an image, in a matrix whose each coefficient corresponds to a "sub-band" (zone of the Fourier domain) and to a position in the image.

A "sub-band" translates an oscillation scale as well as a spatial orientation. It is encoded by a 2D atomic function called a "wavelet", which is a kind of localized and oriented oscillating pulse. Each coefficient is computed by a scalar product between a translated wavelet and the image, and therefore represents the presence of a local component in the image, at one position, for a sub-band.

By the wavelet transform, the image is expressed in an orthogonal basis of 2D atoms, formed by dilations and translations of a scale function ϕ and of three wavelets (ψ^D, ψ^V, ψ^H) expressed as a function of a scale function ϕ_1 1D and a wavelet 1 as follows:

$$\psi^D = \psi_1(x)\psi_1(y)$$
$$\psi^V = \phi_1(x)\psi_1(y)$$
$$\psi^H = \psi_1(x)\phi_1(y)$$
$$\phi = \phi_1(x)\phi_1(y)$$

In practice, the scalar products are produced by filtering (convolutions) of the image by the 4 base atoms, combined with resamplings, which reflect the expansion of these atoms.

3.2 Quaternionic Wavelet Transform (QWT)

QWT [5] is an enhancement of DWT, which provides richer analysis for 2D signals. Unlike DWT, it is almost translational invariant, and its coefficients are expressed in terms of amplitude and phase, much like the coefficients of a Fourier transform.

It is based on the QFT (Quaternionic Fourier Transform), and on the local quaternionic phase of T. [3], which extends to dimension 2 the well-known signal processing tools, by a generalization in the algebra of quaternions H. According to Bülow, this more general algebra is more suitable than C for manipulating 2D signals.

A quaternion is the generalization of a complex number, having three imaginary parts encoded on the imaginary numbers $i; j; k$. We write it in Cartesian representation $q = a + bi + cj + dk$, and its polar writing is, analogously to the complex exponential $q = |q|e^{i\varphi}e^{i\theta}e^{i\psi}$.

It is therefore defined by a module and an argument that contains three angles. The quaternionic argument gives us access to the phase of 2D signals.

The local phase of a 1D signal is known to be extracted by the Hilbert transform (HT) and the complex number argument (see analytical signal). Bülow remarks that it allows to efficiently describe the shape of 1D signals, which is why he creates the quaternionic phase [3], associated with a 2D function, defined using partial Hilbert transforms (HT) (H_1, H_2) and total (H_T) which form the analytical quaternionic signal [5]:

$$f_A(a,b) = f(a,b) + iH_1f(a,b) + jH_2f(a,b) + kH_Tf(a,b)$$

Quaternionic argument of this kind of signal represents the quaternionic phase of f, which describes its local structures at all points.

Integration in Wavelets. The QWT uses the notion of phase in a wavelet decomposition. Characterized from an explanatory quaternionic mother wavelet, the QWT yields quaternionic coefficients whose phase precisely describes the coded structures. The power of description of the image already provided by the decomposition into sub-bands is then completed by an even finer description thanks to the phase. Each sub-band of the QWT can be seen as the analytical signal associated with a narrowband part of the image.

We will keep the terms *localamplitude* (modulus) and *localphase* (argument), of the analytical signal 1D. The amplitude of a coefficient quantifies the presence of a local 2D component, and its phase, represented by three angles, constitutes a complete description thereof.

The amplitude of a coefficient QWT $|q|$, invariant by translation of the image, quantifies the presence of a component, at any spatial position, in each frequency sub-band.

The phase, represented by three angles $(\varphi; \theta; \psi)$, constitutes a complete description of the structure of these components. We will discuss the interpretation of this phase below.

Implantation. From a practical point of view, if the mother wavelet is separable *i.e.* $\psi(a,b) = \psi_h(a)\psi_h(b)$ (this is our case), then the HT 2D are equivalent to HT 1D along the rows and columns of the image. So, considering the Hilbert pairs $(\psi_h, \psi_g = H\psi_h)$ (of wavelets) and $(\phi_h, \phi_g = H\phi_h)$ (of scale functions), the analytical 2D wavelet is written in terms of separable products.

$$\psi^D = \psi_h(a)\psi_h(b) + i\psi_g(a)\psi_h(b) + j\psi_h(a)\psi_g(b) + k\psi_g(a)\psi_g(b)$$
$$\psi^V = \phi_h(a)\psi_h(b) + i\phi_g(a)\psi_h b) + j\phi_h(a)\psi_g(b) + k\phi_g(a)\psi_g(b)$$
$$\psi^H = \psi_h(a)\phi_h(b) + i\psi_g(a)\phi_h(b) + j\psi_h(a)\phi_g(y) + k\psi_g(a)\phi_g(y)$$
$$\phi = \phi_h(a)\phi_h(b) + i\phi_g(a)\phi_h(b) + j\phi_h(a)\phi_g(b) + k\phi_g(a)\phi_g(b)$$

his implies that such a decomposition is very dependent on the orientation of the image in the frame (x, y) (variance by rotation) and that the wavelet is not isotropic. The advantage of the QWT is in its ease of installation by separable filter banks, and in its concept of phase.

The QWT uses the Dual-Tree algorithm [13], a filterbank that uses a Hilbert pair as a 1D mother wavelet. It provides complex analytical coefficients, and the modulus is translationally invariant, for redundancy of only 4:1.

Two complementary filter banks, one utilizing an indeed filter, the other an odd filter, lead to four divisible 2D filter banks, somewhat counterbalanced from each other. These shifts compare hypothetically to the phase shifts of the 2D Hilbert changes specified over. One gets a sub-pixel accuracy, interpreted by implication in the notion of phase shifts of the 2D Hilbert transforms mentioned above. One obtains a sub-pixel precision, translated indirectly in the notion of phase. Initially combined by Kingsbury [13] to establish two complex decompositions (6 oriented sub-bands), the four outputs of the Dual-Tree constitute here the Cartesian components of a quaternionic output. The quaternion algebra H then gives access to the module/argument representation which allows us to separately represent the presence of local components in the image (amplitude), and their structures (phase).

Note that the Dual-Tree carries out an approximation, which makes the coefficients of the QWT approximately analytical, and therefore the extraction of local 2D amplitudes and phases, as well as their interpretation, are in reality approximate.

3.3   Using Wavelets

It appears that DWT's multiscale analysis is well suited for textural images. From each sub-band, one calculates an average, a standard deviation, the total energy, and the average power ... By correctly combining these characteristics, one constitutes a descriptor vector experimentally favorable to characterize the texture well.

Recently, Celik and Tjahjadi [4] used the CWT Dual-Tree, for its (almost) translational invariant modulus and its "oriented" aspect. The extracted descriptor made it possible to obtain better results than with conventional wavelets.

The translational invariance of the modulus ensures that the extracted characteristics are independent of the precise position of the textural patterns, and therefore allows better characterization.

We propose to use the QWT, which also has a translational invariant modulus, and we extend the analysis using the QWT phase.

To calculate the QWT, we use the algorithm described in [5].

4   Extreme Gradient Boosting Methods for AGB Estimation

More recently, Chen and Guestrin (2016) [6] proposed the last avatar of boosting with extreme gradient boosting. The complexity is very sensitive in particular with the number of parameters which it is necessary to take into account in the optimization of the algorithm. The computation costs would become quite prohibitive, also the associated library (XGBoost), available in R, Python, Julia, Scala, and in distributed environments (Spark) offers an efficient parallelization of computations with in particular the possibility of accessing the graphics card (GPU) of the computer and offers an approximate version when big data is distributed.

But, what really encourages interest in this version of boosting is its fairly systematic use in the winning solutions of the Kaggle forecasting contests. Gradient Boosting is a supervised learning algorithm whose principle is to combine the results of a set of simpler and weaker models in order to provide a better prediction. This is also referred to as the model aggregation method. The idea is therefore simple: instead of using a single model, the algorithm will use several which will then be combined to obtain a single result.

It is above all a pragmatic approach which therefore makes it possible to manage both regression and classification problems. The algorithm has a sequential operation. What differentiates it from random forests for example. This sequential principle will certainly make it slower, but above all, it will allow the algorithm to improve by capitalization compared to other methods. At first, He builds a first model and evaluates it (supervised learning). Each individual will at that point be weighted concurring to the execution of the prediction, beginning from the primary evaluation, etc. XGBoost stands out remarkably from other methods in machine learning competitions, but this is not only due to its principle of sequential self-improvement.

This robustness also comes from the fact that XGBoost integrates a large number of modifiable and configurable hyper-parameters for improvement.

5   Implementation

5.1   Test Data

The implementation of our model required the use of a set of satellite images for calibration and testing. Considering the rarity and the difficulties of acquiring real images, we have chosen to use two types of images for the implementation of our model. Thus, given that we only had very few real images, in particular those of the locality of Kumu in the great South of Cameroon (at the rate of three plots) which were the subject of several field studies for measuring the biomass of trees, we chose to calibrate and test our model with simulated DART (Discrete Anisotropic Radiative Transfer) [11] images of the forests of the Congo Basin (precisely on three sites: Congo (176 thumbnails), RCA (105 thumbnails)) and DRC (109 thumbnails)). The model obtained can therefore be validated on the real images mentioned above.

Developed at CESBIO in 1992, the DART model was patented in 2003. It is free of rights for scientific activities and research in general. With the support of CNES, the company Magellium has developed a professional version of the DART model which works under Linux and Windows [11] environments. DART model simulates radiative transfer in the Earth - Atmosphere system, at any wavelength from visible to thermal infrared. It employs an approach that combines ray tracking and the discrete ordinate method. It is suitable for natural and urban environments (forests with different types of trees, urban buildings, rivers, etc.) with or without taking into account the topography and the atmosphere. It simulates the landscape as a 3D matrix of cells that may contain cloudy matter and/or opaque or translucent triangles. Cloudy material is used to simulate leaf vegetation (tree crown, grass, etc.) and the atmosphere. Triangles are used to simulate opaque or translucent surfaces (topography, leaf, woody and urban elements, etc.). On the other hand, DART uses spectral and structural databases (atmosphere, tree leaves, soils, etc.).

A user-friendly GUI graphic interface allows both to enter the parameters of the studied landscape and to visualize the results of the simulations (images, etc.).

5.2   Implementation Strategies

In most applications in the literature, wavelet texture classification methods use either a global energy measure or statistical modulus measures.

First, we therefore compared the performance of the DWT and the QWT by making measurements on their module.

5.3   Descriptor Extraction

After the calculation of the modulus $M_{ij} = |q_{ij}|$ of the wavelet transform of a given image (i and j are the discrete coordinates of a pixel), we consider two measures for each sub-band.

Table 1. Results on Congo, CAR and DRC dataset

Method	Settings	Congo		CAR		DRC	
		AMAE	Gain	AMAE	Gain	AMAE	Gain
Basic FOTO		56590		81890		39760	
FOTO use SVR	RBF Kernel	46103.74	18.53%	66643.02	18.62%	31458.90	20.88%
FOTO use k-NN	K=9	48344.67	14.57%	72857.69	11.03%	33608.78	15.47%
FOTO use k-NN	K=11	48232.02	14.77%	70765.04	13.59%		
FOTO use RF	ntree=50	77554.91	-37.05%	67140.53	18.01%	33079.94	21.95%
FOTO use Attribute selection + SVR	RBF Kernel	45356.84	19.85%	66633.88	18.63%	30519.11	23.24%
Attribute selection + k-NN	K=5	45593.04	19.43%	71077.77	13.20%	33608.78	15.47%
Attribute selection + k-NN	K=7	45280.02	19.99%	70634.69	13.74%		
FOTO + QWT + XGBOOST		**64432.24**	**21.32%**	**40208.12**	**28.95%**	**30193.01**	**24.06%**

Energy:

$$m = \frac{1}{E}\Sigma M_{ij}^2$$

consider E as the entire energy of the image minus that of the low-frequency sub-band. m is used in this normalization as the relative amount of energy in one sub-band compared to others.

The standard deviation:

$$m = \sqrt{\frac{1}{N}\Sigma(M_{ij} - \mu)^2}$$

consider N as the number of pixels in the sub-band, and μ as the average.

6   Results and Discussion

The cross-validation results are almost identical for energy and standard deviation. We arbitrarily choose, for the rest, to keep the standard deviation measure. We present the results in comparison with the other methods. Note that these results are correct, and confirm that the quaternionic wavelet transform is a good method.

6.1   Results

We estimated the error using a tenfold cross-validation scheme on each classification method and each dataset. As an evaluation criterion, we used the mean absolute error (AMAE) i.e. the average of the absolute value of the difference between the actual AGB values and those predicted for all the images of the dataset. The Tables 1 present the results for the Congo, CAR (Central African Republic) and DRC (Democratic Republic of Congo) datasets respectively.

These comes about show us a clear improvement of the FOTO method with the use of QWT and XGBOOST. These improvements, depending on the quality of the data in each game go up to more than 28%.

With a gain of 21.32%, the QWT + XGBOOST algorithm gives the best improvement on the Congo dataset.

With a gain of 24.06%, the QWT + XGBOOST algorithm gives the best improvement on the DRC dataset.

Ditto on the CAR dataset where the QWT + XGBOOST algorithm improves with a gain of 28.95%.

These results prove to us that the new algorithm (QWT + XGBOOST) presented here improves more than all the previous adaptations of FOTO.

6.2   Discussions

The much more complex textural patterns, made up of a set of local components. The QWT is therefore perhaps not the most suitable tool for a "fast" analysis of textures. It seems to us that a spatial measurement on the modulus of the QWT coefficients combined with a study of the QWT phase, would be much more effective for the characterization of the textures and the extraction of the descriptors. This work, with a single standard deviation, opens the way to many possibilities for study in the space field.

7   Conclusion and Perspectives

In this work, we proposed to set up a modern approach permitting to assess the aboveground forest biomass (AGB) on tremendous regions of moo openness. A troublesome task in the field. A method called FOTO was introduced by Couteron [7] and Proisy et al. [16] and has proven to be powerful in giving solid biomass predictions from canopy pictures in several locales of the tropics [14,17]. We investigated the plausibility of progressing the execution of this strategy by nonlinear regression procedures. The performance test of our strategy was carried out on simulated pictures of the forest canopy reference to the characteristics of nearby stands in the DRC (Democratic Republic of Congo), CAR (Central African Republic) and Congo. The results gotten illustrate that our approach is strong and yields with less mistakes than in the linear regression utilized in FOTO. Precision picks up of around 30% have been gotten utilizing the proposed approach.

Acknowledgements. We address our thanks to Professor Maurice TCHUENTE (UMMISCO, Université de Yaoundé I, Department of computer science) and to Professor Louis Aimé FONO, Université de Douala for fruitful discussions.

References

1. Antin, C., Pélissier, R., Vincent, G., Couteron, P.: Crown allometries are less responsive than stem allometry to tree size and habitat variations in an Indian monsoon forest. Trees **27**, 1485–1495 (2013)

2. Barbier, N., Couteron, P., Gastelly-Etchegorry, J., Proisy, C.: Linking canopy images to forest structural parameters: potential of a modeling framework. Ann. For. Sci. **69**, 305–311 (2012)
3. Bulow, T.: Hypercomplex spectral signal representations for image processing and analysis. Ph.d. thesis, Inst. f. Informatik u. Prakt. Math. der ChristianAlbrechts-Universitat zu Kie (1999)
4. Celik, T., Tjahjadi, T.: Multiscale texture classification using dual-tree complex wavelet transform. Pattern Recogn. Lett. **30**(3), 331–339 (2009)
5. Chan, W., Choi, H., Baraniuk, R.: Coherent multiscale image processing using dual-tree quaternion wavelets. IEEE Trans. Image Process. **17**(7), 1069–1082 (2008)
6. Chen, T., Guestrin, C.: XGBoost: a scalable tree boosting system. In: Proceedings of the ACM SIGKDD International Conference on Knowledge Discovery and Data Mining, San Francisco, CA, USA, August 2016
7. Couteron, P.: Quantifying change in patterned semi-arid vegetation by Fourier analysis of digitized aerial photographs. Int. J. Remote Sens. **23**(17), 3407–3425 (2002)
8. Couteron, P., Pelissier, R., Nicolini, E., Paget, D.: Predicting tropical forest stand structure parameters from Fourier transform of very high-resolution remotely sensed canopy images. J. Appl. Ecol. **42**, 1121–1128 (2005)
9. DeFries, R., et al.: Earth observations for estimating greenhouse gas emissions from deforestation in developing countries. Environ. Sci. Policy **10**, 385–394 (2007)
10. Foody, G., Boyd, D., Cutler, M.: Predictive relations of tropical forest biomass from Landsat TM data and their transferability between regions. Remote Sens. Environ. **85**, 463–474 (2003)
11. Gastellu-Etchegorry, J.P., et al.: Dart: Modèle physique 3D d'images de télédéection et du bilan radiatif de paysages urbains dt naturels. Revue Télédéection **8**(3), 159–167 (2008)
12. Tapamo, H., Mfopou, A., Ngonmang, B., Monga, O., Couteron, P.: Linear vs non-linear learning methods: a comparative study for forest above ground biomass, estimation from texture analysis of satellite images. Arima **18**, 114–131 (2014)
13. Kingsbury, N.: Complex wavelets for shift invariant analysis and filtering of signal. Appl. Comput. Harmon. Anal. **10**(3), 234–253 (2001)
14. Ploton, P., et al.: Assessing aboveground tropical forest biomass using Google Earth canopy images. Ecol. Appl. **22**(3), 993–1003 (2012)
15. Proisy, C., et al.: Biomass prediction in tropical forests: the canopy grain approach. In: Remote Sensing of Biomass - Principles and Applications. Temilola Fatoyinbo (2012)
16. Proisy, C., Couteron, P., Fromard, F.: Predicting and mapping mangrove biomass from canopy grain analysis using Fourier-based textural ordination of Ikonos images. Remote Sens. Environ. **109**(3), 379–392 (2007)
17. Singh, M., Malhi, Y., Bhagwat, S.: Biomass estimation of mixed forest landscape using a Fourier transform texture-based approach on very-high resolution optical satellite imagery. Int. J. Remote Sens. **35**(9), 3331–3349 (2008)

Detection and Classification of Underwater Acoustic Events

Caouis Kammegne[1,2(✉)], Theophile Bayet[1,3,4], Timothee Brochier[5], Diop Idy[1,5], Christophe Denis[3,4], and Yann Tremblay[6]

[1] UCAD, IRD, UMMISCO, Dakar, Senegal
kammegnecaouis@gmail.com, theophile.bayet@ird.fr
[2] African Institute for Mathematical Sciences (AIMS), Mbourg, Senegal
[3] Sorbonne Université, IRD, Unité de Modélisation Mathématique et Informatique des Systèmes Complexes, UMMISCO, 93143 Bondy, France
christophe.denis@lip6.fr
[4] Sorbonne Université, LIP6, 75005 Paris, France
[5] IRD, Université Cheikh Anta Diop, UCAD, Sorbonne Université, SU, Unité de Modélisation Mathématique et Informatique des Systèmes Complexes, UMMISCO, Campus UCAD-IRD de Hann, 18524 Dakar, Senegal
timothee.brochier@ird.fr
[6] Institut de Recherche pour le Développement (IRD), Research Unit UMR248 MARBEC, Avenue Jean Monnet, CS 30171, 34203 Sète Cedex, France
yann.tremblay@ird.fr

Abstract. The knowledge of fish assemblage in submarine environments is a keystone for fishery management but remain poorly monitored due to heavy methodological requirements for scientific fish sampling. Passive acoustic monitoring appeared as a promising non intrusive alternative to fish sampling, potentially providing more objective data at a reduced cost, but still rely on heavy expert analysis of the acoustic signal. We propose in this paper to improve passive acoustic monitoring efficiency with deep learning. Using convolutional recurrent neural networks, we built and tested models able to detect two types of fish vocalizations as well as motor engine sounds. The detector had a high F1 score (>0.94) and an error rate (<0.18). These methods are promising tools for the fish communities management as they allow automatic fish sounds detection and classification.

Keywords: Fish sounds · Fish chorus · Underwater acoustic · Passive acoustic monitoring · Sound event detection · Deep learning · CRNN · Engine sounds underwater

1 Introduction

Biodiversity monitoring is the process of establishing the status of and tracking changes in living organisms and the ecological complexes of which they are a part

Supported by UMMISCO.

T. M. Ngatched Nkouatchah et al. (Eds.): PAAISS 2022, LNICST 459, pp. 251–269, 2023.
https://doi.org/10.1007/978-3-031-25271-6_16

[1]. It provides a basis for assessing the integrity of ecosystems, their response to disturbance, and the success of measures taken to conserve or restore biodiversity. According to the United Nations Global Biodiversity Outlook, approximately 80% of the world's marine fish stocks for which quantitative information is available are fully exploited or over-exploited [1]. This over-exploitation, together with a variety of environmental destruction, result in a depletion of biological diversity that brings us closer and closer to a critical threshold that could catastrophically impact the resilience of the ecosystem and associated human communities.

Marine and coastal ecosystems such as mangroves, seagrass beds, salt marshes and reefs are common nursery grounds for a large number of fish and shellfish. They play an important role in maintaining biodiversity, but also in absorbing storm energy, stabilizing sediments, filtering seawater, and tourism [2–4]. Fish biodiversity monitoring is typically carried out by expensive, intrusive scientific fishing operations, that can have a significant effect on the biodiversity in small marine protected areas (MPA). Passive Acoustic Monitoring (PAM) is an emerging alternative for this task, as there are more than 800 species of fish capable of producing sounds [5,6] that are not only species-specific but also contextual (courtship, territorial defense, distress calls). This method is minimally invasive, reduces the risk of altering the behavior of a species of interest, and allows for continuous monitoring of the species in presence [7]. Acoustic sensors offer the advantage of a wider detection area and fewer taxonomic restrictions than optical sensors. As such, they can simultaneously study entire vocalizing animal communities and their acoustic environments [7].

PAM is very useful for monitoring populations over long periods of time, detecting reproductive aggregations, or tracking the spatiotemporal activities of soniferous species [8,9]. The application of PAM in ecology was initially focused on cryptic animal species such as cetaceans and echolocating bats [10,11], but the advent of dedicated acoustic sensors (recorders, ultrasonic detectors, microphones, and/or hydrophones) has expanded the PAM to the study of birds [12], primates [13], and fish [14,15].

Methods to perform automatic Sound Event Detection (SED) are now being developed to process these large audio datasets. Two different approaches stand out in the scientific community: monophonic SED and polyphonic SED [16]. These two approaches differ in their ability to discern a sole event (monophonic) or several simultaneous events (polyphonic) in a single time frame. The latter are better suited to a real-world environment, and are therefore more suitable for fish vocalization detection.

Work using automatic algorithms for PAM can be classified into the three following categories: algorithms based on rules set by experts [17–19], unsupervised clustering algorithms [20,21] which are able to cluster samples into groups according to the dispersion of spectral characteristics and supervised automatic learning algorithms [22]. In this last category, different neural network architectures have been successfully used for automatic fish sound detection, starting with feed-forward neural networks (FNN) [23]. Convolutional neural networks

(CNNs) achieve better performance than FNNs, as they are able to recognize patterns and extract relevant information from time-frequency representations of acoustic signals of different fish species to detect and classify calls [24–27]. Yet other structures were used in previous works, such as recurrent neural networks (RNN) which are good at learning temporal information from two-dimensional input [28] and convolutional recurrent neural networks (CRNN) [16]. CRNN which combines the advantages of both CNN and RNN has been successfully used in several polyphonic SED studies including bird species classification [29], detection and classification of urban sounds and home environments [16,30], and for speech detection [31]. We have not found any study that applies this model in the detection and classification of fish sounds.

In this work, we used a CRNN to automatically detect and classify two fish species' calls and motor sounds from a dataset collected in a marine protected area (MPA) in Senegal, from which partial manual labeling were already performed to evaluate fish assemblage parameters [32]. The question addressed in this paper is whether CRNN can be a used as an automatic alternative for the labeling of fish calls in large datasets, which is an essential step for the construction of indicators.

The paper is organized as follows. The process of data collection and annotation as well as a characterization of the detected sounds is presented in Sect. 2. We also present the architecture of the CRNN used for the task and the metrics to measure the performance of the model, as well as the experiments that were conducted. In Sect. 3, the experimental results and discussions of the results are reported. Section 4 is a summary of the conclusions of this work.

2   Materials and Methods

This section introduces and describes the data that were used during our work and the models developed during our development phase.

2.1   Methodology

There was yet no public dataset containing fish sounds that were captured in a natural environment that was similar to our application field, Senegal's mangroves. We describe in the following sections the data collection and processing as well as annotation choices and process.

Our goal is to automatically detect and classify fish sounds in large data sets, and correspond to a SED problem in a polyphonic environment.

The SED problem can be formulated in two steps, a sound representation step and an event classification step [16]. In the sound representation step, audio features are extracted from a two-dimensional time-frequency representation of the audio signal to form, for each frame t of the signal, a feature vector $x_t \in \mathbb{R}^F$, where $F \in \mathbb{N}$ is the number of features per frame. In the classification step, the model estimates the activity probabilities $p(y_t(k)|x_t, \theta)$ of the sound event classes $k = 1, 2, ..., K$ in frame t, where θ denotes the classifier parameters.

The event activity probabilities are then binarized by thresholding to obtain event activity predictions $\hat{y}_t \in \mathbb{R}^K$. The parameters θ are trained by supervised learning, using a binary-valued vector y_t for each frame obtained from the start and end annotations of sound events in the audio recordings. If the event of a class k is active during frame t, $y_t(k)$ will be set to 1, and 0 otherwise. In the polyphonic SED framework, in a frame t, $y_t(k)$ can be non-zero for several classes of events k since several classes can overlap in time.

The differences in duration between event classes can be exploited as features to distinguish certain events. Some sounds are very compact in time, while others continue for a long time. To exploit these temporal features, the classification method must be able to preserve the temporal context along the sequential feature vectors. Therefore, the input features are presented as a context window matrix $X_{t:t+T-1}$, where $T \in \mathbb{N}$ is the number of frames that defines the length of the temporal context sequence, and the target output matrix is defined by $Y_{t:t+T-1}$.

Collection of Data. The data used in this work are described in [32]. They were collected using an omnidirectional hydrophone with a gain of 13.98 dB and a sensitivity of -169.6 dB, equipped with waterproof data loggers. The hydrophone was deployed in the Bamboung River, an MPA located in the Sine-Saloum Delta at a depth of two to three meters and was set up to continuously record at 44 kHz series of consecutive 4 min audio files. The instrument remained in the water and recorded for 38 h and 15 min, from 12/01/2020 at 7:00 PM to 12/03/2020 at 10:00 AM.

Data Annotation. Data were manually analyzed to determine potential types of fish calls in the dataset. For our study, we identified two calls (the most abundant in the data) that we call A and B and boat engine sounds. The spectrograms of these sounds are shown in Fig. 2.

The sound A consists of a kind of siren with an average duration of 1.45 $\pm$ 0.34 s, it appears most often on the spectrogram with three harmonics, the fundamental 256 Hz, the first and second harmonics 512 Hz 768 Hz respectively. Almost all of its energy is concentrated in the fundamental frequency and the first harmonic. It does not appear impulsively and can be classified as a vocalization. The sound B consists of very fast drumming with an average duration of 0.84 $\pm$ 0.28 s with a frequency range 450 Hz and 2000 Hz, its energy having a greater intensity 450 Hz and 1000 Hz. It appears regularly in two very close pulses, but we also observed isolated pulses. It can be classified in the category of stridulations [34]. The sound of the engine was a continuous noise in a wide range of frequency but whose energy varies according to the distance of the boat from the hydrophone.

The manual annotation of the two calls A and B and of the motor sounds was done using the Audacity software [35] by the authors of this work. We thus constituted for each 4-min recording a metadata file containing the file name, label, start and end time of each event of interest in the recording. The

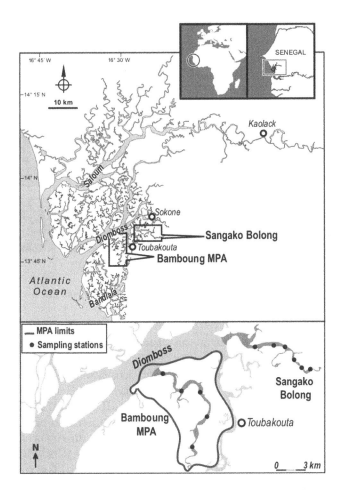

Fig. 1. Location of deployment of the acoustic recording package in the Sine-saloum delta [33]

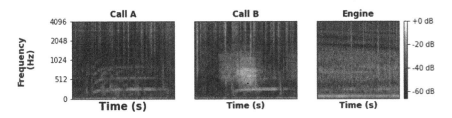

Fig. 2. Spectrograms of isolated sounds of interest annotated on the dataset. Left: fish "A". In the center: fish "B". On the right: an engine

distribution of fish calls was not regular over time, there were periods where fish emit in chorus, with very dense calls with a lot of overlap between them, and periods of low density with almost no overlap Fig. 3. Annotation was very difficult when fish emit sounds in chorus, it becomes near impossible to distinguish start and end times of calls. In these cases, the segment containing overlapping calls of the same species was annotated as one sound event (Fig. 1).

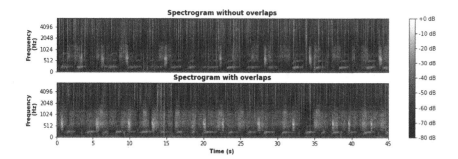

Fig. 3. Spectrograms showing non-overlapping calls at the top and overlapping calls at the bottom

Data Sets. Given the variety in the distribution of calls, we formed three datasets. The first one with a low density of calls (LDD for Low Density Dataset), the second one was made of records with a high density of calls, containing chorus from both A and B species (HDD for High Density Dataset) and the last one was a mixture of a certain proportion of the first two (MDD for Mixed Density Data set). The annotated number of events and duration in seconds of the events of a class of the three data sets are given in the Table 1. The three sets each consist of 36 audio files of 4 min divided into training and validation sets. This repartition concerns only the fish calls, the engine sounds appearing a few times but over long durations of time. We therefore have the same distribution for the motor sounds in the three data sets. A test set was built with a mixed distribution to represent the real distribution.

Table 1. Number and total duration of sound events related to the different classes in the three constructed datasets, according to the event densities observed on the recordings: Low Density Dataset (LDD), High Density Dataset (HDD) and Mixed Density Dataset (MDD), as well as in the test set.

Classes	LDD		HDD		MDD		TEST	
	Nbr	Duration (s)	Nbr	Duration (s)	Nbr	Duration (s)	Nbr	Duration (s)
A	687	926	2680	3811	1555	2181	459	614
B	526	365	2093	3241	1288	1416	288	454
Engine	10	1970	10	1970	10	1970	3	347

Data Processing. For our study, we use as features the coefficients of the log-mel band energies, obtained from the short-time Fourier transform (STFT). We operate with audio signals sampled at 44.1 kHz and the STFT was computed over windows of 2048 samples with an overlap of 50%. This value was chosen because it gives us a good compromise between temporal and spectral resolution on the spectrographs of our sounds. The coefficients of the log-mel band energies are obtained by filtering the STFT power spectrum with a filterbank composed of 128 triangular filters evenly spaced in the mel frequency scale covering 0 to 22,050 Hz, in respect of the Nyquist frequency condition. After calculating the logarithm of the log-mel band energies, each band energy is normalized by subtracting its mean and dividing by its standard deviation calculated over the training set. The normalized mel band energies are finally divided into 256 frames sequences, which accounts to almost 6 s, and the input tensor is $X_{t:t+T-1} \in \mathbb{R}^{T \times F}$ where $T = 256$ is the length of a sequence and $F = 128$ is the number of mel filters. The length T of the sequences is further made variable during parameter search (Sect. 2.3). In addition, the label tensor is defined by $Y_{t:t+T-1} \in \mathbb{N}^{T \times K}$ where K is the number of sound event classes, three in our case.

2.2   Models and Metrics

We present here the models that were used to process the data and the metrics used to measure the performance of the models.

Models. The CRNN used in this work was proposed in [16], and is composed of four parts. The top of the architecture consist of convolution layers that act as feature extractors. These are followed by recurrent layers that receive as input the feature maps of the last convolutional layer, integrate them over time, and thus provide the contextual information. A dense layer reads the outputs of the last recurrent layer and estimates the event activity probabilities for each frame. Finally, the event activity probabilities are binarized with a threshold to obtain event activity predictions. The stack of convolutional, recurrent, and dense layers is trained jointly by backpropagation. The log-mel band energies that are derived from the STFT are used as input features of the network.

Metrics. In this work, we use segment-based metrics defined in [36], representing the active/inactive state for each event class in a fixed length interval. They compare the model output and the label tensor in short time segments. The size of this segment depends on the desired resolution of the model application and the need to mitigate problems related to the annotator's subjectivity when marking the beginning and end of sound events [36]. Based on the activity representation, the following intermediate statistics are defined:

- True positive (TP): both the label and the model output indicate that an event should be active in this segment;

- False positive (FP): the label indicates that an event is inactive in this segment, but the output indicates it as active;
- False negative (FN): the label indicates that an event is active in this segment, but the output indicates it as inactive.

The intermediate statistics are then aggregated over the entire test data set and the metrics are calculated based on the aggregated values. Thus, the first evaluation metric (the F_1 score) is given by:

$$F_1 = \frac{2 \cdot TP}{2 \cdot TP + FN + FP} \tag{1}$$

The second evaluation metric is the error rate. It measures the number of errors in terms of insertions (I), deletions (D) and substitutions (S). To calculate the error rate per segment, errors are counted segment by segment. In a segment k, the number of substitution errors $S(k)$ is the number of events in the label tensor for which a correct event was not generated, but something else was. This is obtained by matching the rate of false positives and false negatives, without designating which erroneous event is substituted for another. The remaining events are deletions and insertions: $D(k)$ is the number of events in the label tensor that were not correctly identified (false negatives after taking substitutions into account) and $I(k)$ the number of events in the model output that are not correct (false positives after taking substitutions into account). This leads to the following formulas:

$$\begin{aligned} S(k) &= min(FN(k), FP(k)) \\ D(k) &= max(0, FN(k) - FP(k)) \\ I(k) &= max(0, FP(k) - FN(k)) \end{aligned} \tag{2}$$

The total error rate is calculated by:

$$ER = \frac{\sum_{k=1}^{K} S(k) + \sum_{k=1}^{K} D(k) + \sum_{k=1}^{K} I(k)}{\sum_{k=1}^{K} N(k)} \tag{3}$$

where K is the total number of segments and $N(k)$ being the number of sound events marked as active in the label tensor on segment k [36].

We use metrics based on segments whose length reduces to 1 second segments (F_{1sec} and ER_{1sec}).

2.3   Sensitivity Tests

To obtain the best detector for our environment, we trained three CRNN models with our three databases by performing a series of experiments.

- **Parametric search.** We perform a hyperparameter search using the randomsearchcv algorithms on predetermined ranges for each training data set. We select for each architecture the hyperparameter configuration that leads to the best results on the validation set, and use this architecture to compute the results on the test set. For each data set, the search is performed on the number of RNN layers number, number of hidden units in these layers, the number of CNN layers, the Max Pooling arrangements after each convolutional layer, and the length of sequences that are fed as inputs to the models, with parameter ranges shown in Table 2. For the max pooling arrangements, the numbers indicate the number of frequency bands at each max pooling step while the time dimension is preserved. For example, the configuration (4, 2, 2) pools for 128 log-Mel bands in input, 8 bands in output in three steps: 128 bands $\longrightarrow$ 32 bands $\longrightarrow$ 16 bands $\longrightarrow$ 8 bands. For all architectures, a batch normalization layer and a dropout rate of 0.25 are added after each convolutional layer. The output layer has one neuron for each class and has the sigmoid function as the activation function. In the convolutional layers, we use filters of size (3, 3); in the recurrent layers, we have opted for GRU architecture, as it has a smaller number of parameters than LSTM. The binary cross entropy is defined as the loss function, and all networks are trained with the Adam function as the gradient descent optimizer. The event activity probabilities are thresholded at $C = 0.5$, to obtain the binary activity matrix used to compute the scores. All networks are trained until overfitting starts to appear: as a criterion, we use the early stop on the validation metric, stopping the training if the score does not improve for more than 25% of the number of epochs defined at the beginning and the parameters are reset to the best performing values during validation.

Table 2. Range of the parameter search for the selected parameters.

Parameter	Parameter range
RNN layers number	1 ; 2 ; 3
Hidden units in the RNN	32 ; 64 ; 128
CNN layers number	2 ; 3 ; 4
Max pooling arrangements	(4,2) ; (4,3) ; (5,2) ; (5,3) ; (4,2,2) ; (4,3,2) ; (5,2,2) ; (5,3,2) ; (5,4,2) ; (5,4,2,2) ; (5,4,3,2)
Length of the sequences (frames)	64 ; 128 ; 256 ; 512

• **Model performance.** We test the optimal models obtained on the three data sets with the test set defined in Sect. 2.1. The objective is to determine which model generalizes better in a real environment with a heterogeneous event distribution.

• **Parametric search on data preprocessing.** We perform another search on the parameters of audio representations with the best architecture by varying the STFT window width and the number of log-Mel filters. The value ranges are 1024, 2048, 4096 and 40, 64, 128 respectively. The goal is to find the best representation of the data in terms of temporal and frequency resolution.

2.4 Application to Large Data Set

As an application, we used the model to evaluate the distribution of calls over the complete 38 h-time series records. First, we compared the average spectrogram with the calls detected by the model during the 38 h of audio recording in the Bamboung records. The average spectrogram was computed by calculating the long-term average spectrogram on 4-min. subsamples, and values were normalized on the 100–2000 Hz band in which A and B calls are visible. Model predictions were transformed and seconds of detection per minutes, and interpolated on the same time axis as the average spectrogram. Second, on a part of the data (24 h) CRNN predictions were compared with manual annotations and power spectral density (PSD) corresponding to A and B calls. Manual annotation of A and B calls was performed on a 30 s subsampling every hour [32], and PSD were extracted from the average spectrogram for the 260–300 Hz and 600–1200 Hz band, corresponding to the maximum energy for calls A and B respectively. The three time series were scaled from 0 to 1. For manual annotation, the maximum number of calls counted per 30 s among the annotated subsamples was 23 for both call types (by accident). Note that these annotated data were not used for the training, so that most of these data were previously unseen by the model. In a second time, specific check was performed in order to verify model predictions at particular hours.

3   Results

We describe here the results of the experiments previously described.

3.1 Parameters Identification and Sensitivity Tests

• Parametric Search Results
Hyperparameters were retained after ten iterations of parametric search using the randomsearchcv tool on each of the three CRNN models. All three models have a training F_1 score greater than or equal to **0.95**. The HDD model trained with the dense data outperforms the others with an F_1 score of 0.98 and has three convolution layers, two recurrent layers of 32 hidden units each, and its input data is sequenced at a length of 256 frames (Table 3).

• Model Performance
The LDD model trained on the eponymous dataset has the best generalization performance with a F_1 score on the test data of **0.949** and an error rate of **0.18** followed very closely by the MDD model ($F_1 = 0.941$ and $E_r = 0.21$). The HDD model, although performing the best in training generalizes very poorly. It has a high rate of event insertion and deletion compared to the other two (Table 4).

However, each model performed differently according to the class. The LDD model outperforms both MDD and HDD in almost all classes. Each class was likely to appear with different classes rather than in isolation due to a polyphonic environment. The detection performance of B by HDD and MDD was

Table 3. Final hyperparameters obtained after the parametric search operation and corresponding evaluation scores for each data set. Each CRNN model is named after the dataset that was used to train it

	LDD	HDD	MDD
RNN layers	1	2	1
Hidden units	64	32	128
CNN layer	3	3	3
Max pooling	(5,4,2)	(5,2,2)	(5,4,2)
Length of the sequence	128	256	128
F_1 validation	0.95	**0.98**	0.96
E_r validation	0.12	**0.08**	0.16

significantly lower than the detection performance of the other classes. This was confirmed by the particularly high number of insertions for this class in both models, **572** for HDD and **217** for MDD. Call A was well detected by all three models, but where LDD and MDD show perfect performance for the detection of the engine, HDD had an F_1 score of only **0.78** with an insertion number of **179** for this class (Table 4).

Table 4. Scores of the three models on the metrics used per event class and on the overall test set. The scores in bold indicate the best performing method on the test set

Scores	LDD				HDD				MDD			
	A	B	Engine	TEST	A	B	Engine	TEST	A	B	Engine	TEST
F_1	0.93	0.91	1	**0.949**	0.90	0.69	0.78	0.77	0.94	0.85	1	0.941
E_r	0.04	0.08	0	**0.18**	0.02	0.40	0.23	0.68	0.02	0.20	0	0.21
D	0	84	0	134	0	71	0	100	0	72	0	178
I	84	16	0	192	41	572	179	1102	45	217	0	190
S	5	13	0	9	7	50	0	66	6	7	0	11

A closer look at the detection capabilities of the models with a comparative study between the neural network outputs for a 35 s sequence of the test set showed that all three models detect the A and B calls well when they overlap, with LDD making the fewest errors. When the motor sound overlaps the A call, LDD is the only one able to detect it all the time, this performance decreases with the increase of the energy in the motor sound until it cannot distinguish the A call from the motor sound anymore (Fig. 4).

• **Parametric Search on Data Preprocessing**
The performance of the model on the test data increased with the number of Mel filters and were higher for a window size of 2048 (Table 5).

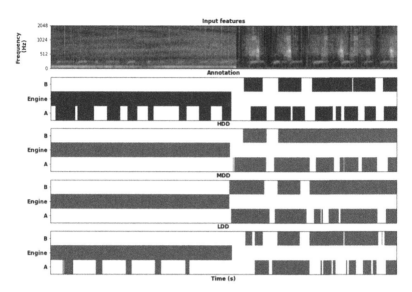

Fig. 4. 35 seconds input feature (Top). Annotations associated to the input features (second from top), outputs for the MDD model (third from top), HDD model (fourth from top) and LDD model (last from top).

Table 5. Performances of the LDD model as a function of the choices made in the preprocessing of the data - variations in N-Mel are performed with a window size of 2048, while variations in the window size are performed with a number of Mel filters fixed at 128.

Scores	Sizew_n			N-Mel		
	1024	2048	4096	40	64	128
F_1	0.91	0.949	0.89	0.89	0.91	**0.949**
E_r	0.17	0.18	0.21	0.30	0.20	**0.18**

3.2 Sound Event Time Series

The LDD model predicted different patterns of time series for the three detected classes. A calls appear in three waves on a day, the first between 00:00 and 06:30, then a second between 08:00 and 12:00, finally the third between 18:00 and 00:00. B calls are emitted between 20:30 and 00:20 and are very intense between 21:30 and 23:30 as we observe call choirs. For both call types, we observe call choirs at certain periods within the waves of calls. The CRNN predictions suggest that calls can reach 55 and 59 s per minutes resp. for A and B calls, which correspond to almost continuous chorus. Motor noise was detected at the beginning and the end of the time series, without surprise since it correspond to the motor of the boat used for the hydrophone deployment, and it was also part of the initially annotated data. More surprisingly, motors noise were detected the 2 December at 5 h 33 and at 17 h 04 for duration 5 min, these detection were confirmed by direct listening of the corresponding sound files. Visual check suggest a good correspondence between apparent signature of A and B calls in the spectrogram and model predictions Fig. 5.

However, periods of low number of A calls (e.g. below 20 s per minutes), not clearly marked in the average spectrogram, although manual annotation confirm the absence of these call (Fig. 6a). For B fish, the signature not very clear in the spectrogram while the pattern is very marked in model predictions, but here also the CRNN successfully detect the call variability, in line with manual annotations (Fig. 6b).

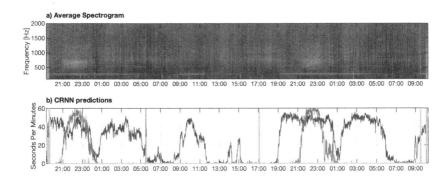

Fig. 5. Comparison of average spectrogram (a) and CRNN sound event detections (b) during the 38 h 15 record in Bamboung station for A and B calls an motor noise corresponding respectively to the blue, red and yellow lines. The average spectrogram was normalized from 0 (dark blue) to 1 (light blue); A and B calls can be visually seen as marked peaks respectively 280 Hz and 600 Hz. (Color figure online)

The observed temporal variability in annotated sequences of A in BBG was significantly correlated with the 260–300 Hz PSD temporal variability ($R = 0.83$ and $P < 10^{-6}$). Similarly, the B temporal variability in BBG was correlated with the 600–1200 Hz PSD, although less significantly ($R = 0.7$ and $P < 10^{-3}$). However, the CRNN sound event detection had a much better correlation with manual annotations, resp. $R = 0.94$ ($P < 10^{-12}$) and $R = 0.92$ ($P < 10^{-9}$) for 'A' and 'B' sounds categories.

4   Discussion

Fish sound production rates can be used as an indicator of the health of marine ecosystems [37]. In the context of rapidly changing marine ecosystems due to various anthropogenic factors combined with big data collection and storage techniques, it is imperative to develop automatic methods for monitoring long-term underwater acoustic biodiversity. Studies have demonstrated the performance and benefits of deeps learning methods in identifying fish sounds [24–26]. In this study, we propose a CRNN to detect two fish calls and boat engine sounds in a

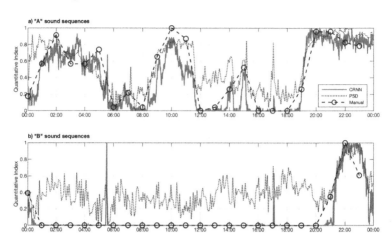

Fig. 6. Comparison of CRNN model predictions (black line), Band pass power spectral density (blue line) and manual annotations (red line with circle markers) time series for a) A and b) B calls for 24 h records in Bamboung station, 2nd December 2020. Power spectral density were averaged on 260–300 Hz and 600–1200 Hz band respectively corresponding to maximum energy band for A and B calls. (Color figure online)

mangrove environment. This study is the first to use this model for fish sound detection. Our model achieves high detection performance with an F1 score of 0.94. However, the implementation of this algorithm for fish sound detection imposes a number of constraints that we discuss here.

One of the basic requirement for machine learning is that the data we want to learn from as well the data to be analyzed must come from the same distribution and be identically and independently distributed [38]. Usually, this is not the case in real data, and data-scientist deal build mixed training data set that combine different distributions that can occur in the complete dataset [39]. In our case we faced this problem as there was a strong variability in fish calls activity, e.g. depending the daytime or nighttime. However, unlike [39] the best predictions were obtained when using one type of distribution, corresponding the lowest fish call density, rather than the high call density nor mixed call density distributions (Table 4). This was unexpected because there was less annotated events in the low call density training set than in the high call density training set, and the distribution was less comparable to the test set than the mixed call density training set Table 1. This singularity seems to arise from our annotation process where, in the case of high density calls, events were not singled out and degraded the resolution of the annotation, which led the high and mixed call density to achieve lower performance. This revealed that a training data set with good precision in identifying the start/end times of active events was more efficient than a training data set including overlapping events, even if mixed with part of dataset without overlapping.

Biological choruses are collective events during which a number of individuals, usually belonging to the same species, simultaneously produce and repeat similar sounds. These are important features of sound production in some species including fish. They were reported to follow daily and seasonal patterns, and to be generally correlated with sunrise and sunset [40], although in our case choruses were observed a large part of the night (Fig. 6). Our approach makes it possible to detect biological chorus based on the duration of the detected event knowing the duration of an isolated event. Since a chorus is made up of several overlapping sounds of the same type, our model detected it as a single sound with a long duration. However, we could not automatically know the number of sounds involved in the chorus. This remains a limitation in evaluating the density of fish sounds. Other methods of detecting biological choruses have been proposed in [41,42] but none of them allow us to know the number of sounds involved in the choruses. It would be interesting to learn specific characteristics at the beginning or end of a sound to allow our detector to isolate overlapping sounds of the same type. To our knowledge this problematic, quite specific to marine bio-acoustics, was not yet tackled in the machine learning literature.

Detecting spectral variations within fish calls duration imply using an adapted representation, or "feature extraction" of the dataset. Indeed, directly using the rough signal (.wav) signal being far to expensive for large dataset analysis [43], a preprocessing of the sound is necessary to extract features. The parameters choices leading to this audio representation strongly impacts the architecture and performance of a deep learning [44] model. In this paper we showed the impact of Mel frequency filters and length of the window for the STFT. Since fish sounds are present in the low ($<2000\,\mathrm{Hz}$) frequencies, a large number of Mel filters allow us to accentuate the resolution of the characteristics in this frequency range, thus always increasing the performance of the model, certainly at an increasing memory cost (not quantified here). The length of the window for the STFT was a more subtle parameter. Indeed, for one of the detected call A the main features are harmonic frequencies, whose resolution and fine scale variations are better seen with a longer STFT window (Fig. 2). For the other detected call B, the main features are rapid drums which can be seen in the spectrogram only using shorter STFT window (Fig. 2). Thus, ideally the audio representation might be adapted to each fish call characteristics in order to get individual annotations of individual calls even in chorus, although in or case an intermediate value appeared as optimal for average model performance (Table 5).

Finally, it should be noted that the precision for automatic detection of the start and end of fish calls might be also impacted by the precision of the manual labelling in the training set. According to [36], the length of the time segments used for the calculation of the evaluation metrics make it possible to reduce the subjectivity, or error, linked to the annotation. In our data fish sounds were often separated by very short time intervals ($<1\,\mathrm{s}$) approaching the length of the segment used for the evaluation metric ($1\,\mathrm{s}$) which may be responsible for the relatively high number of false positives, or insertions (Table 4). Reducing this time segment may allow to reduce these insertion, although more investigation should be conducted to test the model sensitivity for this parameters.

The best model, i.e. the one trained with the low density fish call training set, was used to predict fish calls and motor sound events in the complete (38-h) dataset. The mean spectrogram gives us a rough information about the chorus for the two fish calls, but with a much lower precision than the CRNN detector (Fig. 6). In addition, when fish calls do not happen in choruses the model can also give us an approximation of the number of calls and the start and end times of each call, which are important for calculating, for example, the species sound diversity indices [8, 32]. However, as explained before in the case of chorus, this may not be possible in the current model configuration because overlapping calla would be detected as a continuous call. Specific adaptations in order to train the model to detect specifically call starts or ends could allow to overpass this issue. The model proved its utility for ecological investigations, for example by making clearly appear the A and B calls patterns in the time intervals of 01/12 and 03/12; each call seems to have a specific daily pattern, but a study over a longer period of time is needed to confirm this hypothesis. Also, the model proved its utility for anthropic sound detection as motor noise, which were not expected in the recording area (a marine protected area closed to fisheries). So that a priori the CRNN successfully detected the only motor noise sound event.

This suggest CRNN could be a usefull architecture to analyse sound data collected during passive acoustic monitoring (PAM), potentially helping both for fishing pressure and biodiversity monitoring. Motor sounds could stand as a proxy for fishing pressure, or be used as a proxy to assess the level of compliance of the no-entrance rule in a MPA, an important factor at the time to evaluate the effect of the protection on fish assemblage [33]. Fish assemblage parameters (abundance, richness, diversity) could be obtained if the CRNN was trained for the classification of an increased number of sound class, say 10 in the case of the present dataset [32].

5   Conclusion

The model employed in this study allowed us to automatically detect two fish calls and engine sounds. Our detector achieves an average F1 score (>0.94), which is a very encouraging result and shows the prospects of this approach for monitoring underwater acoustic diversity. We record acoustic data at several other sites in Senegal and have already identified 19 classes of fish calls [32]. We subsequently annotate these records to form high-quality labeled databases that are of crucial importance for the development of machine learning algorithms. We will then train our model to detect all sound classes for a real implementation of this approach, which would allow spatio-temporal monitoring of fish acoustic biodiversity.

References

1. Hirsch, T.: Global biodiversity outlook 3. UNEP/Earthprint (2010)
2. Duke, N., Nagelkerken, I., Agardy, T., Wells, S., Van Lavieren, H.: The importance of mangroves to people: a call to action. United Nations Environment Programme World Conservation Monitoring Centre (2014)

3. Ramesh, R., Banerjee, K., Paneerselvam, A., Raghuraman, R., Purvaja, R., Lakshmi, A.: Importance of seagrass management for effective mitigation of climate change. In: Coastal Management, pp. 283–299. Elsevier (2019)
4. Ellis, J.I., et al.: Multiple stressor effects on coral reef ecosystems. Global Change Biol. **25**(12), 4131–4146 (2019)
5. Kaatz, I.M.: Multiple sound-producing mechanisms in teleost fishes and hypotheses regarding their behavioural significance. Bioacoustics **12**(2–3), 230–233 (2002)
6. Rountree, R.A., Gilmore, R.G., Goudey, C.A., Hawkins, A.D., Luczkovich, J.J., Mann, D.A.: Listening to fish: applications of passive acoustics to fisheries science. Fisheries **31**(9), 433–446 (2006)
7. Gibb, R., Browning, E., Glover-Kapfer, P., Jones, K.E.: Emerging opportunities and challenges for passive acoustics in ecological assessment and monitoring. Methods Ecol. Evol. **10**(2), 169–185 (2019)
8. Carriço, R., et al.: The use of soundscapes to monitor fish communities: meaningful graphical representations differ with acoustic environment. Acoustics **2**, 382–398 (2020)
9. Luczkovich, J.J., Mann, D.A., Rountree, R.A.: Passive acoustics as a tool in fisheries science. Trans. Am. Fish. Soc. **137**(2), 533–541 (2008)
10. Mellinger, D.K., Stafford, K.M., Moore, S.E., Dziak, R.P., Matsumoto, H.: An overview of fixed passive acoustic observation methods for cetaceans. Oceanography **20**(4), 36–45 (2007)
11. Adams, A.M., Jantzen, M.K., Hamilton, R.M., Fenton, M.B.: Do you hear what I hear? Implications of detector selection for acoustic monitoring of bats. Methods Ecol. Evol. **3**(6), 992–998 (2012)
12. Pérez-Granados, C., Traba, J.: Estimating bird density using passive acoustic monitoring: a review of methods and suggestions for further research. Ibis **163**(3), 765–783 (2021)
13. Heinicke, S., Kalan, A.K., Wagner, O.J.J., Mundry, R., Lukashevich, H., Kühl, H.S.: Assessing the performance of a semi-automated acoustic monitoring system for primates. Methods Ecol. Evol. **6**(7), 753–763 (2015)
14. Putland, R.L., Mackiewicz, A.G., Mensinger, A.F.: Localizing individual soniferous fish using passive acoustic monitoring. Ecol. Inform. **48**, 60–68 (2018)
15. Carriço, R., Silva, M.A., Menezes, G.M., Fonseca, P.J., Amorim, M.C.P.: Characterization of the acoustic community of vocal fishes in the azores. PeerJ **7**, e7772 (2019)
16. Cakır, E., Parascandolo, G., Heittola, T., Huttunen, H., Virtanen, T.: Convolutional recurrent neural networks for polyphonic sound event detection. IEEE/ACM Trans. Audio Speech Lang. Process. **25**(6), 1291–1303 (2017)
17. Lin, T.-H., Tsao, Y., Akamatsu, T.: Comparison of passive acoustic soniferous fish monitoring with supervised and unsupervised approaches. J. Acoust. Soc. Am. **143**(4), EL278–EL284 (2018)
18. Ruiz-Blais, S., Camacho, A., Rivera-Chavarria, M.R.: Sound-based automatic neotropical sciaenid fishes identification: cynoscion jamaicensis. In: Proceedings of Meetings on Acoustics 167ASA, vol. 21, p. 010001. Acoustical Society of America (2014)
19. Ricci, S.W., Bohnenstiehl, D.R., Eggleston, D.B., Kellogg, M.L., Lyon, R.P.: Détection et modèles d'appels de sifflets de poisson-crapaud à huîtres (opsanus tau) dans un site de restauration d'huîtres à grande échelle. PLoS ONE **12**, e0182757 (2017)
20. Ozanich, E., Thode, A., Gerstoft, P., Freeman, L.A., Freeman, S.: Deep embedded clustering of coral reef bioacoustics. J. Acoust. Soc. Am. **149**(4), 2587–2601 (2021)

21. Ulloa, J.S., Aubin, T., Llusia, D., Bouveyron, C., Sueur, J.: Estimating animal acoustic diversity in tropical environments using unsupervised multiresolution analysis. Ecol. Indic. **90**, 346–355 (2018)
22. Noda, J.J., Travieso, C.M., Sánchez-Rodríguez, D.: Automatic taxonomic classification of fish based on their acoustic signals. Appl. Sci. **6**(12), 443 (2016)
23. McLoughlin, I., Zhang, H., Xie, Z., Song, Y., Xiao, W.: Robust sound event classification using deep neural networks. IEEE/ACM Trans. Audio Speech Lang. Process. **23**(3), 540–552 (2015)
24. Guyot, P., Alix, F., Guerin, T., Lambeaux, E., Rotureau, A.: Fish migration monitoring from audio detection with CNNs. Audio Mostly **2021**, 244–247 (2021)
25. Malfante, M., Mohammed, O., Gervaise, C., Mura, M.D., Mars, J.I.: Use of deep features for the automatic classification of fish sounds. In: 2018 OCEANS-MTS/IEEE Kobe Techno-Oceans (OTO), pp. 1–5. IEEE (2018)
26. Waddell, E.E., Rasmussen, J.H., Širović, A.: Applying artificial intelligence methods to detect and classify fish calls from the Northern Gulf of Mexico. J. Marine Sci. Eng. **9**(10), 1128 (2021)
27. Piczak, K.J.: Environmental sound classification with convolutional neural networks. In: 2015 IEEE 25th International Workshop on Machine Learning for Signal Processing (MLSP), pp. 1–6. IEEE (2015)
28. Graves, A., Mohamed, A.-R., Hinton, G.: Speech recognition with deep recurrent neural networks. In: 2013 IEEE International Conference on Acoustics, Speech and Signal Processing, pp. 6645–6649. IEEE (2013)
29. Gupta, G., Kshirsagar, M., Zhong, M., Gholami, S., Ferres, J.L.: Recurrent convolutional neural networks for large scale bird species classification. Sci. Rep. **11**, 17085 (2021)
30. Serizel, R., Turpault, N., Eghbal-Zadeh, H., Shah, A.P.: Large-scale weakly labeled semi-supervised sound event detection in domestic environments. arXiv preprint arXiv:1807.10501 (2018)
31. Wolters, P., Daw, C., Hutchinson, B., Phillips, L.: Proposal-based few-shot sound event detection for speech and environmental sounds with perceivers. arXiv preprint arXiv:2107.13616 (2021)
32. Timothée, B., et al.: Passive acoustic monitoring to differentiate fish assemblages in protected vs. exploited African mangrove areas (2022, in press)
33. Sadio, O., Simier, M., Ecoutin, J.-M., Raffray, J., Laë, R., de Morais, L.T.: Effect of a marine protected area on tropical estuarine fish assemblages: comparison between protected and unprotected sites in Senegal. Ocean Coast. Manag. **116**, 257–269 (2015)
34. Parmentier, E., Fine, M.L.: Fish sound production: insights. In: Suthers, R.A., Fitch, W.T., Fay, R.R., Popper, A.N. (eds.) Vertebrate Sound Production and Acoustic Communication. SHAR, vol. 53, pp. 19–49. Springer, Cham (2016). https://doi.org/10.1007/978-3-319-27721-9_2
35. Team Audacity. Audacity (2014)
36. Mesaros, A., Heittola, T., Virtanen, T.: Metrics for polyphonic sound event detection. Appl. Sci. **6**(6), 162 (2016)
37. Munger, J.E., et al.: Machine learning analysis reveals relationship between pomacentrid calls and environmental cues. Marine Ecol. Progress Ser. **681**, 197–210 (2022)
38. Goodfellow, I., Bengio, Y., Courville, A.: Deep Learning. MIT Press, Cambridge (2016)
39. Sarr, J.-M.A., et al.: Complex data labeling with deep learning methods: lessons from fisheries acoustics. ISA Trans. **109**, 113–125 (2021)

40. Parsons, M.J.G., Salgado-Kent, C.P., Marley, S.A., Gavrilov, A.N., McCauley, R.D.: Characterizing diversity and variation in fish choruses in Darwin Harbour. ICES J. Marine Sci. **73**(8), 2058–2074 (2016)
41. Sánchez-Gendriz, I., Padovese, L.R.: A methodology for analyzing biological choruses from long-term passive acoustic monitoring in natural areas. Ecol. Inform. **41**, 1–10 (2017)
42. Lapp, S., et al.: Automated detection of frog calls and choruses by pulse repetition rate. Conserv. Biol. **35**(5), 1659–1668 (2021)
43. Dai, W., Dai, C., Qu, S., Li, J., Das, S.: Very deep convolutional neural networks for raw waveforms. In: 2017 IEEE International Conference on Acoustics, Speech and Signal Processing (ICASSP), pp. 421–425. IEEE (2017)
44. Natsiou, A., O'Leary, S.: Audio representations for deep learning in sound synthesis: a review. In: 2021 IEEE/ACS 18th International Conference on Computer Systems and Applications (AICCSA), pp. 1–8. IEEE (2021)

Plant Diseases Detection and Classification Using Deep Transfer Learning

Olushola Olawuyi and Serestina Viriri[(✉)] [ID]

School of Mathematics, Statistics and Computer Science,
University of KwaZulu-Natal, Durban, South Africa
{221119659,viriris}@ukzn.ac.za

Abstract. Plant diseases have resulted in a significant reduction in the quality and quantity of crop harvests. In extreme circumstances, diseases of plants even prevent the entire crop from germinating. In this paper, a thorough investigation, and review of deep transfer learning and deep convolutional neural networks (CNNs) was done. How-ever, the focus of this research work was to implement a pretrained model (Resnet50) for the detection and classification of plant diseases using ImageNet. Dataset of Corn (maize) and Potato from the plant village plat-form was used to evaluate the performance of the model. The model took in Corn (maize) or Potato leaves as input and then passed them to the preprocessing stage where they are prepared for the Resnet50 model. Preprocessing techniques adopted were data augmentation and segmentation. Finally, the Resnet 50 model was then evaluated and achieved following results: 98.0% accuracy: 77.0% precision: 99.0% and recall: 86.0% F1-score. Initially, the value of the loss was 0.08 but as the training progressed, it reduced to 0.053, improving the accuracy of the model.

Keywords: Disease detection · Deep learning · Deep transfer learning · Convolutional neural network (CNN) · Machine learning

1 Introduction

Agriculture has served as mainstream for the provision of food for human consumption in many countries of the world. Farming is a significant source of income for many countries in the world since the agricultural sector is a backbone for many nations in the world owing to its contributions to the provision of food for people's livelihood, either directly or indirectly. It helps to drive the economy of many countries. The enemy of plants is the diseases that attack the such plant. They affect the plants' productivity or eventual death if timely and proper care using the best method to diagnose the affected plant is not provided. Bacteria, fungi, and viruses cause most of the diseases in plants. The damages caused by these organisms are characterized by visual signs which can be seen on the plant's leaf or stem.

Detection of the plant disease through a manual process of diagnosing the leaf of the plant is inaccurate and can lead to an error in conclusion while determining the diseases

© ICST Institute for Computer Sciences, Social Informatics and Telecommunications Engineering 2023
Published by Springer Nature Switzerland AG 2023. All Rights Reserved
T. M. Ngatched Nkouatchah et al. (Eds.): PAAISS 2022, LNICST 459, pp. 270–288, 2023.
https://doi.org/10.1007/978-3-031-25271-6_17

that the plant carries. Farmers need to monitor plants constantly in order to prevent affected plants from spreading diseases on the farmland to other plants. But oftentimes manual monitoring is challenging, time-consuming and ineffective. Plant diseases cause a considerable amount of agricultural crop yield to be lost due to the quality of the crops that have been reduced. This in turn eventually impacts developing countries because there are fewer qualified experts to identify and treat plant diseases.

Deep learning has demonstrated encouraging results in image classification and is now being used in most industries to solve issues in various ways [1]. Computer vision along with the deep learning (DL) method has proved to be state-of-the-art in handling numerous farming challenges [2]. Image processing methods with machine learning can assist in the accurate identification of symptoms of plant diseases, which can aid farmers in their battle against disease outbreaks. A variety of applications for image processing could be found in agriculture which entails detecting affected plant leaves, locating the diseased point, and identifying the nature of the disease. Plant disease gives a negative impact on the quality of plant products [3].

Vagisha et al. [4]. According to their research work, plant disease detection using Support Vector Machine (SVM), Convolutional Neural Network (CNN), Artificial Neural Network (ANN) and also K-Nearest (KN) Neighbor focused primarily on the most used classification mechanisms. The study showed that the methodology of the Convolutional Neural Network offers greater precision compared to conventional approaches. New techniques and processes are needed to make it easier for scientists and non-scientists to recognize various diseases affecting plants and due to these better techniques need to be explored [5]. In general, the deep transfer learning model and precisely Rsnet50 were used in this research work in detecting and classifying plant leaves' diseases.

This paper is organized as follows: Sect. 2 Review of the existing work, Sect. 3 Describes methods and techniques, Sect. 4 emphasized on the results and discussion and Sect. 5 concludes the paper.

2 Review of Existing Work

2.1 Artificial Intelligence (AI)

Is an aspect of computer science that deals with endowing computers with problem-solving capability. This system makes use of an algorithm to perform a task using their intelligence. This involves making use of machine learning algorithms, deep learning, and neural networks.

2.2 Machine Learning (ML)

ML are mathematical model algorithms used to learn patterns that are embedded in data. ML encompasses computational algorithms which perform pattern classification, recognition, and prediction of data by learning from existing data (training set). ML algorithms can as well be categorized into (3) namely: (1) supervised learning (2) unsupervised learning (3) reinforcement learning.

R. U. Khan et al. [6] in their study focus on machine learning techniques that transitioned from traditional machine learning to deep learning in the last five years with lots

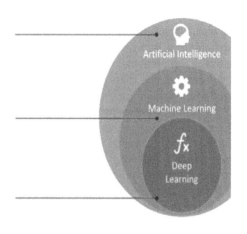

Artificial Intelligence
Any technique which enables computers
to mimic human behavior.

Machine Learning
Subset of AI techniques which use
statistical methods to enable machines
to improve with experiences.

Deep Learning
Subset of ML which make the
computation of multi-layer neural
networks feasible.

Fig. 1. Overview of Artificial intelligence, Machine learning and Deep learning [31]

of datasets about plant diseases thoroughly examined. Difficulties and issues with the current systems were also addressed.

2.3 Deep Learning (DL)

DL is also a machine learning method which allows computers to learn instruction by examples. This technology has a wide range of applications, for instance, most self-driven cars use deep learning technology which helps such vehicles identify traffic signs and differentiate between pedestrians and streetlights. Through the help of a deep learning model, computer systems were able to learn and carry out operations like image classification tasks directly. Saleem et al. [7] used different architectures like deep learning, Faster Region-based CNN (Faster-RCNN), Single Shot Multibox Detector (SSD) and Region-based Fully Convolutional Networks which identified different diseases of the plant.

Deep Learning (DL) based plant disease classification techniques use several CNN models, including AlexNet, GoogleNet, VGGNet, and others. Multiclass classification with several classes requires careful hyperparameter modification when the dataset size is insufficient to prevent overfitting in case the model becomes stuck in a local minimum [8].

Plant disease identification using deep learning along with computer vision has been the focus of much research over the past decade. On a range of datasets, traditional computer vision approaches such as Haar, hog sift, surf, image segmentation, Support Vector Machines (SVM), utilising K-Nearest Neighbours (KNN), K-means, and Artificial Neural Networks (ANN) have all been implemented and used.

Artificial Neural Networks (ANN), decision trees, support vector machines (SVM), with K-means are types of machine learning (ML) techniques which have been used to identify diseases [9]. When an image is captured, it must be translated in form of data before the computer can interpret the content because the computer is not knowledgeable enough to interpret the image directly. It implies that to use the technology, the images must be coded into data type which can be fed to the computer systems.

Reddy et al. [10] identified different species of plants by using colour leaves images and CNN. Five different datasets were used, which include Swedish leaf, Plant Village, Snap leaf, and UCI leaf, with Leaf Snap. Four (4) convolutional layers with two FC layers, with a SoftMax layer, are all used in their model. Three (3) datasets—Flavia, Swedish leaf, with UCI leaf—the method used to achieve great accuracy. Similar to this, Leaf Snap's accuracy is 0.98, whereas Plant Village's data is accurate at 0.900.

CNN model was developed to detect the diseases of tomato plants by using a Plant Village dataset which gives an accuracy of (0.972), although the accuracy gotten was less than the accuracy of the VGG16 model which gives (0.983). But the proposed technique required less than one-fourth of the time required by VGG16 [11].

In the Plant Village dataset used by [12], the researcher made use of (14) different species of cucumber leaves which were analyzed for (7) different diseases. The datasets used were combined to provide a good presentation of the dataset which was collected. The Plant Village dataset was used by the researcher [13] This show how the dataset collected was helpful to have a better understanding of plant diseases.

This research identified five (5) different diseases of cassava-plant [14] the plain convolutional neural network (PCNN), and deep residual network (DRNN) were used. The outcome of the study shows that the DRNN outperformed PCNN with 9.25 per cent. The outcome of the research shows that three diseases and two destructive pests of the cassava plants were identified. In extending the research work in classifying diseases of cassava plants using a transfer-learning approach and then a smartphone-based CNN model 80.6 per cent accuracy was achieved [15].

Adedoja et al. [16] in their study disclosed that the NASNet-based deep CNN model was utilized to classify plant leaf diseases, with a 93.82 per cent accuracy rate. The INC-VGGN technique was utilized by [17] to identify rice and maize leaf diseases. VGG19 was replaced in their method, the last convolutional layer, two (2) inception layers with one (1) global average of pooling layer.

Another study employed deep learning architecture by [18] to classify 13 different plant disease categories. The authors downloaded and enhanced photographs of various disease-affected plants from the internet to boost the number of images for their model training and 96.3% accuracy was attained.

VGG16, ResNet, and Dense Net models were used on a plant village dataset to identify plant disease [19]. Sethy, P.K et al. [13] proposed a technique that deals with disease detection and severity estimation to retrieve unhealthy regions from an image that required a region of interest, a colour-based segmentation technique based on incremental K-means clustering was used.

Sethy, P.K et al. [13] built a feature vector, texture features are extracted using the GLCM approach, and colour features are recovered from the segmented sick leaf region using the RGB colour space. The suggested method deals with identifying diseases from soybean crops, which includes classification and severity assessment, and experimental findings show that SVM performs better in comparison to KNN, with SVM achieving higher accuracy than the KNN classifier.

Kowshik B et al. [20] built customized deep learning for the identification of plant illnesses using simple leaf images of healthy or diseased plants, based on unique convolutional neural network architectures. The models were trained using a publicly available library of 87,848 images under both laboratory and real-world situations in cultivation areas. The dataset includes 25 different plant species in 58 different (plant disease) combinations, as well as some healthy and unhealthy plants.

Research by [3] used two distinct segmentation techniques which are thresholding with K-means clustering algorithm with classification method like artificial neural network (ANN) and feed-forward backpropagation. Digital camera help in capturing plant leaves images on the field and then the image is preprocessed, the original image is segmented, and important features are extracted to identify the infected regions of the plant leaves are extracted using two separate segmentation algorithms.

Plant leaf disease was identified using a variety of segmentation techniques, image thresholding, K-means clustering, and Neural Networks which is been used to create clustering of plant leaf disease classification [3]. Various algorithms were tested on the effects of various diseases of plants and the neural network gave the best accurate result compared to others, based on experimental results that greatly support an accurate result in less computation time. In the context of image classification, it showed how deep neural networks were utilized to recognize plant diseases.

According to [21] in their research work, five (5) distinct architectures were compared: VGG16, ResNet50, InceptionV3, Inception ResNet, and DenseNet169. After the test, it was discovered that ResNet50, use skip connections and residual layer, which produces the best results. According to [22] they examine the research efforts in the domain of image-based plant disease diagnosis with deep learning, as well as the problems that have been encountered in implementing it in the agricultural sector. The authors look at the datasets that were used, the image pre-processing, as well as the deep learning algorithms that were used. Based on a review of the literature, deep learning models built with CNN architectures have achieved high classification accuracies for diagnosing plant illnesses. However, those models tend to fail to generalize images taken in a variety of situations.

Deep learning models, according to [23], have the potential to deliver appropriate outcomes without human interaction, which makes them particularly promising for handling real-time challenges. A system that monitors the farmland frequently was proposed, to identify Crop diseases using a combination of CNN and DNN algorithms [24]. The model is trained using machine learning approaches, which aids in making suitable disease decisions. Their study provides an overview of various disease classification methodologies for crop disease detection, as well as an image segmentation algorithm which can be used for automatic detection and classification of plant leave disease in the future. The proposed algorithm was tested on lots of fruit crops and then the researchers observed similar diseases among the fruit crops. The method used eventually a best result with minimal computational effort providing effectiveness of the algorithm proposed for the detection and classification of the fruit crop disease. The second advantage of their techniques shows that the diseases of plants can be diagnosed early. Increasing recognition rates in the classification process by using convolutional neural networks and deep neural network methods was also another benefit of their system [24].

Deep Learning technique for detecting and classifying plant diseases based on a plant's leaves, in their study, they used classification in numerous phases to eliminate alternatives at each level, resulting in greater prediction accuracy and when extracting a leaf from the input image, a YOLOv3 object detector was employed [25]. Also, a series of ResNet18 models were used to examine the extracted leaves, while Transfer learning was used to train those ResNet18 models. The first layer determines the leaf type, while the second layer looks for diseases that could affect the plant.

In the research work done by [26] Bell pepper and potatoes were classified using the classification model first and analysed the input leaf image and categorized it as healthy or unhealthy. If healthy, the crop name and its recognition of being healthy are noted and if unhealthy, the crop name and the disease associated with it are equally identified. To improve the quality of images in their research work, the method of pre-processing was introduced. Dataset used is then divided into train and test data, with the train data being used to develop the model. After identifying healthy and unhealthy inputs, the trained CNN model accurately classifies and recognizes the crop name and the disease that is affecting the plant.

2.4 Transfer Learning (TL)

It is the technique that is used in image classification and natural language processing tasks. it makes use of features from images for a pre-trained model, which helps so that the new model will not be trained from scratch. Transfer learning techniques can be directly used in making predictions on new tasks or combined in training a new model. When pre-trained models are used in a new model it reduces the training time. TL is very useful when the training dataset is small. It uses weights from pre-trained models to initiate the weights of the new model. Negative transfer is also referred to as the transfer learning field when the transferred knowledge hurts the target learner [14, 27]. Negative transfer can happen for a variety of reasons, which include the source and target domains' relevance, as well as the learners' capacity to identify transferable and useful knowledge across domains [28].

2.5 Convolutional Neural Network (CNN)

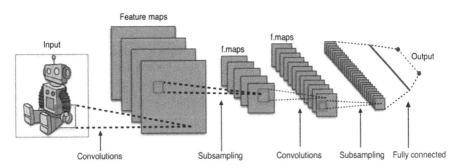

Fig. 2. CNN architecture (Convolutional neural network - Wikipedia)

The architecture of CCN is shown in Fig. 2 above which is mostly used in image processing, image identification, image classification, analysis of video, and processing of natural language. CNN takes images as input and assigns important features/objects to distinguish them. The term 'convolutional' comes from a mathematical technique that entails the convolution of many functions. CNNs have multiple hidden layers, as well as an input layer and an output layer. CNN hidden layers are typically made up of a succession of convolutional layers. The CNNs operate by receiving the input signal first and then processing it. The Input image will be processed through a sequence of the convolution layers with different filters and the signal flow from one layer to the next and is controlled by the control layer. The output will be flattened and then fed into the fully connected layer which connects all other network layers by connecting every neuron from one layer to the neurons of the next layer. As a result, the output will then be classified.

3 Methods and Techniques

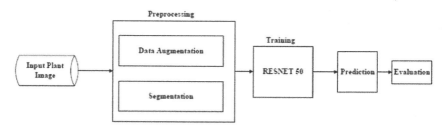

Fig. 3. Proposed model

The proposed model's structure is shown in Fig. 3 above: The model takes in Corn (maize) and Potato plant images as input. The input image is then passed to the preprocessing stage where they are prepared for the Resnet50 model. The adopted preprocessing technique in this study is data augmentation and segmentation. The Resnet50 is then trained and tested after the plant image dataset has been preprocessed. Finally, the proposed model was evaluated.

3.1 Preprocessing

Preprocessing stage is a very important stage that happens before the image data is passed to the deep learning algorithm. This stage helps to prepare data and ensure that the data is passed to a deep learning algorithm in a proper format. This study adopted image augmentation and image segmentation as preprocessing techniques.

3.2 Image Augmentation

A deep learning model works well with large datasets. Image augmentation is a technique of expanding data when an ample amount of data is not available for training a deep learning model. In data augmentation, the plant images were altered to create more datasets for Rent 50 training. The image augmentation technique adopted in this study is rotation, shifting, and blurring.

3.3 Image Rotation

Image rotation is one of the most widely utilized augmentation methods. The data on the image does not change even when it is rotated. If a maize leaf is rotated or viewed from a different angle, it still looks like a maize leaf. Therefore, this strategy was employed to enhance the size of our training data by producing several images rotated at various angles.

3.4 Image Shift

Image shifting is another method of image augmentation technique that was adopted. In this process the position of the objects in the photos was altered by shifting them, to have more training data. The position of each object in the image is mapped to a new location of the output image using the geometric transformation known as "image shift." A result of this is that if an object is at position x,y in the original image, it is moved to a new location X, Y in the new image.

3.5 Image Blurring

Since images come from various sources, their quality varies depending on the source. There could be very high-quality images and very-bad images. This technique was used to increase training data by producing several blurred images.

3.6 Data Segmentation

Image segmentation involves the partitioning of an image into different segments. It is mostly used to locate objects and boundaries which helps to reduce the complexity of the image so that further processing or analysis of the image can be made easier. In the process of this research images belonging to the same category are identified with the same label.

3.6.1 Resnet 50 Model

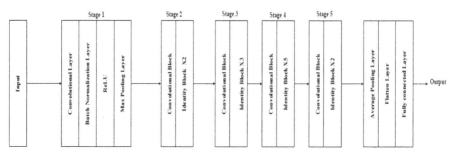

Fig. 4. Resnet50 archetecture

The architectural diagram of Resnet 50 is shown in Fig. 4 above. It consists of five stages each with convolutional and identity blocks. Each convolutional and identity block is made up of 3 convolutional layers respectively. The model implemented the pooling layer two times. The pooling operation implemented are max pooling and average pooling. It constitutes 48 Convolution layers, 1 MaxPool with 1 Average Pool layer. Even though Resnet50 contains 50 layers, it also contains around 23 million trainable parameters, which is substantially lower when compared to other architectures.

3.6.2 Convolutional Layer

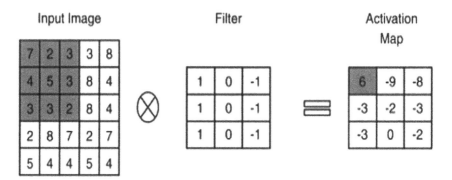

Fig. 5. Convolution operation [30]

The foundation of CNN is a convolutional layer which has a number of filters or kernels, which settings will be learned during the course of the training. Typically, the filters' size is smaller than the original image. Individual filter produces an activation map after it convolves with the image. The dot product that is between each of the elements of the convolution filter with the input is computed at each spatial position as a filter which is moved over the image. Convolution of the filter with the input image yields the first entry of the activation map. This procedure is then repeated for each component of the input image in creating an activation map. Each filter of the activation maps is stacked along the dimension depth to create convolutional layers of the output volume. All activation map element is a neuron's output. Due to this result, every neuron is connected to the discrete local area in the input image and the area's size is the same as the filter's size. Additionally, each neuron in an activation map has certain parameters in common. The convolution operation is shown in Fig. 5 above.

3.6.3 Batch Normalization

Accelerating a deep learning training process can be achieved via batch normalization. According to its statistics in a mini-batch, each layer element in deep learning is normalized with batch normalization to zero means, also with unit variance. Each activation is given learnt scaling plus shifting parameter to increase the network's capacity for representation. When calculating the mean and variance of each hidden unit from each layer across the batch normalizing the units and scaling them using the learned scaling parameter, and then shift them with the learned shifting parameter and mini-batch-based stochastic gradient descent is updated. Equation of batch normalization is as given below where represent ed hidden unit, $\sigma_j{}^2$ is the variance and μ_j is the mean. Learned scaling and shifting parameters are represented by Υ_j and β_j.

$$\hat{h}_j \leftarrow \Upsilon_j \frac{h_j - \mu_j}{\sqrt{\sigma_j^2 + \varepsilon}} + \beta_j \qquad (3.1)$$

Mandal et al. [29].

3.6.4 Max Pooling

In this operation the maximum element on the region of the feature map which is covered by the filter that were selected. Therefore, expected result (output) of max-pooling layer in the feature map which include most prominent features of previous feature map. This was implemented as max pooling 2D layer in Keras.

3.6.5 Average Pooling

In this operation, average of the items in the feature map area that is covered by the filter, is calculated by average pooling. Therefore, average pooling delivers the average of the feature present in each patch.

3.6.6 Residue Block

Given neural network with input x it is important learning true distribution H(x) and residue can be designated as

$$R(x) = \text{output} - \text{input equal to } H(x) - x \qquad (3.2)$$

Mandal et al. [29].

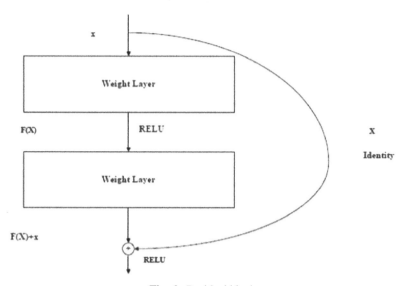

Fig. 6. Residual block

Which can be re-written as

$$H(x) = R(x) + x \qquad (3.3)$$

Mandal et al.[29].

The residue block is attempting to learn the real output H.(x). According to Fig. 6 above, the layers are learning the residual, R(x), because there is connection identity coming due to x while layers in the residual network learn residual (R(x)), and layers in traditional network learn true output (H(x)). Additionally, it's been found that learning residual of input and output, are simpler than learning input alone. Since they are skipped and don't complicate the architecture, the identity residual model permits the reuse of activation functions from earlier levels in this way.

3.6.7 Performance Evaluation

The developed model was evaluated with the following metrics: accuracy, precision, recall, F1-score, and loss. Mathematical formulas are given below.

$$Accuracy = \frac{TN + TP}{TN + FP + TP + FN} \qquad (3.4)$$

$$Precision = \frac{TP}{TP + FP} \qquad (3.5)$$

$$Recall = \frac{TP}{TP + FN} \qquad (3.6)$$

$$F1 - score = \frac{2 * Precision * Recall}{Precision + Recall} \qquad (3.7)$$

TP denote True Positive, TN represent True Negative, FN is the number of False Negative and FP represent False Positive.

3.6.8   Technology Description

Table 1. Technology description

S/N	Technology	Description
1	Kaggle	Online cloud
2	Tensorflow	2.9
3	language	Python 3.9
4	Accelerator	GPU

Table 1 shows the technology description used for the implementation of the model.

3.7   Result and Discussion

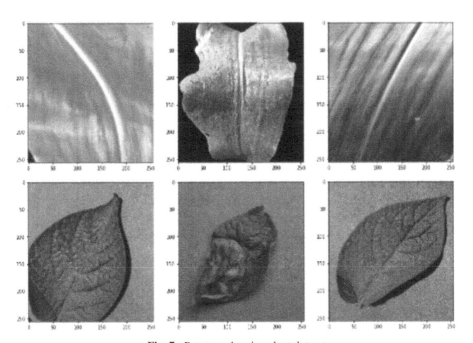

Fig. 7. Potato and maize plant dataset

Figure 7 above shows the dataset for potato and maize. The plant village dataset from Kaggle was used in this study for training and testing the proposed model. Out of numerous plants that were present in the dataset, Corn (maize) and Potato were selected. Random selection of the dataset is as shown below. 80% of images from the dataset were used for training the Resnet50 model, 10% were used for testing and the other 10% were for validation during training.

3.8   Resnet50 Training

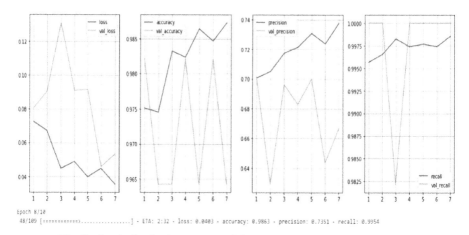

Epoch 8/10
48/109 [========>.................] - ETA: 2:32 - loss: 0.0403 - accuracy: 0.9863 - precision: 0.7351 - recall: 0.9954

Fig. 8. Graph plot for Accuracy Precision-Recall and Loss During Training

The training process of the Resnet model is shown below. A callback function was defined to plot the charts of different metrics performances at end of respective epochs, Training process lasted for 9 epochs since the model convergence was observed in the 9th epoch and at this point, no additional training will increase the model performance. After the end of every epoch, the Resnet50 model is evaluated with validation data. The charts above in Fig. 8 show four performance metrics that were plotted independently for the 8th epoch. Each of the charts contains a score for validation and training. For instance, the first chart illustrates loss and validation loss(val_loss), likewise accuracy, precision, and recall. Validation loss gives the value for the cost function of cross-validation of data while loss gives value for the cost function for training data.

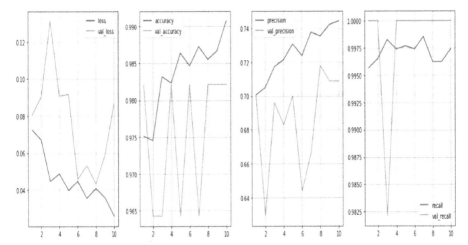

Fig. 9. Graph plot for Accuracy Precision-Recall and Loss During Training in the 9th epoch

The chart in Fig. 9 above illustrates the model performance during training in the 9th epoch. According to the chart above and below the value of loss and validation loss decreases while the value of accuracy, and precision-recall increases, indicating that the model is training well. We aim to stop the training when the loss has gotten to the barest minimum.

3.9 Resnet50 Model Prediction

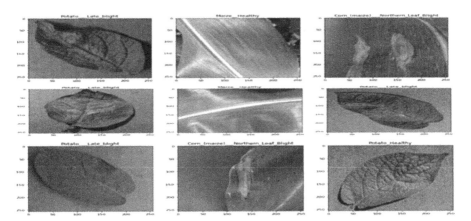

Fig. 10. Model prediction

After the Resnet50 model has been trained well enough, it was subjected to tests and results which showed that it was able to predict maize and potato and their corresponding disease. The model prediction is as shown above in Fig. 10.

4   Results and Discussion

Table 2. Results

Accuracy	Precision	Recall	F1-score	Loss
0.98	0.77	0.99	0.86	0.053

The Model is evaluated using five (5) metrics to show its performance, which are accuracy, precision, recall, f1-score, and loss. Table 2 above shows the result of the performance of the Model. The study found that Resnet50 model was able to predict maize and potato plants, and their diseases with 0.98 accuracies, 0.77 precision, 0.99 recall and 0.86 f1-score. At the training process, the model was evaluated using the loss function of categorical cross-entropy. The higher the value of loss, the higher the model's error. Initially, the value of the loss was 0.08 but as the training progressed it reduced to 0.053.

Table 3. Parameters used for the model implementation

Parameter	Value
Activation function for Input layer	RELU
Activation function for the Output layer	SoftMax
Learning rate	0.01
Batch size	32
Loss function	Categorical cross-entropy
Optimizer	Adam
Number of classes	7

The above Table 3: Shows all parameters used for the model implementation.

Table 4. Distribution of the datasets

Classes	Total number of instances	The number used for Validation	The number used for training	Number used for testing
Healthy maize	1162	116	929	117
Maize Cercospora leaf spot	513	51	410	52
Maize Common rust	1192	119	953	120
Maize Northern Leaf Blight	985	98	788	99
Healthy Potato	152	15	121	16
Potato (Early blight)	1000	100	800	100
Potato (Late blight)	1000	100	800	100

Table 5. Comparison with earlier methods that use pre-trained model using plant image dataset.

Reference	Model	Accuracy
[30]	CNN model (Potatoes)	97.66%
[31]	smartphone-based CNN model (Cassava plant)	80.6%
	ResNet-50 (Cotton)	95.0%
	DenseNet169-MLP Model (Rice Plant)	97.68%
[2]	NASNet-based deep CNN	93.82%
Proposed	Resnet 50 (Maize & Potatoes)	98.0%

Distribution of the datasets is shown in Table 4.

The comparison in Table 5 above shows some of the pretrained model already used in related area of this research work. The accuracy of this proposed work outperforms the earlier techniques which have been used (Fig. 11).

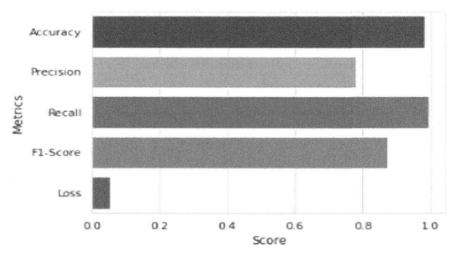

Fig. 11. Chart for the evaluation metric

5   Conclusion

Deep learning has been used for scenarios where significant amounts of unsupervised information are present especially with the development of vast information analysis. The deep learning process has advanced significantly with enormous amounts of unlabeled training data as a capable tool for large-scale information analysis. This research work has conducted a thorough investigation into the identification and classification of plant diseases and reviewed both traditional and cutting-edge methods that have been widely used. Some of the reviews highlighted show the shortcomings and performance rates of the earlier studies. The finding from this research has also helped to implement a model which has helped to detect and classify plant diseases using RESNET 50 of deep learning and CNNs techniques. A pretrained network Resnet 50 model was implemented, to detect and classify plant diseases of Corn (maize) and Potatoes through their respective leaves. A Plant village dataset from Kaggle online platform was used in the training and testing of the model. The numbers of plants that were present in the dataset was distributed in this orders: 80% of the dataset was used for training, 10% was used for testing while the remaining 10% was used for validation during training.

5.1   Contributions

This research work has contributed to the body of knowledge by providing a cutting-edge concept on how we can use a deep learning pretrained model to identify and classify diseases of plants. Here are some of the major contributions:

1. Major contribution of this research paper has shown it to provide a convenient means through which plant diseases can be monitored adequately, thereby circumventing the risk of losing harvest in order to foster an increase in crop yield and farmers' profit.

2. The Resnet50 model has helped to detect and classify Plant leaf diseases.
3. The implementation of the Resnet 50 model will help plant experts to accurately diagnose plant diseases.

References

1. Rahul, S., Amar, S., Kavita, N.Z., Jhanjhi, M., Emad, S.J., Sahil, V.: Plant disease diagnosis, and image classification using deep learning. Comput. Mater. Continua **71**, 2125-2140. (2021). https://doi.org/10.32604/cmc.2022.020017
2. Nilay, G., Atulpatel, A.: Comprehensive study of deep learning architectures, applications and tools. Int. J. Comput. Sci. Eng. **6**(12), 701–705 (2018)
3. The Impact of Plant Disease on Food Security, p. 40 (2012)
4. Vagisha, S., Amandeep, V., Neelam, G.: Classification techniques for plant disease detection. Int. J. Recent Technol. Eng. (IJRTE) **8**(6), 5423–5430 (2020). ISSN 2277-3878
5. Ji, M., Zhang, K., Wu, Q., Deng, Z.: Multi-label learning for crop leaf diseases recognition and severity estimation based on convolutional neural networks. Soft. Comput. **24**(20), 15327–15340 (2020). https://doi.org/10.1007/s00500-020-04866-z
6. Khan, R.U, Khan, K, Albattah, W., Qamar, A.M.: Image-based detection of plant diseases: from classical machine learning to deep learning journey. Wirel. Commun. Mob. Comput. vol. 13 (2021). Article ID 5541859
7. Muhammad, H.S., Sapna, K., Johan, P., Khalid, M.A.: Image-based plant disease identification by deep learning meta-architectures. Plants **9**, 1451 (2020)
8. Sagar, A., Jacob, D.: On using transfer learning for plant disease detection (2020)
9. Zhuang, F.: A comprehensive survey on transfer learning. In: Article in Proceedings of the IEEE (2020)
10. Reddy, S.R.G., Varma, G.P.S., Davuluri, R.L.: Optimized convolutional neural network model for plant species identification from leaf images using computer vision. Int. J. Speech Technol. (2021)
11. Sembiring, A., Away, Y., Arnia, F., Muharar, R.: Development of concise convolutional neural network for tomato plant disease classification based on leaf images. In: Journal of Physics: Conference Series, vol. 1845 (2021). article 012009
12. Samaya, M., Tim, M.J.: Deep learning architectures. Deep learning architectures – IBM Developer (2017)
13. Sethy, P.K., Barpanda, N.K., Rath, A.K., Behera, S.K.: Deep feature-based rice leaf disease identification using support vector machine. Comput. Electron. Agric. **175**, 105527 (2020)
14. Pan, S.J., Yang, Q.: A survey on transfer learning. IEEE Trans. Knowl. Data Eng. **22**, 1345–1359 (2010). https://doi.org/10.1109/TKDE.2009.191.30
15. Ranjan, K.U., Mishra, G.Y., Sandesh, R., Himanshu, P.: The understanding of deep learning: a comprehensive review. Math. Probl. Eng. **2021**, 15 (2021). https://doi.org/10.1155/2021/5548884.34
16. Adedoja, A., Owolawi, P.A., Mapayi.: Deep learning based on NASNet for plant diseases recognition using leave images. In: Computer Science 2019 International Conference on Advances in Big Data, Computing and Data communication Systems (icABCD) (2019)
17. Chen, J., Liu, Q., Gao, L.: Visual tea leaf disease recognition using a convolutional neural network model. Symmetry (Basel), 11, 343 (2019). https://doi.org/10.3390/sym11030343.4
18. Sladojevic, S., Arsenovic, M., Anderla, A., Culibrk, D., Stefanovic D.: Deep-neural-networks-based recognition of plant diseases by leaf image classification. Comput. Intell. Neurosci. (2016). https://doi.org/10.1155/2016/3289801.57

19. Zhao, Z., Wang, H., Yu, X.: Spectral-spatial graph attention network for semisupervised hyperspectral image classification. IEEE Geosci. Remote Sens. Lett. 2021. (2021)
20. Kowshik, B., Savitha, V., Nimosh, M.M., Karpagam, G., Sangeetha, K.: Plant disease detection using deep learning. Int. Res. J. Adv. Sci. Hub (IRJASH), 03(03S) (2021)
21. Abhinav, S., Dheeba, J.: On using transfer learning for plant disease detection (2020). (researchgate.net)
22. Muthukumarana, Aponso, A.C.: (2020),
23. Oyewola, D.O., Dada, E.G., Misra, S., Damaševicius, R.: Detecting cassava mosaic disease using a deep residual convolutional neural network with distinct block processing. PeerJ Comput. Sci. **7**, e352 (2021)
24. Aravind, K.R., Raja, P.: Automated disease classification in (Selected) agricultural crops using transfer learning. Automatika. **61**, 260–272 (2020)
25. Venkataramanan, A., Honakeri, D.K.P., Agarwal, P.: Plant disease detection and classification using deep neural networks. Int. J. Comput. Sci. Eng. (IJCSE) **11**, 40–46 (2019). e-ISSN 0975–3397
26. Harini, S., Savitha, S.K.: Detection and classification of plant diseases using deep learning techniques. Res. Proposal, 58 (2021)
27. Wang, Z., Dai, Z., Poczos, B., Carbonell, J.: Characterizing and avoiding negative transfer. In: Proceedings of IEEE Conference on Computer Vision and Pattern Recognition, Long Beach, June 2019, p. 51 (2019)
28. Mohammed, T.J.: Deep learning: convolutional neural networks (CNNs) (2019). https://medium.com/@b.terryjack/deep-learning-convolutional-neural-networks-cnns-7f7f16341df1
29. Mandal, B., Okeukwu, A., Theis, Y., Masked Face Recognition using ResNet-50 (2021). http://arxiv.org/abs/2104.08997
30. Mostafa, S., Wu, F.X.: Neural engineering techniques for autism spectrum disorder, diagnosis of autism spectrum disorder with convolutional autoencoder and structural MRI images (2021)
31. Cinoy, R.: Understanding artificial intelligence, Machine Learning and Deep learning. l Ponirevo

Light-Weight Deep Learning Framework for Automated Remote Sensing Images Classification

Adekanmi Adegun[1] , Serestina Viriri[1(✉)] , and Jules-Raymond Tapamo[2]

[1] School of Mathematics, Statistics and Computer Science,
University of KwaZulu-Natal, Durban, South Africa
{adeguna,viriris}@ukzn.ac.za
[2] School of Engineering (Computer Engineering), University of KwaZulu-Natal,
Durban, South Africa
tapamoj@ukzn.ac.za

Abstract. Remote sensing images classification plays an important role in a wide range of applications including disaster response, law enforcement, and environmental monitoring. During the past years, significant efforts have been made to develop various machine learning based Computer aided design (CAD) systems for the analysis and classification of these images towards object detection. However, the performance of these systems has been limited due to the complex features of the images. Recently, deep learning methods have achieved promising results in images analysis and classification. These methods however rely heavily on appropriate turning of millions of parameters, which often leads to over-fitting, poor generalization and heavy consumption of computing resources. In this paper, a light-weight deep learning framework has been proposed for remote sensing images classification. The proposed framework consists of two stages: the first stage leverages on an encoder-decoder Network (EDN) to learn the complex features of remote sensing images, with the encoder section learning the local features and the decoder learning the global features. The final classification is carried out in the second stage which employs DenseNet framework. The proposed system was evaluated on the publicly available EuroSAT database. It achieves superior performance of 98% in accuracy, recall, precision and F1-score.

Keywords: Remote sensing images · Deep learning · Encoder-decoder network · Classification

1 Introduction

Remote sensing images possess complex features such as high spatial, temporal, spectral and radiometric resolution. The images are also characterized with coarse resolution, cloud masking, embedded objects and complex background. Thus, performing manual analysis of these images for object detection can be

T. M. Ngatched Nkouatchah et al. (Eds.): PAAISS 2022, LNICST 459, pp. 289–303, 2023.
https://doi.org/10.1007/978-3-031-25271-6_18

very expensive and laborious [1,2]. In addition, big data analysis tasks on of remote sensing images has been limited due to the following challenges:

1. Images are from multiple sources and produced with various data input techniques and various devices such as camera, satellite, drones etc. These devices also vary in qualities such as spatial, spectral, radiometric, and temporal resolutions.
2. Images are also generally heterogeneous in appearance as described in Fig. 1, with high intra-class variance of its elements, and large number of spectral channels due to effects such as cloud masking [2].

So a robust system is required for efficient analysis of these images.

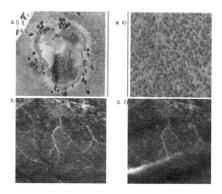

Fig. 1. Challenges: a i) homogeneous image with elephants a ii) heterogeneous image with elephants (WorldView-3 satellite- Addo Elephant National Park, South Africa. (copyright) 2020) b i) and b ii) images with temporal variability. (PROBA-V challenge dataset. Courtesy: ESA ACT)

Conventional machine learning approaches based on handcrafted features extraction algorithms have been used in the past on remote sensing images [3]. These methods include local binary patterns (LBP) [4] and scale-invariant feature transform (SIFT) [5]. Conventional classification methods which are further utilized for the classification of the extracted handcrafted features include Support vector machine (SVM) [6], Artificial Neural Network (ANN) [7], Fisher vectors (FV) [8] and the vector of locally aggregated descriptors (VLAD) [9]. These methods have not been able to achieve optimum performance on remote sensing images due to their inability to extract deep features and also, due to the aforementioned factors.

In the recent past, deep leaning methods have been utilized for objects detection and classification process from remote sensing images as shown in Fig. 2. The most popular approach among these methods is the Convolutional Neural Network (CNN) which relies on convolution layers for the features detection and extraction [3]. CNNs have surpassed traditional methods in images classification and objects detection [3,10]. Their main advantage is in their ability to provide an end-to-end pixel-wise classification that requires very minimal feature engineering. Other deep learning methods such as Deep Belief Networks (DBNs) [11,12] and stacked auto-encoders [11] have also produced promising results in remote-sensing image classification. Deep learning techniques require large amount of memory and computational resources for efficiency [13]. Although the availability of vast amount of GPU has been able to mitigate this effect, developing a robust system that will efficiently manage computing resources with a fast response time is very important in some time-critical decision based systems such as disaster response and law enforcement. Furthermore, there is need to optimize the computational and storage complexities of CAD systems to increase object detection speed and response time for quick decision-making [14]. Efficient management of computational resources will encourage portability of the system on mobile devices and sensors based devices for easy access, most especially in Internet of Things (IoT) based environment for wider coverage. In this research, we propose a light-weight deep learning framework for remote sensing images classification. The proposed framework is able to first detect features and performs pixel-wise classification for segmentation process using an Encoder-Decoder Network. The second part of the framework employs a well-devised light-weight DenseNet block for object classification. The proposed design is aimed at optimizing system performance and minimizing computational resources with reduced usage of computational cost of memory and time.

The organization of this paper is described as follows: Sect. 2 discusses the Related Works and Sect. 3 describes Methods and Techniques. Section 4 discusses the Experimental Results. The last section, conclusions is discussed in Sect. 5.

2 Related Works

Deep learning methods have been utilized for detection and classification of objects from remote sensing satellite images in the past. CNN-based architectures have been mostly deployed for the classification and detection task in the recent past. Fully convolutional neural network (FCN) architecture was employed for object recognition in multispectral satellite imagery by Gudzius et al. [15]. The model was able to generalize across dispersed scenery with 97.67% accuracy over multiple sensors. Classic machine learning techniques based on convolutional network were used for feature extraction, classification of pixels in satellite images by Napiorkowska et al. [16]. The techniques which were originally developed for the ImageNet challenge were then applied to satellite imagery for object detection and classification into three sample classes of roads, palm trees and cars. The system achieved overall accuracy of 96%. Dogan et al. [17] evaluated 11 popular CNN based models for detection of objects classified into 14 in DOTA dataset. The models were trained on 49,053 objects from satellite imagery. RCNN model was then used for object detection tasks.

A convolutional neural network was designed by Goni et al. [18] for multiclass object detection model in satellite images from LandSat-8. The proposed model was trained to identify and detect different sample classes of vegetation, water bodies, road networks and building. Also, five different approaches based on U-Net and Mask R-Convolutional Neuronal Networks models were utilized for object detection and classification of satellite images in SpaceNet dataset [19]. The models achieved an average precision value of 93.7%. A deep learning model was used for classification of conifer and deciduous trees from airborne LiDAR 3D point clouds representing individual trees [20]. The model achieved 90% accuracy for the deciduous trees and 65% accuracy for the coniferous trees. Alkema et al. [21] used a convolutional neural network (CNN) for the detection and recognition of a target species, marsh marigold, from UAV images. The system achieved a single prediction of an MCC of 0.62, recall: 0.85 and precision: 0.72 after training on the flower dataset in 1500 epochs.

Li et al. [22] developed classification methods in urban built-up areas using four deep neural networks (DNNs) CNN, CapsNet, SMDTR-CNN and SMDTR-CapsNet. Their system achieved overall accuracy of 95.0%. Chebbi et al. [23] also deployed deep learning algorithms for feature extraction and classification of remote sensing data. Nguyen et al. [24] deployed a deep learning method, CNN to classify classes of remote sensing images. They performed experiments on a set of satellite image data with their proposed classification method, showing promising results in terms of classification accuracy and classification speed. Basu et al. [25] proposed a classification framework that extracts features from remote sensing images for classification using Deep Belief Network. They performed experiments on SAT-4 and SAT-6 datasets, with the network producing classification accuracy of 97.95% on SAT-4 and 93.6% on SAT-6. Lastly, an investigation of the performance of deep learning over conventional methods for vegetation detection of land covers with grass, shrub, and trees. The objects were then grouped and classified into vegetation and non-vegetation such as roads, buildings [26].

2.1   Research Approach

Our approach combines whole tasks of analysis of remote sensing images which include feature detection, segmentation, features extraction and classification with the optimum use of computing resources. The research aims at optimizing system performance and minimizing computational resources with reduced usage of computational cost of memory and time in analysing remote sensing images. Our contributions include:

1. Encoder-Decoder Network
   The EDN is also able to process complex features such as multi-resolution, coarse appearance and irregular border of remote sensing images through the encoder and decoder units pixel-wisely;
2. DenseNet Classifier
   A DenseNet framework is employed for object classification from remote sensing images. The DenseNet framework is well devised with fewer parameters for accurate and efficient classification of images. The model is also computationally efficient to classify the images. The memory issue with most deep

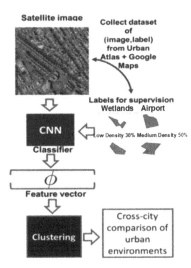

Fig. 2. Diagram illustrating application of Deep Learning techniques for high resolution satellite image analysis [27].

learning framework is mitigated by memory-efficient implementation through the concatenation strategy employed.

3   Methods and Techniques

This section presents the overview of the general methodology adopted in this work.

3.1   Methodology Overview

The process of classification of the data-set towards vegetation detection is categorised into three main stages as shown in Fig. 1:

1. Pre-processing which includes image normalization, noise filtering, spectral analysis, and augmentation.
2. Encoder-Decoder modeling which achieves detection, extraction and pixel-wise classification of features.
3. Image Classification using DenseNet model is the last stage where output from the Encoder-Decoder Network is finally classified.

The above are illustrated in Fig. 3 and further described in detail below:

Pre-processing Stage. The following tasks were performed in the pre-processing stage:

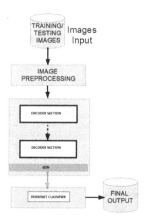

Fig. 3. Framework diagram of the proposed system for remote sensing image analysis.

1. Image size and normalization: The images were prepared in the same scale and resolution through cropping, and resizing. Further, processing such as re-sampling is also performed on the images. The images were then normalized through pixel value mean and standard deviation computation for data centring and data normalization.
2. Noise Removal and Image standardization: The system employed noise removal processes such as morphological operations, contrast and intensity adjustment. Image standardization was also ensured to generally reduce the computation complexity by ensuring that images with multi-sizes and multi-resolution were processed into same scale and resolution (256 × 256) before being sent into the models.
3. Image Augmentation: An augmentation algorithm was also implemented on the images to populate and increase the training data-set.

Encoder-Decoder Network. The Encoder-Decoder Network [28] is a data-driven deep learning framework that is made up of a series of convolutional and pooling layers for feature detection, extraction and pixel-wise classification, as shown in Fig. 4.

DenseNet Model. The DenseNet model is used for overall image classification and for final predictions. It basically utilises dense connections between layers, and composed of Dense Blocks. It is a memory-efficient model with better feature use efficiency and overall excellent performance on classification of images.

3.2 Proposed Model

Encoder-Decoder Network. Feature Detection and Extraction with Encoder-Decoder Network: This is a scalable network that is composed of four

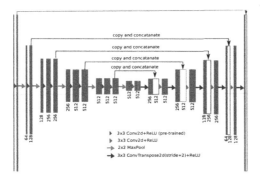

Fig. 4. Framework diagram for the encoder-decoder network [28].

consecutive blocks at both encoder and decoder sections, as described in Fig. 4. Each block of the encoder network is composed of 3 convolution layers and ReLU activation modules [29] with a kernel size of 3×3. The channel sizes for the four blocks are 512, 256, 128 and 64 respectively. The ReLU activation module introduces non-linearity into the operation of the network. This improves the training and execution speed of the model.

The encoder uses 2×2 maxpool modules for features down-sampling. Features maps are extracted from the convolution layers. These are further downsampled by half using the maxpool modules. The outcome pooling indexes are sent into the corresponding layers in the decoder section for upsampling. This is illustrated as

$$Y_i = U(D(x_i : Z_m) : Z_n) \tag{1}$$

where the network starts with an input image, x_i and Y_i is the final output, U is the upsampling module, D is the downsampling module, Z_m is the RELU activation function in the encoder, Z_n is the RELU activation function in the decoder.

In the decoder section, each block of the decoder network is composed of a convolution layer with ReLU activation module and another transpose-convolution layer with ReLU activation module. The stride is set to 2, the padding is not active, and the kernel size is 3×3. The transpose-convolution layers are utilized to upsample feature maps from the encoder section. Throughout the encoder-decoder network, feature maps from the encoder section are simultaneously copied and concatenated with the corresponding output feature maps of the matched decoder section to achieve enriched information and avoid vanishing gradient. The process also restores the lost feature information.

DenseNet Model Architecture. The proposed architecture as shown in Fig. 5 is made up of a fine-tuned network comprising dense blocks which are composed

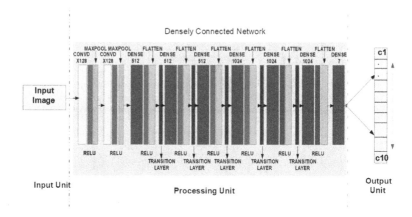

Fig. 5. The basic architectural diagram for DenseNet System design.

of convolution layer, Max Pooling layer and rectified linear unit function (ReLU). The dense blocks and the concatenation process are described as follows:

$$y = C_n([x_0, x_1, ..., x_{n-1}]) \tag{2}$$

where $x_0....x_{n-1}$ denotes the concatenation of the input feature-maps from the convs operators C_n [30].

The conventional approach to improve the performance of deep learning model is to increase the model complexity by increasing the depth of the model networks through the addition of more layers. This can actually lead to network gradient vanishing and exploding. It can also result in non-convergence of the networks [30]. To overcome this challenge, we employ the residual learning approach in dense connected networks [30] to improve the performance of the system. The proposed system explores the potential of the feature reuse via residual learning in the transition layer of the network, which results in condensed models that are easy to train and highly parameter efficient. Feature-maps learned by different layers are concatenated [31] to increase the variation in the input of subsequent layers and improves efficiency.

4 Experimental Results

In this section, various experiments were performed to evaluate the performance of each of the stages of our proposed framework. The evaluated results are displayed and explained below. They are also compared with the existing and similar approaches.

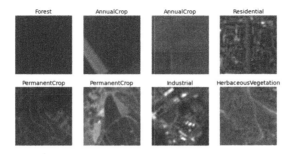

Fig. 6. Sample images from EuroSAT dataset, showing various objects categories of remote sensing images.

4.1 Dataset

The bench-marking EuroSAT [32] dataset used is an open and free satellite data which is based on Sentinel-2 satellite images covering 13 spectral bands and consisting of 10 classes with total 27,000 labelled and geo-referenced images. The dataset contains labelled ground truth of remotely sensed images for the evaluation of the deep learning models. This dataset suites our purpose for this research because it contains various objects categories such as annual crop, permanent crop (e.g., fruit orchards, vineyards or olive groves) and pastures and non-vegetation classes such as road and building images. This dataset contains ten (10) land use and land cover classes with each class containing 2000 to 3000 images with the images measuring 256×256 pixels and spatial resolution of about 30 cm per pixel. This dataset is also characterized with features such as multi-resolution, heterogeneous appearance, high intra-class variance of elements, and large number of spectral channels high intra-class variance inherent to remotely sensed images. Sample images from the dataset are presented in Fig. 6. For the purpose of this research the dataset has been divided into training, testing and validation datasets.

4.2 Results and Discussion

Various experiments were carried out in this section to evaluate the performance of the proposed system. The proposed system was also evaluated against five deep learning models for object classification using performance metrics such as accuracy, precision, recall, and F1-Score on publicly available dataset EuroSAT. The results are discussed in the sections below:

Proposed Model Classification Results. The proposed model achieves an accuracy result of 98.5% on the dataset. The result in Fig. 7 shows that the model performs very well on the high resolution dataset with very low score of the loss percentage. This shows better detection and also implies that the model predicts correctly on most of the sample images in the dataset. The curve in

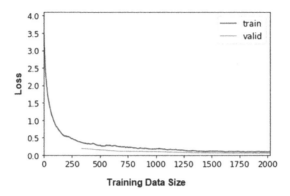

Fig. 7. Training curve diagram showing the loss score for Proposed model on both the training and validation dataset

Fig. 7 also shows that the model does not over-fit, and the performance on both training and validation dataset is good. Also, the classification reports in Fig. 8 shows that the model achieves average precision score of 98%, average recall percentage of 98% and average F1-Score of 98%.

The confusion matrix in Fig. 9 shows the results across all classes for better evaluation of the performance per class. Figure 9 shows the results of the 10-class predictions with the model. In the first category from the confusion matrix result, 581 images of annual crops were correctly classified as annual crops, 585 images of Forest classified correctly as Forest, 596 images of Herbaceous Vegetation classified correctly as Herbaceous Vegetation, 493 images of Highway classified correctly as Highway, 486 images of industrial classified correctly as industrial, 392 images of Pasture classified correctly as Pasture, 462 images of Permanent Crops classified correctly as Permanent Crops, 579 images of Residential places classified correctly as Residential, 491 images of River classified correctly as River and 642 images of sea lakes classified correctly as sea lakes.

Lastly, Fig. 10 shows the image classification output of the sample testing images. The result shows that the model was able to detect the 12 images accurately without missing any of the images.

Models Performance Comparison. Table 1 shows the performance analysis of the proposed model against some popular model on EuroSAT dataset using the Accuracy, Precision, Recall and F1-score metrics. The result shows that the proposed model outperforms other models. Table 2 also shows that our proposed model perform better than some unsupervised deep learning models on EuroSAT dataset across the 10 classes. Lastly, Table 3 shows the parameters size of the proposed model as very light when compared with other models. With our approach, we have been able to reduce tremendously the parameter size of the proposed model. This will reduce the memory requirement and encourage portability. It also improves the overall processing performance of the system.

```
                          precision   recall  f1-score   support

            AnnualCrop       0.98      0.98      0.98       591
                Forest       0.98      1.00      0.99       587
   HerbaceousVegetation      0.97      0.98      0.97       611
               Highway       0.99      0.99      0.99       500
            Industrial       1.00      0.98      0.99       496
               Pasture       0.98      0.96      0.97       408
         PermanentCrop       0.97      0.95      0.96       484
           Residential       0.98      1.00      0.99       581
                 River       0.99      0.98      0.98       499
               SeaLake       0.99      1.00      1.00       643

              accuracy                           0.98      5400
             macro avg       0.98      0.98      0.98      5400
          weighted avg       0.98      0.98      0.98      5400
```

Fig. 8. A diagram showing the classification reports of Proposed model on testing dataset

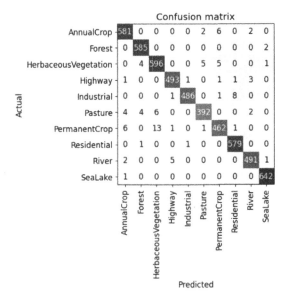

Fig. 9. A diagram showing the classification performance of the Proposed model on testing dataset using confusion matrix

Conclusively, our newly devised and well-structured model with features such as residual networks and features re-usability performs well on complex dataset such as remote sensing images. Also, the re-usability features of these two models allows them to perform efficiently with limited training dataset.

Table 1. Performance analysis(%) and comparison of the deep learning methods on EuroSAT Dataset.

Methods	Accuracy	Precision	Recall	F1-score
Proposed model	98.5	98	98	98
ResNet50	96.5	96	96	96
InceptionV3	75	75	75	75
EfficientNet	65	66	65	65
VGG16	79	79	79	79

Table 2. Class-wise F1 scores(%) obtained by the existing methods (Unsupervised learning methods) against our proposed model on the EuroSAT Dataset.

Methods	DGGAN [33]	MARTA GAN [33]	CNN+PCA [33]	Proposed
Annual crop	67.15	67.01	72.89	98
Forest	83.20	86.54	89.78	99
Heb. vegetation	69.69	68.60	78.37	97
Highway	29.50	34.47	40.15	99
Industrial	78.52	79.63	82.53	99
Pasture	65.63	66.31	73.73	97
Permanent crop	63.84	62.32	67.43	96
Residential	68.18	63.41	71.55	99
River	77.73	90.11	81.93	98
Sea lake	97.42	99.67	98.84	99

Table 3. Comparison of the parameters size of various deep learning methods used on EuroSAT Dataset.

Algorithm	Parameters
Proposed model	2,961,066
ResNet101	44,611,648
InceptionV3	23,897,056
EfficientNet	5,329,532
VGG19	11,117,632

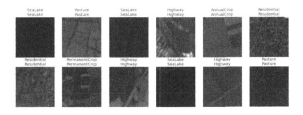

Fig. 10. A diagram showing the classification performance of the Proposed model on sample dataset

5 Conclusion

We have proposed, an efficient light-weight deep learning framework for effective detection and classification on high resolution remote sensing images. Our proposed model was evaluated against four (4) state-of-the-art deep learning models on the same dataset. The proposed model was able to efficiently overcome the challenges such as multi-resolution, heterogeneous appearance and large number of spectral channels. The model is also able to mitigate the challenges of heavy reliance of deep learning methods on appropriate turning of millions of parameters, which sometimes leads to over-fitting, poor generalization and heavy consumption of computing resources. The experiments also show that the model generally perform well on remote sensing images dataset when tested and evaluated on publicly available EuroSAT datasets. It achieves a superior performance of average accuracy score of 98%.

References

1. Al-Doski, J., Mansor, S.B., Khuzaimah, Z.: Improved land cover mapping using landsat 8 thermal imagery. In: IOP Conference Series: Earth and Environmental Science, vol. 540, no. 1, p. 012022. IOP Publishing (2020)
2. You, Y., Cao, J., Zhou, W.: A survey of change detection methods based on remote sensing images for multi-source and multi-objective scenarios. Remote Sens. **12**(15), 2460 (2020). pp. 1–40
3. Özyurt, F.: Efficient deep feature selection for remote sensing image recognition with fused deep learning architectures. J. Supercomput. **76**(11), 8413–8431 (2020)
4. Brahnam, S., Jain, L.C., Nanni, L., Lumini, A. (eds.): Local Binary Patterns: New Variants and Applications, vol. 506. Springer, Heidelberg (2014). https://doi.org/10.1007/978-3-642-39289-4
5. Lindeberg, T.: Scale invariant feature transform, p. 10491 (2012)
6. Awad, M., Khanna, R.: Support vector machines for classification. In: Efficient Learning Machines, pp. 39–66. Apress, Berkeley (2015)
7. Zupan, J.: Introduction to artificial neural network (ANN) methods: what they are and how to use them. Acta Chim. Slov. **41**, 327–327 (1994)
8. Csurka, G., Perronnin, F.: Fisher vectors: beyond bag-of-visual-words image representations. In: Richard, P., Braz, J. (eds.) VISIGRAPP 2010. CCIS, vol. 229, pp. 28–42. Springer, Heidelberg (2011). https://doi.org/10.1007/978-3-642-25382-9_2

9. Jégou, H., Douze, M., Schmid, C., Pérez, P.: Aggregating local descriptors into a compact image representation. In: 2010 IEEE Computer Society Conference on Computer Vision and Pattern Recognition, pp. 3304–3311. IEEE (2010)

10. Benali Amjoud, A., Amrouch, M.: Convolutional neural networks backbones for object detection. In: El Moataz, A., Mammass, D., Mansouri, A., Nouboud, F. (eds.) ICISP 2020. LNCS, vol. 12119, pp. 282–289. Springer, Cham (2020). https://doi.org/10.1007/978-3-030-51935-3_30

11. Signoroni, A., Savardi, M., Baronio, A., Benini, S.: Deep learning meets hyperspectral image analysis: a multidisciplinary review. J. Imaging 5(5), 52 (2019)

12. Kim, J.W.: Classification with deep belief networks (2013). https://www.ki.tu-berlin.de/fileadmin/fg135/publikationen/Hebbo_2013_CD.pdf

13. Adegun, A.A., Viriri, S.: FCN-based DenseNet framework for automated detection and classification of skin lesions in dermoscopy images. IEEE Access 8, 150377–150396 (2020)

14. Huang, R., Pedoeem, J., Chen, C.: YOLO-LITE: a real-time object detection algorithm optimized for non-GPU computers. In: 2018 IEEE International Conference on Big Data (Big Data), pp. 2503–2510. IEEE (2018)

15. Gudžius, P., Kurasova, O., Darulis, V., Filatovas, E.: Deep learning-based object recognition in multispectral satellite imagery for real-time applications. Mach. Vis. Appl. 32(4), 1–14 (2021). https://doi.org/10.1007/s00138-021-01209-2

16. Napiorkowska, M., Petit, D., Marti, P.: Three applications of deep learning algorithms for object detection in satellite imagery. In: IGARSS 2018–2018 IEEE International Geoscience and Remote Sensing Symposium, pp. 4839–4842. IEEE (2018)

17. Dogan, F., Turkoglu, I.: Comparison of deep learning models in terms of multiple object detection on satellite images. J. Eng. Res. (2021)

18. Goni, I., Ahmadu, A.S., Malgwi, Y.M.: Multi-class object detection model in satellite images using convolutional neural network. Communications 9(1), 1–5 (2021)

19. Mohanty, S.P., et al.: Deep learning for understanding satellite imagery: an experimental survey. Front. Artif. Intell. 3, 85 (2020)

20. Hamraz, H., Jacobs, N.B., Contreras, M.A., Clark, C.H.: Deep learning for conifer/deciduous classification of airborne LiDAR 3D point clouds representing individual trees. ISPRS J. Photogramm. Remote. Sens. 158, 219–230 (2019)

21. Alkema, S.: Aerial plant recognition through machine learning (2019)

22. Li, W., Liu, H., Wang, Y., Li, Z., Jia, Y., Gui, G.: Deep learning-based classification methods for remote sensing images in urban built-up areas. IEEE Access 7, 36274–36284 (2019)

23. Chebbi, I., Mellouli, N., Farah, I.R., Lamolle, M.: Big remote sensing image classification based on deep learning extraction features and distributed spark frameworks. Big Data Cogn. Comput. 5(2), 21 (2021)

24. Nguyen, T., Han, J., Park, D.-C.: Satellite image classification using convolutional learning. In: AIP Conference Proceedings, vol. 1558, no. 1, pp. 2237–2240. American Institute of Physics (2013)

25. Basu, S., Ganguly, S., Mukhopadhyay, S., DiBiano, R., Karki, M., Nemani, R.: DeepSat: a learning framework for satellite imagery. In: Proceedings of the 23rd SIGSPATIAL International Conference on Advances in Geographic Information Systems, pp. 1–10 (2015)

26. Ayhan, B., et al.: Vegetation detection using deep learning and conventional methods. Remote Sens. 12(15), 2502 (2020)

27. Albert, A., Kaur, J., Gonzalez, M.C.: Using convolutional networks and satellite imagery to identify patterns in urban environments at a large scale. In: Proceedings

of the 23rd ACM SIGKDD International Conference on Knowledge Discovery and Data Mining, pp. 1357–1366 (2017)

28. Iglovikov, V., Shvets, A.: Ternausnet: U-net with VGG11 encoder pre-trained on ImageNet for image segmentation. arXiv preprint arXiv:1801.05746 (2018)

29. Agarap, A.F.: Deep learning using rectified linear units (ReLU). arXiv preprint arXiv:1803.08375 (2018)

30. Huang, G., Liu, Z., Van Der Maaten, L., Weinberger, K.Q.: Densely connected convolutional networks. In: Proceedings of the IEEE Conference on Computer Vision and Pattern Recognition, pp. 4700–4708 (2017)

31. Du, C., Wang, Y., Wang, C., Shi, C., Xiao, B.: Selective feature connection mechanism: concatenating multi-layer CNN features with a feature selector. Pattern Recogn. Lett. **129**, 108–114 (2020)

32. Helber, P., Bischke, B., Dengel, A., Borth, D.: EuroSAT: a novel dataset and deep learning benchmark for land use and land cover classification. IEEE J. Sel. Top. Appl. Earth Observ. Remote Sens. **12**(7), 2217–2226 (2019)

33. Kang, J., Fernandez-Beltran, R., Duan, P., Liu, S., Plaza, A.J.: Deep unsupervised embedding for remotely sensed images based on spatially augmented momentum contrast. IEEE Trans. Geosci. Remote Sens. **59**(3), 2598–2610 (2020)

AI applications and Smart Systems Technologies

DeepMalOb: Deep Detection of Obfuscated Android Malware

Zakaria Sawadogo[1,2]($\boxtimes$) (iD), Jean-Marie Dembele[2], Attoumane Tahar[1],
Gervais Mendy[1] (iD), and Samuel Ouya[1] (iD)

[1] LITA (Laboratoire d'Informatique, de Télécommunications et Applications),
Université Cheikh Anta Diop de Dakar, Dakar, Senegal
{attoumane.tahar,gervais.mendy,samuel.ouya}@ucad.edu.sn
[2] LANI (Laboratoire d'Analyse Numérique et Informatique),
Université Gaston Berger, Dakar, Senegal
{sawadogo.zakaria,jean-marie.dembele}@ugb.edu.sn

Abstract. The detection of malware android became very crucial with the use of obfuscation techniques by developers of malicious applications. In the literature several approaches have been proposed to take into account certain techniques. But it is difficult to take into account all obfuscation techniques because of mutations and this is a critical challenge for cybersecurity. In this contribution, we proposed an approach to detect obfuscated malicious applications. This approach is based on the memory dump process. This process helps to discover the behaviour of obfuscated applications while they are executing without targeting a particular obfuscation technique. We implemented our application using supervised neural networks. We tested and selected hyper-parameters to train our detection model. The different results obtained by the evaluation metrics such as accuracy, precision, recall and F1 score, are excellent with high values around 99%.

Keywords: Android malware detection · Obfuscation techniques · Deep learning · Cybersecurity · Machine learning · Memory dump

1 Introduction

Application developers used obfuscation techniques to protect themselves against hacking. Indeed, their main purpose was to defend against hacking attempts and protect against common attacks, such as code injection, reverse engineering and falsification of users' private data [1].

Today, obfuscation techniques are a subject of interest to researchers. In fact, developers of malicious Android applications use obfuscation techniques against the detection models of researchers or to evade anti-malware products [2].

This is confirmed by Bit-defender's report that malicious Android app developers have been using COVID-19 related keywords to mask data leakage apps. The report states that more than 85% [3,4] tracking apps are leaking data.

T. M. Ngatched Nkouatchah et al. (Eds.): PAAISS 2022, LNICST 459, pp. 307–318, 2023.
https://doi.org/10.1007/978-3-031-25271-6_19

In the literature, several types of obfuscation techniques exist including Rename obfuscation, data obfuscation, control flow obfuscation, encryption, etc. These techniques are the most cited in the literature and they contained other sub-techniques [2]. Several authors base their approach on one or more of these obfuscation techniques. However, most of these approaches do not take all obfuscation techniques into account.

It is clear from the literature review that there are many challenges related to the detection of obfuscation malware.

- The majority of the proposed detection approaches focuses on some techniques of obfuscation, which limit their efficiency.
- The growth of obfuscated malicious applications that bypass detection and antivirus approaches.
- The constant changing obfuscation techniques could make the models obsolete.

In this work, we are interested in memory dumping for the detection of obfuscated malware. The memory analysis is capable of detecting unconventional malware [5]. We therefore used debug mode for the memory dump process because of the memory volatility. This allows us to more accurately represent what a user would have executed at the instant of the malware attack. According to Sihwail et al. 2018 [6], memory analysis is a promising technique for malware detection and is used to provide a better understanding of the malicious code. Our contribution is an approach that enables the detection of malicious applications without specifically selecting an obfuscation technique. It also allows considering the mutation of the different types of obfuscation used by the developers of malicious applications. In this proposal, we make the following contributions:

1. An efficient approach to the detection of obfuscated malicious applications independently of the obfuscation techniques.
2. An excellent evaluation of our approach based on the multi-layer perceptron algorithm which is a supervised neural network algorithm.

We organized our paper as follows: We start with an introduction in Sect. 1. In Sect. 2, we present the state of the art on Android malware detection. In Sect. 3, we describe our approach to obfuscated malware detection. We presented our implementation environment, data-set and evaluation metrics in Sect. 4. We show the results of the implementation of our approach in Sect. 5. In Sect. 6, we will make a comparative study of our work with the literature. The last section concludes the paper.

2   Related Work

Mirzaei et al. 2019 [7] proposed AndrODet, a mechanism to detect three types of obfuscation in Android applications: ID renaming, string encryption and control flow obfuscation.

Alireza et al. 2019 [8] found that there is a methodological problem in the experimental evaluation of the ability of the AndrODet system to detect the string encryption.

According to Alireza et al., AndrODet's ability to detect string encryption was evaluated with a dataset from the training dataset. However, the authors of AndrODet did not take into account the fact that many samples are very similar. And this could introduce a risk that the model derived from these samples may not be generalizable to all types of string encryption detection. For Alireza et al., the AndrODet approach instead learns to classify samples according to the features of each malware family.

Li et al. 2019 [9] proposed Obfusifier, a system based on obfuscation-resistant features extracted from non-obfuscated applications, while the system is still effective in detecting obfuscated malware. They report that their system can obtain accuracy, recall and F-measurement in excess of 95% for detection of obfuscated Android malware.

According to Li et al., the features on which their model is trained are extracted from unobfuscated applications, but they do not say in the paper how these features can characterize obfuscated malicious applications.

Guo et al. 2020 [10] proposed an approach based on dynamic extraction of the entire layout tree, called WALTDroid. They claimed that their approach can better resist the obfuscation effect.

Zhang et al. 2021 [2] conducted a study in which they summarized which obfuscation approaches are most popular for protecting their software against code theft and tampering. But also those that are to bypass anti-malware products and detection systems.

Alessandro et al. 2018 [11] showed through a survey how the application of several obfuscation techniques affects the effectiveness of widely used machine learning based malware detection approaches coupled respectively with static and dynamic analysis.

Yusheng et al. 2018 [12], worked on a malware classification method based on virtual memory dumping. Their classification method focused on backdoor malware, leaving the other types of malware.

Sihag et al. 2021 [13] proposed BLADE, an obfuscation-resistant malware detection system based on opcode segments. They proposed a system that allows the characterization of features that are resistant to obfuscation techniques through opcode segments.

Sihwail et al. 2018 [6], investigated the types of malware and detection methods. They also reviewed three types of malware analysis techniques: static, dynamic and hybrid. Their study found that in the face of obfuscation techniques used by malware to evade detection, memory analysis can tell us about the activities taking place in the system.

In the light of the literature review on the detection of obfuscated applications, some challenges exist, as we indicated in Sect. 1. It is in this context that we propose an approach to detect obfuscated malware without targeting a particular obfuscation technique.

In Sect. 3, we present our approach called **DeepMalOb** which is a system that allows from the data retrieved from memory dump to detect malicious obfuscated applications without focusing on a particular technique. Thus, we take up the challenge of one of the limitations that has been raised in the literature which is that the proposed detection approaches are mostly focused on some obfuscation technique, which limits their performance.

3   Proposal Approach to Detection of Malware Obfuscated

In this section, we first present our approach to obfuscated malware detection, and then we explain the supervised neural network model we used.

3.1   Proposed Approach to the Detection of Obfuscated Malware

Our approach can be subdivided in the following seven steps: (also describe in Fig. 1)

- In step 1, we create a data-set composed of real-life scenarios simulations of the memory dump process. This data-set is composed of malicious and benign applications. The malware used are the ones that are widespread in the real world.
- In step 2, we clean the data impurities, we put the data on the same scale. At the end of this step, we have features ready to be used for the training. This data-set will be split in two: training data-set and test data-set. We do not select features in this step because we are using a deep learning algorithm.
- In step 3, we implement a supervised neural network model (more details in Subsect. 3.2) to build our obfuscated malware detection approach. This step will train our model from the training data. And provide us with a model capable of obfuscated malware detection.
- In step 4, we test our model with the test data to obtain its score.
- In steps 5 and 6, we prepare non-training and non-test data through none labeled data cleaning up.
- In step 7, we evaluate our model with data from previous steps and compare it with the performance obtained with the test data in step 4.

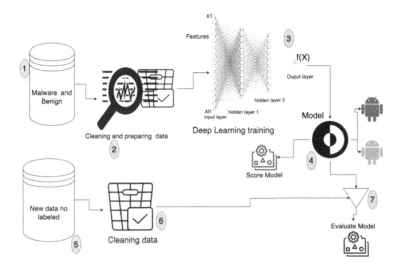

Fig. 1. Approach to detection of malware obfuscated

3.2   Supervised Neural Network Model

Artificial neural networks are machine learning techniques based on the function [14–17] and operation of the human brain. The use of neural networks in machine learning has given rise to deep learning [18]. This technique has the advantage of using multiple layers of neural networks to perform data processing and calculations on a large amount of data. Deep learning generally works by using three types of neural network layers:

Input layer - This layer consists of as many neurons as there are input features. Hidden layer - This can consist of one or more hidden layers of multiple neurons. Output layer - This layer can be composed of one or more neurons in accordance with the type of output.

Deep learning can be divided into two groups, namely unsupervised and supervised deep learning. In our case we used the Multilayer Perceptron (MLP) [19] which is a supervised deep learning algorithm for the implementation of our approach. MLP has the facility to perform non-linear model learning and also the capacity to learn models in real-time. We defined a neural network whose input layer consists of neurons $N_1, N_2...N_n$ corresponding to the features $x_1, x_2...x_n$ in step 2 of our approach (Fig. 1). After this input layer, we defined two hidden layers whose neurons of the first layer are $\frac{n}{2}$ and $\frac{n}{4}$ for the second hidden layers with **n** number of neurons of the input layer. Finally, we defined an output neuron that takes the decision to classify the application according to the information received from the previous neurons.

4   Experiment Setup

In this section, we present the description of the used data set, then we will describe our implementation environment. And finally we describe the various evaluation metrics that we will use to evaluate our model.

4.1   Data Set Description

In our implementation we used CIC-MalMem-2022 [20] which is a new obfuscated malware repository. It focuses on the simulation of real-life scenarios. The malwares used are widespread in the real world (Fig. 2), consisting of spyware, ransomware and Trojans, it provides a balanced data set that can be used to test obfuscated malware detection systems. Our data set contains a total of 58,596 applications of which 29,298 are benign and 29,298 are malicious. Figure 2 shows the total count of each malware family from each malware category.

Malware category	Malware families	Count
Trojan Horse	• Zeus	• 195
	• Emotet	• 196
	• Refroso	• 200
	• scar	• 200
	• Reconyc	• 157
Spyware	• 180Solutions	• 200
	• Coolwebsearch	• 200
	• Gator	• 200
	• Transponder	• 241
	• TIBS	• 141
Ransomware	• Conti	• 200
	• MAZE	• 195
	• Pysa	• 171
	• Ako	• 200
	• Shade	• 220

Fig. 2. Data set description

4.2   Experience Environment

We experimented with a MacBook Pro (13-inch, M1, 2020) with the following features: 16 GB of RAM with the M1 chip. We installed Anaconda Navigator which includes several development tools and a Python library for machine learning.

4.3   Evaluation Metrics

In the area of machine or deep learning, there are several metrics for model validation. We can use the metrics of the confusion matrix [21] or other metrics depending on the quality of the data set [22].

Our dataset is composed of two classes (positive and negative class) and is balanced. We will use the metrics of the confusion matrix. In what follows, we will consider good software as a positive class and malware as a negative class. Let us define the terms below:

True positive Tp: The number of good software that were correctly predicted to be good software;

True negative Tn: The number malware that were correctly predicted to be malware;

False positive Fp: The number of good software but were wrongly predicted to be malware.

False negative Fn: The number malware but were wrongly predicted to be good software.

The sum of the terms Tp, Tn, Fp and Fn gives the total of the data set used for training. These are also exclusive of each other. We calculated the evaluation metrics from Tp, Tn, Fp and Fn.

ACCURACY represent the quotient of perfectly predicted to the total number of samples in the test data-set.

$$ACCURACY = \frac{Tp + Tn}{Tp + Fp + Fn + Tn} \tag{1}$$

PRECISION is the quotient of all samples that were perfectly predicted to be positive among all positive samples.

$$PRECISION = \frac{Tp}{Tp + Fp} \tag{2}$$

RECALL is the ratio of all correctly predicted positive samples to all positive samples and those incorrectly predicted as positive.

$$RECALL = \frac{Tp}{Tp + Fn} \tag{3}$$

The combination of Eqs. 2 and 3 provides a more complete evaluation metric. We call metric **F1-Score.**

$$F1 - Score = 2 * \frac{PRECISION * RECALL}{PRECISION + RECALL} \tag{4}$$

5   Results and Analysis

We present the results of our implementation and comment on these results in this section. For the implementation, we used the supervised Multi-layer perceptron neural network with four layers. Two hidden layers, an input layer and an output layer.

5.1 Choice of Hyper-Parameters

We tested the different activation functions (logistic, tanh, relu) and optimiza-tion functions (lbfgs, sgd, adam) [23] in finding the functions that give the best performance. We have excellent results with the relu function and Adam's opti-mizer. Also we modified some hyperparameters:

- **learning_rate**, we switched to **adaptive**, which allows the updating of weights during training
- **learning_rate_init** $= 10^{-4}$, this hyperparameter controls the updating of weights.
- **max_iter=500**, this hyperparameter determines the number of iterations until convergence of the solver.

Table 1. Performance results of the model depending on the choice hyperparameters

	Accuracy	Training scores	Testing scores
logistic, lbfgs	54.00	54.14	54.30
logistic, sgd	55.00	54.46	54.57
logistic, adam	54.00	54.15	54.30
tanh, lbfgs	55.00	54.95	55.00
tanh, sgd	54.00	54.43	54.53
tanh, Adam	55.00	54.57	54.63
relu, lbfgs	**98.00**	**98.37**	**98.18**
relu, sgd	50.00	50.01	49.94
relu, Adam	**99.00**	**99.21**	**99.29**

The results presented the Table 1 shows that we obtain the best performance when we use the relu activation function with the optimizers lbfgs and adam. With the couple (relu, adam) we get more than 99% for the training performance metric, test performance and model accuracy.

5.2 Interpretation of Results

We applied our approach to a data set that was obtained on a simulation as close to the real world as possible using obfuscated malware prevalent in the real world. Our approach is also interesting because we did not target a particular obfuscation technique, but recovered the data from the memory dump process. This process allows us to recover the behaviours of applications during execution.

Figures 3 and 4 show the evaluation results of our DeepMalOb approach which are very good as we have performances that are as high as 99% for each evaluation metric. If we refer to the Eqs. 1, 2 and 3, our approach minimizes False Positives (Fp) and False Negatives (Fn). This shows that DeepMalOb perfectly

	precision	recall	f1-score	support
Benign	1.00	0.99	0.99	5973
Malware	0.99	1.00	0.99	5747
accuracy			0.99	11720
macro avg	0.99	0.99	0.99	11720
weighted avg	0.99	0.99	0.99	11720

Fig. 3. Report classification

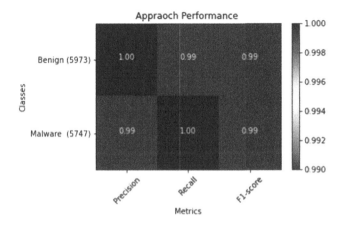

Fig. 4. Approach training performance

detects both classes. Evaluating our approach, which we proposed and described in the Sect. 3.1, showed high performance, which is encouraging regarding the effectiveness of our approach. This shows that the approach is capable of detecting obfuscated malware applications. At the same time, the high performance may hide shortcomings, so we remain cautious. To remove any doubt, we plan to run further tests using other data sources and also to make a comparative study with other algorithms and taking into account a variety of factors.

6   Discussion

In the literature, one can find some interesting work on memory dumping and detection of malicious applications.

The paper Mal-Xtract of Charles Lim et al. 2016 [24] for emulation system based memory analysis to detect the end of the unpacking routine achieves a performance of 97%. This approach is based on similarity algorithms.

Yusheng et al. 2018 [12] proposed a classification method based on visual memory dump of malware. The authors focused on backdoor malware and used classification algorithms such as K-NN and random forest and achieved the accuracy of 95%.

Authors Ahmet et al. 2020 [25] proposed a method based on memory dumping and computer vision to detect malware. In their approach, they use multiple learning and dimension reduction techniques as well as algorithms such as Random Forest, linear SVM and XGBoost and achieved the accuracy of 96.39%. However, it has not been applied to Android malware or obfuscated applications. In this paper, we proposed DeepMalOb which implements a supervised neural network algorithm that allowed us to achieve 99% performance for the evaluation metrics (Accuracy, Precision, Recall, F1-score). Our DeepMalOb approach thus outperforms several works in the literature. Moreover, our approach does not focus on a single obfuscation technique.

7 Conclusion

We proposed an approach named DeepMalOb that will detect obfuscated malicious applications. This approach is based on the memory dumping process. This process allows recovering the behaviors of obfuscated malwares during their execution without targeting a particular obfuscation technique. Our contribution is an answer to one of the challenges encountered in the literature, specifically that proposed approaches for detecting obfuscated Android malware are limited to certain obfuscation techniques. We implemented DeepMalOb using supervised neural networks. We fine-tuned our detection model and select the best hyperparameters. The different results obtained by the evaluation metrics such as accuracy, precision, recall and F1 score are excellent with values as high as 99%. These high performance evaluation metrics of our model show that it is capable of detecting obfuscated malicious applications. Our DeepMalOb approach outperforms several obfuscated android malware detection approaches but most importantly we do not target a specific obfuscation technique. For our system retrieves its analysis data from the memory dump process which then allows understanding the behavior of obfuscated applications. We plan to run more simulations to further evaluate our model.

Acknowledgment. Our work was sponsored by the Partnership for Skills in Applied Science, Engineering and Technology - Regional Scholarship and Innovation Fund (PASET-RSIF).

References

1. Ebad, S.A., Darem, A.A., Abawajy, J.H.: Measuring software obfuscation quality-a systematic literature review. IEEE Access **9**, 99024–99038 (2021)
2. Zhang, X., Breitinger, F., Luechinger, E., O'Shaughnessy, S.: Android application forensics: a survey of obfuscation, obfuscation detection and deobfuscation techniques and their impact on investigations. Forensic Sci. Int. Digit. Investig. **39**, 301285 (2021)

3. Malicious android apps capitalizing on covid-19 promon. https://promon.co/security-news/malicious-android-apps-are-capitalizing-on-covid-19/. Accessed 15 Dec 2020

4. Sawadogo, Z., Mendy, G., Dembelle, J.M., Ouya, S.: Android malware classification: updating features through incremental learning approach (UFILA). In: 2022 24th International Conference on Advanced Communication Technology (ICACT), pp. 544–550. IEEE (2022)

5. Hargreaves, C., Chivers, H.: Recovery of encryption keys from memory using a linear scan. In: 2008 Third International Conference on Availability, Reliability and Security, pp. 1369–1376. IEEE (2008)

6. Sihwail, R., Omar, K., Ariffin, K.A.Z.: International journal of advanced science, engineering and information technology IJASEIT. Int. J. Adv. Sci. Eng. Inf. Technol. **8**(4-2), 1662–1671 (2018)

7. Mirzaei, O., de Fuentes, J.M., Tapiador, J., Gonzalez-Manzano, L.: ANDRODET: an adaptive Android obfuscation detector. Futur. Gener. Comput. Syst. **90**, 240–261 (2019)

8. Mohammadinodooshan, A., Kargén, U., Shahmehri, N.: Comment on "AndrODet: an adaptive Android obfuscation detector". arXiv preprint arXiv:1910.06192 (2019)

9. Li, Z., Sun, J., Yan, Q., Srisa-an, W., Tsutano, Y.: Obfusifier: obfuscation-resistant android malware detection system. In: Chen, S., Choo, K.-K.R., Fu, X., Lou, W., Mohaisen, A. (eds.) SecureComm 2019. LNICST, vol. 304, pp. 214–234. Springer, Cham (2019). https://doi.org/10.1007/978-3-030-37228-6_11

10. Guo, J., Liu, D., Zhao, R., Li, Z.: WLTDroid: repackaging detection approach for android applications. In: Wang, G., Lin, X., Hendler, J., Song, W., Xu, Z., Liu, G. (eds.) WISA 2020. LNCS, vol. 12432, pp. 579–591. Springer, Cham (2020). https://doi.org/10.1007/978-3-030-60029-7_52

11. Bacci, A., Bartoli, A., Martinelli, F., Medvet, E., Mercaldo, F., Visaggio, C.A.: Impact of code obfuscation on android malware detection based on static and dynamic analysis. In: Proceedings of the 4th International Conference on Information Systems Security and Privacy (ICISSP), pp. 379–385. INSTICC, SciTePress (2018)

12. Dai, Y., Li, H., Qian, Y., Xidong, L.: A malware classification method based on memory dump grayscale image. Digit. Investig. **27**, 30–37 (2018)

13. Sihag, V., Vardhan, M., Singh, P.: BLADE: robust malware detection against obfuscation in android. Forensic Sci. Int. Digit. Investig. **38**, 301176 (2021)

14. Ramachandran, P., Zoph, B., Le, Q.V.: Searching for activation functions. arXiv preprint arXiv:1710.05941 (2017)

15. Werbos, P.J.: Backpropagation through time: what it does and how to do it. Proc. IEEE **78**(10), 1550–1560 (1990)

16. Cortes, C., Mohri, M., Rostamizadeh, A.: L2 regularization for learning kernels. arXiv preprint arXiv:1205.2653 (2012)

17. Zhang, Z., Sabuncu, M.: Generalized cross entropy loss for training deep neural networks with noisy labels. Adv. Neural Inf. Process. Syst. **31** (2018)

18. Hush, D.R., Horne, B.G.: Progress in supervised neural networks. IEEE Signal Process. Mag. **10**(1), 8–39 (1993)

19. Taud, H., Mas, J.F.: Multilayer perceptron (MLP). In: Camacho Olmedo, M.T., Paegelow, M., Mas, J.-F., Escobar, F. (eds.) Geomatic Approaches for Modeling Land Change Scenarios. LNGC, pp. 451–455. Springer, Cham (2018). https://doi.org/10.1007/978-3-319-60801-3_27

20. Carrier, T., Victor, P., Tekeoglu, A., Lashkari, A.H.: Detecting obfuscated malware using memory feature engineering. In: Mori, P., Lenzini, G., Furnell, S. (eds.) Proceedings of the 8th International Conference on Information Systems Security and Privacy (ICISSP 2022), Online Streaming, 9–11 February 2022, pp. 177–188. SCITEPRESS (2022)
21. Handling imbalanced datasets in machine learning — by baptiste — towards data science. https://towardsdatascience.com/handling-imbalanced-datasets-in-machine-learning-7a0e84220f28. Accessed 15 Dec 2022
22. Sawadogo, Z., Mendy, G., Dembele, J.M., Ouya, S.: Android malware detection: investigating the impact of imbalanced data-sets on the performance of machine learning models. In: 2022 24th International Conference on Advanced Communication Technology (ICACT), pp. 435–441. IEEE (2022)
23. Kingma, D.P., Ba, J.: Adam: a method for stochastic optimization. arXiv preprint arXiv:1412.6980 (2014)
24. Kane, S.N., Mishra, A., Dutta, A.K.: Preface: international conference on recent trends in physics (ICRTP 2016). J. Phys: Conf. Ser. **755**(1), 5 (2016)
25. Bozkir, A.S., Tahillioglu, E., Aydos, M., Kara, I.: Catch them alive: a malware detection approach through memory forensics, manifold learning and computer vision. Comput. Secur. **103**, 102166 (2021)

Reconfigurable Intelligent Surfaces: Redefining the Entirety of Wireless Communication Systems in Leaps and Bounds

Peter Ogolla🆔 and Olutayo Oyerinde(✉)🆔

School of Electrical and Information Engineering, University of the Witwatersrand,
Braamfontein, Johannesburg, Gauteng, South Africa
peterogolla1@students.ac.za, olutayo.oyerinde@wits.ac.za

Abstract. The next-generation wireless networks are poised to undergo major shifts in their underlying technologies. This is unavoidable if they are to support the new and advanced services that are geared towards the provision of the ultimate user experience through hyperconnectivity, which is only achievable through wireless networks characterized by ultra-high reliability and data rates, negligible latencies, and very low error rates. The reconfigurable intelligent surface (RIS) has been earmarked as the novel antenna technology for future wireless networks with applications spanning from wireless communication, localization, and radio sensing. This paper explores the RIS technology by delving deeper into the reasons that make the RIS an attractive prospect for next-generation wireless networks and highlighting some of the considerations that need to be made while integrating RISs into communication networks. Simulation results considering a single-input single-output (SISO) communication system show that significant improvements in spectral efficiency can be achieved when the RIS is incorporated. Increasing the number of RIS elements results in a rise in spectral efficiency. The results further demonstrate that the enhancement impact of RIS is particularly great in cases where the direct path between the transceivers is very weak.

Keywords: Reconfigurable intelligent surfaces · Next-generation wireless networks · Metasurface · Compressive sensing · Artificial intelligence

1 Introduction

Mobile networks have been on a continuous path of rampant evolution since their inception in 1979. At the center of the evolution are the changing demands arising from the need for increasingly complex services compared to the available requirements. This has often necessitated a major shift in the technology of the day. With the commercial rollout of fifth generation (5G) mobile networks ongoing, discussions and research activities around the next-generation communication networks are already in full swing. Distinctive services that are geared towards the provision of the ultimate user experience through hyperconnectivity have been identified. These have all been positioned

© ICST Institute for Computer Sciences, Social Informatics and Telecommunications Engineering 2023
Published by Springer Nature Switzerland AG 2023. All Rights Reserved
T. M. Ngatched Nkouatchah et al. (Eds.): PAAISS 2022, LNICST 459, pp. 319–331, 2023.
https://doi.org/10.1007/978-3-031-25271-6_20

under the Internet of Everything (IoE) umbrella. The realization of these services, however, requires advanced device form factors and advanced wireless networks characterized by extremely high reliability, negligible error rates ($\sim 10^{-7}$), hyper-fast data rates (1 Tbps), and extremely low latencies (< 10 ms). This is essential to support the diverse kind of devices across both the downlink and uplink channels. To maximize throughput and reduce latencies, previous generations of wireless networks focused optimization efforts solely on the endpoints through sophisticated designs. The wireless propagation channel between the transmitter and receiver has long been considered uncontrollable. The confinement of optimization efforts to the endpoints, however, limits the achievable enhancements, especially with the stringent demands associated with the next-generation networks.

The constraint has led to a major shift in the focus of research efforts. More attention is now being given to the previously untouched wireless medium. Initial studies have shown that huge performance gains can be unearthed if the wireless environment is controllable. The result has been the emergence of the smart radio environment (SRE) concept, which is also known as "Wireless 2.0" or the Intelligent Radio Environment (IRE). Here, the transmitters, receivers, and wireless channels are all considered optimization variables [1] that can be exploited in the next generation of wireless networks. Future wireless networks are expected to use the terahertz frequency spectrum. At these frequencies, signals encounter severe attenuation due to atmospheric absorption and free-space path losses. To compensate for this, enormous antenna arrays are required at the transmitter. Since traditional antennas use relay technology, this implementation will inadvertently translate into very high-power consumption. As a result, a key requirement for the realization of the SRE concept is the development of a novel antenna technology that will effectively support the signal propagation at these high frequencies while consuming ultra-low power.

2 Motivation

Research efforts are pointing in the direction of metamaterials as the possible answer to the novel antenna problem for future wireless communication systems. This is due to their small size, geometry, structure, and their inherent abilities to manipulate electromagnetic waves [2]. The three main implementations of metamaterial-based antennas are the metasurface lens, the metamaterial antenna, and the reconfigurable intelligent surface (RIS) [2]. The first two rely on dedicated radio-frequency chains to adjust the direction of the impinging wave. They can thus be considered active devices since they require a separate power source to operate. On the other hand, the RIS does not require a dedicated power source for normal operation. This along with other attractive features that will be discussed in subsequent sections makes the RIS a front runner in the race for novel antenna technology for next-generation wireless networks.

3 Reconfigurable Intelligent Surface

Also going by other names such as Large Intelligent Surface (LIS), software-defined surface (SDS), and Intelligent Reconfigurable Surface (IRS), the RIS is essentially a low-cost, energy-efficient, two-dimensional (2-D) array of electronically large, nearly passive reflective elements made of electromagnetic materials. Each element that comprises the RIS has the inherent capability of smartly controlling the phase and/or the amplitude of the impinging electromagnetic wave using unnatural properties like anomalous reflection, perfect absorption, and negative refraction [3]. The elements are controllable individually or as a group. This is often done through a local control unit (RIS controller) attached to the RIS through control or backhaul links. The RIS controller actively communicates with the other nodes in the network, such as the base station (BS), user equipment (UE), and RIS, and dynamically alters the phase or reflection profile of the RIS to steer the outgoing signal in the desired direction without the limitation of Snell's law of reflection. The resultant outgoing signals are constructively merged at the receiver, resulting in improved total received signal power [4] and expanded network coverage.

Apart from phase and amplitude, other wave parameters that can be dynamically adapted by the RIS include wave polarization, time delay, and frequency. The RIS achieves all of these without the need for complex encoding, decoding, or radio frequency (RF) operations, as is the case in conventional phased arrays. It is also worth noting that the RIS does not generate any signals of its own but only affects the signals sent between the transceivers. As much as these two factors are advantageous from both power and noise perspectives, the passivity of the RIS complicates certain analytical tasks such as the acquisition of instantaneous channel state information, which remains an active area of research. Overall, the RIS can effectively, proactively, and smartly reconfigure the wireless propagation environment, resulting in high spectral efficiency, better-received signal quality through beamforming, and expanded network coverage and capacity even for high mobility channels such as unmanned vehicle channels, without the need for complex signal processing. RIS also plays a crucial role in enhancing the overall channel quality by alleviating wireless channel issues such as interference, channel hardening, and fading's thereby enhancing the overall channel quality.

3.1 RIS Operation

The RIS can be operated as a reconfigurable lens, a reconfigurable mirror, or a hybrid combination of the two. When operating as a lens, the impinging wave is focused through refraction while when used as a reconfigurable mirror, the incident wave is anomalously reflected in the desired direction based on the configured phase profiles of the RIS elements. The ability of a single RIS to operate in the hybrid mode – simultaneously both as a mirror and as a lens – not only allows widely spaced users to be served by a single transmitter but also reduces the power requirements for the transmitter. The hybrid operating mode hasn't been well studied in as much as it is likely to be the most beneficial mode since it provides full range coverage compared to the individual modes which only serve users in each plane. These realizations have different use cases and design considerations. The different operating modes are illustrated in Fig. 1.

The implementation of the RIS is often split into two major branches: conventional reflect-arrays and metasurfaces [5]. Reflect arrays are the simplest to implement and utilize a large number of elements, each with dimensions comparable to the wavelength of the impinging wave. Every element of the RIS receives a point of the impinging

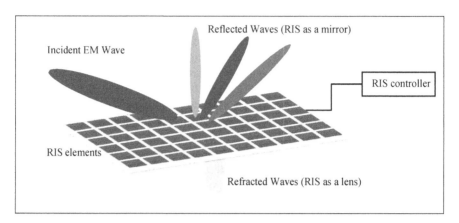

Fig. 1. Typical RIS structure detailing the operation modes

wave and either diffusely scatters it in all directions within the operating plane or does a phase shift and steers all rays towards a specified direction. For this implementation to be effective, however, there is a need to have a large number of RIS elements working together as a unit. Metasurfaces [6] implementation on the other hand, is more complex. It utilizes the great degrees of freedom arising from the numerous densely packed meta-atoms with subwavelength dimensions and spacing to control the impinging waves. The underlying structures of the meta-atoms and the subsequent electromagnetic response of the metasurface can be changed in real-time. Their makeup comprises several layers of the reconfigurable metasurface with individual dimensions being significantly larger than the corresponding wavelengths [5].

The elements that make up the RIS are often arranged as triangular or rectangular lattices, with the distance between them ranging from a tenth to half a wavelength. When in operation, the RIS elements can be reconfigured in one or more of the following ways: mechanically through physical stretching; functionally using materials such as graphene and liquid crystal; optically using an optical pump; electronically using diodes and transistors; or thermally. Electronic reconfiguration is the most widely used approach due to the associated low power and hardware costs, quick response rates to the fast-changing wireless channel, and lower reflection-related losses. Varactors are used when multiple phase shift levels are required since the frequently used positive-intrinsic-negative (PIN) diodes are capable of only two levels – the ON and OFF states. As much as the varactors have this huge advantage, their utilization is limited owing to the high implementation costs which arise from the wide range of biasing voltages required. This is further exacerbated by the large number of elements that are required for a single practical RIS implementation. The performance of the RIS elements (and consequently the RIS) is largely dependent on the fabrication material used and the correlation between the individual elements. In light of this, the verification of the selected channel models is therefore essential.

The RIS is widely considered as a large-scale array of phase shifters functioning without dedicated radio resources. This means that it can neither send pilot symbols nor directly estimate wireless channels when used in a communication system. It only requires negligible power and digital signal processing capabilities for the configuration of its surfaces. The latter only happens during the programming and control stages, with no power requirement during the normal operation phase [1]. The reconfigurable intelligent surfaces do not provide any power amplification. As a result, RISs are said to be nearly passive.

The functioning of RISs is through the creation of virtual links between the transmitter and receivers, which achieves the dual role of improving coverage, especially when the line-of-sight (LOS) is blocked and providing reliable data rates through spatial multiplexing. This ability of RISs to smartly reconfigure the wireless channel means that the propagation environment can now be considered as a deterministic space, which opens a myriad of optimization opportunities for the next-generation wireless networks [7].

3.2 RIS Features

The attractive features of RISs that are key to their increased application are highlighted in [8] and [7]. To start with, their passive nature means that they do not require dedicated power sources. Coupled with their lightweight and the ease with which they can be fabricated into different shapes, RIS can be deployed in many areas, such as on building facades, decorative paintings, furniture, and apparel. The introduction of RIS to a communication system ensures that the users that are in the "service dead zones" because of obstacles can be serviced. This is achieved through the virtual line-of-sight links between the transceivers that go around the obstacles. This results in the expansion of the network coverage and an improvement in both the spectral efficiency and the received signal-to-interference-plus-noise ratio (SINR). When deployed at the edge of a cell, the RIS achieves the double role of facilitating the suppression of co-channel interference between adjacent cells and enhancing the received signal power for the users at the edge of the cell. RISs are also very useful when it comes to bolstering physical layer security. They achieve this by canceling the signal at the eavesdropper station, leaving only legitimate users to receive the signal.

RISs fundamentally achieve full-duplex transmission without the need for power amplifiers, analog-to-digital converters, or digital-to-analog converters. The non-reliance on power amplifiers to shape the impinging signal makes them more energy-efficient compared to conventional relay systems such as those employed in massive multiple-input multiple-output (MIMO) systems, which often require large numbers of high-resolution phase shifters and complex feeding networks that inadvertently translate to high hardware and power costs [3]. This also means that RISs neither introduce nor magnify noise when used in the network. These two factors give the RIS an edge over the conventional active antennas. However, to get the same amount of antenna gain with the RIS as you would with conventional phased arrays, a large number of antenna elements is required [9]. Additionally, the introduction of an extra device in the form of the RIS into an already complex radio environment results in extra channels that further increase the channel and location estimation overheads [4].

Being a contiguous surface, any single point within the RIS can shape the impinging signal. This significantly improves the reliability of the RIS. RISs also have a full-band response, meaning that they can function at any operating frequency and can work with the existing hardware and wireless network standards without any alterations. This makes them both easy to use and integrate into a communication system. A good mix of a small number of base stations and a larger number of RISs can easily result in a scalable, low-cost hybrid network. The passive nature and associated low costs of the RIS means that RISs can be densely packed and interconnected to improve both coverage and performance without the need for complex management of interference between them [10]. Deployments that have incorporated double RISs for instance, have been seen to have better performance when compared to situations where a single RIS is used. Additionally, higher spatial multiplexing gains arising from greater channel ranks are achievable when multiple RISs are used.

3.3   RIS Applications

A lot of existing literature [1, 11, 12] focuses on the role that RIS plays in enabling and improving terrestrial communication, radio sensing, wireless power transfer, and localization. The problems associated with the integration of RIS into communication systems are also highlighted in existing works [13]. This work does not seek to replicate the existing works. On the contrary, we provide only a few examples for context purposes.

At the core of the next-generation networks is the utilization of high-frequency bands – millimeter wave (mmWave) and micrometer wave (μmWave) – for wireless communication owing to the large bandwidths that they present. The biggest challenge here is that the signals are highly susceptible to obstructions, and their natural propagation paths are generally sparse due to the combined effects of large penetration and path losses and low scattering [11]. To compensate for these effects, smaller, numerous, and densely packed antennas are required. Conventional antenna arrays are not ideal due to their large size, high power consumption, and the fact that the relay technology is still far from maturity. This creates a niche that can be effectively filled by the RIS. In addition to the other features that make the RIS a suitable antenna candidate, it is also considered electronically large, which means that the footprint required for the realization of RIS is very small. This facilitates RIS deployment.

The application of RIS technology is not limited to terrestrial communication but can improve performance in non-terrestrial networks (NTNs), deep space networks (DSNs), underwater systems, and confined spaces such as underground mining tunnels. In NTNs, for instance, the RIS can be integrated to bring about boosts in received signal strength for geostationary orbit (GEO) satellites, and improvements in beamforming and power efficiency in middle earth orbit (MEO) satellites [14]. RISs have been proposed to replace both reflect and phased arrays for extended tracking of orbiters and near-earth satellites due to their superior steering abilities, passive beamforming capabilities, and compatibility with size, weight, and power (SWaP) requirements [14]. The nimbleness and low power consumption make the RIS a suitable candidate for extending the average flight duration of high-altitude platform systems (HAPS) at significantly lower operational costs. The network coverage, throughput, and energy efficiency can be increased without many modifications as the massive surfaces of HAPS provide ideal facades for the installation of many RISs. The effective roll-out of RISs in NTNs requires that the physical design of individual systems and the corresponding aerodynamics be considered. As in terrestrial systems, the propagation losses and the number of required RIS phases should also be considered. The space environment also has specific factors that affect communication, such as solar scintillation, sharp temperature fluctuations, solar winds, dust storms, and coronal mass ejections which must also be factored in.

RIS-aided wireless signal transmission in challenging environments namely underground, underwater, disaster, and industrial environments has been extensively studied in [15]. Through the incorporation of RISs in underground tunnels, for instance, the signal blocking probability can be significantly reduced with further improvements achievable through the proper configuration of the RIS phase profiles, an increase in the number of RISs, and optimization of the location and size of the RIS relative to the position and size of the obstacles [16]. The RIS range in the underground tunnels can also be increased if the distance between RIS and the transmitter is increased at a given blocking probability.

The integration of terrestrial and non-terrestrial communication systems will be fundamental for next-generation wireless networks. Based on its nature and functionality, the RIS remains a key enabling technology for the expansion of coverage in the space-air-ground-sea networks. In high mobility scenarios, RISs can be used to effectively mitigate the effects of Doppler spread and multipath fading. The latter can be eliminated if all reflectors in each wireless channel are RIS-coated, consequently leading to improved received signal power.

3.4 RIS Outlook

As already partly mentioned, further developments in mobile communications require a rethinking of the current technologies. Enhancement of network coverage through increasing the density of active nodes raises deployment, power, and maintenance-related costs and results in severe interference issues that need complex mitigation approaches. This situation is further exacerbated by the high propagation losses at high frequencies, which would ideally call for more active nodes to compensate for the losses. The associated high costs and signal processing complexities are further increased by having many antennas at the active nodes like the base stations and access points in the form of technologies such as massive MIMO. RIS is well-poised to handle these issues based on properties and attractive features already highlighted. The incorporation of RISs into a communication system opens new and enormous opportunities in localization, communication, and sensing.

From a localization perspective, for instance, RIS exhibits immense potential to improve the accuracy with which the position and orientation of the user can be measured. It does this by providing significant boosts in both the position and orientation error bounds. Due to poor signal propagation at high frequencies arising from channel sparsity and atmospheric absorption, RIS assists the communication by not only providing the required beamforming through coordinated phase shifts but also aids in correctly locating the UE with greater precision even in cases where the LOS between the transceivers is missing or blocked. Additionally, the ability to deploy multiple RIS units within a network without interference increases these benefits by orders of magnitude. It has also been seen that localization and mapping functions can be significantly improved when the deployed RIS density in each coverage area is high.

Successful RIS deployment, however, requires a few factors to be considered prior to roll-out. First and foremost, the right channel model must be selected. This often depends, among other factors, on the selected RIS implementation. The three main channel models that are often considered are the dyadic backscatter, spatial scattering, and large-scale path loss models [5]. A thorough review of the channel models has been done in [17]. The choice of the channel model including the effects of polarization, the shape of the beams, path losses, and spreads, largely affects the integrity of the results and effective deployment of the RIS. The frequency band where the RIS is implemented, and the mode of operation are vital factors to consider when selecting the channel model. RIS operates in receive, transmit, or reflect modes. These factors need to be thoroughly studied to get the best out of the RIS.

Proper and reliable design of the reflection and phase matrices to provide beam-forming and/or cancellation of interference both in the near and far-end communication scenarios is important. The accuracy and performance of communication and localization receive huge boosts if the RIS phase profiles are properly designed. This, however, is no mean task and several research efforts are ongoing to find the best possible solutions for optimization of power [18], data rates, SINR, and energy efficiency [19]. The phase profile needs to be jointly designed with multiple transmitters for an effective balance between lessening the intra-cell and inter-cell interference and achieving the desired power levels of the received signal.

The algorithms that work for small RISs might not hold for very large RISs. As a result, there is a need for coming up with more efficient algorithms. Techniques such as compressive sensing (CS) and artificial intelligence (AI) are showing great promise towards the achievement of this. For instance, the application of machine learning (ML) capabilities to RIS-assisted communications systems has been seen to significantly improve the performance of the systems. The choice of the appropriate ML model is core to the effective balance between performance and complexity. Improvements in SNR, for instance, require proper passive beamforming configuration of the RIS to construc-tively combine the many virtual links at the transceivers, especially for MIMO systems. The result is high-dimensional inputs for supervised learning models, translating to high computational complexity. Unsupervised models can be used to address this. In [20], an unsupervised learning model is introduced and achieves 95% complexity reduction with only a 2% drop in spectral efficiency in comparison to the alternating optimization (AO) approach for a RIS-assisted MIMO system. Reliable passive beamforming is achieved with only a few layers and nodes with no requirement for data labels.

Another factor is the accurate acquisition of the channel state information (CSI). Partial or full knowledge of the wireless channel is crucial if the benefits that come with RIS are to be actualized. Channel estimation (CE) is, however, complex, and challenging. This is due to the passive nature of the RIS, meaning that it is unable to transmit or process pilots that could otherwise be used for channel estimation; the massive number of reflecting elements and their associated channel coefficients that need to be estimated; and the dependency that exists between the RIS performance and CSI. The main CE approaches for RIS systems fall into three general categories. In the first case, a few RIS elements are made active to assist with the channel estimation. As much as this simplifies the CE problem, it increases estimation errors and the power consumption of the RIS. In the second case, the RIS is treated as fully passive, and the CE problem involves the estimation of the cascaded channel. Though popular, the inability to have the channels between the RIS and the different nodes separately estimated prevents full utilization of the RIS, especially in scenarios where the tracking of the movement of the user is required. The third approach focuses on beam searching using codebooks. The explicit channel estimation is foregone in this case. Beam searching using predefined codebooks, in addition to having a few active RIS elements to send pilots supported by powerful compressive sensing and machine learning techniques, has shown great potential. Hierarchical codebooks, for instance, have shown superior performance in both localization and communication in RIS-assisted networks. Accurate acquisition of CSI remains vital in the design and optimization of the reflection matrices. For channel estimation, it is important that the operating mode of the communication system – whether time-division duplex (TDD), or frequency-division duplex (FDD), or both – is considered.

Lastly, there is a need to formulate a proper strategy for the practical deployment of the RIS. The strategy should seek to rip the benefits of a reduction in costs while expanding the capacity and coverage of the network. This will entail decisions on whether to use active or passive arrays or a mix of the two; and whether to operate the RIS in receive or transmit versus reflect mode [10]. Additionally, consideration must be made as to where the RIS needs to be placed. The gains and relative motion patterns come into play when deciding on whether the RIS needs to be closer to the transmitter or the receiver. The further the RIS is from the transceivers, the greater the path loss. This can be mitigated by using a chain of RISs. However, consideration needs to be made of the number and spacing of the RISs so that their use is not counterproductive.

There are options to deploy the RIS as a centralized unit whereby all the reflecting elements are placed close to the transmitter, or a decentralized unit that involves clustering the RISs near each user in the network. The decision will revolve around the maximization of beamforming gains and distribution of gains among users. When coming up with the deployment strategy, the associated costs, propagation environment, user distribution, and usage patterns need to be factored in. For instance, as much as the RIS can be densely packed owing to the low hardware and power costs with few active nodes being used, the increased complexity can be a factor that deters such an implementation [10]. Localization approaches and their corresponding accuracy need to consider where the RIS is placed with respect to the transceiver – whether it is in the near-field or the far-field. For large antenna arrays, for example, it is common to assume that the RIS is in the far-field, yet it could in fact be well in the near-field. Additionally, useful position information is often carried in the spherical wavefront, which can be left unexploited if the planar wavefront is used instead (Table 1).

3.5   RIS Capacity and Spectral Efficiency

To demonstrate the effect of the RIS in a communication system, the simplest case of a single input single output (SISO) communication system is considered in this article. In this case, both the transmitter and the receiver are equipped with a single antenna, respectively. The setup used for the simulations is shown in Fig. 2.

For the simulation, the SISO system is considered to be operating in the downlink. A bandwidth of 20 MHz is used while the transmit power and the noise figures are set to 10 mW and 13 dB respectively. The number of antennas at the transmitter and receiver

Table 1. Summary of RIS reconfiguration, application areas and implementation considerations

RIS reconfiguration methods	Reconfigurable signal parameters	RIS application areas	RIS implementation factors
Mechanical Functional Optical Electrical Thermal	Phase Amplitude Polarization Time delay Frequency	Terrestrial communication Non-terrestrial networks Deep space networks Underwater networks Confined underground spaces	Channel model to be used Design of phase and reflection profiles Acquisition of accurate CSI Overall RIS gains being targeted (strategic)

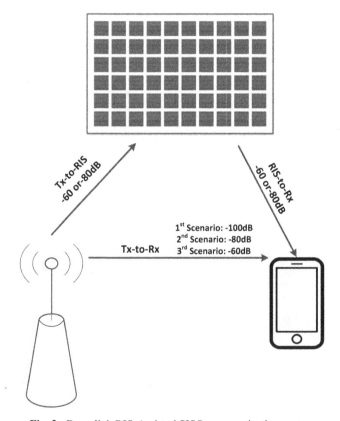

Fig. 2. Downlink RIS-Assisted SISO communication system

are both unitary, while the number of reflective elements for the RIS is set at 2000. The amplitude reflection coefficient of each RIS element is set to 1. The three scenarios considered are based on the overall path loss, with the values being -100 dB, -80 dB, and -60 dB. The results are shown in Fig. 3.

The capacity of the channel between the transmitter and the receiver is often given based on the Shannon's channel capacity formula below, where C represents the system capacity; N_tN_r refers to the number of antennas at the transmitter and receiver respectively (both of which are 1 for the SISO system); B is the bandwidth, and $\frac{S}{R}$ refers the signal to noise ratio (SNR).

$$C = N_tN_rB \log_2\left(1 + \frac{S}{R}\right) \tag{1}$$

As can be observed from Eq. (1), the channel capacity is dependent on SNR. Also, as already highlighted, one of the key motivations for using RIS is its ability to enhance communication through passive beamforming. It does this by reflecting or refracting the impinging signal such that the reflected signal is directed in the desired direction as opposed to scattering in all directions. As a result, the signal power is concentrated and directed toward the receiver. Since there is a lot of scattering, reflection, and diffraction in the wireless propagation channel, the received signal is often attenuated and only a portion of the transmitted signal power is received at the receiver. The SNR is thus impacted, and consequently, the capacity of the communication system. The incorporation of the RIS brings considerable improvements since it picks up the weak signals and, based on the configured phase profile, steers the impinging waves anomalously to the receiver, resulting in increased received signal power and improved SNR. With other factors constant, the capacity of the communication system is thereby expanded when RIS is incorporated.

The second part, which is also covered by simulations in this article, is the spectral efficiency of the SISO communication system. The gains in spectral efficiency are compared for the system with and without the RIS. The work also investigates the effect that the number of RIS elements and the signal power has on spectral efficiency. As can be observed from Fig. 3, higher performance gains in spectral efficiency are realized where communication is assisted through the RIS. The spectral efficiency increases as the number of RIS elements grows. This can be attributed to the fact that RISs smartly influence incident radiation through individual elements. When many of these elements are closely packed, the collective effect is very significant.

The impact of the RIS is very visible as the quality of the direct link deteriorates. The performance gains related to the spectral efficiency are highest at -100 dB and lowest at -60 dB. This underpins the fact that RIS is more beneficial and should be used when the link between the transmitter and the receiver is very weak. This scenario could occur where the LOS is partially or completely blocked, thereby causing significant path losses. As already discussed, electromagnetic signal propagation at the high frequencies that are associated with the next-generation networks is highly susceptible to blockages. Consequently, weak LOS or non-LOS occurrences will be common. RIS displays the huge potential to aid in communication in this harsh environment. This will not only improve communication but also significantly reduce the hardware and power costs associated with having a high density of active nodes, which would otherwise have to be installed to compensate for the losses in the absence of RISs.

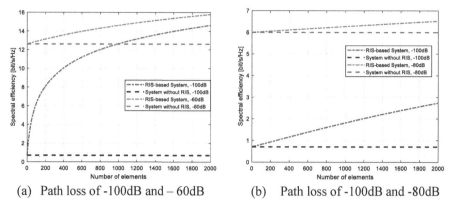

(a) Path loss of -100dB and – 60dB   (b) Path loss of -100dB and -80dB

Fig. 3. Comparative Spectral efficiency of RIS SISO system and the system without RIS, operating in a weak cascaded channel (Path loss $= -100$ dB), and a stronger cascaded channel (Path loss $= -60$ dB and -80 dB)

4 Conclusion

The RIS structure, features, implementation, and design considerations have been highlighted in this article. The immense benefits that the integration of the RIS into a communication system have also been delved into while also looking at the reason behind the RIS being considered a suitable novel antenna technology for the next generation wireless networks. The main objective of this article is to provide the audience with an overview of the RIS technology, its desirable features, application areas, and the decisions that need to be made while incorporating RISs into future wireless communication systems. With the commercial roll-out of 5G already ongoing, this article seeks to contribute to the current research on the next-generation communication systems by bringing in one place valuable resources that will continue to be built upon.

References

1. Di Renzo, M., et al.: Smart radio environments empowered by reconfigurable intelligent surfaces: how it works, state of research, and the road ahead. IEEE J. Sel. Areas Commun. **38**(11), 2450–2525 (2020)
2. Samsung Research: 6G: the next hyper connected experience for all. Samsung (2020)
3. Xu, S.: Reconfigurable intelligent surface-based wireless communications: antenna design, prototyping, and experimental results (2020)
4. Zheng, B., Zhang, R.: Intelligent reflecting surface-enhanced OFDM: channel estimation and reflection optimization. IEEE Wireless Commun. Lett. **9**(4), 518–522 (2019)
5. ElMossallamy, M.A., Zhang, H., Song, L., Seddik, K.G., Han, Z., Li, G.Y.: Reconfigurable intelligent surfaces for wireless communications: principles, challenges, and opportunities. IEEE Trans. Cogn. Commun. Netw. **6**(3), 990–1002 (2020)
6. Chen, H.T., Taylor, A.J., Yu, N.: A review of metasurfaces: physics and applications. Rep. Prog. Phys. **79**(7), 076401 (2016)
7. Basar, E., Di Renzo, M., De Rosny, J., Debbah, M., Alouini, M.S., Zhang, R.: Wireless communications through reconfigurable intelligent surfaces. IEEE Access **7**, 116753–116773 (2019)

8. Liu, Y., et al.: Reconfigurable intelligent surfaces: principles and opportunities. IEEE Commun. Surv. Tutor. **23**(3), 1546–1577 (2021)

9. Dai, L., et al.: Reconfigurable intelligent surface-based wireless communications: antenna design, prototyping, and experimental results. IEEE Access **8**, 45913–45923 (2020)

10. Wu, Q., Zhang, S., Zheng, B., You, C., Zhang, R.: Intelligent reflecting surface-aided wireless communications: a tutorial. IEEE Trans. Commun. **69**(5), 3313–3351 (2021)

11. De Lima, C., et al.: Convergent communication, sensing and localization in 6G systems: an overview of technologies, opportunities and challenges. IEEE Access **9**, 26902–26925 (2021)

12. Renzo, M.D., et al.: Smart radio environments empowered by reconfigurable AI meta-surfaces: an idea whose time has come. EURASIP J. Wirel. Commun. Netw. **2019**(1), 1–20 (2019). https://doi.org/10.1186/s13638-019-1438-9

13. Alsabah, M., et al.: 6G wireless communications networks: a comprehensive survey. IEEE Access **9**, 148191–148243 (2021)

14. Tekbıyık, K., Kurt, G.K., Ekti, A.R., Yanikomeroglu, H.: Reconfigurable intelligent surfaces in action for non-terrestrial networks. arXiv preprint arXiv:2012.00968 (2020)

15. Kisseleff, S., Chatzinotas, S., Ottersten, B.: Reconfigurable intelligent surfaces in challenging environments: underwater, underground, industrial and disaster. IEEE Access **9**, 150214–150233 (2021)

16. Chen, C., Pan, C.: Blocking probability in obstructed tunnels with reconfigurable intelligent surface. IEEE Commun. Lett. **26**(2), 458–462 (2021)

17. Huang, J., et al.: Reconfigurable intelligent surfaces: channel characterization and modeling. arXiv preprint arXiv:2206.02308 (2022)

18. Wu, Q., Zhang, R.: Intelligent reflecting surface enhanced wireless network via joint active and passive beamforming. IEEE Trans. Wirel. Commun. **18**(11), 5394–5409 (2019)

19. Huang, C., Zappone, A., Alexandropoulos, G.C., Debbah, M., Yuen, C.: Reconfigurable intelligent surfaces for energy efficiency in wireless communication. IEEE Trans. Wirel. Commun. **18**(8), 4157–4170 (2019)

20. Nguyen, N.T., Nguyen, L.V., Huynh-The, T., Nguyen, D.H., Swindlehurst, A.L., Juntti, M.: Machine learning-based reconfigurable intelligent surface-aided MIMO systems. In: 2021 IEEE 22nd International Workshop on Signal Processing Advances in Wireless Communications (SPAWC), pp. 101–105. IEEE (2021)

A New Class of DC-Free Run-Length Limited Codes

Elie Ngomseu Mambou[1], Jules M. Moualeu[2], and Theo G. Swart[1(✉)]

[1] Department of Electrical and Electronic Engineering Science,
University of Johannesburg, P.O. Box 524, Auckland Park 2006, South Africa
{emambou,tgswart}@uj.ac.za
[2] School of Electrical and Information Engineering, University of Witwatersrand,
Johannesburg 2000, South Africa
jules.moualeu@wits.ac.za

Abstract. The conventional 4B6B run-length limited (RLL) code recommended by the IEEE 802.15.7 standard for visible light communication (VLC) is memory consuming as it must be stored at both the encoder and decoder; additionally, it can only be decoded through maximum likelihood (ML) decoding which is costly in terms of computational complexity. In this paper, a new class of structured DC-free RLL code without using lookup tables is proposed. A case study of the 4B6B code that achieves better error correction performance compared to the conventional 4B6B codes in a concatenated scheme, is investigated. Through simulations and analysis, it has been established that polar codes and convolutional codes concatenated with the proposed 4B6B code outperforms most existing schemes at high signal-to-noise ratio (SNR) in terms of bit-error rate (BER) and frame-error rate (FER). At a FER of 10^{-4}, the concatenated polar codes of length 128 with the proposed 4B6B code outperforms the same structure when using the traditional 4B6B code by 0.6 dB while maintaining the same complexity for encoding and decoding processes.

Keywords: DC-free · Run-length limited codes · Look-up tables · Polar codes · Maximum likelihood decoding · Visible light communication

1 Introduction

With the upcoming fourth industrial revolution, the world is witnessing a growing demand on the deployment of wireless services, leading to an exponential increase of mobile data traffic. To this end, the radio frequency (RF) spectrum is limited by a shortage of usable radio frequencies. Visible light communication (VLC) is an evolving communication technology that has emerged as a complement to RF-based communications. The VLC refers to a short range optical wireless communication via lighting beam sources such as a light-emitting diode (LED). It presents several advantages such as higher security, low cost of deployment and bigger unregulated bandwidth [1]. Despite this benefits, VLC suffers

T. M. Ngatched Nkouatchah et al. (Eds.): PAAISS 2022, LNICST 459, pp. 332–341, 2023.
https://doi.org/10.1007/978-3-031-25271-6_21

from several issues including flickering and uncontrolled light dimming. The light flickering occurs when there are long runs of similar bits, i.e. several adjacent zeros or ones. The flickering can be mitigated by run-length limited (RLL) codes such as the Manchester, 4B6B and 8B10B codes as per the IEEE 802.15.7 standards for VLC [2]. RLL codes have found applications in various fields such as optical and magnetic recording devices, high-speed local area networks, noise reduction in VLSI systems, etc. RLL codes are very often concatenated with modern forward error correction codes because of their limited error correction performance [3–5].

The *eMiller* code presented an improved copy of the traditional Miller code in [3]. This code improves the VLC channel based on error correction ability compared to few conventional RLL codes. However, the decoding of the eMiller code via the Viterbi algorithm brings extra complexity compared to the Miller code. A class of $(n-1)/n$ rate RLL codes was presented in [4]. A trellis code was generated for (d, k)-RLL codes with $k \in \{3, 4, 5, 6, 7\}$ and $d = 0$, where d and k represents the minimum and maximum consecutive zeros in a code, respectively. It was reported that the error correction performance of such codes improves with increasing run-length k. This increase of k could perturb the flicker-free property of a VLC channel depending on the system optical clock rate. A 5B10B RLL code was proposed in [5]. This is a mapping of the 5-bit code to selected balanced instances of the 10-bit code based on distance properties. A *balanced word* is a sequence where the number of zeros equals that of ones. This code has a better error correction performance than the Manchester code and 4B6B RLL codes at the cost of a more complex decoding. Moreover, the spectral efficiency of the proposed 5B10B code equals that of the Manchester code which adds a redundancy of the same length as the payload.

As aforementioned, the design of good RLL codes in terms of performance and complexity, remains a challenge in VLC systems. In this paper, we propose a class of 4B6B RLL code that has a better error correction performance than the traditional one in a concatenated VLC system in the high signal-to-noise (SNR) ratio regime. The proposed code is structured and can hence be decoded using a faster and simpler decoder than the *maximum likelihood* (ML). Furthermore, the decoding of the proposed RLL code is faster as it can be done in parallel.

The remainder of this paper is structured as follows. Section 2 gives some background on the underlying topic. In Sect. 3, the new class of 4B6B RLL code is presented, followed by the analysis and discussions on Sect. 4. Finally, the paper is concluded in Sect. 5.

2 Background

2.1 RLL Codes in VLC Channel

The block diagram of a conventional VLC channel at 50% dimming is depicted in Fig. 1. This is a concatenated system made of FEC and RLL codes. The payload u of length K is jointly encoded by the FEC and RLL encoders, then modulated through an on-off keying (OOK) scheme. The obtained signal y of length N is conveyed through a VLC additive white Gaussian noise (AWGN) channel. At the receiver, likelihood ratio (LR) values are perceived as r, then the original word is recovered back after the OOK demodulation, the RLL and FEC decoding operations are applied sequentially.

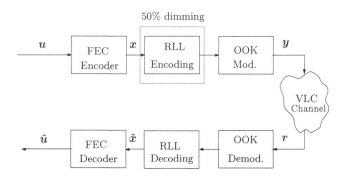

Fig. 1. Flicker-free VLC channel at 50% dimming.

The use of RLL codes in VLC has been recommended in [2] to enforce a flicker-free channel at 50% dimming. These RLL codes include the Manchester or 1B2B code, the 4B6B code and the 8B10B code. A κBηB RLL code consists of mapping the κ-bit code to selected instances of the η-bit code. In case of the 1B2B or the 4B6B code, these selected instances are balanced. There are $\binom{\eta}{\eta/2}$ instances of balanced codewords for a given η-bit code. The Manchester code transforms bits "0" and "1" into codewords "01" and "10", respectively. Table 1 shows the conventional 4B6B RLL code as per [2]; only 16 balanced 6-bit codewords are used, while the remaining 4 are allocated as follows: 111000 and 000111 are reserved for the idle time pattern whereas 110100 and 001011 are reserved for the preamble. The 8B10B RLL code is a combination of the 3B4B and 5B6B codes following some running disparity (RD) properties. A single error that occurs in the channel can produce at most an error burst of 5 bits, corresponding to the maximum run-length of 8B10B code versus 4 bits for the 4B6B code.

Because RLL codes are non-linear, they are mostly decoded through a *maximum likelihood* decoding technique. The posteriori bit probability based on OOK modulation with AWGN is estimated as follows

$$p(r_i|y_i = \lambda) = \frac{1}{\sqrt{2\pi\sigma^2}}e^{-\frac{(r_i-\lambda)^2}{2\sigma^2}}, \tag{1}$$

where σ^2 is the channel variance, $\boldsymbol{y} = (y_1, y_2, \ldots, y_N)$ and $\boldsymbol{r} = (r_1, r_2, \ldots, r_N)$ are the transmitted and received signals, respectively and $\lambda = \{0, 1\}$.

The κBηB RLL decoder receives as input $\boldsymbol{r} = (\boldsymbol{r}_1, \boldsymbol{r}_2, \ldots, \boldsymbol{r}_{\frac{N}{\eta}})$ with $\boldsymbol{r}_i = \{r_{i,1}, r_{i,2}, \ldots, r_{i,\eta}\}$ corresponding to the transmitted matrix $\boldsymbol{y} = (\boldsymbol{y}_1, \boldsymbol{y}_2, \ldots, \boldsymbol{y}_{\frac{N}{\kappa}})$

with $\boldsymbol{y}_i = \{y_{i,1}, y_{i,2}, \ldots, y_{i,\kappa}\}$. The decoding of RLL codes is achieved through an *a posteriori probability (APP)* estimator which is a soft-input soft-output (SISO) decoding technique. This is done by computing the reliability matrix $\mathcal{P} = [\boldsymbol{P}_1, \boldsymbol{P}_2, \ldots, \boldsymbol{P}_N]$ where $\boldsymbol{P}_i = \{P_{i,j}, 1 \leq j \leq 2^\kappa\}$, is the posterior probability vector of the transmitted bit λ_i being λ_j (bit at position j). Assuming a uniform distribution of transmitted bits λ_i, the entries of $\mathcal{P}$, $P_{i,j}$, are computed using Bayes' rule

$$P_{i,j} = \frac{p(r_i|\lambda_i = \lambda_j)p(\lambda_i = \lambda_j)}{p(r_i)}. \tag{2}$$

Moreover, the η-bit codeword probability is given by

$$p(\boldsymbol{r}_i|\boldsymbol{y}_i) = \prod_{z=1}^{\eta} p(r_{i,z}|y_{i,z}). \tag{3}$$

Table 1. Traditional 4B6B code as defined in [2].

4B	6B	4B	6B	4B	6B	4B	6B
0000	001110	0100	010101	1000	011001	1100	110010
0001	001101	0101	100011	1001	011010	1101	101001
0010	010011	0110	100110	1010	011100	1110	101010
0011	010110	0111	100101	1011	110001	1111	101100

2.2   Error Correction Analysis of RLL Codes

The bit-error probability of an RLL code, P_b varies with its distance profile. Let W be the distance profile of a $(\kappa, \eta, \delta_{\min})$ RLL code, where $\delta_{\min}$ is the minimum Hamming distance. W can be expressed by a Z-polynomial as follows

$$W(Z) = \sum_{\delta=0}^{n} A_\delta D_\delta Z^\delta, \tag{4}$$

with A_δ being the average number of erroneous source bits for every wrongly decoded codeword and D_δ being the number of codewords at distance δ of the correct codeword. The distance profile is also referred to as the *weight enumerating function (WEF)* in [6].

A union bound for RLL code is derived from its distance profile. Considering an OOK modulation through an AWGN channel with a soft-input maximum likelihood (ML) decoding of RLL codes, the upper bound on P_b is derived as [6]

$$P_b \leq \frac{1}{\kappa} \sum_{\delta=0}^{\eta} A_\delta D_\delta \mathcal{Q}\left(\sqrt{\delta R \frac{E_b}{N_0}}\right) < \frac{1}{\kappa} W\left(e^{-R\frac{E_b}{2N_0}}\right), \tag{5}$$

where E_b/N_0, denotes the energy signal per noise ratio, R refers to the code rate and $\mathcal{Q}(\cdot)$, the complementary Gaussian integral function.

The distance profile of the Manchester code or 1B2B RLL code is easily derived as $W_{1B2B} = Z^2$; that of the conventional 4B6B code is given by $W_{4B6B} = 14.75Z^2 + 14.2Z^4 + 3Z^6$.

3   Improved RLL Code

Inspired by Knuth's parallel algorithm [7] for balancing a code, we propose an $l\text{B}\lceil l + \log_2 2l\rceil\text{B}$ RLL coding (l being the length of the payload and $\lceil \cdot \rceil$ is the ceiling operation) where l and $\lceil l + \log_2 2l\rceil$ are positive even integers. Knuth's balancing algorithm consists of flipping the first e bits ($1 \le e \le N$) of a sequence $\boldsymbol{x}$ until a balanced state is reached, then the balancing index e is appended as redundancy $\boldsymbol{p}$ to the obtained codeword $\boldsymbol{x}'$ and the concatenated codeword $\boldsymbol{x}'\boldsymbol{p}$ is transmitted. Note that a redundancy of $\log_2 l$ is required by Knuth's algorithm. However, for a full balancing (encoded payload with prefix together), one extra bit is needed as shown in [8], leading to a redundancy of $\log_2 2l$. The appended redundancy follows a Gray coded progression [9].

Theorem 1. *A DC-free $l\text{B}\lceil l + \log_2 2l\rceil B$ RLL code can always be obtained through an inverting process and without need for lookup tables.*

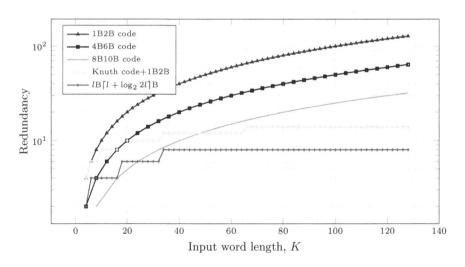

Fig. 2. Redundancy in terms of word length.

Proof. Consider the balancing of a binary word $\boldsymbol{x}$ of length l. It requires exactly $\log_2 l$ bits to uniquely index each bit position of $\boldsymbol{x}$.

It has been shown in [10] that at least one occurrence of balanced output is obtained when adding a set of *balancing sequences* $\boldsymbol{b}(z)$ to a word $\boldsymbol{x} \oplus_2 \boldsymbol{b}(z)$, with $1 \le z \le 2l$, '$\oplus_2$' being the binary addition and z, the iterator through all balancing sequences. Let $\sigma(z)$ denote the sum after the z-th balancing sequence has been added to $\boldsymbol{x}$. $\sigma(z)$ follows a $(1,1)$-random walk with $1 \le z \le 2l$. Moreover, it was established that $\sigma(z)$ is bounded as $\min\{\sigma(z)\} \le \beta^l \le \max\{\sigma(z)\}$ [9], where min and max refer to the minimum and the maximum respectively and $\beta^l = l/2$ is the balanced value. Therefore, $\min\{\sigma(z)\} \le \beta^l - 1$ and $\max\{\sigma(z)\} \ge \beta^l + 1$. Through flipping of $\boldsymbol{x}$, a sequence $\sigma(z)$ can always be found such that $\beta^l - 1 \le \sigma(z) \le \beta^l + 1$. Since the Gray encoded indexes follow also a $(1,1)$-random walk, we conclude that a redundancy of $\log_2 2l$ is enough to balance $\boldsymbol{x}$. This completes the proof.

Example 1. A DC-free 8B12B RLL code can be derived through an inverting process and without the use of lookup tables according to Theorem 1. Consider the following payload $\boldsymbol{x} = 11010011$ to be encoded into a DC-free 8B10B RLL code.

The encoding happens as follows:

①$11010011 \rightarrow 010100110\boldsymbol{00}\mathit{0}$
②$01010011 \rightarrow 000100110\boldsymbol{01}\mathit{0}$
③$00010011 \rightarrow 001100110\boldsymbol{11}\mathit{0}$

Lines ⓘ refer to the i-th inversion bit in $\boldsymbol{x}$, where $i \in \{1,2,3\}$; the bold bits are Gray indexes whereas the italic bit is the additional bit to control the balancing value.

Following the same logic, we can obtain a DC-free 4B7B RLL code but with a little trick, we can simplify it to a DC-free 4B6B RLL code as follows:

- For a word starting with a '0', index positions, e where $e \in \{1,2,3,4\}$, are encoded as: $1 \rightarrow 01$, $2 \rightarrow 10$, $3 \rightarrow 00$ and $4 \rightarrow 11$.
- For a words starting with a '1', index positions are: $1 \rightarrow 01$, $2 \rightarrow 10$, $3 \rightarrow 11$ and $4 \rightarrow 00$.

A DC-free 4B6B RLL code as presented in Table 2 is constructed with no lookup table or enumerative coding. The underlined bits represents the inverted portion and bold bits, the encoded position of the balancing index according to previous guidelines.

Table 2. Proposed DC-free 4B6B RLL code.

4B	6B	4B	6B	4B	6B	4B	6B
0000	110010	0100	110001	1000	011100	1100	001011
0001	100101	0101	100110	1001	010110	1101	010101
0010	101001	0110	101010	1010	011010	1110	011001
0011	110100	0111	100011	1011	001101	1111	001110

4   Analysis and Discussions

4.1   Redundancy Study

An efficient VLC channel also requires an optimal LED power dissipation. In other words, the generated redundancy during transmission should be as low as possible for power saving purposes while increasing the channel throughput. Figure 2 depicts a comparison of redundancies against input word lengths for various DC-free RLL codes. Note that all odd redundancies are rounded up to the next even number and redundancies produced by Knuth's balancing algorithm are balanced through the 1B2B code. For any $\kappa B\eta B$ RLL code, only length multiples of κ were considered.

It can be observed from Fig. 2 that redundancies of 1B2B, 4B6B and 8B10B RLL codes versus input word lengths follow a logarithmic progression as well as that of Knuth's algorithm and the proposed $l B\lceil l + \log_2 2l\rceil B$ code but at different slopes. However the proposed RLL code outperforms all existing ones in terms of redundancy and so, improves the channel throughput.

4.2   Error Correction Performance

The distance profile of the new 4B6B RLL code is given by $W_{P4B6B} = 13.5Z^2 + 15.25Z^4 + 3.25Z^6$. The coefficient of Z^2 for W_{P4B6B} is smaller than that of W_{4B6B}, this means that the proposed code has an improved distance profile leading to a better error correction performance in a concatenated regime as explained in [6].

Figure 3 shows uncoded run-length limited codes where $N = 32$. The maximum likelihood decoding was used for RLL codes (1B2B, 4B6B) and Viterbi algorithm (VA) with trellis codes (eMiller and $(0, 4)$ $2/3$ RLL). In order to perform a fair comparison between various schemes, graphs from Fig. 3 was generated in terms of energy per symbol E_s/N_0 because, the normalization over E_s/N_0 instead of energy per bit E_b/N_0 adjusts for additional energy considered to transmit parity symbols; therefore, all codes are transmitted using the same amount of energy although they have different rates. The proposed 4B6B RLL code performance is similar to that of the conventional 4B6B code and slightly worse that than the 1B2B code at SNR values greater than 10 dB.

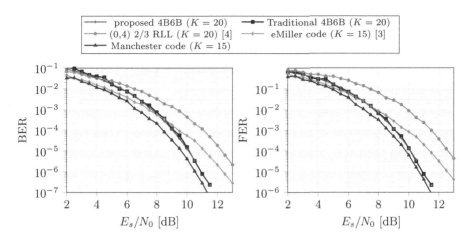

Fig. 3. Uncoded run-length limmited codes with $N = 32$.

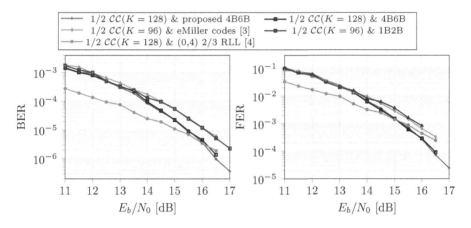

Fig. 4. Convolutional coded RLL codes for $N \approx 384$.

Figure 4 shows the convolutional coded RLL for various schemes. A 1/2-rate convolutional code ($\mathcal{CC}$) with the generator code as $(13, 15)_8$. The proposed 4B6B code outperforms every referenced schemes for the SNRs above 16 dB both in terms of the BER and the FER. Figure 5 presents different polar coded RLL schemes. The successive cancellation (SC) algorithm was used to decode polar codes ($\mathcal{PC}$) while the Bahl-Cocke-Jelinek-Raviv (BCJR) algorithm was used for decoding of trellis codes used as inner codes. The frozen set and length-matching of $\mathcal{PC}$ are based on the standardized 5G polar code. Similar to the previous graph, the proposed 4B6B code is very competitive at high SNR, from 10 dB upwards for both BER and FER cases, moreover they are only comparable to $\mathcal{PC}$ & 1B2B and $\mathcal{PC}$ & 4B6B. At a BER of 10^{-6}, the proposed 4B6B RLL code presents gains in dB of 0.2 and 0.5 against $\mathcal{PC}(128, 64)$ & $(0,4)$ 2/3 RLL [4],

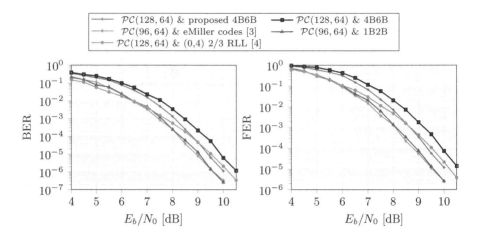

Fig. 5. Polar coded RLL codes for $N \approx 192$.

and $\mathcal{PC}(128, 64)$ & conventional 4B6B while the $\mathcal{PC}(96, 64)$ & eMiller [3], and $\mathcal{PC}(96, 64)$ & Manchester outperforms the proposed 4B6B code by 0.5 dB.

5   Conclusion

A new class of DC-free RLL code was proposed for VLC channels. The main advantage is that the code is structured and can be decoded with a less complex decoder than the MAP. Furthermore, the error correction performance is appealing in some instances. A case study of the 4B6B RLL code was presented which has an improved distance profile than the original 4B6B code and generates less redundancy at large input lengths. Simulations reveal that the proposed 4B6B RLL code outperforms most schemes at high SNR for concatenated systems with polar and convolutional codes as outer codes. A future work will consist of exploiting the inverting process of proposed RLL codes to design an optimal decoder with a performance close to ML decoding.

References

1. Pathak, P., Feng, X., Mohapatra, P.: Visible light communication, networking and sensing: a survey, potential and challenges. IEEE Commun. Surv. Tutor. **17**(4), 2047–2077 (2015)
2. Yoon, S.H., et al.: IEEE standard for local and metropolitan area networks—Part 15.7: short-range optical wireless communications. IEEE Std, pp. 1–407 (2019)
3. Lu, X., Li, J.: New Miller codes for run-length control in visible light communications. IEEE Trans. Wirel. Commun. **17**(3), 1798–1810 (2018)
4. Li, Z., Yu, H., Shan, B., Zou, D., Li, S.: New run-length limited codes in on–off keying visible light communication systems. IEEE Wirel. Commun. Lett. **9**(2), 148–151 (2020)

5. Reguera, V.A.: New RLL code with improved error performance for visible light communication. arXiv preprint arXiv:1910.10079 (2019)
6. Benedetto, S., Biglieri, E.: Principles of Digital Transmission: With Wireless Applications. Kluwer Academic/Plenum Publishers (1999)
7. Knuth, D.E.: Efficient balanced codes. IEEE Trans. Inf. Theory **32**(1), 51–53 (1986)
8. Mambou, E.N., Esenogho, E., Ferreira, H.C.: Improving the redundancy of Knuth's balancing scheme for packet transmission systems. Turk. J. Elec. Eng. Comp. Sci. **27**, 2579–2589 (2019)
9. Mambou, E.N., Swart, T.G.: A construction for balancing non-binary sequences based on Gray code prefixes. IEEE Trans. Inf. Theory **64**(8), 5961–5969 (2018)
10. Swart, T.G., Weber, J.H.: Efficient balancing of q-ary sequences with parallel decoding. In: 2009 IEEE International Symposium on Information Theory, pp. 1564–1568. IEEE, Seoul (2009)

Affective Computing

Conversational Pattern Mining Using Motif Detection

Nicolle Garber and Vukosi Marivate[✉]

Department of Computer Science, University of Pretoria, Pretoria, South Africa
vukosi.marivate@cs.ac.za

Abstract. The subject of conversational mining has become of great interest recently due to the explosion of social and other online media. Supplementing this explosion of text is the advancement in pre-trained language models which have helped us to leverage these sources of information. An interesting domain to analyse is conversations in terms of complexity and value. Complexity arises due to the fact that a conversation can be asynchronous and can involve multiple parties. It is also computationally intensive to process. We use unsupervised methods in our work in order to develop a conversational pattern mining technique which does not require time consuming, knowledge demanding and resource intensive labelling exercises. The task of identifying repeating patterns in sequences is well researched in the Bioinformatics field. In our work, we adapt this to the field of Natural Language Processing and make several extensions to a motif detection algorithm. In order to demonstrate the application of the algorithm on a dynamic, real world data set; we extract motifs from an open-source film script data source. We run an exploratory investigation into the types of motifs we are able to mine.

Keywords: Natural Language Processing · Pattern mining · Motif mining · Conversational analysis

1 Introduction

Motif discovery can be phrased as the detection of 'functionally significant short, statistically overrepresented subsequence patterns in a set of biological sequences' [1]. More simply, we can think of a motif as an abstract generalisation of short repeating subsequences in a collection of sequences. These repeating subsequences contain variations from each other and from the motif that tries to describe them. Technically, this introduces challenges. However; when applied to conversations, this allows us to capture various dynamics and different ways in which people's conversation can evolve. The focus of our work is to capture repeating conversational patterns through the use of motif detection. We demonstrate this by focusing on open source film scripts of a comedy genre.

© ICST Institute for Computer Sciences, Social Informatics and Telecommunications Engineering 2023
Published by Springer Nature Switzerland AG 2023. All Rights Reserved
T. M. Ngatched Nkouatchah et al. (Eds.): PAAISS 2022, LNICST 459, pp. 345–361, 2023.
https://doi.org/10.1007/978-3-031-25271-6_22

Successful motif detection in conversations can prove useful in many applications. Critically, finding conversational cues can assist with intelligent conversation labelling. This has wide applications in various business domains with service centres dealing with a customer base through text using chat-bots, customer agents or even phone transcripts. We can start to think of instructive cues for chat-bots, determining themes of customer sentiment development or service requests. On social media platforms such as Twitter, mining motifs may uncover recognizsable cues which might assist in event detection. In any context, quantifying conversation gives us the power to abstract, index and search. This helps us to extract important things in any domain.

We turn to the field of Bioinformatics, in which motif detection forms a large and fundamental part of understanding important biological sequence structures such as DNA and proteins. We attempt to transfer the idea of a motif representing a structural unit into the idea of a structural unit of a conversation.

Conversation in a real world goal-oriented setting (such as in business), contains a particular set of goals and therefore is likely to have a more limited set of conversational cues. It is therefore expected that clearer motif patterns might emerge. Likely, if it is observed that conversational motif mining is successful on a more varied dataset, we can have increased confidence in its application in a more targeted setting. We simulate this idea by application in a broad and varied conversational setting such as an open-sourced dataset of film scripts. We focus our attention on one particular genre of the film scripts in order to constrain the diversity of the underlying conversations. It is well known that the comedy movie genre makes good use of tropes and movie motifs [13].

In addition, it is clear after some experimentation that the comedy genre has the largest set of conversations of any genre, which allows for richer sequence data in order to run motif detection. We investigate the types of motifs we are able to extract.

There are two larger components that constitute the motif mining pipeline. Firstly, we need to convert the conversational text data into meaningful sequences. The second part of the pipeline consists of the application of motif detection on top of these sequences. Our paper is structured as follows: the second section provides a view of previous work done in the Bioinformatics and Natural Language Processing (NLP) domains. Next, we describe the motif mining pipeline in the methodology section. The results section is split into two parts: the first deals with the conversion of conversations into sequences while the second deals with the motif mining algorithm. We show the reader a view of the motif mining algorithm on generated data after which we investigate the film scripts dataset results. Finally, we follow a brief summary, discussion of the method, results and possible extensions in the conclusion.

2   Background

In this section, we cover the concept of a motif, how it has been used and how we would like to leverage it. The reader might be interested to note that while motif detection associates very highly with the field of Bioinformatics, the concept is being applied in a number of different areas. For example, motifs can help to uncover network structures which can find application not only in Bioinformatics but in communications and software engineering [2]. The former two are active areas of research and there are several survey papers on both of these [3–5, 14, 16] for example. Motif detection has been used in [6] by the authors to understand information processing in the brain via motif detection through variational autoencoders. Motif learning was used in a very interesting way by the authors of [17] who use motif-based methods in order to discover higher-order similarities in heterogeneous information networks for use in recommender systems.

A motif is a characterization of a short subsequence of DNA [16]. This sequence typically indicates a significant biological structure such as DNA binding sites for regulatory proteins [16] (a common application in the field). Segments of DNA which are used for transcription processes are called genes and the information contained in these helps with making proteins. In many cases, the transcription process is a function of the genes of a sequence and finding these patterns is one of the most important and challenging fields of molecular biology and computer science [16].

The challenges of motif detection lie in the fact that any real data as in DNA sequence data (or in our case conversational sequences) contains noise. In biological sequences, this is expressed as mutations, insertions or deletions of nucleotides [16]. Additionally, motifs can either occur in the same gene or in multiple genes. Some genes may not have them [16]. More traditional techniques search for exactly one motif per sequence. This may miss some motifs or conversely detect motifs in sequences which may not contain them. Since most motif detection algorithms look for some type of global commonality between motifs in sequences, sequences that do not have this motif would add noise to this process. For these reasons, motif detection algorithms typically need to be more complex than pattern matching or brute force algorithms.

We focus on a category of earlier approaches used which were found to work better with longer motifs [16]. These are probabilistic models which make use of some type of position weight matrix. Each position of a motif is represented by the various probabilities of a 'letter' (sequence element) in that position. This type of structure deals better with weakly constrained positions where variation is likely [16]. These methods are not guaranteed to find a global optimum and make use of more local search technique methods [16]. An example of a way to measure a subsequence as a motif has been described by Tompa as explained by the review paper authors of [16]. The probability of finding a motif s in N number of sequences can be characterised with a statistical significance test which includes the formulation of a z-score. This is asymptotically normally distributed with mean 0 and standard deviation 1. This score makes it possible to compare different motifs. The z-score is as follows:

$$M_s = \frac{(N_s - NP_s)}{\sqrt{(Np_s)(1 - p_s)}} \tag{1}$$

where N_s is the number of sequences containing occurrence of s (sequence motif) and p_s is the probability of at least one motif s in a sequence [16]. While there have been more sophisticated motif detection methods developed, our work focuses on some of the earlier or more classical techniques. This is intended as an introductory experiment into the concept of motif mining in conversations.

2.1 Conversational Mining

Analysing conversations can be thought of in the context of the broader field of Natural Language Processing (NLP). There is no single accepted definition of NLP; however, the general meaning is quite consistent. That is: a set of computational techniques aimed at understanding, summarising and representing text. This is done with the aim of striving towards human-like capabilities of generating and processing text for a diverse set of tasks [7].

The most common type of work done in computational fields with regards to conversations is various methods and enhancements for dialogue systems which maintain dialogue state and can be used for generative conversational agents. The survey paper [8] performs a good investigation of advances in the space by dividing dialogue systems into task-oriented and non-task oriented models. The work in [27] focuses on surveying different aspects of spoken language understanding in order to build better conversational systems. The recent work [18] addresses building a domain driven bot by separating content selection for candidate responses from response composition. This was integrated into the Google assistant. The task of dialogue generation is approached in [19] by a hierarchical variational memory network. This aims to abstract variations as well as long-term dependency modeling such as is necessary for dialogue state tracking. A different approach is followed in [20] where multi-turn conversation is modeled using a dense semantic matching network which leverages context-response pairs to find an optimal candidate. An important aspect of research in dialogue systems includes examining evaluation metrics of generative models. The authors of [28] provide recommendations for building metrics that perform better than the technical metrics created for machine translation in this domain.

Some earlier work [9] places focus on performing analysis on conversational patterns in social media. The focus of the work is the examination of product launches on Twitter. Conversational analysis is leveraged in order to create concept maps to compare conversations. A concept map is defined as a network that follows the conceptual progression of a conversation (in this context) by keyword representation which can lead to the discovery of topic clusters which are related to each other. The approach appears to be quite handcrafted - requiring specific pre-processing for the domain and the creation of domain-specific dictionaries. Traditional network analysis is applied in order to extract the concept map and topic flows. Semantic complexity cannot be modelled through single keywords and the abstract structures that are extracted are vague. The notion of conversational structure abstractions is not brought forward. For example, the abstraction is extracted in the form of a word cloud. Another example of analysis-style work is from a more recent paper which leverages a social media

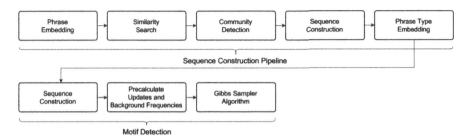

Fig. 1. Modular representation of pipeline for conversational motif mining strategy

platform Gab in order to detect 'echo-chamber' patterns by [21]. The structural abstraction of conversations which we extract in the form of motifs is extracted in this work in the form of cascades. This is a directed graph where the set of vertices represent content (posts, replies, quotes) and the edges represent replies and quotes (or interactions with content). This structure evolves over time with the original post forming a 'root node' of sorts and subsequent interactions form levels. While these cascades are able to model linear and non-linear interactions, there is only brief work done on modelling the content and conversational queues (in the form of hashtags) and most emphasis is placed on response time and spread modelling of the different types of cascades.

We see that motifs are not applied to conversations, to the best of our knowledge. In fact, the conversational pattern mining field appears saturated with work on dialogue management systems, bots, assistants, dialogue act prediction and question answering. There seems to be an opportunity for creating more data mining techniques for conversation. We can do this in order to begin understanding generic structures of conversations for modelling or extraction. It seems as though there is less work developed on converting conversations into either embeddings (as we have done) or even discrete representations over time. Motifs assist with understanding generic conversational structures which can be used for a host of use cases - from segmentation of important parts of conversation, to search, to understanding, to prediction, to visualisation to clustering. With the understanding of generic structures of conversation, just as in Bioinformatics, we can begin to assess individual deviation from global structures, build anomaly detection, understand human conversations in a domain better - particularly conversational queues in goal-oriented domains or even queues displaying negative conversational patterns to detect on social media.

3   Methodology

We begin our pipeline by structuring conversational text into sequence data. We present the higher level pipeline components in Fig. 1.

We have two larger pipeline components: sequence creation and motif detection. In the sequence creation component, we find embeddings for the phrases on a sentence level. In the traditional use of motif detection, the sequences consist of categorical elements. We aim to create an analogue to this by grouping similar phrases together to form generic phrase types. The volume of data produced during this process necessitates an efficient clustering technique. We therefore perform community detection on phrases and their most similar neighbours. The communities found in this way are representative of similar phrases. For simplification, we produce a low dimensional representation of each phrase type by finding the centroid of the classes and performing dimensionality reduction. This forms the sequence base upon which we are able to run the motif detection pipeline.

The motif detection pipeline is built on the Gibbs sampler framework [12]. We describe the extensions needed for transferability from the Bioinformatics to the conversational text domain.

3.1 Sequence Creation Process

From each of the spoken phrases, we aim to find a generic "phrase type". This is: an abstract class capturing the semantic, emotional and conversational meaning of a phrase within the context of the conversation. The high-level steps in this process look as follows:

1. Phrase level embeddings are constructed.
2. A graph is created using the embeddings. Communities within this graph are extracted and represented as centroids.
3. Simpler representations are created using dimensionality reduction.

Embedding Construction. We find phrase level embeddings in order to capture the dynamics of spoken phrases in a conversation. This is done by performing word level embeddings, followed by sentence embeddings. The good structure of the text we are dealing with (minimal spelling mistakes, special characters and mixed languages) enables us to leverage pre-trained embeddings. This avoids the resource expensive task of training our own embeddings or fine-tuning.

Word vector representations are derived using the well known continuous bag of words (CBOW) model where each word is represented by a bag of character n-grams [22]. From here, phrase embeddings are obtained by encoding the FastText word embeddings with the InferSent model [23].

Community Detection for Creation of Phrase Classes. For the creation of the classes representing 'phrase types', we turn to unsupervised methods.

Each of the spoken utterances is represented by a high dimensional vector $x \in \mathbb{R}^{4096}$. This vector contains a lot of information (4096 dimensional space). The motif detection algorithm works by scanning over multiple sequences with a moving window and finds optimal alignment by looking at where the motifs achieve the greatest similarity. Working with four thousand dimensional sequences is infeasible for analysis and it is not interpretable. Each sentence embedding on its own does not tell us the abstract conversational class this phrase belongs to. We have a continuous spectrum of vectors $x \in \mathbb{R}^{4096}$ which do not capture a more hierarchical structure. We construct abstract classes with information about the conversational function of the class, for example: greeting phrases, displays of empathy, pause cues. In order to find these classes, we perform semantic grouping. Since the dataset is too large to perform simple clustering on, we perform the following succession of tasks:

1. Run an index on the dataset for fast KNN query [24] (we use NMSLIB with angular distance).
2. For each phrase in the dataset, search for the 10 nearest neighbours based on angular distance.
3. Create a dataset in which each row has phrase, neighbour and angular distance. This forms the structure on top of which a graph is built. The phrase is the source node, the neighbour is the target node and the edge weight is represented by angular distance.
4. Extract communities from groups of common phrases that form. The community is represented as a centroid of the embeddings of the phrases within it. This is done by making use of the community info_map algorithm [11].

After obtaining phrase embeddings which represent the nodes in our graph, we find the edges by detecting the 10 closest neighbours by angular distance. The KNN classifier as described by [10] is a decision rule based classifier which assigns a classification to an unlabeled point based on the classification of the nearest classified points. We make use of NMSLIB [24]: Non-Metric Space Library which is specifically designed for efficient similarity search based on various non-metric spaces. It is very fast and efficient. We make use of the angular distance defined by:

$$d(x, y) = \arccos\left(\frac{\sum_{i=1}^{n} x_i y_i}{\sqrt{\sum_{i=1}^{n} x_i^2} \sqrt{\sum_{i=1}^{n} y_i^2}}\right)$$

It is found that this distance works the best when dealing with our embeddings. Additionally, it is known that cosine distance works well with embeddings produced by models where the objective function was represented by a dot product with softmax. The algorithm uses Hierarchical Navigable Small World Graphs (HNSW) which builds a representation of stored elements incrementally through proximity graphs. This search technique has a logarithmic complexity with very high performance. The KNN algorithm is implemented with search for the 10 nearest neighbours of every phrase.

By utilising the KNN techniques, we find close relationships of phrases. If many phrases share many neighbours this will be well captured in a graph structure. Phrases fall into communities where there are many similar phrases. Because we model this on a phrase level, these will capture conversational queues. In addition, because of the quality of embeddings used, any semantic similarity, as well as syntactic similarity is captured within the communities.

The community info_map algorithm was first introduced in 2008 by the authors of [11]. The idea here is to minimise the map equation (objective function) over all partitions of the network. We use this algorithm as a base to obtain our community clustering (which in our application case consists of 3232 communities). There are many smaller communities which may be very similar to larger ones. We use the extracted centroids of the communities with dimensionality reduction as opposed to using categorical representations for the communities for the following reasons:

1. We lose relational information of clusters relative to other clusters.
2. We lose meaning about the clusters.
3. We are forced to deal with the clusters in a categorical manner which has many implications for the motif detection algorithm.

Simplification of Phrase Class Representation. We have calculated 'phrase classes' in which each phrase can map to a more abstract representation. As we have discussed above, we map each class to a vector by calculating the centroid of each phrase within a community. The challenge at this point is to find a dimensionality reduction technique that will adequately represent each community in relation to all other communities. We focus on conserving the pairwise distances between the centroids. Manifold learning is a good approach for this task as we are dealing with a high dimensional space which will benefit from a non linear method. In order to select the best algorithm, we select the one that maximises the correlation of pairwise cosine distances before and after reduction. We tune the parameters by grid search. The Uniform Manifold Approximation and Projection (UMAP) algorithm developed in [29] is a non-linear dimensionality reduction technique. It enjoys good speeds (scalability) and a greater preservation of global structure. We now have representations of phrases in conversational sequences. We map each phrase into its 'phrase type' class. This class has a vector representation in five dimensions in a euclidean space with cosine distances preserved.

3.2   Motif Detection

In this part of the pipeline we focus on detecting the development of conversational cues that follow a generic pattern common to most or all of the movies.

We look at the Gibbs sampling method [12]. Gibbs sampling methods have been used at length for motif detection. The authors describe the benefits of the implementation as N linear run time for N sequences as well as allowing for increased variability among the patterns that are found. The latter is useful for modelling human conversations which are not a prescribed set of exact rules. For example, in a standard greeting sequence, there may be a generic pattern which includes the following turns:

1. Character1: greeting phrase
2. Character2: greeting phrase
3. Character1: generic response phrase
4. Character2: generic response phrase
5. Character1: queue for initiation of specific topic
6. Character1: response of initiation of specific topic

If a third character is introduced, the pattern will likely change. However; it will still form an instance of a generic greeting queue. In gene sequences, this variation is caused by factors such as mutation and as such it is a consideration of the underlying algorithm.

Gibbs Sampler Algorithm. In the base algorithm [12], each sequence is assumed to have exactly one motif. The Markov assumption is also applied. Given a set of N sequences $S_1, ..., S_N$, we look for segments of the sequences which are most similar to each other. The segment is of fixed length W. The measure of similarity of the sequences is one which maximises the ratio of pattern (motif) probability to background probability. When we have a good alignment of motifs or positions in each sequence where the segment maximises this ratio, we stop the iterations of the algorithm.

This ratio is:

$$A_x = \frac{Q_x}{P_x}$$

A_x is described as the probability that a sequence z contains a motif at position x (foreground probability over background probability). At each iteration, one of the sequences is held out. The window is tested at each position of the sequence by calculating the probability P_x of generating the sequence using background probability. The probability profile elements $q_{i,j}$ [12] are described by:

$$q_{i,j} = \frac{(c_{i,j} + b_j)}{(N - 1 + B)} \tag{2}$$

where the c term represents the count of amino acids that occur in the ith position and the b term is the background frequency of the amino acid. A random segment is selected from all the window candidates according to the weights A_x at each x. Over time, $q_{i,j}$ begin to reflect a pattern existing in other sequences. The segment probabilities A_x become more strongly characterised and the algorithm tends to favour further positions in other sequences that confirm these patterns.

There are several constraints of the motif algorithm. These include:

- Constraining each sequence to have exactly one instance of a motif.
- A fixed pattern of length W.
- A fixed sequence length.
- The algorithm is stopped after a number of iterations as opposed to a convergence criterion.

These are considerable limitations which have practical effects not just on our particular application but on most applications we could consider motif mining for. In particular for real life scenarios, we may have some sequences like some time series or conversations which we think may contain a pattern. We don't know beforehand what the pattern looks like or which sequences have it. The first constraint means that sequences that do not have the same pattern as others get considered equally to others and may throw off the pattern detection because it would affect global alignment scores. It also means that if a sequence has more than one instance of the same pattern, this would not be picked up by the algorithm - a separate match algorithm would have to be run post hoc. A fixed motif size is difficult to fine tune. We may not know what type of motif we are looking for and there may be a vast range of possibilities to choose from. Fixed motif lengths may also impose too tight a constraint on the detection of a global pattern against local sequence patterns. For example, some sequences may express a motif with more noise in between its elements and be longer than others. The next constraint, a fixed sequence length is at times not a practical limitation. In our application, our movie conversations are of different lengths. In order to shape sequences to the same size we may need to add extra consideration to how and where we cut them and this might result in information loss. The last assumption is a beneficial one which allows us to consider using the method in the first place. There is support for variation within the motifs which is ideal for conversations and any time series, as we have mentioned before. The fact that the algorithm is heuristic but does not have built in convergence criteria imply that it is fairly easy to stop the algorithm prematurely or conversely have very long and unnecessary run times which add marginal or no improvement.

We build on the implementation of [30] with some extensions. Firstly, we address the challenge of implementing motif detection in a completely different setting such as conversational mining. Secondly, we make extensions to the original algorithm that allow it to work not only in this setting but in other multivariate time series settings. This may allow a practitioner to overcome a seasonality constraint in searching for time series patterns and look for irregular patterns in a way that is more robust to noise. We start the description with a high level explanation of the additions we have made and then a brief holistic discussion of the entirety of the algorithm. We make the following adjustments:

1. Adaptation for use on any sequences (In Bioinformatics there is a finite set of elements in the sequences (typically "A", "T", "G", "C").
2. Adaptation for use on varied sequence lengths.
3. Adaptation for algorithm to consider sequence elements which are not categorical.
4. Extraction of a global motif which characterises most of the underlying instances.
5. Ability to calculate a local sequence alignment to the global pattern.

A high level description of the algorithm is as follows: we randomly hold out one sequence at a time and find an optimal window placement on the sequence (what we refer to as local alignment) while determining its impact globally (global alignment). This is done iteratively and randomly, allowing window selection on each hold out sequence to start improving global alignment and thereby improve local alignment and so on. The probabilistic implementation allows for variations in local alignment while still finding optimal global alignment. The set of best motifs are only updated when a motif on the holdout sequence is found to improve the global score. The algorithm begins with random initialisation of a set of windows on each sequence. These windows are of length k - the motif length. We then take our set of sequences and select a random hold out sequence. We calculate an optimal placement on the sequence by sliding the window on the sequence and choosing a best probabilistic score. Once this window is selected on the holdout sequence, its impact in relation to all the other windows on all the other sequences is assessed. If this global score is improved by the hold out sequence contribution, the motif for the hold out sequence is replaced, otherwise the procedure continues and another holdout sequence is selected. This is following the Gibbs sampling procedure.

Extensions. In transitioning from the case of DNA bases or amino acids which typically involve 4 classes to a setting in which we have thousands of classes, we consider some extensions. We adjust for the class probabilities tending to zero as the ratio of classes to sequence length grows. The probability of observing any element is obtained from an updated dictionary. Any observation of the element itself adds a count of one. The most similar elements to it (elements with a cosine similarity of greater than cut-off of 0.995) add a proportionately scaled partial count of less than one. When constructing the probability profile for each position, we add all observed instances of the element and all similar elements across the sequences in this position. We also no longer consider a joint probability of observing all the elements of the current window in the motif set. Instead, we calculate the marginal probability of these elements. These probabilities are weighted with an update scheme. For every element in the vocabulary, we add the probabilities of all the most similar elements as observed by a cosine similarity greater than a selected cut-off point. This updated dictionary is precomputed. An example of the updates can be seen in Fig. 2.

We calculate the global pattern which is used for comparison of each motif in the current set. Each position considers the element with the heaviest count (similarity updates considered). Each position is compared across motifs to the global pattern. We transform it to scale between zero and one. We construct a score vector which accumulates these alignments per position. Each position has the added similarities and is normalised by dividing by the number of motifs. The score vector is then transformed to a single global score by summing individual elements and dividing by k. The score vector and k are interpretable. The global pattern is instructive in the understanding of the dataset and the patterns that are found. This structure tells us what motif abstraction looks like. We are also able to cluster our sequences based on how well each motif aligns locally to the global pattern and use this to select the highest aligning local patterns.

4   Results

In this section, we consider an experiment which demonstrates the functionality of the motif detection algorithm. Subsequently, we look at the performance of the conversational motif detection pipeline on a real world dataset.

Original Community (index 5) similarity score: 1	Most similar Community (index 24) similarity score: 0.9963924583208448	2nd most similar (index 30) similarity score: 0.9928539706375146	Not similar (index 8) similarlity score: 0.5089499668686416
No.	There's no witnesses...	Nothing.	Eric?
No.	No, thanks.	Nothing's with me.	Marty...
No.	No, sir.	Never!	Doug...
No.	No, sir.	Nothing comes.	Marty...
No!	No, sir.	Nothing.	Marty...
No, to you--M'sieu <u>Monescu</u>.	No, no.	See? Nothing.	Scooby?
No, m'sieu!	No, no.	Nothing at all?	Scooby?
No. <U>Knots</U>!	No, no.	Nothing.	Jeff. Jeff.
No!	No, thanks.	Nowhere.	Jeff!
No.	No thanks.	Nothing happened.	Jeff!
No way.	No, Mr. Charles.	Nobody.	Gus?
No.	No... no.	Nothing sweetheart.	Gus?
No way.	No!	Nothing, I guess...	Chris!
No.	Well--uh--yes and no.	Nobody. Sooze.	Chris -- Chris -- !
No...	No, sir?	Nothing.	Nick!
No?	Sir! No Sir!	Nothing.	Jimmy!
No!	No, Slink --	Nothing.	<U>Denby!</U>--Are you Chad Denby? John Belushi...
... No!	No rain.	Nothing.	<u>Jim</u> Belushi...
No, it's Dr. Fronkonsteen!	No Jonathan.	Nothin'.	Jim Belushi...?
No.	No, Fred ereck	Nothing.	Jim West.

Fig. 2. Illustration of the need to consider the closeness of our conversational classes

4.1 Motif Detection Results

In order to demonstrate how motif detection works, we generate data with motifs and observe whether they are detected. The dataset generated mimics what the motif detection module would expect in our pipeline. We generate 22 sequences and introduce 50 vocabulary' elements. Each element is a uniformly random two dimensional vector: $x \in [-1, 1], y \in [0, 1]$. The motif elements are generated not to be too similar to each other by creating vectors no more than 0.4 cosine similarity. The representative classes of the motif elements are $[3, 5, 7]$. With this set of sequences, we run the motif detection algorithm. We visually display the results in Fig. 3(a):

We detect every instance of an artificially planted motif except one. The global pattern score is 0.88993719 and the global pattern is as expected: 3,5,7. We can see in Fig. 3(b) that the angles between the motif elements are all quite similar. This is the shape of the motif in the space if we think of it visually. In the real world example, we have higher dimensional vectors so it is not as easy to visualise.

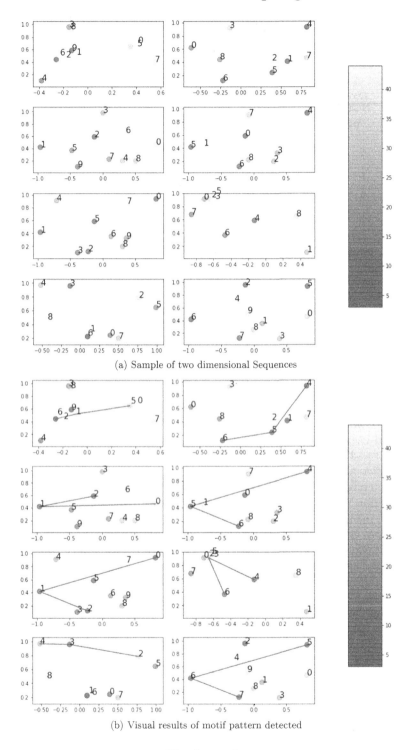

(a) Sample of two dimensional Sequences

(b) Visual results of motif pattern detected

Fig. 3. sample

Result: BestMotifs, GlobalPattern, Score
initialisation - random windows on sequences=*BestMotifs*
;
for *i=0* → *numSeeds* **do**
  if *CurrentSet* > *BestMotifs* **then**
    BestMotifs = CurrentSet
    for *j=0* → *N* **do**
      select random holdout;

      probabilistic selection of the optimal window placement
      if *currentSet* > *BestMotifs* **then**
      | select window on holout
      else
      | continue
      end
    end
  else
  | continue
  end
end

4.2 Application

We apply our method to the Cornell Movie–Dialogs Corpus [15] which is a set of conversational movie scripts extracted from 617 movies. We are working with a diverse domain and types of conversations. The language in movie scripts is clean and easy to process, thus allowing us to focus on the pipeline concepts instead of text wrangling. Our use case involves exploring a movie script dataset with particular focus on the comedy genre.

Using embedded phrases, we construct the graph explained in the methodology section. We found 3232 communities. We drop any communities with less than five members in them. We are left with 1442 communities. We find the centroids of the communities in the original space and reduce the dimensionality by focusing on preserving the cosine similarities between the centroids. We obtain a 0.6 correlation of pairwise cosine distances using UMAP. We obtain 97 sequences after some cleaning mapping to 841 phrase type classes. This occurs because of the phrases that do not map to larger communities which we omit. We extract the longest subsequence of a sequence which has no gaps larger than two consecutive phrases.

Upon running the algorithm with different initialization, different results are obtained. We detect a global pattern consisting of the following classes: [100, 0, 66, 1, 185]. This has an alignment score of 0.84346919 (with the detected motifs). The underlying classes are interesting and fit a comedy type of script. The community of the detected classes look as follows:

Table 1. Table showing an example of motifs detected from comedy movies

Motif Position 1	Motif Position 2	Motif Position 3	Motif Position 4	Motif Position 5
Well, I hope you've changed	Yeah, and for yours. I'm sure you've changed	...namely a personality	So how are you?	I'm okay
The reason?	I see	Sit down	What?	Miss Van Cartier
Huh?	I say we don't want to appear	Oh, that	What do you think you're doing?	Why, I'm assisting you, sir
Do uh... do you understand what I'm saying?	Yes	Good. Or should I speak slower?	Yes	Do you follow or should I speak slower?
Are you kidding me?	Seems like a nice place	It is, if you like idiots	What do you mean?	Really?
I would have said do	Aye, but you know him well	That's what you tell me	What have you heard?	Is it? Is it really?

1. Huh? [confusion]
2. Yeah/Yes/Oh/Yep/yes?/yes! [generic type of class allowing for variation - nothing specific]
3. Tell me/tell me again/that's what you tell me [statement/prompt for further information]
4. What?/Doing what?/What happened?/The reason?/what! [exclamation of disbelief or question for further information]
5. You okay? [concern/display of consideration]

In general, there are slight deviations in individual motifs found across the sequences. The overall tone and message remains quite clear. The motif detected is of a conversation between characters - some inquiry and an explanation. Individual motifs are expressions of a higher representation of a conversational cue. Since typically it is difficult to separate conversations from emotions, we pick up variations on an emotional theme. An example of what some of these phrases look like can be seen in Table 1. We see the individual variations in the instance motifs and the overarching patterns.

5 Conclusion

We have shown in our work that it is possible to use motif detection in a different setting in order to extract conversational patterns. We are able to view the results, local alignment scores of the motif and a global pattern. Local alignment scores can assist in selecting the most relevant sequences while the global pattern reveals what the motif abstraction is. In future work, we aim to develop a benchmark and evaluation strategies which are able to better diagnose and quantify results.

Acknowledgements. The authors want to acknowledge the contribution of ABSA bank which sponsors the Data Science Chair.

References

1. Köhler, S., Seitzer, P., Facciotti, M.T., Ludascher, B.: Improved motif detection in large sequence sets with random sampling in a Kepler workflow. Procedia Comput. Sci. **9**, 1999 (2012)
2. Meira, L.A., Maximo, V.R., Fazenda, A.L., da Conceicao, A.F.: An improved network motif detection tool. arXiv preprint arXiv:1804.09741 (2018)
3. Ciriello, G., Guerra, C.: A review on models and algorithms for motif discovery in protein-protein interaction networks. Brief. Funct. Genomic. Proteomic. **7**(2), 147–156 (2008)
4. Wong, E., Baur, B., Quader, S., Huang, C.-H.: Biological network motif detection: principles and practice. Briefings Bioinform. **13**(2), 202–215 (2012)
5. Hu, J., Li, B., Kihara, D.: Limitations and potentials of current motif discovery algorithms. Nucleic Acids Res. **33**(15), 4899–4913 (2005)
6. Kirschbaum, E., et al.: Learned motif and neuronal assembly detection in calcium imaging videos. arXiv preprint arXiv:1806.09963 (2018)
7. Cambria, E., White, B.: Jumping NLP curves: a review of natural language processing research [review article]. IEEE Comput. Intell. Mag. **9**(2), 48–57 (2014)
8. Chen, H., Liu, X., Yin, D., Tang, J.: A survey on dialogue systems: recent advances and new frontiers. ACM SIGKDD Explor. Newsl. **19**(2), 25–35 (2017)
9. Lipizzi, C., Iandoli, L., Marquez, J.E.R.: Extracting and evaluating conversational patterns in social media: a socio-semantic analysis of customers' reactions to the launch of new products using twitter streams. Int. J. Inf. Manag. **35**(4), 490–503 (2015)
10. Dudani, S.A.: The distance-weighted k-nearest-neighbor rule. IEEE Trans. Syst. Man Cybern. **SMC-6**(4), 325–327 (1976)
11. Rosvall, M., Bergstrom, C.T.: Maps of random walks on complex networks reveal community structure. Proc. Natl. Acad. Sci. **105**(4), 1118–1123 (2008)
12. Lawrence, C.E., Altschul, S.F., Boguski, M.S., Liu, J.S., Neuwald, A.F., Wootton, J.C.: Detecting subtle sequence signals: a Gibbs sampling strategy for multiple alignment. Science **262**(5131), 208–214 (1993)
13. McDonald, J.T.: Romantic Comedy: Boy Meets Girl Meets Genre, 2nd edn. Columbia University Press, New York (2007)
14. Ribeiro, P., Silva, F., Kaiser, M.: Strategies for network motifs discovery. In: 2009 Fifth IEEE International Conference on e-Science, pp. 80–87. IEEE (2009)
15. Danescu-Niculescu-Mizil, C., Lee, L.: Chameleons in imagined conversations: a new approach to understanding coordination of linguistic style in dialogs. In: Proceedings of the 2nd Workshop on Cognitive Modeling and Computational Linguistics, pp. 76–87 (2011)
16. Das, M.K., Dai, H.-K.: A survey of DNA motif finding algorithms. BMC Bioinform. **8**(S7), S21 (2007)
17. Zhao, H., Zhou, Y., Song, Y., Lee, D.L.: Motif enhanced recommendation over heterogeneous information network. In: Proceedings of the 28th ACM International Conference on Information and Knowledge Management, pp. 2189–2192 (2019)
18. Szpektor, I., et al.: Dynamic composition for conversational domain exploration. In: Proceedings of the Web Conference 2020, pp. 872–883 (2020)
19. Chen, H., Ren, Z., Tang, J., Zhao, Y.E., Yin, D.: Hierarchical variational memory network for dialogue generation. In: Proceedings of the 2018 World Wide Web Conference, pp. 1653–1662 (2018)

20. Li, Y., Yu, J., Wang, Z.: Dense semantic matching network for multi-turn conversation. In: 2019 IEEE International Conference on Data Mining (ICDM), pp. 1186–1191. IEEE (2019)
21. Bagavathi, A., Bashiri, P., Reid, S., Phillips, M., Krishnan, S.: Examining untempered social media: analyzing cascades of polarized conversations. In: Proceedings of the 2019 IEEE/ACM International Conference on Advances in Social Networks Analysis and Mining, pp. 625–632 (2019)
22. Mikolov, T., Grave, E., Bojanowski, P., Puhrsch, C., Joulin, A.: Advances in pretraining distributed word representations. In: Proceedings of the International Conference on Language Resources and Evaluation (LREC 2018) (2018)
23. Conneau, A., Kiela, D., Schwenk, H., Barrault, L., Bordes, A.: Supervised learning of universal sentence representations from natural language inference data. In: Proceedings of the 2017 Conference on Empirical Methods in Natural Language Processing, Copenhagen, Denmark, pp. 670–680. Association for Computational Linguistics (2017). https://www.aclweb.org/anthology/D17-1070
24. Boytsov, L., Naidan, B.: Engineering efficient and effective non-metric space library. In: Brisaboa, N., Pedreira, O., Zezula, P. (eds.) SISAP 2013. LNCS, vol. 8199, pp. 280–293. Springer, Heidelberg (2013). https://doi.org/10.1007/978-3-642-41062-8_28
25. Author, F., Author, S.: Title of a proceedings paper. In: Editor, F., Editor, S. (eds.) CONFERENCE 2016. LNCS, vol. 9999, pp. 1–13. Springer, Heidelberg (2016). https://doi.org/10.10007/1234567890
26. LNCS. http://www.springer.com/lncs. Accessed 4 Oct 2017
27. Gašić, M., Hakkani-Tür, D., Celikyilmaz, A.: Spoken language understanding and interaction: machine learning for human-like conversational systems (2017)
28. Liu, C.-W., Lowe, R., Serban, I.V., Noseworthy, M., Charlin, L., Pineau, J.: How not to evaluate your dialogue system: an empirical study of unsupervised evaluation metrics for dialogue response generation (2016)
29. McInnes, L., Healy, J., Melville, J.: UMAP: uniform manifold approximation and projection for dimension reduction (2018)
30. Sczopek, S.: DNA Motif Finding via Gibbs Sampler (2017). https://github.com/sczopek/Python-Sample-Motif-Finding-via-Gibbs-Sampler/commits/master

Facial Expression Recognition with Manifold Learning and Graph Convolutional Network

Olufisayo Ekundayo[1] , Serestina Viriri[1,2(✉)] , and Reolyn Heymann[2]

[1] School of Mathematics, Statistics and Computer Science,
University of KwaZulu-Natal, Durban, South Africa
`viriris@ukzn.ac.za`
[2] Department of Electrical and Electronic Engineering Science,
University of Johannesburg, Johannesburg, South Africa
`rheymann@uj.ac.za`

Abstract. Facial Expression Recognition (FER) has the ability to detect human affect state. Most of the methods employed for FER task do not really consider the correlation among FER data labels to resolve data annotation and ambiguity problems. Label Distribution Learning (LDL) application to FER considerably address this, but only in the presence of data with distribution labels. Therefore, methods that would recover label distribution from logical labels are required. This work is presenting a graph-based label enhancement approach with manifold learning and Graph Convolutional Network (GCN) for facial expression recognition. The manifold learning approach transforms FER data as a graphical problem, where the data points are considered as nearest neighbours represent graph nodes, with the motive of representing the distances along the edges of the neighbouring graph with the approximate distances along the manifold. This process uses the nearest neighbour graph to learn the geometric structure in FER data, which also learn the possible correlation among the data labels. The graphical convolutional network is employed to incorporate the information provided in the manifold learning and the logical description of the data to classify the nodes of the graph using the information of the nearest neighbours. The experiment conducted on the Binghampton University-3D Facial Expression (BU-3DFE) and the Cohn Kanade extension (CK+) data shows that the model gives promising results.

Keywords: Facial Expression Recognition · Manifold learning · Graph Convolutional Network · Label distribution learning · Label enhancement

1 Introduction

As one of the prominent research fields in cognitive computing and Computer Vision (CV), FER has produced positive and promising research results that

T. M. Ngatched Nkouatchah et al. (Eds.): PAAISS 2022, LNICST 459, pp. 362–378, 2023.
https://doi.org/10.1007/978-3-031-25271-6_23

encourage its public acceptance and applications. FER application list is not limited to medicine, security, marketing and education. Recently, [20] presented a work that captured student emotional state in real-time in a virtual class. They incorporate emotion recognition into virtual learning. The successes recorded in FER so far could be attributed to the extensive research on developing robust FER models and the quality and quantity of available FER datasets. FER could be divided into three main aspects: the data, the model and the annotation, which is the description of the data classes. In the literature, little consideration is given to the data annotation aspect. The prevailing data annotation in FER is the grouping of FER data into logical labels of six or seven classes, as proposed by Ekman and Friesel [9]. Nevertheless, the logical label of FER datasets requires the hands of experts, which is expensive and time-consuming. Also, human errors like annotation inconsistency and bias are probably inevitable due to the ambiguous nature of FER datasets. Another shortcoming with the logical labels is the inability to consider the correlation among labels.

Label distribution learning and label enhancement techniques have been employed in the literature to mitigate the ambiguity nature and the label correlation challenges in FER [4,15]. Among the label distribution enhancement algorithms, graph-based models have reported promising results. The graph-based model for label enhancement relies on the assumption that data features and data labels have smooth variations along the graph's edges. While label propagation algorithms aggregate node labels over the edges in the graph, the manifold learning algorithms present distance along the edges with the approximate distance along the manifold. [4] reported that the graph algorithms that have a strong local linear assumption and strong smoothness assumptions are not suitable for image input and deep neural features. But Isomap manifold is a global manifold learning that preserves geometric features of data in a lower-dimensional space [26].

This work presents a graph-based label enhancement approach with manifold learning and Graph Convolutional Network (GCN) for facial expression recognition. The manifold learning approach transforms FER data as a graphical problem, where the data samples form the graph nodes, and the edges of the neighbouring graph are represented with the approximate distances along the isomeric manifold. The Isomap employs the image-based Euclidean distance and geodesic algorithm to learn the geometric structure and the correlation among data annotations. GCN propagates data features along the edges of the neighbouring nodes, incorporates the information provided in the manifold learning and the logical description of the data, and classifies the graph's nodes into six basic emotions using a semi-supervised approach.

Our contributions include the following:

- Incorporate inductive and transductive learning to model the correlation among facial expression labels and recover emotion distributions from logical labels.
- The Isomap manifold learning is employed to learn the correlation among FER data annotations by computing the similarity distance of neighbouring

nodes. The correlation is modelled with the objectives that nodes closed in the manifold are likely to have similar annotation.

- Graph Convolution Network is used in a semi-supervised manner to propagate data features along the edges of the neighbouring nodes and thus learn emotion distribution from the neighbouring nodes.

The proposed method is similar to the method in [5] and [13] by using a manifold algorithm for data similarity computation. However, our approach is different from the work of [5] by using Isomap manifold, which preserves the global representative features in the data and also minimises parameter tuning challenge. The main parameter is K, which is the number of neighbouring nodes that determines the topological stability. Also, the proposed model is different from the work of [13] by computing image-based Euclidean distance that makes the model robust against short-circuit error caused by general Euclidean distance used in [13].

This work is organised as follows: Sect. 2 contains the review of some recent works in FER that considered label annotation challenges in FER model; Sect. 3 presents a discussion of the proposed model starting from Isomap manifold to GCN model. A detail account of the experiments is presented in Sect. 4, which provides information about the datasets, data preprocessing techniques and the experiments' procedures. The results of the experiments are presented and thoroughly discussed in Sect. 5, and the discussion also includes comparisons of the proposed model with some existing standard methods and visualisation of the model output. Section 6 is the conclusion of this work.

2 Related Works

The three main aspects of Facial Expression Recognition (FER) research are the data, the model and FER data annotations. Researchers have thoroughly considered diverse ways to resolve the limitation in FER from data and model points of view.

Initially, static data in their hundreds were the only available data in the field, and they were collected in a controlled environment. The laboratory collected data limits the performance of FER because FER developed in a controlled environment fails to be generalised to the real world. The introduction of sequence and temporal data give room for emotion recognition and the corresponding intensity estimation. The advent of deep learning, especially Convolution Neural Network (CNN), poses a great demand on the volume of learning data to make an appropriate FER model. With internet facilities, data collection is now accessible, which mitigates the challenges with data availability. Likewise, different models have been proposed in the literature for optimal FER. Among the existing models, deep learning models have records of superior performance. Variants of deep learning models consider for FER implementation include CNN, Generative Adversarial Network (GAN), Multitasking Convolution Neural Network (MCNN), Cascaded Convolutional Neural Network (CCNN), to mention a few. The deep networks have successfully contributed immensely to achieving a robust FER. Still, the deep networks only considered the logical labels in their classification task. Most of the existing methods fail to incorporate correlation among data labels. Using logical labels make the models not capture the ambiguous nature in FER datasets.

Recently, Multilabel Learning (ML) methods have been adopted in FER to account for FER label ambiguity. Group Lasso Regularised Maximum Margin (GLMM) proposed by [30], considered the fact that the Action Unit (AU) at different affective states is triggered in the same region of the face. GLMM used the feature extracted for different expressions at the same region to classify them into a zero or non-zero, making it possible for a group to contain different expressions. The global solution of the model was achieved by a function called Maximum Margin Hinge loss. GLMM was later enhanced to Adaptive Group Lasso Regression [31] to assign a continuous value to the distribution of expression present in a non-zero group. GLMM shows its superior performance compares with some existing ML methods from the experiment conducted on s-JAFFE. [18] is another prominent multilabel approach to FER, LI and Deng [18] introduced a multilabel deep learning model termed Deep Bi-Manifold CNN (DBM-CMM). The model preserves the local affinity of deep emotion features and the manifold structure of emotion labels, while learning the discriminating feature of multilabel expression. The deep network training is supervised by softmax cross-entropy loss jointly with the bi-manifold loss for feature discriminating enhancement. This model resolves data ambiguity accurately from RAF-ML data and generalised well with existing multilabel data through the incorporated adaptive mechanism. Nevertheless, the multilabel approach could only resolve the ambiguity problem but could not account for the intensity of the recognised emotions.

Label inconsistency and ambiguity challenges are lately considered using the LDL approach. LDL application to FER requires the construction of distributed labels of each of the facial expression instances; as found in [25,27,33]. Jia et al. [15] preserved the correlation among FER data label locally using EDL-LRL (Emotion Distribution Label-Low Ranking label correlation Locally), which forms a low-rank structure that alleviates the complexity in emotion correlation, with an assumption that low-rank structure represents the label space. The experiments conducted on label distribution datasets (s-JAFFE and s-BU3DFE) show the proposed model's prominence. The model considers the correlation among the label locally on data with a distribution label. Abeere et al. [1] proposed a feature hybrid based model called EDL-LBCNN, which hybridised Local Binary Convolution (LBC) features and Convolution Neural Network (CNN) features train with Kullback-Leibler loss and optimise with ADMM (Alternating Direction Method of Multipliers). The outcome of the experiment on the s-JAFFE dataset shows its promising performance. Zhang et al. [29] proposed a Correlated Emotion Label Distribution Learning (CELDL) model for infrared facial expression recognition. The model initially computes the correlation between expression images using cosine similarities and finally learns the basic emotion in infrared expression with deep CNN. This method is domain-specific, as the model performance was reported only on infrared features. The above LDL models require FER data with distribution labels, and the generalisation of the methods to in-the-wild data and data with a logical label is a challenge.

Chen et al. [4] proposed a label enhancement model to recover label distribution from the logical data annotations. The model generates an auxiliary label space from action units and facial landmarks. This method minimises the problem encountered in Graph Laplacian Label Enhancement (GLLE) model using approximate KNN for building the approximate KNN (akNN) graphs that generate the auxiliary labels. Deep CNN was used as the backbone of the proposed system. The experiments conducted on some laboratory-controlled data (CK+, Oulu-CASIA, CFEE, MMI) and in-the-wild (AFFNET, RAF, SFEW) data proved the system's efficiency over existing methods with an assurance of label consistency and consideration of label ambiguity. The model did not report the intensity of the recognised emotions. There is a need for methods in the field that could recover the distribution label from logical annotations of data to resolve label ambiguity, inconsistency and intensity estimation.

Graph Neural Networks (GNN) is presently gaining attention because of their efficiency in graphical structure problems. A thorough investigation of GNN models is available in [32]. GCN proposed by [17] is one of the variants of GNN, and it has been used diversely in image-related tasks such as image classification [12], image semantic segmentation [19], region classification [6] and object detection [14]. GCN could be implemented for supervised, unsupervised or transductive learning depending on the task, the availability, and the integrity of the available data.

In this work, we propose a manifold learning model as a graph-based label enhancement approach to learn the correlation among data labels, and GCN is employed as a semi-supervised model to recover the emotion distribution from the logical labels of the datasets to address annotation inconsistency, ambiguity and expression intensity estimation challenges in FER.

3   Manifold Graph Convolutional Network Model

This section contains manifold learning and graph convolutional network model description for facial expression recognition task.

3.1   Isomap Manifold

Isomap manifold represents a high dimensional dataset in a low dimensional space with the preservation of the fundamental relationship among the data [22,23]. Facial expression data are non-linear and high dimensional, which make them candidate of dimensionality reduction algorithm. Assuming FER data $X \in R^{M \times N}$, such that $X = \{x_1, x_2, \ldots\ldots\ldots, x_n\}$. Isomap manifold tends to find a lower dimensional space m and embed X samples, that is, $X \in R^{m \times N}$. The manifold achieved the embedding of facial expression data into low dimensional space by using the global topological information of feature space to obtain similarity distance about data points x_i. Euclidean distance is reported to be susceptible to short circuit edge problem [3], which implies that it could provide neighbours along the external space that are not neighbours along the manifold. To avoid the short circuit edge problem, and degradation in isomap performance in the presence of noise. We employ the image based euclidean distance proposed in [3]. Each expression image is first transformed linearly using (1) where σ the width parameter is taken to be 1. Assuming two images x and y, then the Euclidean distance between them is given as:

$$d^2(x, y) = \sum_{i,j=1}^{MN} g_{i,j}(x_i, y_i)^T G(x, y) \tag{1}$$

where the image vector $g_{ij} = \frac{1}{2\pi\sigma^2}\exp\left[\frac{-(|P_i - P_j|^2)}{2\sigma^2}\right]$ and symetric matrix $G = (g_{ij})_{MN \times MN}$, P_i, P_j are pixels and $|P_i - P_j|$ is the distance P_i and P_j on the image lattice. Also $u = G^{\frac{1}{2}}x$ and $G^{\frac{1}{2}} = \alpha\gamma^{\frac{1}{2}}\alpha$. α is the orthogonal matrix whose column vector are eigenvectors of G and $\gamma^{\frac{1}{2}}$ is the diagonal matrix which contains the eigenvalue of G.

The distances between the transformed images are computed from (2).

$$d(x) = (x_i - x_j)^T G(x_i - x_j) = (u - v)^T(u - v) \tag{2}$$

The nearest neighbourhood graph is constructed from the computed distances d(x), and the Dijkstra algorithm (the shortest algorithm) finds the shortest path along the neighbourhood graph to compute non-neighbouring data points. The application of multidimensional scaling generates the low dimensional vector space.

3.2   Graph Convolution Network

Graph Convolution Network (GCN) has intrinsic ability to work directly on a graph related problem, and this motivates us to apply GCN for node classification using the available information through Isomap manifold.

Generally, GCN works by propagating node features along edges of the neighbouring graph, through which it learns the latent representative features in each node for node classification. Assuming a data X with $N \times F$ matrix and $N \times N$ adjacency matrix G, where N is the number of X samples, and F is the number of features in each sample of X, then GCN latent layers are given as:

$$H^i = f(H^{(i-1)}, A) \tag{3}$$

where f is GCN propagation rule which computes a node features from the neighbouring nodes without including the node information and transform it with the application of weight W and the activation function σ, the expression is shown in (4) below:

$$f(H^i, A) = \sigma(AH^{i-1}W^{i-1}) \tag{4}$$

To include the node feature in the node aggregation in (2), A is modified by adding Identity matrix to A as $\hat{A} = A + I$, and also multiply with the inverse degree of $\hat{A}$ denoted as D^{-1}, D^{-1} in (5) to resolve the possible problem attributed to gradient explosion, which could emanate from the degree of the node because the feature value increases with the node degree. Multiplying D^{-1} with the representing features normalises the feature representation, and thus making the feature representation aggregation invariant to node degree.

$$f(H^i, A) = \sigma(D^{-1}\hat{A}D^{-1}H^{i-1}W^{i-1}) \tag{5}$$

The adjacency matrix only assigns one as the edge weight in the original GCN, which would possibly misguide the label's prediction in the presence of adjacent nodes of different labels. To avoid this, a similarity graph that assigns different edge weights to different neighbour nodes should be used with GCN as an aggregate of neighbour nodes' information.

This work uses distance generates along the Isomap manifold as the similarity graph for GCN aggregation of neighbour nodes' information. The objective function is computed using a multidimensional scale that runs on the geodesic distance to generate the co-ordinate of the Euclidean space. Given the Multidimensional Scaling (MDS) function $z \in R^{n \times k}$ then the objective function in (7) is obtained from the derivative of (6).

$$MDS = argmin\frac{1}{2}\sum_{n}^{i=1}\sum_{n}^{i=i+1}(||x_i - x_j|| - ||z_i - z_j||)^2 \tag{6}$$

where $||x_i - x_j||$ is the original distance in d-dimensional space, and $||z_i - z_j||$ is the k-dimensional data points such that the original distances are preserved.

$$f(z) = \sum_{n}^{i=1}\sum_{n}^{i=i+1} s_{ij}\left(-\frac{z_i - z_j}{\sqrt{(z_i - z_j)^2}}\right) \tag{7}$$

where $s_{ij} = ||x_i - x_j|| - ||z_i - z_j|| = \sqrt{(x_i - x_j)}^2 - \sqrt{(z_i - z_j)}^2$. The Isomap distances at the lower dimensional space also preserve distance and similarity proportionality relationships; that is, the higher the distance, the lower the similarity between nodes and the lower the distance, the higher the similarity. The computed similarity matrix represents the edge weight between nodes, which in turn help to construct a graph with the appropriate information about adjacent nodes.

If the computed similarity graph is represented with $\Theta = \Theta_{ij}$, where Θ_{ij} is the similarity between $node_i$ and $node_j$. Then, replacing the adjacency graph A in (4) with the computed similarity graph, Θ generate an updated version of (4) as presented in (8).

$$f(H^i, \Theta) = \sigma(\Theta H^{i-1}W^{i-1}) \tag{8}$$

The similarity graph models the correlations among emotions, assuming that data points close in the low dimensional space should have the same label description. Given the feature matrix E and the manifold similarity graph θ, GCN could predict the required emotion distribution in facial expression images. The output layer of GCN is now expressed in (9), which is the final output weight given as W^i

$$W^i = softmax(\sigma(\Theta E W^{i-1}))\tag{9}$$

Algorithm 1: Manifold-GCN Algorithm

Input: : Expression images $X \in R^n$, k (number of Kneighbour nodes)
Output: : description degree of y to x such that $\sum_y d^y = 1$

1 Compute the linear transformation of each expression image $x_i \in X$ by multiplying x_i with the eigenvalue and eigenvector of the symmetric matrix of the image vector.
2 Compute distances for every pair of x_i, x_j using Eq. (2).
3 Generate neighbouring graph with geodesic algorithm.
4 Find the shortest path for every none neighbouring data points using Dijkstra algorithm.
5 the similarity graph $\theta = \theta_{i,j} = d_G(x_i, x_j)$.
6 Replace Adjacency graph $\in f(H^i, A)$ with the similarity graph θ
7 Perform the classification with softmax function as given in Eq. (9)

Figure 1 is the framework description of MGCN.

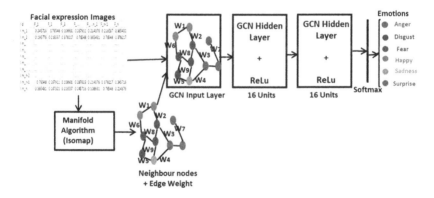

Fig. 1. Architectural description of manifold GCN model.

4   Experiment

This section presents details of the experiments from data preprocessing, feature representation and label enhancement and emotion classification.

4.1 Datasets

This study considers two FER datasets, which are BU-3DFE [28] and Cohn Kanade Extension (CK+) [21].

Binghampton University -3D Facial Expression (BU-3DFE) contains 2500 emotion data collected from 100 subjects in which 40% are male, and the remaining 60% are female. Although BU-3DFE is static and controlled, it is regarded as in-the-wild-data because of the different races, ethnicities, and ages of subjects in the data.

Cohn Kanade (CK+). CK+, unlike the BU-3DFE dataset, is a sequence dataset; it consists of 7 expressions (Anger, Disgust, Contempt, Fear, Happy, Neutral, Sadness, Surprise) and the neutral face. CK+ contains 593 frames, whereby 327 are labelled out of them. The frames are produced by 127 subjects, of which 65% are female, and 35% are male. CK+ has been employed severally, virtually in all categories of facial expression recognition tasks. In this study, we are only considering six basic emotions.

4.2 Data Preprocessing

Isomap performance is affected by noise. To ameliorate this effect, we employed a face detection algorithm and normalisation techniques available in OpenCV [2] to minimise redundant information in the data. The Haar-like cascades are used for face detection, and a standard equalisation algorithm is used for contract normalisation. Figure 2 shows the information preserved in BU-3DFE data before and after preprocessing. Figure 2a shows the effect of light intensity variation on the manifold visualisation of unpreprocessed data, and Fig. 2b reflect the importance of the application of light normalization to the data in manifold visualisation.

4.3 Experimental Setup

The images are the graph's nodes; the edges and their respective weight are generated via the Isomap manifold. We achieved the model implementation by using stellargraph [8] and keras with tensorflow 2.2 as backend [7]. ADAM optimiser [16] is employed at the training phase of the model with a learning rate of 0.03, dropout of 0.25, weight decay (L2 regularisation) of $5e^{-4}$. The Manifold GCN model has two hidden graph convolutional layers with ReLu activation function, and the output layer for nodes classification is the softmax activation function. For each of the datasets, less than 10% are randomly selected as label data, 16% as evaluation data, and the remaining data are used as test data. The summary of the data is available in Table 1. The training process takes a maximum of 100 epochs, and we also use the early stopping function to stop the training after a consistent increase in loss values. The experiment results are presented from an average of 10 runs.

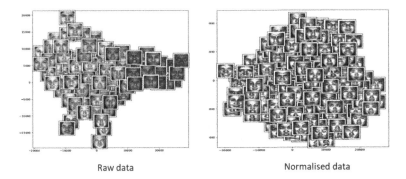

Raw data   Normalised data

Fig. 2. Figure showing Isomap transformation performance of raw expression images on the left and the preprocessed images of BU-3DFE on the right.

The first phase of the experiments is the model performance evaluation with parameter tuning, and we observe the system's performance with different K values, optimisers, and learning rates. Furthermore, we compare the system's performance with some existing models developed for label enhancement distribution learning for FER. We conclude the experiment by visualising the embedding vectors in our model.

Table 1. The summary of data distribution in the Manifold GCN model.

Data	Nodes	Edges	Classes	Train	Evaluation	Test
BU-3DFE	2400	2400	6	50	150	2200
CK+	593	593	6	50	100	443

5   Experimental Results and Discussion

The training and the evaluation accuracy and loss of the model are shown in Fig. 3. The model performance on the test datasets in this work is presented as multiclass confusion matices in Fig. 4 and Fig. 5, and from the confusion matrices we compute accuracy, F1-Score, average precision, average recall metrics as given in Eq. 10, Eq. 11, Eq. 12 and Eq. 13 respectively. The outcomes of the computations are detailed in Table 2. The comparison study with some existing models is presented in Table 3, and we compare the model with some baseline methods on the datasets using accuracy as the metrics for performance evaluation. The proposed method has an outstanding performance on BU-3DFE data. The model performance on CK+ is promising compare to other models. This implies that consideration of similarity measures accounted for by our model positively affects the system's performance.

$$accuracy = \frac{TP + TN}{FP + FN + TP + TN} \tag{10}$$

$$F1 - Score = 2 * \frac{Precision * Recall}{precision + Recall} \tag{11}$$

where Precision $= \frac{TP}{TP+FP}$ and recall $= \frac{TP}{TP+FN}$.

$$AveragePrecision = \frac{TotalPrecision}{no_o f_c lasses} \tag{12}$$

$$averagerecall = \frac{Totalrecall}{no_o f_c lasses} \tag{13}$$

TP simply means True Positive, TN means True Negative, FP means False Positive and FN means False Negative.

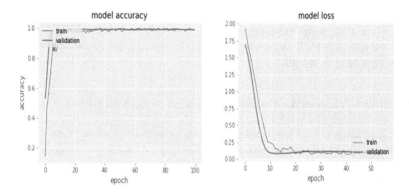

Fig. 3. The right figure is the training and validation accuracy graph, while the left figure is the training loss and the validation loss of the model performance.

Table 2. The Performance of the manifold GCN model on datasets based on test accuracy(%) and loss values.

Model	Database	Accuracy	F1_Score	Average Precision	Average Recall
Manifold GCN	BU-3DFE	98.80%	0.97	0.97	0.98
	CK+	97.20%	0.96	0.96	0.97

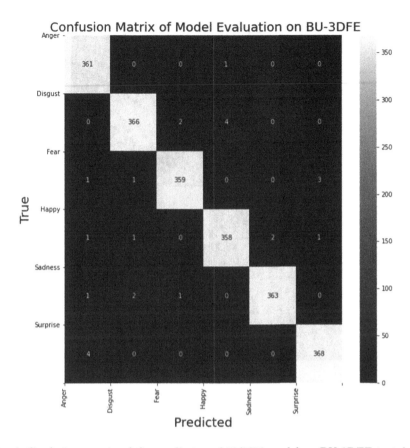

Fig. 4. Confusion matrix of the prediction of MGCN model on BU-3DFE test data

Table 3. The performance of the manifold GCN model compare with existing models on CK+ data.

Author	Method and contribution	Number of classes	Accuracy
[24]	E3DNET	7	80.36
[18]	DBMNET	7	85.27
[10]	Deep Forest	6	93.07
[4]	LDL-ALSG	7	93.08
[20]	CDLLNET	7	87.42
[11]	MA-FER	7	83.28
Proposed Model	**Manifold GCN**	**6**	**97.20**

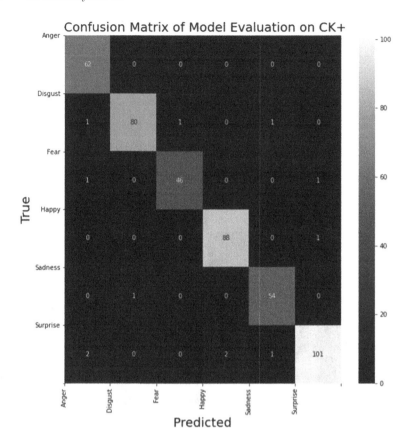

Fig. 5. Confusion matix of the prediction of MGCN model on CK+ test data

Experiment Result for k Values and Parameter Setting. We consider increasing
the number of k(neighbour) parameters and observe the effect on the model
performance. K values are increased in the multiple of two, that is, set {2,4,6,8}
as presented in Table 4. We observe that the model gives stable and optimal
results for the datasets when k = 4 and deduce that the more the neighbour
size, the more difficult the classification task. This is suspected to be a result
of accommodating members with different features that introduce information
that misguides the central node classification. For our model parameters, we
conducted a manual search between three optimisation functions (Stochastic
Gradient Descent (SGD), ADADELTA, ADAM) and learning rate was varied
between 0.1 and 0.5 step by 0.1, 0.001 and 0.005 step by 0.001, and lastly 0.0001
and 0.0005 step by 0.0001. We also search for the dropout value between 0.25
and 0.5. We obtained optimal results with ADAM optimiser, 0.003 learning rate,
and 0.25 dropout.

Table 4. Table showing the model performance at different values of k.

Database	K = 2	K = 4	K = 6	K = 8
BU-3DFE	94.03%	98.80%	87.53%	80.16%
CK+	94.72%	97.20%	86%	72.59%

Model Visualization. Graph convolutional network is implemented as a semi-supervised model, couple with manifold enhancement the model is capable of learning correlation among labels and hence resolves data inconsistencies. The model's output is the softmax activation function, softmax approximately gives the proportion of each emotion in the expression face, and removing the threshold enables the model to recover the emotion distribution from logical labels. Sample of the model prediction is presented in Fig. 6. We employed Isomap low dimensional data embedding technique to visualise features in the hidden layers of our model. Isomap has the tendency to map high dimensional data feature with similar label to the corresponding low dimensional space. The classification output is viewed based on the categories of different colours, where each colour represent a particular class. Figure 7 provides information about the hidden layers of the proposed model. The closeness of colours with different labels speaks volume about the correlation and the distribution of emotion in facial expression.

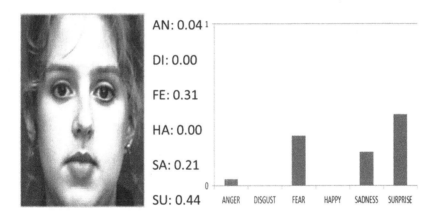

Fig. 6. Sample of manifold GCN prediction of CK+ data

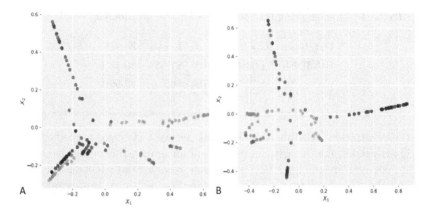

Fig. 7. A is the 2-dimensional visualization result of the model information of BU-3DFE data, and B is the 2-dimensional visualization of what the model learns of CK+ data. (Color figure online)

6   Conclusion

This work implements label enhancement for facial expression distribution learning. We adopt inductive technique, which is manifold learning to account for the similarities and correlations among FER data, which help compute distance similarity for graph convolution networks to substitute for adjacency matrix. The model performs optimally on both the CK+ and BU-3DFE datasets, visualising the data with Isomap dimensional reduction indicates that the model learns the correlation appropriately among data classes and hence resolve data inconsistencies. This study is conducted in a controlled environment, that is, on laboratory prepared data. Future work would consider more challenging environments like data in the wild or dynamic environments. The computation of distance similarities is an inductive process in isolation from the semi-supervised learning GCN, such that GCN could only make predictions based on the prior knowledge of seen data.

References

1. Almowallad, A., Sanchez, V.: Human emotion distribution learning from face images using CNN and LBC features. In: 2020 8th International Workshop on Biometrics and Forensics (IWBF), pp. 1–6 (2020). https://doi.org/10.1109/IWBF49977.2020.9107940
2. Bradski, G.: The OpenCV library. Dr. Dobb's J. Softw. Tools **25**, 120–123 (2000)
3. Chen, J., Wang, R., Shan, S., Chen, X., Gao, W.: Isomap based on the image Euclidean distance, vol. 2, pp. 1110–1113 (2006). https://doi.org/10.1109/ICPR.2006.729
4. Chen, S., Wang, J., Chen, Y., Shi, Z., Geng, X., Rui, Y.: Label distribution learning on auxiliary label space graphs for facial expression recognition. In: 2020

IEEE/CVF Conference on Computer Vision and Pattern Recognition (CVPR), pp. 13981–13990 (2020). https://doi.org/10.1109/CVPR42600.2020.01400

5. Chen, S.-B., et al.: Graph convolutional network based on manifold similarity learning. Cogn. Comput. **12**(6), 1144–1153 (2020). https://doi.org/10.1007/s12559-020-09788-4

6. Chen, X., Li, L.J., Fei-Fei, L., Mulam, H.: Iterative visual reasoning beyond convolutions, pp. 7239–7248 (2018). https://doi.org/10.1109/CVPR.2018.00756

7. Chollet, F., Allaire, J., et al.: R interface to Keras (2017). https://github.com/rstudio/keras

8. CSIRO Data61: Stellargraph machine learning library (2018). https://github.com/stellargraph/stellargraph

9. Ekman, P., Friesen, W.V.: Constant across cultures in the face and emotion. J. Pers. Soc. Psychol. **17**(2), 124–129 (1971). https://doi.org/10.1037/h0030377

10. Ekundayo, O., Viriri, S.: Deep forest approach for facial expression recognition. In: Dabrowski, J.J., Rahman, A., Paul, M. (eds.) PSIVT 2019. LNCS, vol. 11994, pp. 149–161. Springer, Cham (2020). https://doi.org/10.1007/978-3-030-39770-8_12

11. Gan, Y., Chen, J., Yang, Z., Xu, L.: Multiple attention network for facial expression recognition. IEEE Access **8**, 7383–7393 (2020). https://doi.org/10.1109/ACCESS.2020.2963913

12. Garcia, V., Bruna, J.: Few-shot learning with graph neural networks (2017)

13. He, T., Jin, X.: Image emotion distribution learning with graph convolutional networks, pp. 382–390 (2019). https://doi.org/10.1145/3323873.3326593

14. Hu, H., Gu, J., Zhang, Z., Dai, J., Wei, Y.: Relation networks for object detection (2017)

15. Jia, X., Zheng, X., Li, W., Zhang, C., Li, Z.: Facial emotion distribution learning by exploiting low-rank label correlations locally. In: 2019 IEEE/CVF Conference on Computer Vision and Pattern Recognition (CVPR), pp. 9833–9842 (2019). https://doi.org/10.1109/CVPR.2019.01007

16. Kingma, D.P., Ba, J.: Adam: a method for stochastic optimization. CoRR abs/1412.6980 (2014). http://dblp.uni-trier.de/db/journals/corr/corr1412.html#KingmaB14

17. Kipf, T.N., Welling, M.: Semi-supervised classification with graph convolutional networks. In: Proceedings of the 5th International Conference on Learning Representations, ICLR 2017 (2017). https://openreview.net/forum?id=SJU4ayYgl

18. Li, S., Deng, W.: Blended emotion in-the-wild: multi-label facial expression recognition using crowdsourced annotations and deep locality feature learning. Int. J. Comput. Vis. **127**, 884–906 (2018). https://doi.org/10.1007/s11263-018-1131-1

19. Liang, X., Lin, L., Shen, X., Feng, J., Yan, S., Xing, E.: Interpretable structure-evolving LSTM, pp. 2175–2184 (2017). https://doi.org/10.1109/CVPR.2017.234

20. Liu, T., Wang, J., Yang, B., Wang, X.: Facial expression recognition method with multi-label distribution learning for non-verbal behavior understanding in the classroom. Infrared Phys. Technol. **112**, 103594 (2021). https://doi.org/10.1016/j.infrared.2020.103594

21. Lucey, P., Cohn, J., Kanade, T., Saragih, J., Ambadar, Z., Matthews, I.: The extended Cohn-Kanade dataset (CK+): a complete dataset for action unit and emotion-specified expression, pp. 94–101 (2010). https://doi.org/10.1109/CVPRW.2010.5543262

22. Samko, O., Marshall, D., Rosin, P.: Selection of the optimal parameter value for the Isomap algorithm. Pattern Recogn. Lett. **27**, 968–979 (2006). https://doi.org/10.1016/j.patrec.2005.10.017

23. Tenenbaum, J., Silva, V., Langford, J.: A global geometric framework for nonlinear dimensionality reduction. Science (New York, N.Y.) **290**, 2319–2323 (2001). https://doi.org/10.1126/science.290.5500.2319
24. Wu, Z., Chen, T., Chen, Y., Zhang, Z., Liu, G.: NIRExpNet: three-stream 3D convolutional neural network for near infrared facial expression recognition. Appl. Sci. **7**(11) (2017). https://doi.org/10.3390/app7111184
25. Xi, X., Zhang, Y., Hua, X., Miran, S.M., Zhao, Y.B., Luo, Z.: Facial expression distribution prediction based on surface electromyography. Expert Syst. Appl. **161**, 113683 (2020). https://doi.org/10.1016/j.eswa.2020.113683. http://www.sciencedirect.com/science/article/pii/S0957417420305078
26. Xie, G., Shi, H., Yin, B., Kang, Y., Shao, C., Gui, J.: Robust l-isomap with a novel landmark selection method. Math. Probl. Eng. **2017** (2017). https://doi.org/10.1155/2017/3930957
27. Xing, C., Geng, X., Xue, H.: Logistic boosting regression for label distribution learning. In: 2016 IEEE Conference on Computer Vision and Pattern Recognition (CVPR), pp. 4489–4497 (2016). https://doi.org/10.1109/CVPR.2016.486
28. Yin, L., Wei, X., Sun, Y., Wang, J., Rosato, M.: A 3D facial expression database for facial behavior research, vol. 2006, pp. 211–216 (2006). https://doi.org/10.1109/FGR.2006.6
29. Zhang, Z., Lai, C., Liu, H., Li, Y.F.: Infrared facial expression recognition via Gaussian-based label distribution learning in the dark illumination environment for human emotion detection. Neurocomputing **409**, 341–350 (2020). https://doi.org/10.1016/j.neucom.2020.05.081. http://www.sciencedirect.com/science/article/pii/S0925231220309322
30. Zhao, K., Zhang, H., Dong, M., Guo, J., Qi, Y., Song, Y.: A multi-label classification approach for facial expression recognition. In: Visual Communications and Image Processing, Kuching, Malaysia. IEEE (2013). https://doi.org/10.1109/VCIP.2013.6706330
31. Zhao, K., Zhang, H., Guo, J.: An adaptive group lasso based multi-label regression approach for facial expression analysis. In: International Conference on Image Processing (ICIP), Paris, France, pp. 1435–1439. IEEE (2014). https://doi.org/10.1109/ICIP.2014.7025287
32. Zhou, J., et al.: Graph neural networks: a review of methods and applications. AI Open **1**, 57–81 (2020). https://doi.org/10.1016/j.aiopen.2021.01.001. https://www.sciencedirect.com/science/article/pii/S2666651021000012
33. Zhou, Y., Xue, H., Geng, X.: Emotion distribution recognition from facial expressions. In: Proceedings of the 23rd ACM International Conference on Multimedia, MM 2015, pp. 1247–1250 (2015)

Speech Emotion Classification: A Survey of the State-of-the-Art

Samson Akinpelu$^{(\boxtimes)}$ and Serestina Viriri

School of Mathematics, Statistics and Computer Science,
University of KwaZulu-Natal, Durban, South Africa
222068579@stu.ukzn.ac.za, viriris@ukzn.ac.za

Abstract. Technological advancement and rapid growth in Artificial Intelligence (AI) with the corresponding non-availability of sufficient dataset for training the machine learning algorithms has paved the way for applying deep learning techniques for classifying human emotion from auditory speech. The study presents a full survey of the state-of-the-art algorithms and approaches for performing speech emotion classification. Comparative analysis of existing methods for extracting features from the speech signal, a critical review of the performance evaluation of specific algorithms developed for carrying out speech emotion analysis, coupled with the study of evaluation metrics used for performance analysis is presented. The major strength and weaknesses of the algorithms examined were highlighted. Ultimately, the best-performing algorithm can be inferred from the comparison. This paper provides a survey with the utmost aim of revealing how most deep learning techniques outperform conventional algorithms for speech emotion classification.

Keywords: Classification · Speech emotion · Performance metrics · Deep learning · Classifiers

1 Introduction

Auditory speech interaction seems to be the most simple and convenient mode of human communication. In addition to linguistic information such as connotation and dialect type, speech signals carry a wealth of non-linguistic information such as facial expressions, speech emotion, and so on. Speech emotion classification [1] (SEC) has become increasingly important in affective computing and human-machine interactions in recent years, as a result of notable advancements in computer vision, artificial intelligence, and machine learning. In many publications, it is also popularly known as speech emotion recognition (SER). Speech emotion classification entails recognizing the emotional feature of speech regardless of the actual meaning. Though individuals can achieve this task as a natural component of verbal communication, the possibility of accomplishing this automatically and more accurately using a computer device is still research in progress [2,3]. The innovation by which a computer can automatically and

© ICST Institute for Computer Sciences, Social Informatics and Telecommunications Engineering 2023
Published by Springer Nature Switzerland AG 2023. All Rights Reserved
T. M. Ngatched Nkouatchah et al. (Eds.): PAAISS 2022, LNICST 459, pp. 379–394, 2023.
https://doi.org/10.1007/978-3-031-25271-6_24

accurately understand human emotion through speech has piqued the interest of several researchers. SEC is particularly beneficial in applications that require normal human-machine interaction, such as e-learning, customer support and online movies, where the response of the user is determined by the detected emotion [4]. It is also helpful for in-car board systems, where the system can use information about the driver's mental state to initiate vital safety measures [5]. It can also be used as a clinical diagnosis for patients who are suffering from a mental disorder. It is applicable in automatic translation systems where the speaker's emotional state is a factor in communication between parties. However, the lack of a sufficient label dataset to train machine learning algorithms, in identifying human emotion has encouraged the application of deep transfer learning [6]. The specific contribution of this study is to compare several cutting-edge and state-of-the-art techniques for classifying emotion from speech signals. We carried out a comprehensive survey of eliciting emotion from human auditory speech using the conventional approach of classification, neural network and deep learning techniques. Possible combinations of the traditional approach of classification and deep learning (Convolutional Neural Network and Recurrent Neural Network) also known as ensemble methods for improved classification accuracy were highlighted. Researchers in the speech emotion domain and affective computing will be thoroughly furnished with the growth of research in emotion classification and enhancement in models for more accurate recognition of emotion from this study.

1.1 Emotion Classification

Emotion is a positive or negative mental state that is linked to a sequence of physiological activities. Emotions describe an individual's psychological condition. It is impossible to separate it from man, as it is exhibited at one point or another. Emotion is a dominant factor in human attitudinal behaviour and comportment, according to scientific findings. Personality theory, which reveals human actions and inactions, has a significant relationship with the emotional state of people.

The obvious reason why emotion classification has attracted so many scholars in the last decade is that man and his emotional traits are inextricably linked. It influences the creation of higher levels of awareness during embryogenesis and determines the content and structure of consciousness throughout a lifetime [7]. Majorly, emotion falls into two categories, which are positive (happiness, surprise, excitement) and negative (sadness, anger, disgust, fear) emotions respectively.

Emotions, like any other neurobiological activity, range in intensity from low to high. SADNESS, HAPPINESS, DISGUST, ANGER, SURPRISE, and FEAR are the six main categories of emotion identified by Paul Ekman's study as depicted in Fig. 1. Disgust and anger, for example, may combine to generate a new emotion called con-tempt and so when these six basic emotions unified, there is a likelihood for more complex emotions to emerge [8].

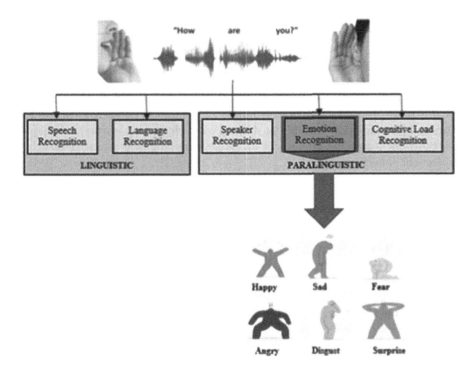

Fig. 1. General framework of emotion classification

Certain real-life scenarios have shown that emotion is transferable (though not always), and the explicit purpose of human social interaction will be meaningless without an accurate classification of emotion [9]. Many relationships and societal groups have been battered because of the inability to manage emotional outbursts. A variety of methods for classifying emotion have been developed, including facial image expression, audio speech, and behavioural traits just to mention a few, however, the focus of this study is on speech utterance [5].

The remaining section of this study is as follows. Section 2 entails a discussion on speech emotion classification with corresponding classification algorithms. Section 3 discusses various evaluation metrics for emotion classification models. A critical review of state-of-the-art methods of emotion classification was carried out in Sect. 4 and Sect. 5 concludes the study.

2   Speech Emotion Classification

The study of emotional attributes from speech signals is known as speech emotion classification (SEC). It is the most prevalent and suitable means of recognizing human emotion, therefore it's no surprise that it's attracting a growing number of scholars with the potential to expand research in Human-Computer Interaction (HCI). To detect emotional content from a speech signal, various approaches such as Mel-frequency cepstrum coefficient (MFCC), log-mel, prosodic and spectrogram have been applied to extract speech features before classification into different emotions takes place [9,10].

The following reasons have made speech emotion classification a thought-provoking task. Foremost, it is uncertain which features of the speech signal can be optimally used for differentiating between emotions. The variation introduced by different speakers, speaking styles, and tempo has added another obstacle because these properties have a huge impact on commonly extracted features like pitch and formants [11]. Insufficient dataset with which deep learning techniques can be trained and the absence of an indigenous language ascent dataset are subjects of concern in SEC.

A comparison of several techniques and their performance using some well-known evaluation metrics is carried out in this study. The performance of several techniques used in the main conference on emotion classification was also investigated in this work. The task was divided into three main components: dataset preprocessing and augmentation, feature extraction, and emotion classification (sad, happy, angry, etc.). The accuracy of performance evaluations as well as other evaluation measures was critically examined.

2.1 Speech Emotion Classifiers

With a broad range of research articles published a few years ago, the subject of classification algorithms and techniques has been deemed a significant aspect of Machine Learning (ML). The term "classification" in ML has typically been used in a broad sense, encompassing supervised, unsupervised, and semi-supervised learning algorithms. The goal of unsupervised learning is to find and analyze the structure of unlabeled data. Each data input is pre-assigned a class label in supervised learning, to which speech emotion classification also belongs [12,13].

The classification techniques usually require a split of the dataset into training and testing data. In the recent past, there has been a notable development in research for the development of multiclass classification algorithms and techniques for speech emotion classification. One of the popular classification algorithms is rule-based which classifies data by using a group of "if... then..." rules. It follows a set of conditions having conjunctions of attributes, before arriving at a conclusion. A decision tree is a primary example of rule-based classification [14] (Mulongo Pihlqvist, 2018; Jasmeet-Kaur, 2020) [15]. Other classification algorithms that have been used in the time past are Support Vector Machine (SVM), Hidden Markov Model (HMM), Artificial Neural Network (ANN) and K-Nearest Neighbour (KNN). Majorly, classification algorithms are subdivided into four categories: Binary, Multiclass, Multi-label and Imbalanced classification as depicted in Fig. 2. These algorithms and their combinations have been applied to emotion classification by various researchers and their performance

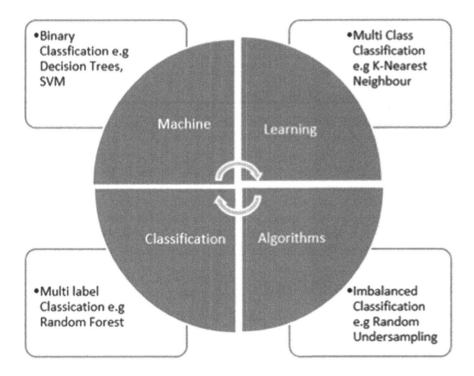

Fig. 2. Categories of classification algorithm

verified using certain standard evaluation metrics [12]. A comparison between these algorithms is shown in Table 1.

2.2 Support Vector Machine (SVM)

SVM is a typical supervised machine learning algorithm that performs well in many classification problems. It uses distinct patterns by splitting hyperplane and kernel functions in modelling non-linear decision margins. SVM ensures that margins between various classes of the dataset (emotional features) are maximized by constructing the best hyperplane. SVM was utilized in [16] to classify three distinct human emotions (happy, sad and neutral) from Berlin Emo-DB and Chinese speech emotion corpus. In their experiments, emotional speech features (Mel-frequency Cepstral Coefficient, energy and pitch) were extracted from the speech signals, and they achieved 91.3% and 95.1% on both datasets respectively. SVM performs classification on input data [17] using Eqs. 1 and 2.

$$k(c, c_i) = (\gamma c^t c_i + m)^d \tag{1}$$

$$c = \sum_{i=1}^{n} w_{gi} k(c_i, c) + b \tag{2}$$

where m is a constant, k represents the kernel function, c is the input data, w_{gi} represents a weight, with b as a bias, c_i is the support vector and d denotes the degree of the polynomial function γ.

2.3   Hidden Markov Model (HMM)

As its name implies, HMM follows the Markov process with an unobserved event in the statistical Markov model in which the probability of a new event relies on the previous event. The word "hidden" denotes the ineptness to recognize the process that produces the event at a certain moment in time. Then, using the framework in conjunction with the target realities of the current event, it is possible to utilize a likelihood to predict the subsequent event. HMM has been successfully used to classify speech emotions in [18] where an accuracy rate of 89.2% was recorded and they established the fact that recognition of emotion with log frequency coefficient features is higher than human vocal tract features.

2.4   K-Nearest Neighbor (KNN)

K-NN is a classification algorithm that is based on propinquity (nearness). It is a supervised classifier known for its convenience and ease of implementation in tackling classification tasks. It performs the classification of data using Euclidean Distance as indicated in Eq. 3.

$$d(x, y) = \sqrt{\sum_{i=1}^{N} (x_i - y_i)^2} \tag{3}$$

where x, y represents two points in Euclidean space, x_i, y_i represents the vectors of Euclidean and N represents the N-th space. The value of k (k-nearest) determines which class the will data be assigned to, among its neighbours. In [19], KNN and artificial neural networks were applied in classifying emotions from a speech corpus that was centred on two different languages. An accuracy of 69.89% was recorded with KNN after the experiment was carried out using linear prediction and frequency cepstral coefficient (feature) and Hurst parameters.

2.5   Decision Tree (DT)

The decision tree is based on a divide and conquers algorithmic approach most suited for a no-linear classification problem. It can be simply described as a tree structure, having several nodes, leaves, roots and branches. DT in a classification task accepts discrete values based on binary recursive partitioning, which involves dividing the data into subsets and then further dividing those subsets into smaller subsets. The method then terminates the procedure once all the requirements have been successfully completed and the subset data is sufficiently homogeneous. A decision tree approach was applied in [20] for the

Table 1. Summary of comparison of State-of-the-art algorithm

Algorithm	Brief description	Strength	Weakness	Author
SVM	It's a linear model that can be used to solve classification and regression problems. The essential concept is that two classes are separated by a hyperplane defined by its normal vector and bias [21]	Performs well when there is a clear margin of distinction between classes. Highly effective when the dimensionality exceeds the number of samples. It conserves memory	It suffers from over-fitting with a large dataset Fails, when the dataset contains more noise, such as overlapping target classes	Vladimir Vapnik in the 1970s
HMM	This is a statistical model that describes the sequences of events. It consists of a Markov chain whose internal behaviours and states remain hidden from the observer [22]	Its principle can be adapted to many tasks [23]	Highly expensive in terms of computational time and memory consumption [24]	Baum L. E and Petrie, 1966
KNN	This is a form of machine learning algorithm that can handle classification and regression problems. K-represent the number of neighbours [25]	It is not cumbersome to implement. i.e., simple and easy. Also, it has no assumption	It has the major drawback of being substantially slower as the size of the data in use grows. It is a lazy learning algorithm [15]	Evelyn Fix and Joseph Hodges in 1951
Decision Trees	DT is a classifier that recursively partitions data space in such a way that it can be described as a collection of related rules. It is usually made up of various nodes that symbolize a branch of a rooted tree. [26]	Simple, easy to understand and robust to outliers	Not suitable for large datasets because it results in overfitting. Prone to the wrong prediction as a result of noise [27]	Around 1970s s (First Version) Breiman, Stone, Friedman, and Olshen

classification of speech emotion and an accuracy rate of 82.9% was achieved on the EmoDB speech corpus.

3   Performance Evaluation Metrics for the State-of-the-Arts Classification Algorithms

When evaluating and comparing different classification models' multiclass problems, performance metrics are immensely important. Many measures can be used to evaluate a multi-class classifier's performance [28]. The performance of various speech emotion classification algorithms on speech corpus is presented in this paper. Several metrics for analyzing the output quality of speech emotion classification algorithms are employed to evaluate the classification results. Confusion matrix, sensitivity, specificity, accuracy, Mathew Correlation Coefficient (MCC), and average precision are all commonly used metrics for evaluating algorithm performance. There are four essential parameters in getting these metrics:

True positives (TP): Is a key parameter in evaluation metrics which shows whether an observation predicted to belong to a class really belongs to that class i.e., $TP \rightarrow (M \in Y) = 1$, where M is the predicted value and Y is the actual value and 1= +ve, 0 = -ve.

True negatives (TN): Usually indicate that the predicted observation not belonging to a class does not actually belong to that class in the real sense i.e., $TN \rightarrow (M \notin Y) = 0$

False positives (FP): As its name implies, happens when the prediction shows that an outcome belongs to a class when it does not, in the real sense. In other words, both the prediction and the actual are not having the same data point i.e., $FP \rightarrow (M = 1, Y = 0)$

False negatives (FN): This happens when the prediction indicates a false identity of observation of not belonging to a class when it belongs to that class i.e., $FN \rightarrow (M = 0, Y = 1)$
The proper combination of these parameters can then be used as the basis for computing the metrics mentioned above, as follows:

Confusion Matrix: Is a summary of prediction results on a classification task. The number of correct and wrong predictions are reported with count values and simplified by each class. It is one of the easiest means of determining the performance of a classification algorithm.

Accuracy: It can be represented by the ratio of correct predictions to total predictions. The accuracy score function from the "sci-kit learn" python library can be used to compute the accuracy of a classification algorithm or model. Mathematically:

$$Accuracy = \frac{TP + TN}{TP + FP + TN + FN} \tag{4}$$

Specificity: It is the ratio of actual negative to predicted negative

$$Specificity = \frac{TN}{FP + FN} \tag{5}$$

Sensitivity: This is the ratio of actual positives to predicted positives.

$$Sensitivity = \frac{TP}{TP + TN} \tag{6}$$

Precision: It is the ratio of relevant samples that are true positives out of all the samples which were predicted to belong in a certain class.

$$Precision = \frac{TP}{TP + FP} \tag{7}$$

Mathews Correlation Coefficient (MCC): The quality of multiclass classification in machine learning is measured using MCC. Because, it considers both true and false positives and negatives, regardless of class size, it is commonly viewed as a balanced metric. It stores correlation coefficients between -1 and $+1$, with $+1$ indicating a perfect prediction, 0 indicating an average random prediction, and -1 indicating a reverse prediction. It is defined as follows:

$$MCC = \frac{(TP.TN) - (TP.FN)}{\sqrt{(TP + FP).(TP + FN).(TN + FP).(TN + FN)}} \tag{8}$$

Alternatively, given a matrix C with k classes, MCC can be computed as:

$$MCC = \frac{c \times s - \sum_k^K p_k \times t_k}{\sqrt{(s^2 - \sum_k^K p^2)(s^2 - \sum_k^K p_k \times t_k^2)}} \tag{9}$$

where;

$c = \sum_k^K C_k k$ represent sum of correctly predicted elements

$s = \sum_i^k \sum_j^K C_i j$ represent cumulative sum of elements

$p_k = \sum_i^K C_k i$ total number of occurrences of class k prediction

$t_k = \sum_i^K C_k i$ number of true occurrence of class k

However, the high performance of a given method or algorithm can be measured by corresponding high sensitivity and specificity. Investigation from this study reveals that MCC has not witnessed huge application as others in both binary and multi-class classification problems.

4   Speech Emotion Classification: A Critical Analysis of State-of-the-Art Techniques and Algorithms

Various Deep Neural Network (DNN) algorithms for speech emotion classification have been developed and applied in the past. DNN has a general framework of an input layer, several hidden layers and an output layer. Speech features are usually extracted through the hidden layer of a typical deep-learning algorithm for speech emotion classification. This section describes how some algorithms have been used to classify emotions using one or more speech corpus, and their corresponding performance. Table 2 shows the performance evaluation results of these algorithms. In [29] a machine learning approach (KNN, SVM, DT and Random Forest) for classifying speech emotion from the speech signal was presented. MFCC was used in extracting the features from the spectrogram because of its dimensionality and computational time reduction capability it possessed. Average accuracy of 75%, 90% sensitivity and 91% of specificity was reported after an experiment was carried out using TESS and KEEL speech datasets. However, most of the algorithms used in this work in detecting emotion from the speech were conventional and may not be able to handle a large dataset as obtainable in neural network techniques. Also, only MFCC cannot yield a high recognition rate of emotion.

Using a Recurrent Neural Network (RNN) and Multi-Head attention-based mechanism, [30] proposed a multimodal-based approach for SEC. The proposed approach is based on two different forms of speech representations: the MFCC of an audio signal and word embedding from text data. They achieve state-of-the-art performance on the IEMOCAP, MELD, and CMU-MOSEI datasets by training these features in temporal space. Though a higher rate of accuracy was recorded, no fine-tunning in the model was adopted and also other speech features like chroma and prosodic were not captured. The algorithm is susceptible to gradient vanishing and difficulty in training.

In [31], a Multi-scale discrepancy adversarial network for cross-corpus speech emotion classification that uses various timelines of deep speech features to simultaneously train a collection of hierarchical domain discriminators and an emotion classifier in an adversarial training network was proposed. To determine cross-corpus efficiency, the research was bench-marked on three major speech datasets (IEMOCAP, CASIA, and MSP), each of which contained two different languages (English and Chinese). Although there was considerable improvement, no baseline comparison was carried out.

A robust and versatile deep learning emotion recognition system based on the analysis of speech signals using a combination of MFCC, HNR, ZCR and TEO parameters with SVM at first and later with Auto-Encoder (AE) was proposed in [32]. An RML (Ryerson Multimedia Lab) emotion corpus consisting of 720 auditory human emotional expression samples of Anger, Disgust, Happy, Fear, Surprise and Sad were employed. About six languages were contained in the corpus used for this work. They show that auto-encoder dimension reduction can improve recognition rate with an accuracy score of 74.07% and 72.83% for both methods as against another baseline approach of emotion classification. The ability to maintain the same accuracy score and recognition rate with multiple speech databases of larger samples is of major concern in this work.

In the work of [33], an improved speech emotion classification using transfer learning with spectrogram augmentation was presented. Transfer learning is a deep learning technique that leverages a pre-trained neural network model. It usually yields better results even with a small dataset. A pre-trained ResNet model was adopted in their work and features were extracted from high-resolution log-Mel spectro-grams using the convolution layer of the neural network model. Additional data samples were generated through spectrogram augmentation. The performance evaluation of their work was carried out on the interactive emotional dyadic motion capture (IEMOCAP) dataset and the result indicated that transfer learning with spectrogram augmentation can improve the rate of emotion recognition. However, the mode of fine-tuning of pre-trained neural network model which is the major key in transfer learning was not stated. Also, loss of feature or distortion on the spectrogram image can occur if the augmentation technique of the data sample is not efficient. This work did show a comparison of the original spectrogram data and augmented ones if the quality remains the same before feeding it into the CNN model adopted. Both facial and audio data were utilized in [6] to perform embedding extraction and fine-tuning a transfer learning model for multimodal emotion classification. Despite the poorer performance of the visual modality compared to the speech modality, after fine-tuning the Convolution Neural Network (CNN)-14, the fusion of both inputs yielded 80.08% emotion classification accuracy.

Zhang et al. [34] applied DCNN-BLSTMwA for enhanced speech motion classification. Speech samples were first preprocessed by data enhancement and dataset balancing. Their model was pre-trained on ImageNet architecture to generate the segment-level features. Eventually, the Deep Neural Network (DNN) was fed with learned high-level emotional features in order to predict human emotion. The result of the performance analysis of the proposed model was carried out on two popular speech databases (EMO-DB and IEMOCAP). An average score of 87.86% and 68.50% for Sensitivity and Specificity was recorded respectively. The work shows high performance in recognition, but the model tends to require high computational time and a large dataset. To improve the accuracy of a speech emotion classification, a novel feature reduction approach was proposed in [35]. They used OpenSMILE-2.3.0 to extract speech feature sets, such as the waveform, Mel/Bark spectrum, FFT spectrum, speech quality, signal energy, and formant, to mention but a few for a total of 384-dimensional features, at the feature extraction stage of their work. The result showed an accuracy score of 83.70%. Dangol et al. [36], proposed a 3D-CNN-based LSTM network with a relation-aware attention mechanism for speech emotion classification. The peculiar situation of overfitting was overcome by oversampling and deep learning black box techniques. A higher accuracy score of 81.05% in detecting mood disorders was achieved after the training of the model. Atila & Şengür, [37] applied 3D CNN-LSTM and attention for accurate classification of speech emotion. In their proposed method, six 3D CNN, two batch normalizations, five ReLu activation, three 3D max pooling and one LSTM layer were used. An experiment was carried out on three datasets (RAVDESS, RML, SAVEE). The novel approach achieved 94.17% sensitivity and 99.09% specificity which proved the efficiency of their model.

Table 2. Summary of comparison of State-of-the-art algorithm

Techniques	Year	Dataset	No. Emotion	Reported accuracy
ANN-LSTM [38]	2017	LDC	4	87.5%
ANFIS-MLP [10]	2017	Berlin EOMD	3	72.5%
Multi-SVNN [39]	2018	Berlin EOMD	–	81.37%
Deep RNN [40]	2018	IEMOCAP	4	70.0%
Deep CNN-LSTM [41]	2019	USC-IEMOCAP	3	52.90%
Transfer Learning SoundNet [3]	2019	MASC	6	73.6%
2D, 3D CNN-LSTM [42]	2019	AEFW	7	60.9%
Deep learning 39 MFCC-HNR-ZCR-TEO [32]	2020	RML	6	72.5%
Transfer learning Siamese NN [42]	2020	RAVDESS, CREMA, eENTER-FACE05	4	50.0%
CNN-LSTM [36]	2020	IEMOCAP, Berlin EOMD, SAVEE	4	84.6%
MFCC-NSL [43]	2020	Synthetic	4	84.25%
HSF-DNN, MS-CNN, LLD-RNN [44]	2020	IEMOCAP	4	53.6%
Deep learning GoogleNet	2020	DEAP	3	83.59%
3D CNN-LSTM [37]	2021	RAVDESS, RML, SAVEE	8	96.18%
3D CNN-Esemble learning [45]	2021	DEAP	Valence/Arousal	96.13%
Transfer learning CNN-14 from PAN [6]	2021	RAVDESS	8	76.58%
Deep learning fusion spatial feature [46]	2021	IEMOCAP, RAVEDESS	4, 8	77.5%
Transfer learning Wav2vec2.0 [47]	2021	RAVDESS	8	80.46%
EEG-BiLSTM-DRNN [48]	2022	DEAP, SEED, IDEA	8	59.0%
CNN-BiLSTM-MLP-FSL [49]	2022	Prototype utterance	–	39.0%
DCERNet-SVM [50]	2022	DEAP	4	93.0%

5   Conclusion

Human auditory speech possessed innate features for accurate prediction of emotion, as compared to facial expression, hence the reason why SEC has been attracting huge researchers globally in the past decades. The state-of-the-art techniques for speech emotion classification have been critically and analytically surveyed in this study. The performance of some algorithms as well as evaluation metrics for speech emotion classification were investigated. The strengths and weaknesses of these algorithms were also examined. It was observed that the application of machine learning techniques such as deep learning and transfer learning for performing analysis on speech signals gives a better performance in speech analysis most especially in the classification of speech emotion. The growth of research in speech emotion classification has indeed witnessed a sporadic increase in the last five years and yet is still increasing, through the application of deep learning as it was revealed through some scientific journals, online repositories and archives.

References

1. Pham, N., Dang, D., Nguyen, S.: A method upon deep learning for speech emotion recognition. J. Adv. Eng. Comput. **4**, 273–285 (2020). https://doi.org/10.25073/jaec.202044.311
2. Chenchah, F., Lachiri, Z.: Speech emotion recognition in acted and spontaneous context. Procedia Comput. Sci. **39**(C), 139–145 (2014). https://doi.org/10.1016/j.procs.2014.11.020
3. ElShaer, M.E.A., Wisdom, S., Mishra, T.: Transfer learning from sound representations for anger detection in speech (2019). arXiv:1902.02120
4. Papakostas, M., Giannakopoulos, T.: Speech-music discrimination using deep visual feature extractors. Expert Syst. Appl. **114**, 334–344 (2018). https://doi.org/10.1016/j.eswa.2018.05.016
5. El Ayadi, M., Kamel, M.S., Karray, F.: Survey on speech emotion recognition: Features, classification schemes, and databases. Pattern Recogn. **44**(3), 572–587 (2011). https://doi.org/10.1016/j.patcog.2010.09.020
6. Luna-Jiménez, C., et al.: A proposal for multimodal emotion recognition using aural transformer on RAVDESS. Appl. Sci. MDPI **12**, 327 (2022). https://doi.org/10.3390/app12010327
7. Izard, C.: Emotion theory and research: highlights, unanswered questions, and emerging issues. Annu. Rev. Psychol. **60**(3955), 1–25 (2009). https://doi.org/10.1146/annurev.psych.60.110707.163539
8. Ekman, P.: Basic-Emotions by Paul Ekman. Book Chapter, San Franciso, USA (1993)
9. Lu, Y.: Transfer learning for image classification (2019). https://tel.archives-ouvertes.fr/tel-02065405
10. Motamed, S., Setayesh, A., Rabiee, A.: Speech emotion recognition based on a modified brain emotional learning model. Biologically Inspired Cogn. Archit. **19**, 32–38 (2017). https://doi.org/10.1016/j.bica.2016.12.002
11. Wang, Y., Boumadane, A., Heba, A.: A Fine-tuned Wav2vec 2.0/Hubert Benchmark For speech emotion recognition, speaker verification and spoken language understanding (2021). arXiv:2111.02735

12. Pérez-Ortiz, M., Jiménez-Fernández, S., Gutiérrez, P.A., Alexandre, E., Hervás-Martínez, C., Salcedo-Sanz, S.: A review of classification problems and algorithms in renewable energy applications. Energies MDPI **9**(8), 607 (2016). https://doi.org/10.3390/en9080607

13. Vijaya, R., Reddy, K., Ravi-Babu, U: A Review on Classification Techniques in Machine Learning (2018). www.ijarse.com

14. Mulongo, B., Pihlqvist, F: Speech emotion recognition: using rule-based methods and machine learning for short answer scoring. KTH Royal Institute of Technology, trita-eecs-ex (2018). https://www.kth.se/en

15. Jasmeet-Kaur, A.: Databases, features and classification techniques for speech emotion recognition. Int. J. Innovative Technol. Exploring Eng. **9**(6), 185–190 (2020)

16. Seehapoch, T., Wongthanavasu, S.: Speech emotion recognition using support vector machines. In: Proceedings of the 2013 5th International Conference on Knowledge and Smart Technology, KST, vol. 6(2), pp. 101–108 (2013). https://doi.org/10.1109/kst.2013.6512793

17. Farooq, M., Hussain, F., Baloch, N., Raja, F., Yu, H., Zikria, Y.: Impact of feature selection algorithm on speech emotion recognition using deep convolutional neural network. Sensors **20**(21), 1–18 (2020). https://doi.org/10.3390/s20216008

18. New, T.L., Foo, S.W., De Silva, L.C.: Detection of stress and emotion in speech using traditional and FFT based log energy features. In: ICICS-PCM Proceedings of the 2003 Joint Conference of the 4th International Conference on Information, Communications and Signal Processing and 4th Pacific-Rim Conference on Multimedia, vol. 3, pp. 1619–1623 (2003)

19. Rejith, S., Manju, K. G.: Speech based emotion recognition in Tamil and Telugu using LPCC and Hurst parameters- a comparative study using KNN and ANN classifiers. In: Proceedings of IEEE International Conference on Circuit, Power and Computing Technologies, ICCPCT, pp. 1–6 (2017)

20. Yuncu, E., Hacihabiboglu, H., Bozsahin, C.: Automatic speech emotion recognition using auditory models with binary decision tree and SVM. In: Proceedings of International Conference on Pattern Recognition, pp. 773–778 (2014). https://doi.org/10.1109/ICPR.2014.143

21. Schnall, A., Heckmann, M.: Feature-space SVM adaptation for speaker adapted word prominence detection. Comput. Speech Lang. **53**, 198–216 (2019). https://doi.org/10.1016/j.csl.2018.06.001

22. Mao, S., Tao, D., Zhang, G., Ching, P.C., Lee, T.: Revisiting hidden Markov models for speech emotion recognition. In: ICASSP 2019 IEEE International Conference on Acoustics, Speech and Signal Processing (ICASSP), vol. 2, pp. 6715–6719 (2019)

23. Chakraborty, C., Talukdar, P.: Issues and limitations of HMM in speech processing: a survey. Int. J. Comput. Appl. **141**, 13–17 (2016). https://doi.org/10.5120/ijca2016909693

24. Degirmenci, A.: Introduction to Hidden Markov Models (2014). https://scholar.harvard.edu/files/adegirmenci/files/hmm_adegirmenci_2014.pdf

25. Venkata Subbarao, M., Terlapu, S.K., Geethika, N., Harika, K.D.: Speech emotion recognition using k-nearest neighbor classifiers. In: Shetty D., P., Shetty, S. (eds.) Recent Advances in Artificial Intelligence and Data Engineering. AISC, vol. 1386, pp. 123–131. Springer, Singapore (2022). https://doi.org/10.1007/978-981-16-3342-3_10

26. Liu, Z., Wu, M., Cao, W., Mao, J., Xu, J., Tan, G.: Impact of feature selection algorithm on speech emotion recognition using deep convolutional neural network. Sensors **273**, 271–280 (2018). https://doi.org/10.1016/j.neucom.2017.07.050

27. Kim, M., Yoo, J., Kim, Y., Kim, H.: Speech emotion classification using tree-structured sparse logistic regression. Interspeech **12**, 1541–1545 (2015). https://doi.org/10.21437/Interspeech.2015-337

28. Grandini, M., Bagli, E., Visani, G.: Speech emotion detection using machine learning techniques (2020). arXiv:2008.05756

29. Sundarprasad, N.: Metrics for multi-class classification: an overview (2018). https://doi.org/10.31979/etd.a5c2-v7e2

30. Ho, N., Yang, H., Kim, S., Lee, G.: Multimodal approach of speech emotion recognition using multi-level multi-head fusion attention-based recurrent neural network. IEEE Access **8**, 61672–61686 (2020). https://doi.org/10.1109/ACCESS.2020.2984368

31. Wanlu, Z., Wenming, Z., Yuan, Z.: Multi-scale discrepancy adversarial network for cross-corpus speech emotion recognition. Virtual Real. Intell. Hardw. **3**(1), 57–76 (2022). https://doi.org/10.1007/s40747-021-00637-x

32. Aouani, H., Ayed, Y.: Speech emotion recognition with deep learning. Procedia Comput. Sci. **176**, 248–260 (2020). https://doi.org/10.1016/j.procs.2020.08.027

33. Padi, S., Sadjadi, S., Sriram, R., Manocha, D.: Improved speech emotion recognition using transfer learning and Spectro-gram augmentation. In: ICMI- Proceedings of the International Conference on Multimodal Interaction, pp. 645–652 (2021). https://doi.org/10.1145/3462244.3481003

34. Zhang, H., Gou, R., Shang, J., Shen, F., Wu, Y., Dai, G.: Pre-trained deep convolution neural network model with attention for speech emotion recognition. Front. Physiol. **12**, 643202 (2021). https://doi.org/10.3389/fphys.2021.643202

35. Zhang, Z.: Speech feature selection and emotion recognition based on weighted binary cuckoo search. Alex. Eng. J. **60**(1), 1499–1507 (2019). https://doi.org/10.1016/j.aej.2020.11.004

36. Dangol, R., Alsadoon, A., Prasad, P.W.C., Seher, I., Alsadoon, O.H.: Speech emotion recognition UsingConvolutional neural network and long-short TermMemory. Multimed. Tools Appl. **79**(43), 32917–32934 (2020). https://doi.org/10.1007/s11042-020-09693-w

37. Atila, O., Şengür, A.: Attention guided 3D CNN-LSTM model for accurate speech-based emotion recognition. Appl. Acoust. **182**, 108260 (2021). https://doi.org/10.1016/j.apacoust.2021.108260. Frontiers in Physiology, 12

38. Thirukumaran, S., Archana, A.F.C.: Speech emotion classification analysis using short-term features. Fron. Physiol. J. Sci. EUSL **8**(1), 13–22 (2017)

39. Mannepalli, K., Sastry, P., Suman, M.: Emotion recognition in speech signals using optimization based multi-SVNN classifier. J. King Saud Univ. Comput. Inf. Sci. **34**, 384–397 (2018). https://doi.org/10.1016/j.jksuci.2018.11.012

40. Chernykh, V., Prikhodko, P. Emotion recognition from speech with recurrent neural networks (2018). arXiv:1701.08071v2. [CsCL]

41. Cho, J., Pappagari, R., Kulkarni, P., Villalba, J., Carmiel, Y., Dehak, N.: Deep neural networks for emotion recognition combining audio and transcripts (2019). arXiv:1911.00432

42. Ren, M., Nie, W., Liu, A., Su, Y.: Multi-modal correlated network for emotion recognition in speech. Vis. Inform. **3**(3), 150–155 (2019). https://doi.org/10.1016/j.visinf.2019.10.003

43. Uddin, M., Nilsson, E.: Emotion recognition using speech and neural structured learning to facilitate edge intelligence. Eng. Appl. Artif. Intell. **94**, 103775 (2020). https://doi.org/10.1016/j.engappai.2020.103775

44. Yao, Z., Wang, Z., Liu, W., Liu, Y., Pan, J.: Speech emotion recognition using fusion of three multi-task learning-based classifiers: HSF-DNN, MS-CNN and LLD-RNN. Speech Commun. **120**, 11–19 (2020). https://doi.org/10.1016/j.specom.2020.03.005

45. Salama, E.S., El-Khoribi, R.A., Shoman, M.E., Wahby Shalaby, M.A.: A 3D-convolutional neural network framework with ensemble learning techniques for multi-modal emotion recognition. Egypt. Inform. J. **22**(2), 167–176 (2021). https://doi.org/10.1016/j.eij.2020.07.005

46. An, X., Ruan, Z.: Speech Emotion Recognition algorithm based on deep learning algorithm fusion of temporal and spatial features. J. Phys.: Conf. Ser. **1861**(1), 012064 (2021). https://doi.org/10.1088/1742-6596/1861/1/012064

47. Pepino, L., Riera, P., Ferrer, L.: Emotion recognition from speech using Wav2vec 2.0 embeddings (2021). arXiv:2104.03502

48. Joshi, V., Ghongade, R., Joshi, A., Kulkarni, R.: Deep BiLSTM neural network model for emotion detection using cross-dataset approach. Biomed. Signal Proc. Control **73**, 103407 (2022). https://doi.org/10.1016/j.bspc.2021.103407

49. Guibon, G., Labeau, M., Lefeuvre, L., Clavel, C.: Few-shot emotion recognition in conversation with sequential prototypical networks. Softw. Impacts **12**, 100237 (2022). https://doi.org/10.1016/j.simpa.2022.100237

50. Pusarla, A., Singh, B., Tripathi, C.: Learning DenseNet features from EEG based spectrograms for subject independent emotion recognition. Biomed. Signal Proc. Control **74**, 103485 (2022). https://doi.org/10.1016/j.bspc.2022.103485

Intelligent Transportation Systems

Forward Obstacle Detection
by Unmanned Aerial Vehicles

Hervé B. Olou[1](✉), Eugène C. Ezin[1,2], Jean Marie Dembele[3,4],
and Christophe Cambier[4]

[1] Institut de Mathématiques et de Sciences Physiques, University of Abomey-Calavi,
Porto-Novo, Benin
{herve.olou,eugene.ezin}@imsp-uac.org
[2] Institut de Formation et de Recherche en Informatique,
University of Abomey-Calavi, Abomey-Calavi, Benin
eugene.ezin@uac.bj
[3] Unité de Formation et de Recherche de Sciences Appliquées et de Technologies,
University of Gaston Berger, Saint-Louis, Senegal
jean-marie.dembele@ugb.edu.sn
[4] Unité de Modélisation Mathématique et Informatique des Systèmes Complexes,
Institut de Recherche et de Développement, Dakar, Senegal
christophe.cambier@ird.fr

Abstract. The automation of unmanned aerial vehicles is an active
research area. Among different techniques for Unmanned Aerial Vehicle (UAV) automation, obstacle detection is gaining attention to ensure
UAV safety flights. This paper presents an algorithm that can be embedded on an UAV to detect forward obstacles. This algorithm is based on
a fast and accurate object detection model combining CenterNet and
MobileNetV2. This model is pre-trained on the Microsoft COCO 2017
dataset and allowed us to identify obstacle zone in images from the UAV's
front camera. After obstacle detection, this algorithm proposes new directions to be followed by the UAV. These directions are left, right, or up to
avoid obstacles. The proposed algorithm detects obstacles and proposes
new directions to avoid obstacles by only using a frontal camera. It is
sized to be embedded on Raspberry Pi 4b and runs in about 800 ms.
It may be combined with the UAV's coordinates and mission path to
regenerate a new mission path in an unknown environment.

Keywords: Unmanned aerial vehicle · Obstacle detection ·
CenterNet · MobileNetV2 · Raspberry Pi

1 Introduction

Unmanned aerial vehicles or drones are no longer used only in the military field.
Thanks to technological advances, they are inexpensive, small, and user-friendly.

Supported by the Digital Science and Technology Network (DSTN).

T. M. Ngatched Nkouatchah et al. (Eds.): PAAISS 2022, LNICST 459, pp. 397–410, 2023.
https://doi.org/10.1007/978-3-031-25271-6_25

Many of them are used for civilian purposes such as delivery services, photography, inspection, agriculture, etc. But for missions like inspection, they should be piloted by experts to avoid piloting errors during flight. Many applications exist to allow an Unmanned Aerial Vehicle (UAV) to fly without human intervention. Applications like Litchi [1], Skygrid [2] and MavenPilot [3] are autonomous flight applications for DJI drones [4]. They are generally used to plan missions with waypoints using the GPS coordinates of the UAV and the planned flight plan. These applications are only adapted to DJI drones and do not take into account obstacle detection and avoidance. They only follow the predefined waypoints and this plan can be modified after the detection of an obstacle.

Obstacle detection and obstacle avoidance are active research areas. Many researchers have proposed solutions to enable an UAV to detect and avoid obstacles in real-time. These solutions are usually based on the use of data from onboard sensors or images from the drone's front camera. By using onboard sensors such as Ultrasonic, Lidar, and Radar sensors, they calculate the distance between the drone and a frontal object. If this distance is small, the drone's next actions should be defined. But these sensors must be used with caution, as they can be affected by external factors like angular range, pressure change, moving sensor, and object [5]. Moreover, solutions based on many sensors are avoided due to limitations in energy, memory, and computational resources [6].

The monocular camera is inexpensive, lightweight, and has low power consumption. It comes as an alternative to the previous limitations cited. In many research works, researchers have embedded it in the UAV front and proposed deep learning based models to detect and avoid frontal obstacles by using images from this camera [6,19,26,27,29]. Deep learning techniques have excellent performance in extracting information from images [7]. But these techniques are also computationally expensive.

In this work, we focus only on solution-based on deep learning to detect and avoid frontal obstacles. By making a trade-off between model performance and execution speed, we propose an algorithm that detects and proposes new directions possibility in real-time to allow the UAV to execute a regenerated path algorithm. This algorithm is run on a lower computational resource.

The remainder of this paper is organized as follows: Sect. 2 presents related work. Section 3 shows the methodology used to implement our approach. Section 4 presents fast object detection models. Section 5 describes the proposed approach. Section 6 shows the experimental results of our work followed by their discussion. Section 7 presents the conclusion and future work.

2   Related Work

Kanellakis and Nikolakopoulos reviewed the use of computer vision techniques on Unmanned Aerial Vehicles (UAVs) [25]. The review was conducted on attitude control, position estimation, and obstacle detection. They mentioned that cameras are used for range measurement tasks, obstacle avoidance, and mapping. Unfortunately, the existing computer vision techniques used with UAVs are computationally expensive.

In [26], Valencia and Kim presented a method based on video streams to detect obstacles. Video streams from the frontal camera are sent to the base station via WiFi for obstacle detection. Their technique divides the received image into several squares; calculates the intensity of each square, and compares the intensity with a certain threshold to detect and locate obstacles. This technique has been tested virtually on a Gazebo simulator [8].

Raheem Nhair and Al-Assadi in [27] proposed a technique to avoid obstacles using a monocular camera by using computer vision techniques to identify the free areas around the obstacle first. Then, the next path of the drone is indicated. Their technique segments image into five and based on the number of white pixels in each segment, they indicate the area with obstacles or not.

From [25–27], the time and space complexity of computer vision algorithms are present. Machine learning techniques can provide a solution to these complexity problems and enable drones to quickly react.

Chen et al. in [29] proposed a navigation system based on object detection and deep reinforcement learning by using data from a monocular camera mounted on the UAV. They used MobileNetV2 with SSDLite for object detection. This object detection model allows them to speed up the learning process and avoid bad prediction errors thus avoiding crashes. The next action is chosen by combining the main information of the map and the predictions made. It uses the current position of the drone, the distance of the drone from the different nearby objects, and the prediction of the movement made previously based on the detection of the boxes.

In [21], Smolyanskiy assembled their UAV for autonomously following trails in forests. They used YOLO [9] model to detect pets and people on the trail.

Anand and Kumawat used CNN for object detection and position tracking in real-time using Raspberry Pi [19]. They proposed an efficient method of object identification based on shape and its real-time motion using the OpenCV library of programming roles primarily for computer vision and the Raspberry Pi with a camera module.

Pyo et al. presented in [20] a front collision warning for vehicles. It is used to detect the vehicle in front. Then, the distance between these vehicles is calculated to define the next action of the vehicle.

In [22], Chen et al. proposed an object detection, localization, and tracking system for smart mobility applications like traffic road and railway environments. By comparing, You Only Look Once (YOLO) [9] V3 and Single Shot Detector [23] (SSD) to determine which one is adapted to their project. Then, they apply SSD to determine if the trajectory of a pedestrian or vehicle can lead to a dangerous situation.

3 Methodology

This work aims to propose an approach that presents new directions for an autonomous Unmanned Aerial Vehicle (UAV) based on the obstacle position in the image from UAV frontal camera. This algorithm should be run in real-time on lower computational resources like Raspberry Pi 4b. To achieve this goal, we proceeded as follows :

- We start by identifying a fast object detection model that can be run on Raspberry Pi 4b. This model should be able to detect cars, pedestrians, cats, dogs, trees, traffic lights, buildings, birds, etc.
- We then propose an algorithm to detect objects as obstacles to the UAV. An avoidance zone is identified to propose commands which must be executed by avoiding collision between the UAV and the obstacles.
- Finally, new directions are proposed based on the free space in the image. Free space is calculated thanks to the obstacle zone size and image size.

4   Fast Object Detection

Obstacle detection is the detection of any objects which can interrupt an UAV during the flight. A collision with such objects can affect the integrity of the UAV during a mission. These objects may be persons, pets, buildings, trees, etc. In this section, we present existing object detection models. According to the platform, these models' architectures are different. We focus on models running on the CPU platform.

Object detection models have two main parts: a backbone for extracting semantic features and a head for classes prediction and object bounding boxes [12].

Backbones are commonly pre-trained on ImageNet [10] or Microsoft COCO [11] datasets. The most representative backbone are SqueezeNet [30], MobileNet [15,16], or ShuffleNet [17]. MobileNetV2 is designed to be faster and more accurate than ShuffleNet and MobiletNetV1 for feature extraction tasks.

On another hand, we have two types of head: one-stage detector and two-stage detector. As one-stage detector, the most representative models are YOLO [9], SSD [23], and RetinaNet [24]. The most representative two-stage object detector is the R-CNN series (faster R-CNN [31], Mask-RCNN [32], etc.). The latter is commonly known to be more accurate than the former but their execution time is slow due to the bounding box refinement operation during the second stage. This operation is more time-consuming as compared to one-stage detectors [13].

In recent works, researchers develop the anchor-free one-stage detector. The most representative is the CenterNet. It is an end-to-end differentiable, simpler, faster, and more accurate than corresponding bounding box based detectors [18].

In [14], they provide a collection of detection models pre-trained on the Microsoft COCO 2017 dataset [11]. These models are presented with their execution speed in milliseconds and their mean average precision (mAP) on the Microsoft COCO dataset. They don't describe how the experiment was done. Table 1 presents faster models of this collection.

As we can see in Table 1, the model combining MobileNetV2 as backbone, and CenterNet as head is faster than others. It has the second best mean average precision (mAP). In this work, we use it to implement our approach.

Table 1. Fast models from the collection of detection models pre-trained on the COCO 2017 dataset

Model name	Speed	COCO mAP
SSD MobileNet v2 320 × 320	19	20.2
SSD MobileNet V1 FPN 640 × 640	48	29.1
SSD MobileNet V2 FPNLite 320 × 320	22	22.2
CenterNet + MobileNetv2 + FPN (512 × 512)	6	23.4

5   Proposed Approach

In this section, we present the proposed approach. Figure 1 shows the flow chart of the proposed approach.

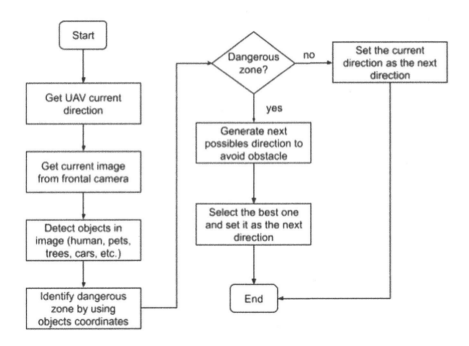

Fig. 1. Flow chart of the proposed approach.

The proposed approach consists of getting the current direction of the UAV and the current image from the UAV frontal camera to estimate the best direction in order to avoid the frontal obstacle. As presented in Algorithm 1, it is mainly based on three functions: avoid_zone(), free_directions(), and best_direction().

Algorithm 1: The proposed approach's algorithm

Data: *image_width, image_height, current_image, current_direction*
Result: *new_direction*
red_zone ← avoid_zone(current_image);
if *(red_zone != NULL)* **then**
| directions ← free_directions(image_width, image_height, red_zone) ;
| new_direction ← best_direction(directions) ;
else
| new_direction ← current_direction;
end

5.1   Presentation of the Function avoid_zone()

avoid_zone() function detects objects in the current image from the frontal camera and returns the dangerous zone in this image by combining the central detected objects box. Its input parameter is the current image from the front camera. Algorithm 2 presents avoid_zone() function algorithm.

As mentioned previously, the CenterNet+MobileNetV2+FPN object detection model is used to detect objects present in images. This model returns different objects' classes and boxes representing each object's position in the image.

Dangerous zone is represented by a box named *red_zone* in Fig. 2. It is represented by a unique box that combines all detected objects in the center of the image by the object detection model. Let's mention that the *red_zone* must be avoided by the UAV.

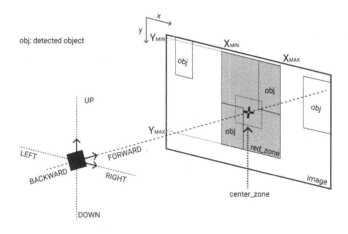

Fig. 2. Image from the frontal camera of drone

The big frame in Fig. 2 represents the current image from the frontal camera and the object detection. The black square with arrows represents the UAV. It

---

Algorithm 2: Function avoid_zone()

Data: *center_zone, current_image*
/* avoid_zone function gets current_image and returns red_zone   */
Function avoid_zone(*current_image*):

    int red_zone[] $\leftarrow$ Array();
    boxes $\leftarrow$ object_detection_model(current_image) ;
    for *(int i $\leftarrow$ 0; i < sizeof(boxes); i++)* **do**
        if *(boxes[i]["X_{max}"] $\geq$ center_zone["X_{min}"] and boxes[i]["X_{min}"] $\leq$ center_zone["X_{max}"])* **and** *(boxes[i]["Y_{max}"] $\geq$ center_zone["Y_{min}"] and boxes[i]["Y_{min}"] $\leq$ center_zone["Y_{max}"])* **then**
            if *(red_zone = NULL)* **then**
                red_zone["X_{max}"] $\leftarrow$ boxes[i]["X_{max}"] ;
                red_zone["X_{min}"] $\leftarrow$ boxes[i]["X_{min}"] ;
                red_zone["Y_{max}"] $\leftarrow$ boxes[i]["Y_{max}"] ;
                red_zone["Y_{min}"] $\leftarrow$ boxes[i]["Y_{min}"] ;
            else
                if *(red_zone["X_{max}"]<boxes[i]["X_{max}"])* **then**
                  | red_zone["X_{max}"] $\leftarrow$ boxes[i]["X_{max}"] ;
                end
                if *(red_zone["X_{min}"]>boxes[i]["X_{min}"])* **then**
                  | red_zone["X_{min}"] $\leftarrow$ boxes[i]["X_{min}"] ;
                end
                if *(red_zone["Y_{max}"]<boxes[i]["Y_{max}"])* **then**
                  | red_zone["Y_{max}"] $\leftarrow$ boxes[i]["Y_{max}"] ;
                end
                if *(red_zone["Y_{min}"]>boxes[i]["Y_{min}"])* **then**
                  | red_zone["Y_{min}"] $\leftarrow$ boxes[i]["Y_{min}"] ;
                end
            end
        end
    end
    return red_zone;
end

---

can move forward, backward, up, down, left, and right. To simplify the figure, we do not represent rotation angle (turn left or right). The boxes with solid borders and empty fill represent objects detected by the selected model with a high confidence value.

By default, the UAV is planned to move forward which represents the center of the frame. That zone is named *center_zone* and it is represented by a dashed square and the operator plus. That zone must be a safe zone.

If no object is detected, *avoid_zone* function will return null value. Else, the coordinates of detected objects are used to identify those which are in front of the UAV and represent a danger. We only focus on obstacles present in the image center (named *center_zone*). By combining the coordinates of the objects present at the center of the image, we obtain the *red_zone*, a global box with all obstacles.

The coordinate of this box is obtained by using Eq. 1:

$$red\_zone = central\_zone \cup boxes\_in_i \tag{1}$$

with *boxes_in$_i$* the set of obstacles intersect, and *central_zone* the coordinate of the central box in the frame.

If the *red_zone* is empty, that means no object is detected in the center of the image so the current direction is not changed. Otherwise, the UAV direction must change. The next step is to detect the *directions* in which the UAV may be redirected to avoid the *red_zone*.

5.2   Description of free_directions() and best_direction() Functions

free_directions() function detects the possible directions in which the UAV can be redirected to. *red_zone*, and the current image height and width are used by this function to detect these directions. In this work, the possible directions are left, right, and up. These correspond to the proportion of each side of the current image (respectively left, right, and top). Algorithm 3 depicts the *free_directions* function algorithm.

Algorithm 3: Function free_directions()

Data: *image_width, image_height, red_zone*
/* free_directions returns next possibles directions to avoid
   obstacle   */
Function free_directions(*image_width, image_height, red_zone*):
    float directions[] ← Array() ;
    directions["up"] ← red_zone["Y_{min}"] / image_height ;
    directions["left"] ← red_zone["X_{min}"] / image_width ;
    directions["right"] ← 1 − (red_zone["X_{max}"] / image_width) ;
    return directions;
end

The possible directions are calculated by using Eqs. 2, 3, and 4:

$$left = \frac{X_{min}}{W_f} \tag{2}$$

$$right = 1 - \frac{X_{max}}{W_f} \tag{3}$$

$$up = \frac{Y_{min}}{H_f} \tag{4}$$

with W_f the width of the frame (image); X_{min}, X_{max}, Y_{min} and Y_{max} the *red_zone* box coordinates; and H_f the height of the frame (image).

best_direction() function compares directions and chooses the best direction based on their value. The side with the high proportion is selected as the new direction of the UAV to avoid that zone. Algorithm 4 presents the *best_direction* function algorithm.

Algorithm 4: Function best_direction()

Data: *directions*
/* best_direction gets directions and returns the best direction to avoid obstacle   */
Function best_direction(*directions*):
    float best_value ← -1.0 ;
    string def_directions[] ← ["up","left","right"] ;
    string direction ← "up" ;
    int i ← 0 ;
    while *(i < 3)* **do**
        if *(directions[def_directions[i]] > best_value)* **then**
            best_value ← directions[def_directions[i];
            direction ← def_directions[i] ;
        end
        i++ ;
    end
    return direction;
end

By default, if the *red_zone* fills the whole frame, the UAV moves upward. So *new_direction* is up.

6   Experimental Results and Discussion

In this section, we present hardware specifications, model and processing, and tests on some images on Raspberry Pi 4b followed by a discussion of the execution time, the obstacle nature, and the new direction.

6.1   Hardware Specifications

Our goal is to detect obstacles in real-time by using priceless equipment. Then tests are made on Raspberry Pi 4b with 8 GB RAM and 1.2 GHz Quad Core CPU processor.

6.2   Model and Processing

As mention in Sect. 4, CenterNet+MobileNetV2+FPN (512 × 512) is speed and has excellent performance. We download the pre-trained model on the Microsoft COCO 2017 dataset, the associated metadata, and the labels file. We then convert the model to TensorFlow Lite (TFLite) to obtain a smaller model. TFLite is TensorFlow's lightweight solution for mobile and embedded devices [28]. It enables on-device machine learning inference with low latency and small binary size.

6.3   Test on Raspberry Pi 4b

For tests, we chose two images from the collision dataset [33]. Figure 3 presents these pictures. The left picture presents a parked truck while the second one is a parked car.

(a) Parked truck   (b) Parked car

Fig. 3. Tests pictures

We run the converted CenterNet+MobileNetV2+FPN (512 × 512) model on these pictures. The detection result is presented in Fig. 4.

In the first picture, the model perfectly detects the parked truck, three persons, and a car. In the right picture, the model detects the car and a house as a train (error).

Then, we apply our approach to detect dangerous zone and propose the new direction in each picture. We start by the Fig. 3(a). The result is presented in Fig. 5.

Only the truck is detected here as a danger. Then to avoid it, the next possible directions are :

right : 0.0
left : 0.36
up : 0.0

The best direction is to move to the left.

Then, we apply our approach to Fig. 3(b). The result is presented in Fig. 6.

(a)   (b)

Fig. 4. Object detection in tests pictures

Fig. 5. Dangerous zone detection in Fig. 3(a)

Fig. 6. Dangerous zone detection in Fig. 3(b)

Only the car is detected here as a danger. Then to avoid it, the next possible directions are :

right : 0.31
left : 0.26
up : 0.41

The best direction is to move up.

Our approach runs on Raspberry Pi 4b in about 800 *milliseconds* (*ms*).

6.4 Discussion

Obstacles detection in real-time is a challenge on Raspberry Pi 4b. This work presents some advantages and weaknesses. Discussion is made according to execution time, obstacle nature, and new direction.

Execution Time: Our approach detects obstacles and proposes the new direction in about 800 ms. This execution time is satisfying compared to other deep learning approaches on Raspberry Pi 4b. But it must be improved to allow obstacle avoidance and new path generation in real-time by the Unmanned Aerial Vehicle (UAV).

Obstacle Nature: The proposed approach detects forward obstacles and proposes a new direction to avoid them. It detects both moving and stationary obstacles. But the nature and the previous movement of the obstacle are not taken into account in the proposed new direction. These can be helpful in an unknown environment.

New Direction: This approach proposes the new direction based on the current image and the obstacles detected ahead. It is a fast algorithm that can be run on small computing resources and will always propose a safe direction. But its accuracy depends on the object detection model. If the objects are perfectly detected, the best direction to avoid the obstacles will be proposed. This proposal may not be the optimal direction.

7 Conclusion and Future Work

In this paper, we presented an approach to detect forward obstacles and propose next possible directions for an Unmanned Aerial Vehicle (UAV). It is based on CenterNet+MobileNetV2+FPN for obstacle detection. This model is accurate and adapts to lower computational resources. Our approach runs in about 800 *milliseconds* (*ms*) on Raspberry Pi 4b.

In a mission performed by an autonomous unmanned aerial vehicle, the mission path, and GPS coordinates are usually known. The next step in this work is to combine the mission path, the current coordinates of the UAV, and the new directions proposed by our algorithm to regenerate the mission path. All this must be done in real-time.

Acknowledgements. This publication was made possible through the Digital Science and Technology Network (DSTN) supported by Institut de Recherche et de Développement (IRD) and Agence Française de Développement (AFD). We would like to thank the African Center of Excellence (CEA) SMIA at the University of Abomey-Calavi in Benin and the CEA MITIC at the University of Gaston Berger in Senegal for their support.

References

1. Litchi. https://flylitchi.com/. Accessed 8 June 2022
2. Skygrid flight control. https://www.skygrid.com/flight-control/. Accessed 8 June 2022
3. Mavenpilot. https://www.mavenpilot.com/. Accessed 8 June 2022
4. DJI. https://dji.com/. Accessed 8 June 2022
5. Singh, N.A., Borschbach, M.: Effect of external factors on accuracy of distance measurement using ultrasonic sensors. In: 2017 International Conference on Signals and Systems (ICSigSys), pp. 266–271. IEEE (2017)
6. Lee, H.Y., Ho, H.W., Zhou, Y.: Deep learning-based monocular obstacle avoidance for unmanned aerial vehicle navigation in tree plantations. J. Intel. Robot. Syst. **101**(1), 1–18 (2020). https://doi.org/10.1007/s10846-020-01284-z
7. Albawi, S., Mohammed, T.A., Al-Zawi, S.: Understanding of a convolutional neural network. In: 2017 International Conference on Engineering and Technology (ICET), pp. 1–6 IEEE (2017)
8. Gazebo. http://gazebosim.org/. Accessed 8 June 2022
9. Redmon, J., Divvala, S., Girshick, R., Farhadi, A.: You only look once: unified, real-time object detection (2016). https://doi.org/10.48550/arXiv.1506.02640
10. Russakovsky, O., et al.: ImageNet large scale visual recognition challenge. Int. J. Comput. Vis. **115**(3), 211–252 (2015). https://doi.org/10.1007/s11263-015-0816-y
11. Lin, T.-Y., et al.: Microsoft COCO: common objects in context. In: Fleet, D., Pajdla, T., Schiele, B., Tuytelaars, T. (eds.) ECCV 2014. LNCS, vol. 8693, pp. 740–755. Springer, Cham (2014). https://doi.org/10.1007/978-3-319-10602-1_48
12. Bochkovskiy, A., Wang, C.-Y., Liao, H.-Y.M.: YOLOv4: optimal speed and accuracy of object detection. ArXiv200410934 Cs Eess (2020)
13. Chen, C., Liu, M., Meng, X., Xiao, W., Ju, Q.: RefineDetLite: a lightweight one-stage object detection framework for CPU-only devices. In: 2020 IEEE/CVF Conference on Computer Vision and Pattern Recognition Workshop CVPRW, pp. 2997–3007 (2020). https://doi.org/10.1109/CVPRW50498.2020.00358
14. Hongkun, Y., et al.: TensorFlow Model Garden. https://github.com/tensorflow/models. Accessed 8 June 2022
15. Howard, A.G., et al.: MobileNets: efficient convolutional neural networks for mobile vision applications. ArXiv170404861 Cs (2017)
16. Sandler, M., Howard, A., Zhu, M., Zhmoginov, A., Chen, L.-C.: MobileNetV2: inverted residuals and linear bottlenecks. ArXiv180104381 Cs (2019)
17. Zhang, X., Zhou, X., Lin, M., Sun, J.: ShuffleNet: an extremely efficient convolutional neural network for mobile devices. ArXiv170701083 Cs (2017)
18. Zhou, X., Wang, D., Krähenbühl, P.: Objects as points. ArXiv190407850 Cs (2019)
19. Anand, G., Kumawat, A.K.: Object detection and position tracking in real time using Raspberry Pi. Mater. Today Proc. **47**, 3221–3226 (2021)

20. Pyo, J., Bang, J., Jeong, Y.: Front collision warning based on vehicle detection using CNN. In: 2016 International SoC Design Conference (ISOCC), pp. 163–164. IEEE (2016). https://doi.org/10.1109/ISOCC.2016.7799842

21. Smolyanskiy, N., Kamenev, A., Smith, J., Birchfield, S.: Toward low-flying autonomous MAV trail navigation using deep neural networks for environmental awareness. ArXiv170502550 Cs (2017)

22. Chen, Z., Khemmar, R., Decoux, B., Atahouet, A., Ertaud, J.-Y.: Real time object detection, tracking, and distance and motion estimation based on deep learning: application to smart mobility. In: 2019 Eighth International Conference on Emerging Security Technologies (EST), IEEE (2019). https://doi.org/10.1109/EST.2019.8806222

23. Liu, W. et al.: SSD: Single Shot MultiBox Detector, vol. 9905, pp. 21–37 (2016)

24. Lin, T.-Y., Goyal, P., Girshick, R., He, K., Dollár, P.: Focal loss for dense object detection (2018). https://doi.org/10.48550/arXiv.1708.02002

25. Kanellakis, C., Nikolakopoulos, G.: Survey on computer vision for UAVs: current developments and trends. J. Intell. Robot. Syst. 87, 141–168 (2017). https://doi.org/10.1007/s10846-017-0483-z

26. Valencia, D., Kim, D.: Quadrotor obstacle detection and avoidance system using a monocular camera. In: 2018 3rd Asia-Pacific Conference on Intelligent Robot Systems (ACIRS), pp. 78–81. IEEE (2018). https://doi.org/10.1109/ACIRS.2018.8467248

27. Raheem Nhair, R., Al-Assadi, T.A.: Vision-based obstacle avoidance for small drone using monocular camera. IOP Conf. Ser. Mater. Sci. Eng. 928, 032048 (2020)

28. TensorFlow Lite — ML for Mobile and Edge Devices. https://www.tensorflow.org/lite. Accessed 3 July 2022

29. Chen, Y., Gonzalez-Prelcic, N., Heath, R. W.: Collision-free UAV navigation with a monocular camera using deep reinforcement learning. In: IEEE 30th International Workshop on Machine Learning for Signal Processing (MLSP), pp. 1–6. IEEE (2020). https://doi.org/10.1109/MLSP49062.2020.9231577

30. Iandola, F. N. et al.: SqueezeNet: AlexNet-level accuracy with 50x fewer parameters and < 0.5 MB model size (2016). https://doi.org/10.48550/arXiv.1602.07360

31. Ren, S., He, K., Girshick, R., Sun, J.: Faster R-CNN: towards real-time object detection with region proposal networks. In: Advances in Neural Information Processing Systems, vol. 28. Curran Associates Inc (2015)

32. He, K., Gkioxari, G., Dollár, P., Girshick, R.: Mask R-CNN (2018). https://doi.org/10.48550/arXiv.1703.06870

33. Loquercio, A., Maqueda, A.I., Del-Blanco, C.R., Scaramuzza, D.: DroNet: learning to fly by driving. IEEE Robot. Autom. Lett. 3, 1088–1095 (2018)

Multi-agent Reinforcement Learning Based Approach for Vehicle Routing Problem

Jagdeep Singh[1], Sanjay Kumar Dhurandher[2], Isaac Woungang[3(✉)], and Telex Magloire N. Ngatched[4]

[1] Department of Computer Science and Engineering, Sant Longowal Institute of Engineering and Technology, Longowal, India
[2] Department of Information Technology, Netaji Subhas University of Technology, New Delhi, India
[3] Department of Computer Science, Toronto Metropolitan University, Toronto, Canada
iwoungan@ryerson.ca
[4] Faculty of Engineering and Applied Science, Grenfell Campus, Memorial University, St. John's, Canada
tngatched@grenfell.mun.ca

Abstract. Multi-Vehicle routing to service consumers in dynamic and unpredictable surroundings such as congested urban areas is a difficult operation that needs robust and flexible planning. Value iteration networks hold promise for planning vehicle routing problems. Conventional approaches aren't usually constructed for real-life settings, and they are too slow to be useful in real time. In comparison, the Vehicle Routing Problem with Value Iteration Network (VRP-VIN) offers a neural network model based on graphs that can execute multi-agent routing in a highly dispersed but connected graph with constantly fluctuating traffic conditions using learned value iteration. Furthermore, the model's communication module allows vehicles to work better in a cooperative manner online and can easily adapt to changes. A virtual environment is constructed to simulate real-world mapping by self-driving vehicles with uncertain traffic circumstances and minimal edge coverage. This method beats standard solutions based on overall cost and run time. Experiments show that the model achieves a total cost difference of 3% when compared with a state-of-art solver having global information. Also, after being trained with only 2 agents on networks with 25 nodes, can easily generalize to a scenario having additional agents (or nodes).

Keywords: Reinforcement learning · Vehicle routing problem · Value iteration networks · Graph attention layer · Multi-agent communication

1 Introduction

As vehicles grow increasingly widespread, one of the most basic issues is understanding how to navigate a fleet of vehicles to perform a specified job. Also,

T. M. Ngatched Nkouatchah et al. (Eds.): PAAISS 2022, LNICST 459, pp. 411–422, 2023.
https://doi.org/10.1007/978-3-031-25271-6_26

the huge population densities in our cities today put all existing infrastructure, especially urban transportation networks, under strain. With the progression of services like e-commerce and vehicle sharing, these congested cities' transportation demands have also gotten more complicated. So, it is very important to route vehicles in way so as to reduce overall cost, time, and congestion. Different methods [1] have been proposed to route vehicles. One of the classic methods in which a single agent is entrusted with determining the shortest path between a set of sites and destinations is known as Travelling Salesperson Problem. The multi-agent approach to this problem is called the Vehicle Routing Problem (VRP) [2]. In VRP, multiple agents try to find an optimal route by visiting a set of locations exactly once. Even after having a huge number of solvers, they are primarily built to perform planning offline and cannot modify solutions when used online. They are, however, often evaluated on simple planar network benchmarks with limited exploration in multi-agent environments. Furthermore, none of these solutions were created for dynamic contexts where online communication may be quite advantageous.

The Value Iteration Networks [3] have excellent planning capability and can generalize better in a diverse set of tasks. Its purpose is to discover a policy that optimizes expected returns. The value function peak at the goal, so the high-value function mean the destination. In the attention mechanism, only a subset of the input characteristics (value function) is meaningful for a specific label prediction (action). It is also well known that attention improves learning performance by lowering the effective number of network parameters used during learning. We have given a fleet of cars in a multi-agent environment. We have to determine the minimum total cost for mapping a given graph under traffic conditions, such that all routes are traversed not less than a defined number, and this number is not known prior. The Vehicle Routing Problem value iteration network is a distributed neural network designed for managing multiple vehicles intended to complete a specific task. Each agent has a value iteration module to carry out its own planning with the help of communication between agents via an attention mechanism. The dense adjacency matrix [4] is used for encoding paired edge information to accelerate information sharing and allow for more complex encoding since our focus is on sparse road graphs. Using actual traffic flow simulation, we illustrate the usefulness of VRP-VIN on actual road maps derived from eighteen different cities around the world. A random sub-graph of those cities was used to produce training and evaluation examples comprising real-world mapping difficulties, and then a random number is selected, which determines how many times each node in each graph is covered [5,6]. The fleet will be unaware of this knowledge until they reach this number. We use the total time taken for traversal as our major evaluation criterion, demonstrating that this technique outperforms both conventional VRP solvers and recently suggested deep learning models. Moreover, VRP-VIN adapted effectively to the graph size and agent count.

The paper is organized as follows: Sect. 2 gives us detailed literature on value iteration networks. The proposed Model is presented in Sect. 3. An evaluation of the proposed model is available in Sect. 4. Finally, Sect. 5 represents the conclusion and future work of the proposed work.

2 Related Work

In [8], Tamar et al. proposed a neural network incorporated with a planning module. They can learn to plan and can anticipate planning-related outcomes, such as reinforcement learning. They are based on a differential estimation of the value-iteration algorithm using CNN. Value iteration is a technique based on the Markov decision process. The MDP's purpose is to discover a policy that in turn optimizes our expected return. V_n (state value function at iteration n) converges to V* (ideal state value function) using the value iteration technique as n approaches infinity [6]. The VI module in the VIN takes advantage of the fact that each iteration of VI can be visualized as previous V_n and the reward function passes through a convolutional and max pooling layer. The Q function for every channel in the convolution layer refers to a specific action. As a result, K iterations of VI are equivalent to K times of applying a convolutional layer.

In [9], Lu et al. suggested a distributed cooperative routing method (DCR) based on evolutionary game theory to coordinate vehicles. This solution combines edge computing and intelligence to run on roadside units. Nash equilibrium is achieved under DCR. No vehicle can find a path more suitable than the one currently under Nash equilibrium [7].

In [10], Tang et al. proposed a reinforcement learning model with multi-agents for a centralized vehicle routing in order to improve the spatial-temporal coverage. Two reinforcement learning: proximal policy optimization and deep q-learning have been used to create routing policies. A centralized routing method is proposed for vehicular mobile crowd-sensing systems (VMCS) to expand their range of sensing based on MARL. The author initiates by customizing an environment for reinforcement learning in order to get the maximum feasible spatial-temporal coverage based on user preferences for various regions. They designed two MARL algorithms based on the Deep Q network [14] and Proximal Policy Optimization (PPO) [15]. Then, they do comparisons and sensitivity analyses to figure out how well the two methods work for VMCS problems.

In [11], Niu et al. Proposed a Multi-Agent Graph-attention Communication (MAGIC). It is a novel multi-agent reinforcement learning algorithm with a graph-attention communication protocol having a Scheduler to aid the challenge of when and to whom messages should be sent, and a Message Processor employs Graph Attention Networks (GATs) [12] comprising dynamic graphs for handling communication signals. A combination of a graph attention encoder and a differentiable attention mechanism [16] is used to develop the scheduler that provides dynamic, differentiable graphs to the Message Processor, allowing the Scheduler and Message Processor to be trained at the same time.

3   System Model

In this section, the solution to the Vehicle Routing Problem with Value Iteration Network has been discussed in detail. Vehicle Routing Problem with Value Iteration Network (VRP-VIN) has two main components:

- Asynchronous communication module [17] saves messages sent by agents in a temporary unit and retrieves information via agent-level attention method. This information is received by the value iteration network for path planning in the future.
- Value iteration network operates locally on each node repeatedly to calculate the value of traveling to each node for its next route. After that, LSTM [20] planning unit with attention mechanism repeatedly refines the node features and produces a value function associated with each node. The next destination will be selected on the basis of the value function, so the node with the highest value function will become the next destination.

Figure 1 represents the flowchart of the proposed model VRP-VIN The proposed VRP-VIN model is dynamic in nature. In order to do this, VRP-VIN includes a communication module based on the attention mechanism, in which attention is now focused on the agents as opposed to the street segment earlier in the VI module. Whenever an agent acts, it outputs some communication vector: $y^{(i)}$. It is subsequently transmitted to each agent using $Z^{(K)}$, the value iteration module's final encoding. The communication vector [18] is expressed as a set of node attributes in order to obtain the topology of the street graph. At the receiver end, each sender's current communication vector is stored temporarily. Every agent has an attention layer that compiles data from the receiver's inbox, whenever an agent wants to take a new action.

The Routing Path [19] can be represented as a strongly connected graph (G) with edges (E) and vertices (V), where we want to generate a routing path for D agents $\{R^{(i)}\}_{i=1}^{D}$, and each vertex in the graph is traversed D_v time across all agents. Until a specific number is reached, D_v is unknown to the agents, and local traffic information [13] is the only thing that can be observed. Each agent collects surrounding environment observation and information gathered from other agents and then outputs the next step's route.

A route is defined as a sequence of action $R(i) = [s_0^i, \ldots, s^N]$, where s_0^i represents routing steps taken by agent 'i' in time t, indicating the next node to traverse, and each step represents an intermediary destination [20]. The strategy of a single agent can be described as a function of the graph of the road network; surrounding environment observation b_t^i; the communication messages sent by other agents y_t^j; and, the current status of an agent j_t^i. The mathematical Eq. 1 are as follows:

$$s_t^i, y_t^j = f(G, b_t^i, \{y_{t-1}^j\}_{j=1}^{M}; j_t^i), \qquad (1)$$

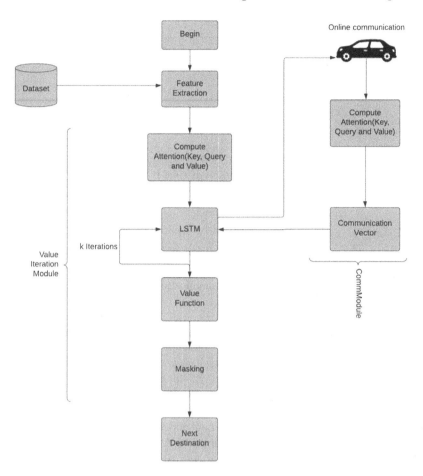

Fig. 1. Flowchart of proposed VRP-VIN Model

Consider a traffic model D determines how long it takes to travel a route, we want our system to accomplish the following goal:

$$min_R(i) \sum_{X=1...L} D(R^i),$$ (2)

subject to

$$\sum_i T(R^i, v) \geq T_v, v$$ (3)

where $T(R, v)$ tells how many times a node v should be visited in path R.

It is worth noting that the model is resilient and failure-proof as the model runs locally on all the agents, which allows it to scale better with the number of agents.

Symbol	Representation
t	Current timestamp
G	Graph of road map
L	No of Agents
n	No of graph nodes
f	Policy of Routing and Communication
π	Routing Policy
F	Time Cost given a route R
o	Agent i's observation at time t
s	Agent i state at time t
a	Agent i action at time t
m	Message vector sent by agent 'i' at time t
D_v	No of times node v needs to be visited
Z_i	At the kth value iteration, Agent i's node feature
Y_i	Agent i's input communication feature

The road network [21] is represented by a tightly linked graph G(V, E). Each graph node represents a street segment, and each agent's goal is to choose a node to be its next destination. Initial node features are refined by passing them through a graph neural network [22] for specific iterations. Then, these features are turned into a value function, and the next destination is the node with the highest value. Let $Z = (z_1, z_2, ..., z_n)$ represents a vector with initial node features, where n denotes number of nodes, and $Y = y_1, y_2, ..., y_n$ denote the node features of the input communication. A linear layer encodes node input features to produce an initial feature for the value iteration module [2]:

$$Z^0 = (Z||Y)W_{enc} + b_{enc} \tag{4}$$

We conduct the following iterative update across neighboring nodes at each planning iteration 'z' using an attention LSTM:

$$Z^{(k+1)} = Z^{(k)} + LSTM(Att(Z^{(k)}, A); H^{(k)}) \tag{5}$$

where K denotes the number of value iteration steps, hidden states $H^{(t)}$ in LSTM, and adjacency matrix A. Floyd Warshall method [23] is employed to compute dense distance matrix, which is then used as an input to this model, rather than using the adjacency matrix as an input to the network. This ensures that our model uses more useful information. The Floyd-Warshall algorithm generates a matrix, $D_{i,j} = d(v_i, v_j)$, which represents the shortest path between any two nodes in terms of pairwise distance. This matrix is then normalized to create a dense adjacency matrix. $A = (D - \mu)/\sigma$ where μ is the mean of the elements of D and σ is the standard deviation of the elements.

The graph attention layer(GAL) [24] is responsible for the exchange of information within a graph. The attention module used in VRP-VIN is a transformer layer that receives adjacency matrix and node features, then outputs modified features. First, the values of the key, query, and value function for each node are calculated.

$$Q^{(k)} = Z^{(k)} W_q + b_q, \tag{6}$$

$$K^{(k)} = Z^{(k)} W_k + b_k, \tag{7}$$

$$V^{(k)} = Z^{(k)} W_v + b_v \tag{8}$$

The node feature vector is multiplied by the weight vector to calculate the key, query, and value. Then we form an attention matrix A_{att} by computing attention between the node and each other nodes.

$$A_{att} = Q^{(k)}.K^{(k)T} \tag{9}$$

To express edge features, we mix adjacency matrix A and attention matrix A_{att} in a multi-layer neural network g as shown below.

$$A(k) = softmax(g(A_{att}^{(k)}, A)) \tag{10}$$

The values of new nodes are calculated by merging the values generated by the other nodes in the merged attention matrix according to the attention. The output of GALs is sent into the LSTM module.

$$Z^{(k+1)} = Z^{(k)} + LSTM(A^{(k)}V^{(k)}; H^{(k)}) \tag{11}$$

Before decoding, the entire procedure is performed for a fixed no. of iterations, k = 1.....K.

Each node feature is translated into a scalar value function on the graph after iterating the attention LSTM module for K iterations. Then SoftMax function is applied across the rest of the nodes to derive action probabilities, masking off the value of any node that is not required to be visited anymore because they're fully traversed.

$$\pi(s_i; j_i) = softmax(Z^K W_{dec} + b_{dec}) \tag{12}$$

Now, the node with the highest probability value is chosen as the next destination. With the help of the shortest path algorithm, a full path is constructed by linking the latest node with the node chosen as the next destination. The graph weight is calculated by dividing the length of a road segment by the average speed of the car driving it. It shows how long it is expected to take to drive from one road segment to the next.

There are 22,814 directed road graphs in the collection, which were collected from 18 cities on six continents. For testing, we pick a different location, and for validation, we utilize 10% of the training set. We also include actual traffic situations and mapping issues in this benchmark. Extra problems fall into three groups: random revisits, realistic traffic, and asynchronous execution (Figs. 2, 3 and 4).

4 Evaluation

A 3-layer MLP with 16 dimensions each, with ReLU activation is utilized to combine the dot-product attention with the distance matrix. The encoding vectors have a 16-dimensional size. Adam optimizer is used to set the model's learning rate during training to be 1e−3. The decay rate is set as 0.1 per 2000 epochs. The model is trained for 5000 epochs. Each of the 50 graphs in our batch size has a maximum of 25 nodes. We just use two agents to train our network and one to nine agents to analyze it [25]. LKH3 is the best-performing iterative solver with available data. First, the solver chooses the best route for precisely covering all nodes exactly once. After that, the solver determines a new optimal route across each of the nodes that still need to be traversed. Until every node has been completely mapped, this is repeated. Basically, the solver does VRP traversals until the required number of nodes has been visited. If an agent had been given global knowledge of every hidden state, this is the best possible performance that could have been obtained. By giving the LKH3 solver information about every hidden variable and doing an optimal plan search, the solution is discovered. By duplicating the nodes and raising the node's edge weights affected by traffic congestion, we alter the adjacency matrix. GATs [12] exchange complex information between the nodes based on the attention mechanism. Normally, GAT architectures, on the other hand, presume that all edges have equal weight rather than encoding the information about the distance matrix, which restricts their potential. Although GATs aren't always made to address TSP or VRP issues, they are still among the most cutting-edge options for graph and network encoding (Tables 1 and 2).

Table 1. Total cost (runtime in hrs)

| | No of vehicles | | | |
No of nodes	1	2	3	4
20	1.1	1.1	1.4	1.9
30	1.2	1.4	1.8	2.2
40	1.4	1.6	2	2.6
50	2	2.2	2.6	3.2
60	2.1	2.3	2.7	3.3
70	2.2	2.4	2.8	3.5
80	2.6	2.9	3.2	4
90	2.9	3	3.6	4.2
100	3.5	3.8	4.3	5.1

The performance of VRP-VIN is the best over a range of agent counts and graph sizes. Notably, this technique with 25 nodes and two agents using reinforcement learning achieves a total cost of around 3% when compared with oracle.

Table 2. Average traversal cost on real graphs; Time cost (hrs); Runtime (ms)

	25 Nodes, 1 Vehicle				25 Nodes, 2 Vehicles		
Method	Cost	Gap	Runtime	Method	Cost	Gap	Runtime
Oracle	1.16	0.00%	71.3	Oracle	1.28	0.00%	438
LKH3	1.26	8.84%	71.2	LKH3	1.8	40.50%	438
GAT	1.53	32.50%	43	GAT	1.56	21.60%	29.1
VRP-VIN(IL)	1.37	18.00%	62.8	VRP-VIN(IL)	1.42	11.30%	66.6
VRP-VIN(RL)	1.25	8.17%	62.8	VRP-VIN(RL)	1.32	2.87%	56.6
	50 Nodes, 2 Vehicles				100 Nodes, 5 Vehicles		
Method	Cost	Gap	Runtime	Method	Cost	Gap	Runtime
Oracle	1.85	0.00%	902	Oracle	3.19	0.00%	2430
LKH3	2.54	37.30%	902	LKH3	6.14	92.50%	2430
GAT	2.58	39.70%	38	GAT	5.43	70.20%	38.2
VRP-VIN(IL)	2.21	19.00%	71.5	VRP-VIN(IL)	4.36	36.70%	72.8
VRP-VIN(RL)	2.12	14.50%	71.4	VRP-VIN(RL)	4.62	44.90%	72.8

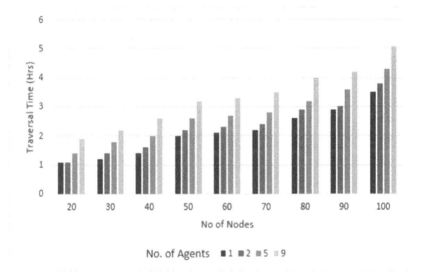

Fig. 2. Total cost graph

We discovered that the model that included imitation and reinforcement learning outperformed all rival models. The model's overall generalization to multiple agents and larger graph sizes is outstanding. Each traversal's cost is distributed across the agents in a fairly equal manner. The method performs significantly better than the current state-of-the-art, LKH solver. The overall cost increases marginally when the number of agents is increased, demonstrating high scalability. When dealing with more agents, the models trained with reinforcement

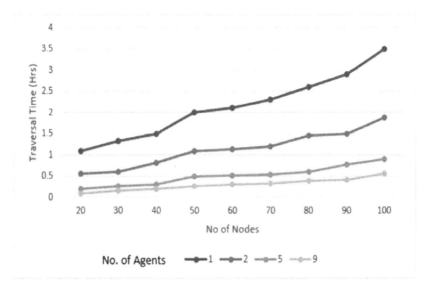

Fig. 3. Cost per agent (runtime in hrs)

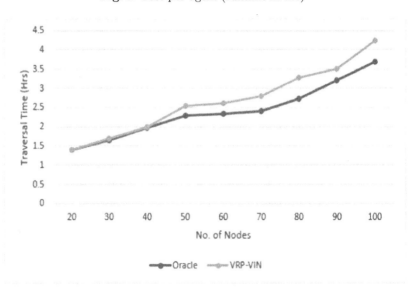

Fig. 4. Oracle vs VRP-VIN (runtime in hrs)

learning have the excellent generalizing capability. Increasing the number of value iterations further increases the performance.

5   Conclusion

The proposed VRP-VIN model can easily route multiple vehicles online in a real-world environment with dynamic obstacles. This model beats all current approaches on real road graphs by leveraging the learned value iteration transitions and a communication protocol based on an attention mechanism. Also, it can be scaled up or down to different numbers of agents and nodes without requiring retraining. Communication is a key component in multi-agent systems learning coordinated behavior. So, Future studies will involve a more in-depth examination of the information stored in the communication and its semantic value. There will also be further research into approaches that will allow this system to operate on huge graphs.

References

1. Pflueger, M., Agha, A., Sukhatme, G.S.: Rover-IRL: inverse reinforcement learning with soft value iteration networks for planetary rover path planning. IEEE Robot. Autom. Lett. **4**(2), 1387–1394 (2019)
2. Toth, P., Vigo, D.: The vehicle routing problem. SIAM, Toronto (2002)
3. Wu, Z., Pan, S., Chen, F., Long, G., Zhang, C., Philip, S.Y.: A comprehensive survey on graph neural networks. IEEE Trans. Neural Netw. Learn. Syst. **32**(1), 4–24 (2019)
4. Tampere, C.M., Corthout, R., Cattrysse, D., Immers, L.H.: A generic class of first order node models for dynamic macroscopic simulation of traffic flows. Transp. Res. Part B: Methodol. **45**(1), 289–309 (2011)
5. Sewall, J., Wilkie, D., Merrell, P., Lin, M.C.: Continuum traffic simulation. Comput. Graph Forum **29**(2), 439–448 (2010)
6. Singh, J., Dhurandher, S.K., Woungang, I.: Multi-agent reinforcement learning based efficient routing in opportunistic networks. In: 2020 IEEE 17th India Council International Conference (INDICON), New Delhi, December 2021, pp. 1–6. IEEE
7. Kool, W., van Hoof, H., Welling, M.: Attention, learn to solve routing problems!. In: 7th International Conference on Learning Representations, ICLR, New Orleans, LA, USA (2019)
8. Tamar, A., Levine, S., Abbeel, P., Wu, Y., Thomas, G.: Value iteration networks. In: Advances in Neural Information Processing Systems, NIPS, Barcelona, Spain, vol. 29, pp. 2154–2162 (2016)
9. Lu, J., Li, J., Yuan, Q., Chen, B.: A multi-vehicle cooperative routing method based on evolutionary game theory. In: 2019 IEEE Intelligent Transportation Systems Conference (ITSC), Auckland, New Zealand, pp. 987–994 (2019)
10. Tang, B., Li, Z., Han, K.: Multi-agent reinforcement learning for mobile crowdsensing systems with dedicated vehicles on road networks. In: 2021 IEEE International Intelligent Transportation Systems Conference (ITSC), Indianapolis, IN, USA, pp. 3584–3589 (2021)
11. Niu, Y., Paleja, R., Gombolay, M.: Multi-agent graph attention communication and teaming. In: Proceedings of the 20th International Conference on Autonomous Agents and Multiagent Systems (AAMAS 2021), Online, IFAAMAS, pp 964–973 (2021)

12. Velickovic, P., Cucurull, G., Casanova, A., Romero, A., Lio, P., Bengio, Y.: Graph attention networks. In: 6th International Conference on Learning Representations, ICLR, Vancouver, Canada (2018)

13. Li, J., et al.: A traffic prediction enabled double rewarded value iteration network for route planning. IEEE Trans. Veh. Technol. **68**(5), 4170–4181 (2019)

14. Sykora, Q., Ren, M., Urtasun, R.: Multi-agent routing value iteration network. In: International Conference on Machine Learning, pp. 9300–9310, November 2020

15. Yun, S., Jeong, M., Kim, R., Kang, J., Kim, H.J.: Graph transformer networks. In: Advances in Neural Information Processing Systems 32, NeurIPS, Vancouver, Canada, pp. 11983–11993 (2019)

16. Vaswani, A., et al.: Attention is all you need. In: Advances in Neural Information Processing Systems, NIPS, Long Beach, CA, USA, vol. 30, pp. 6000–6010 (2017)

17. Dhurandher, S.K., Singh, J., Nicopolitidis, P., Kumar, R., Gupta, G.: A blockchain-based secure routing protocol for opportunistic networks. J. Ambient. Intell. Humaniz. Comput. **13**(4), 2191–2203 (2022). https://doi.org/10.1007/s12652-021-02981-9

18. William, R.J.: Simple statistical gradient-following algorithms for connectionist reinforcement learning. Mach. Learn. **8**(3–4), 229–256 (1992)

19. Helsgaun, K.: An extension of the Lin-Kernighan-Helsgaun TSP solver for constrained traveling salesman and vehicle routing problems. Roskilde University, Roskilde (2017)

20. Hochreiter, S., Schmidhuber, J.: Long short-term memory. Neural Comput. **9**(8), 1735–1780 (1997)

21. Jiang, J., Lu, Z.: Learning attentional communication for multi-agent cooperation. In: Advances in Neural Information Processing Systems, NeurIPS, Monteral, Canada, vol. 31, pp. 7265–7275 (2018)

22. Erdogan, G.: An open source spreadsheet solver for vehicle routing problems. Comput. OR **84**, 62–72 (2017)

23. Gupta, J.K., Egorov, M., Kochenderfer, M.: Cooperative multi-agent control using deep reinforcement learning. In: International Conference on Autonomous Agents and Multiagent Systems, AAMAS, São Paulo, Brazil, pp. 66–83 (2017)

24. Gupta, N., Singh, J., Dhurandher, S.K., Han, Z.: Contract theory based incentive design mechanism for opportunistic IoT networks. IEEE Internet Things J., 1–11 (2021)

25. Issariyakul, T., Hossain, E.: Introduction to Network Simulator 2 (NS2). In: Issariyakul, T., Hossain, E. (eds.) Introduction to Network Simulator NS2, pp. 1–18. Springer, Boston (2009). https://doi.org/10.1007/978-0-387-71760-9_2

An On-Site Collaborative Approach of Road Crash Data Collection

Awa Tiam, Ibrahima Gueye$^{(\boxtimes)}$, and Oumar Niang

Ecole Polytechnique de Thiès, LTISI, Thies, Senegal
{igueye,oniang}@ept.sn
http://www.ept.sn

Abstract. After occurrence of a road crash, the on-site investigation is organized by officers to help establishing the responsibilities of the individuals in case of legal procedures and/or to collect data for crash information system. This investigation often involves road lane closure which may cause travelling delays, traffic jams and even expose road crash responders to subsequent crashes. Globally, long investigation crash scenes have negative impact on mobility services, hence negatively impacting countries economies.

Studies have linked the closure duration to different aspects of the crash. Methods and tools have been studied to lower the time spent for on-site crash investigation.

In this paper, we present the architecture of a collaborative collection strategy for road crash data collection. The objective of this system is to lower the time spent to collect data by allowing multiple users to be involved in this process. Different tests have been conducted. The results show the effectiveness of this system.

Keywords: Road crash · Data collection · Collaborative data collection

1 Introduction

The on-site road crash data collection is necessary because certain types of data are point-in-time elements that need to be collected on-site in order to be accurate for further analysis. Road surface conditions, partial work zones or insurance information are among those elements.

In recent years, crash data collection processes have been widely revisited. Researches have demonstrated the effectiveness of computerized collection of crash data in reducing the noise and automatizing data transport to storage centers skipping the step of manual data entry [2–4]. A review of crash data collection methods for developed and developing countries show that digital data collection approaches are reliable and time saving for data collection and compilation [1].

However, when done by a single officer, collecting crash data may be time-consuming. In fact, crash data guides contain a various number of data elements

© ICST Institute for Computer Sciences, Social Informatics and Telecommunications Engineering 2023
Published by Springer Nature Switzerland AG 2023. All Rights Reserved
T. M. Ngatched Nkouatchah et al. (Eds.): PAAISS 2022, LNICST 459, pp. 423–437, 2023.
https://doi.org/10.1007/978-3-031-25271-6_27

that need to be collected. This made on-site crash data collection quite challenging. Furthermore, when a crash occurs, the scene investigation requires closing roadway for significant amount of time. Studies have shown that this closure duration may vary depending on multiple factors. The roadway closure also causes some problems such as traffic jams, travelling delays, subsequent crashes and incident responders exposure to subsequent crashes. In Senegal, the authority in charge of the regulation of mobility in Dakar has conducted a survey on mobility and transport [5]. This study has shown that in Dakar town, traffic jams have an estimated negative impact of 1% of the national GNP. Moreover, the negative impacts of the mobility dysfunctions represent 5% of the GNP, the same value for the contribution of the transportation sector to the country economy.

Montella et al. [4] proposed the use of computerized collection to speed up the collection time. The results show that this particular objective was not met but the data quality has been enhanced. Photogrammetry and 3D laser scanning [6–8] are also used to take pictures of the crash scene and to retrieve data points subsequently. These techniques have shown efficiency in collecting data from crash scenes. However, they require further processing steps to retrieve the data points, they do not necessarily give the full spectrum of data and present sometimes some financial drawbacks.

In this work, we propose a collection approach based on collaboration to speed up the time spent to collect data. Hence, multiple officers can be involved in the collection of a road crash data elements. The main purposes of the system is to split down the amount of work of collecting crash data and to decrease time spent in collecting those data by using affordable hardware and software. Moreover, by decreasing time spent to collect data, the system will allow to collect more data elements on-site and traffic could resume more quickly. Our system relies on the use of novel data storage and process facilities such as NoSQL and wireless communication technologies for collaborative synchronization. Crash data descriptors (crash general characteristics, road description, involved vehicles and persons description) have been modeled in order to lower the relations between them in the saving stage. So these different entities can be saved separately.

This paper is structured as follows: we first make a review on the techniques and ways of lowering the time spent for site data gathering in road accident data management and related areas, we then present the core concepts and description of the collaborative data collection system. The testing of the proposed strategy and corresponding results are finally presented.

2   Background

There exist many different data transfer technologies with mobile phone's systems. We ran our experiments with Android. In Android, data transfer can be achieved through WIFI-Direct [9] also known as WiFi-P2P, WiFi-Aware or Bluetooth. The WiFi-Direct technology allows data to be transmitted between mobile phone terminals via WiFi without an intermediate access point. The WiFi-Aware is a technology similar to WIFI-P2P except it does not require the authentication protocol from the group owner which does not exist in this implementation. The transferable data volume is less voluminous than the one in WiFi-Direct. Although, for the transfer of heavy data, it is possible to initiate a network with the notion of group owner. The Bluetooth technology [10] allows devices to communicate with each other in wireless manner. Bluetooth technology is commonly used in transferring data, generally files, over a network between two or more devices using the short-range Radio frequency. The speed of information transfer is faster via WiFi than Bluetooth. The energy consumption of WIFI-Direct technology is 40 times higher than the Bluetooth one. Both technologies support service discovery. In this work, Bluetooth technology has been used to ensure data transfer. In our collaborative approach, a team of on-site collectors are located in the same physical place, so the coverage area of the different technologies has been neglected in the process. The size of data we need to transfer is also negligible compared to files.

The Couchbase Lite database [11] is a document-like NoSQL mobile database installed on mobile devices.

The Couchbase Sync Gateway [12] is a synchronization server used to replicate data entered through Couchbase Mobile. The replication protocol used by the server is based on web-sockets. The Android ViewModel [13] helps ensuring UI data is not lost in case of a call or application restart or even screens rotations. Android MutableLiveData [14] is a life-cycle-aware observable data holder. The pair Viewmodel/LiveData help sharing data between fragments in an Android powered mobile application.

3   Related Work

Rabbani et al. [1] have conducted a review on road crash data collection systems in developing and developed countries. Manual and digital data collection approaches were particularly highlighted. Digital approaches are said to be reliable and time saving for data collection and compilation. The use of cameras or mobile applications were recommended to improve the accuracy of the Police records of road crash data collection.

A team of researchers of the University of Kentucky in cooperation with the Kentucky Transportation Cabinet [7] have studied the highway crash scene closure duration depending of various parameters such as the type of crash, the number of units involved, the involvement of trapped occupants, the speed limit, the injury severity and the number of fatalities. The results show that fatal crashes generally have longer closure duration; the closure duration increases as the number of fatalities and number of units; the closure duration is longer when an occupant was trapped; as the limit increases above 40, the closure duration also increases. Finally, the closure severity increases as the injury severity increases. They have also identified electronic data collection to be one of the best practices for crash site investigation. To reduce the time taken to investigate crash sites, they recommend among other actions to implement in-vehicle computers in law enforcement vehicles to verify and record information quickly and to evaluate the use of bar codes and magnetic stripes on driver's licenses and vehicles to help quickly obtain information for accident reporting. The Transportation Research Laboratory[1] have studied and tested the use of a commercial 3D laser scanning to rapidly collect data on site [8]. The process consists of taking two or three laser scans of an incident scene. These scans provide a complete three dimensional model of the scene, which provides hundreds of thousands of data points. The system requires post-processing which can be increased by the filter of excessive data not relevant to the investigation. Authors emit considerations about cost-effectiveness of applications with laser scanning regarding the high investment costs of the development; and also the technology do not provide the full spectrum of data capture.

Unmanned aerial vehicle (UAV) are widely used in many practical uses cases. Recent research trends show the use of UAVs in Wireless Sensor Network (WSN) as an auxiliary tool [15]. Collaborative sensing imply that when a single UAV is involved in the collection process, the problem of UAV's low energy may cause data collection to be incomplete. Multi-UAVs has been proposed to shorten the data collection time of UAVs by the mean of UAV-sensor association schema [16–19].

In web-crawling domain, there are often the limitations of online social network (OSN) sites such as the request rate based on IP. Crowd-crawling has been defined and proposed to allow several researchers from multiple research group to collect data from OSN sites in a collaborative way [20].

Montella et al. [4] have studied the use of mobile computerized applications to lower the time spent to collect data on-site. Their system consists of a web-based data collection system using input fields. They were able to test the entire system with Police officers. Their results show that the objective of speeding up time spent to collect data on-site was not met but the data quality has been widely ameliorated. In their recommendations, they have identified the need of parallel collection process and making this process able to be done offline.

While there are multiple studies on computerizing road crash data collection systems, there are less documented studies about shortening the time spent to collect data using these tools.

4   The Collaborative Collection System

In this paper, we present the architecture of a collaborative crash data collection strategy. The purpose is to leverage on-site crash data collection by allowing multiple officers to work on the process. The collaborative collection strategy is part of an ongoing global work which means to build a crash data system for use in Senegal. This global system (Fig. 1, Fig. 2) is composed of a mobile application called *JAR*, a synchronization server, a central database server and a web application for data analyses. The functional requirements of this system are listed herein:

---

[1]   https://www.trl.co.uk/.

- the system is intended to be used by road safety actors (Police officers, fire-fighters, ...)
- the system must provides access to a computerized form of a crash collection guide (crash general characteristics, vehicle characteristics, road description and person information)
- the system will allow to take photos and videos from crash scenes
- the crash identifier must be deduced automatically by the application
- the crash identifier must be unique in the database as it is used as part of a key for all crash documents
- the data entered by mobile application users must be persisted in a database
- the mobile application must be able to be used offline
- multiple users must be able to collect data for the same crash instance
- users must be able to add persons and vehicles depending on their involvement in a crash
- users must be able to take photos and videos of the crash scene - users must be able to choose from pre-filled values

The non-functional requirements of the system, mainly regarding the database and the synchronization server, imply the deployment on cloud providers. The collaborative collection strategy is conceptually based on below concepts:

- The system repositories are JSON-document like NoSQL databases. Unlike relational databases where relations between entities may force a certain order and organization in data, document based data stores can go beyond these limitations. Thus, we can have documents holding different types of values in the same and unique table
- The mobile application offers a visualization of a road crash data collection guide. There are four types of entities: 'Accident' or general crash characteristics, 'Vehicle' or involved vehicles description, 'Road' or road description and 'Person' for involved persons description. Each of these entities corresponds to a specific type of document. These entities are visualized using Android fragments
- The crash identifier is deduced using the location (GPS coordinates), the time of crash and the administrative location of crash in general characteristics
- This mobile application *JAR* is able to make available the crash identifier deduced from crash general characteristics to the other fragments with use of Android ViewModel/MutableLiveData
- As we can save documents individually, we need to link them for further analysis. The crash identifier is used to link all the documents to the corresponding crash instance

Therefore, we deduced that if multiple users of the application can have the crash identifier, they can collect data for the same crash instance.

The collaborative collection strategy is achieved by sharing the crash identifier among a team of collectors using the Bluetooth technology. A team is defined by one or more agents working on site in collecting data. One of the team members must act as a leader. A leader is responsible for entering crash general characteristics and so the crash identifier will be generated at his level. This identifier is shared among the other collectors. The central database NoSQL nature allows us to achieve data saving without worrying about relations between the different data elements. Once the identifier is shared, it is up to the team members to define the collection plan. This collection plan consists of deciding which part of the crash description will be handled by each team member. This central database offers distributed, fault-tolerant and resiliency capabilities for saved data. The mobile application offers offline-first capability which ensures users to work in connectivity constrained areas. Thus entered data are first saved locally in mobile terminal and with the availability of Internet connectivity, data are synchronized in central database level. Conflicts may arise due to the collaboration. They are handled by the system at local and synchronization level.

4.1 Repositories

There are several data repositories used in this system:

- A Couchbase Lite database acts as our local database. An instance is created in each mobile phone where JAR is launched. When a user click on the save button, the content of the view is used to construct an object which in turn is converted to a document and then saved in local database. Documents saved in local databases are synchronized by the synchronization server to the central database with Internet availability
- A Couchbase server is used to build our central database. This cluster is composed of a set of three nodes each acting as a docker container running a Couchbase server image. A bridge network provides DNS resolution between containers instead of IP resolution. This network provides isolation, which means containers out of this network can not communicate with containers that belong to the network. The data entered through the collection interface and synchronized by the synchronization component are saved in the final database. The purposes of a cluster-based database instead of one single node is to ensures scalability, high-availability and resiliency semantics. Data are distributed across the cluster nodes. Which means that each document has a main node which holds the document and then the two other nodes which have copies of this specific document. This process is known as replication. This ensures that if a specific nodes goes down, clients can still query data
- When users collect data using the mobile application, data are first saved in the local database. With Internet availability, data are saved in the remote central database. This process is called synchronization. This synchronization is made using a server running as a Docker container. This Docker container uses a Couchbase Sync Gateway image. The synchronization server and the database belong to the same docker bridge network

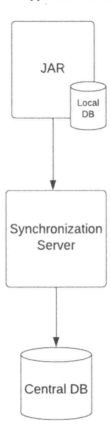

Fig. 1. System modules include a mobile application which holds a local database, a synchronization server and a remote central database.

4.2 Sharing Crash Identifier

The mobile application is configured with a specific UUID. This UUID will be shared by all the instances of the mobile application. This UUID will be used at discovery level by the Bluetooth component. When starting the sharing process, *JAR* only displays devices that have already been connected over Bluetooth with the team leader device. This has been done to prevent displaying an important number of devices not important to have in the sharing process. The Fig. 3 depicts the sequential actions of the crash identifier sharing. Team leader informs data elements of the tab *Accident*. This tab is traduced as a fragment with different inputs to describe general characteristics of a crash: weather conditions, light conditions, situation of the crash from the roadway, etc. Then, the team leader validates data elements of the tab *Accident*. While validating, the system generates the crash identifier from the location, the names of the cities, departments, the crash time and also creates a document using the different inputs' values and the crash identifier as a key. The created document is then saved in

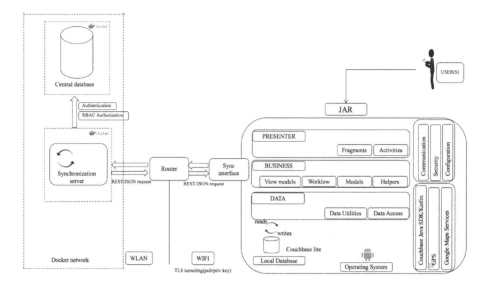

Fig. 2. System architecture

local database. The generated crash identifier is recorded in the view model and saved as a live data. The other fragments, which are listening for this specific Livedata, retrieves the crash identifier and fill the corresponding entry in their respective views. The team leader initiates the sharing of the crash identifier by clicking the corresponding floating action button in the *Accident* fragment. This button is only used in the case of parallel collection. In this stage, all collectors have been identified and they mobile phones have been paired via Bluetooth. The application displays a list of terminal (name, MAC address) recognized by the team leader's terminal. This means that all the terminals running the application, recognized by the team leader's terminal and in the Bluetooth coverage area are displayed on the team leader's screen. The concept of recognition refers to the fact that there has already been a connection between the displayed terminals and the team leader's terminal. The process of discovering new terminals is not implemented because we would end up with a potentially large number of terminals that are not interesting to display. The team leader selects the terminal(s) individually. The crash identifier is sent to each selected terminal. The crash identifier is saved in the collector's instance ViewModel as a Livedata. The accident identifier is automatically filled in the appropriate field on the receiving terminal from the ViewModel. After crash identifier has been shared among all the collectors each of them is supposed to collect specific data describing the crash. It is up to the team members to set up the collection plan.

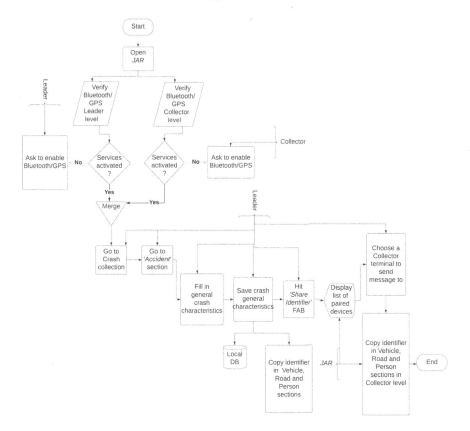

Fig. 3. Sharing crash identifier

4.3 Conflicts Resolution

Warned persons are supposed to use this data entry mode, mainly Police officers who are aware of the task of collecting data from crash scenes. This behavior is desirable because it prevents multiple persons collecting the same data for the same crash. However, there can still be situations where conflicts may arise. In this system, we have a unique replicator which is the synchronization server. We can have conflicts at the local level in mobile database and at replicator level. Mobile application is configured with push only replication. Mobile application users do not have the possibility to delete documents. The document identifiers are constructed using Table 1 scenario: the sequence numbers of vehicles and persons are simply ordinal numbers to numerically identify the involved vehicles and persons. The *region* and *department* are unit administrative locations. Figure 4 depicts the algorithm for conflicts resolution. A team of collectors are located on site and the situation of having two different teams collecting data for the same accident is less likely to arrive. We list hereafter the conflicts scenarios that may arise. There can be other scenarios not identified during tests.

Table 1. Each document has an identifier used to uniquely identify it in database.

Key	Document key	Document typology
CrashID	ACC_region_department_date_hour	Crash general characteristics
VehicleID	Vehicle_CrashID_sequentialNumber	Vehicle details
RoadID	ROAD_CrashID	Road description
PersonID	Person_CrashID_vehicleSequentialNumber_sequentialNumber	Person details

— An officer saves inadvertently an already saved document. By clicking more than one time the save button for example. — An officer can also make modifications on locally filled and saved values. For example, the officer saves a document and afterwards makes modifications on certain fields and saves the document again. In local database level, we apply the *Last Writes Wins* strategy. We saw this kind of conflict resolver adequate to deal with conflicts at the same local level. The *Last Writes Wins* algorithm uses timestamps to determine the last write transaction. The last update of document will be considered. In replication level, conflicts may arise when multiple clients (officers) save or update the same document concurrently. The last write is rejected with an error handled by

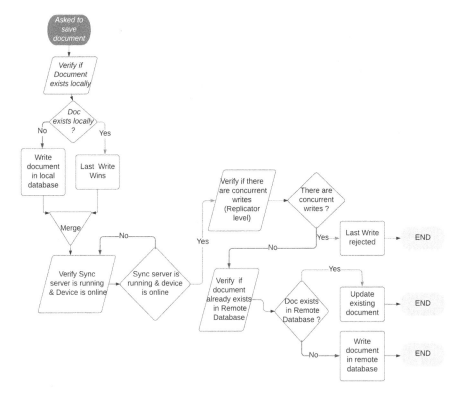

Fig. 4. Conflicts may arise during document saving

the application. If a modification is made on an already replicated document(i.e. exists on remote database) from a client, existing document is updated.

4.4 Security

Synchronization process use web sockets and is so using the Internet to synchronize data from the mobile database to the central database. Hence, the data transfer channel needs to be secured. The mobile application authenticates itself to the synchronization server by using a username/password authentication method. A supplementary secure layer has also been added. A TLS self-signed certificate is pinned in the mobile application. This certificate has been generated using the openssl command line tool. The generated certificates (public and private key) are also configured in synchronization server and copied to container in launch time. The mobile application authenticates using its public key bundled in the application. Communications between the synchronization server and central database server are secured by the use of a role based access control authentication and authorization. An RBAC user is created at database level and credentials are configured in the synchronization server configuration file. This configuration file is used at container startup.

5   Testing of the Collaborative Collection

Table 2 details the hardware and software used to test the collaborative collection system. First, the mobile application is installed in two mobile equipment (a Huawei Nova smartphone and a X_TIGI JOY7 Mate tablet). Then various tests were conducted. The synchronization server has been installed as a docker container in the same physical host as the database cluster of three nodes. In the collaborative process, the smartphone will act as the leader. The Tablet will act as a collector. Prior to the tests, the two equipment were paired via Bluetooth. Table 3 depicts the test stages that were conducted. We focus our tests on the collaborative strategy. The test of the other aspects of the system were not presented in this paper.

Table 2. Hardwares and softwares.

Usage	Version	Properties
Leader	Huawei Nova 3i	Android 8.1 (Oreo) upgradable to Android 9
Collector	X-TIGI-JOY7 Mate	Android 8.1.0
Synchronization server	macOS Mojave 10.14.6.	Processor 2,2 GHz Intel Core i7 Memory 16 Go 2400 MHz MHz DDR4
Central database	macOS Mojave 10.14.6.	Processor 2,2 GHz Intel Core i7 Memory 16 Go 2400 MHz MHz DDR4
Containerization	Docker desktop	Engine 19.03.13 Edition Community

Table 3. Test phases.

Test stage	User story	Status	Result
Mobile application deployment		Done	OK
Visualizing crash, vehicle, person and road	User must be able to visualize the tabs	Done	OK
Display list of discovered devices	User must be able to see a list of discovered devices over Bluetooth	Done	OK
Choose a device and send message	The leader must be able to select a specific device and send a message	Done	OK
Receive a message from leader	A collector has capability to receive crash identifier from the leader	Done	OK
Automatic filling of crash identifier	The crash identifier has to be filled automatically by the application	Done	OK
Saving documents details	Users can save details for crash, vehicle, person and road	Done	OK
Update documents details	Users can update details for already saved documents	Done	OK

5.1   Results

Figure 5 shows the sharing of crash identifier between our leader and collector. The leader (here left and center screens) has completed the general crash characteristics description in left. The check floating action button has been used to validate the data element for crash details. The system has generated the identifier and filled the corresponding field in crash fragment. The up-arrow floating action button has been used to share the identifier. The center screen shows a

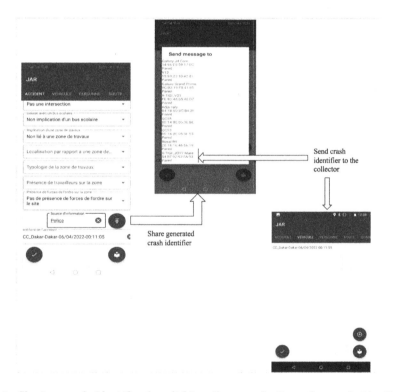

Fig. 5. Sharing crash identifier by clicking the save button, the crash identifier is deduced and filled in

list of paired devices in leader's screen. The last one corresponds to our active collector. After selection, the identifier is sent and filled in the collector's vehicle, road and person fragments.

Results in Fig. 6 shows the actual use of the collaborative system. The crash identifier is available on the leader and collector's screens in all fragments level. So each of them can collect data related to vehicle, person and road details indifferently.

Fig. 6. The identifier is automatically filled in the collector instance

6   Conclusion and Future Work

An on-site post-crash investigation may result in travel delays, traffic jams, or even subsequent crashes. These consequences are most likely to arrive as the road lane closure duration increases. Hence, studies have focused on the task of lowering time spent on-site after the occurrence of a road crash. In this paper, we present the architecture of a collaborative collection strategy for road crash data collection. The objective of this system is to lower the time spent to collect data by allowing multiple users to be involved using affordable hardware and software. Different tests had been conducted. The results show the effectiveness of the system. In our ongoing work, we plan to perform a comparative study with other forms or systems of crash data collection. This comparative study will help us highlight the pluses of this architecture.

References

1. Rabbani, M.B.A., Musarat, M.A., Alaloul, W.S., Ayub, S., Bukhari, H., Altaf, M.: Road accident data collection systems in developing and developed countries: a review. Int. J. Integr. Eng. **14**(1), 336–352 (2022)
2. Campisi, T., Galatioto, F., Franco, P., Barone, R.: A new approach for road accident data acquisition: the K_Road app (2013)
3. Derdus, K.M., Ozianyi, V.G.: A mobile solution for road accident data collection. In: Proceedings of the 2nd Pan African International Conference on Science, Computing and Telecommunications (PACT 2014), pp. 115–120 (2014). https://doi.org/10.1109/SCAT.2014.7055140
4. Montella, A., Chiaradonna, S., Criscuolo, G., De Martino, S.: Development and evaluation of a web-based software for crash data collection, processing and analysis. Accid. Anal. Prev. (2017). https://doi.org/10.1016/j.aap.2017.01.013
5. World Bank. (2001). PPTASS Technical Note Nř19
6. Pagounis, V., Tsakiri, M., Palaskas, S., Biza, B.: 3D laser scanning for road safety and accident reconstruction. In: Proceedings of the XXIIIth International FIG Congress, pp. 8–13 (2006)
7. Walton, J.R., Barret, M.L., Agent K.R.: Evaluation of methods to limit the time taken to investigate crash sites (2005)
8. Forman, P., Parry, I.: Rapid data collection at major incident scenes using three dimensional laser scanning techniques. In: Proceedings IEEE 35th Annual 2001 International Carnahan Conference on Security Technology (Cat. No.01CH37186) (2001). https://doi.org/10.1109/.2001.962814
9. Google Developer Guide. https://developer.android.com/training/connect-devices-wirelessly/wifi-direct. Accessed 30 Jan 2022
10. Bluetooth Official website. https://www.bluetooth.com/learn-about-bluetooth/tech-overview/. Accessed 30 Jan 2022
11. Couchbase Lite. https://docs.couchbase.com/couchbase-lite/current/index.html. Accessed 30 Jan 2022
12. Sync Gateway. https://docs.couchbase.com/sync-gateway/current/introduction.html. Accessed 30 Jan 2022
13. Android ViewModel. https://developer.android.com/topic/libraries/architecture/viewmodel. Accessed 30 Jan 2022
14. Android LiveData. https://developer.android.com/topic/libraries/architecture/livedata. Accessed 30 Jan 2022
15. Zhang, F., Liu, H., Ma, Z., Yang, Y., Wan, X.: Study of UAV application in wireless sensor networks. In: 3rd International Conference on Mechanical, Electronics, Computer, and Industrial Technology (MECnIT), pp. 343–348 (2020). https://doi.org/10.1109/MECnIT48290.2020.9166681
16. Wang, Y., Hu, Z., Wen, X., Lu, Z., Miao, J.: Minimizing data collection time with collaborative UAVs in wireless sensor networks. IEEE Access **8**, 98659–98669 (2020). https://doi.org/10.1109/ACCESS.2020.2996665
17. Wang, Y., et al.: Multi-UAV collaborative data collection for IoT devices powered by battery. In: 2020 IEEE Wireless Communications and Networking Conference (WCNC), pp. 1–6 (2020). https://doi.org/10.1109/WCNC45663.2020.9120646
18. Khodaparast, S.S., Lu, X., Wang, P., Nguyen, U.T.: Deep reinforcement learning based energy efficient multi-UAV data collection for IoT networks. IEEE Open J. Veh. Technol. **2**, 249–260 (2021). https://doi.org/10.1109/OJVT.2021.3085421

19. Alfattani, S., Jaafar, W., Yanikomeroglu, H., Yongacoglu, A.: Multi-UAV data collection framework for wireless sensor networks. In: 2019 IEEE Global Communications Conference (GLOBECOM), pp. 1–6 (2019). https://doi.org/10.1109/GLOBECOM38437.2019.9014306

20. Ding, C., Chen, Y., Fu, X.: Crowd crawling: towards collaborative data collection for large-scale online social networks. In: Proceedings of the first ACM conference on Online social networks (COSN 2013). Association for Computing Machinery, New York, pp. 183–188 (2013). https://doi.org/10.1145/2512938.2512958

Author Index

Printed in the United States
by Baker & Taylor Publisher Services